UNIX® Filesystems
Evolution, Design, and Implementation
(VERITAS Series)

The **WILEY** *advantage*

Dear Valued Customer,

We realize you're a busy professional with deadlines to hit. Whether your goal is to learn a new technology or solve a critical problem, we want to be there to lend you a hand. Our primary objective is to provide you with the insight and knowledge you need to stay atop the highly competitive and ever-changing technology industry.

Wiley Publishing, Inc., offers books on a wide variety of technical categories, including security, data warehousing, software development tools, and networking — everything you need to reach your peak. Regardless of your level of expertise, the Wiley family of books has you covered.

- For Dummies – The *fun* and *easy* way to learn
- The Weekend Crash Course –The *fastest* way to learn a new tool or technology
- Visual – For those who prefer to learn a new topic *visually*
- The Bible – The *100% comprehensive* tutorial and reference
- The Wiley Professional list – *Practical* and *reliable* resources for IT professionals

The book you hold now, *UNIX Filesystems: Evolution, Design, and Implementation,* is the first book to cover filesystems from all versions of UNIX and Linux. The author gives you details about the file I/O aspects of UNIX programming, describes the various UNIX and Linux operating system internals, and gives cases studies of some of the most popular filesystems including UFS, ext2, and the VERITAS filesystem, VxFS. The book contains numerous examples including a fully working Linux filesystem that you can experiment with.

Our commitment to you does not end at the last page of this book. We'd want to open a dialog with you to see what other solutions we can provide. Please be sure to visit us at www.wiley.com/compbooks to review our complete title list and explore the other resources we offer. If you have a comment, suggestion, or any other inquiry, please locate the "contact us" link at www.wiley.com.

Thank you for your support and we look forward to hearing from you and serving your needs again in the future.

Sincerely,

Richard K. Swadley
Vice President & Executive Group Publisher
Wiley Technology Publishing

UNIX® Filesystems:
Evolution, Design, and Implementation
(VERITAS Series)

Steve D. Pate

Wiley Publishing, Inc.

Publisher: Robert Ipsen
Executive Editor: Carol Long
Developmental Editor: James H. Russell
Managing Editor: Angela Smith
Text Design & Composition: Wiley Composition Services

This book is printed on acid-free paper. ∞

Published by Wiley Publishing, Inc., Indianapolis, Indiana
Published simultaneously in Canada

For general information on our other products and services please contact our Customer Care Department within the United States at (800) 762-2974, outside the United States at (317) 572-3993 or fax (317) 572-4002.

Wiley also publishes its books in a variety of electronic formats. Some content that appears in print may not be available in electronic books.

Library of Congress Cataloging-in-Publication Data:

ISBN: 0-471-16483-6

10 9 8 7 6 5 4 3 2 1

Contents

Foreword

It's over 30 years ago that the first Edition of UNIX was released. Much has changed since those early days, as it evolved from a platform for software development, to the OS of choice for technical workstations, an application platform for small servers, and finally the platform of choice for mainframe-class RISC-based application and database servers.

Turning UNIX into the workhorse for mission-critical enterprise applications was in no small part enabled by the evolution of file systems, which play such a central role in this Operating System. Features such as extent-based allocation, journaling, database performance, SMP support, clustering support, snapshots, replication, NFS, AFS, data migration, incremental backup, and more have contributed to this.

And the evolution is by no means over. There is, of course, the ever present need for improved performance and scalability into the realm of Pbytes and billions of files. In addition, there are new capabilities in areas such as distributed single image file systems, flexible storage allocation, archiving, and content-based access that are expected to appear during the next few years.

So if you thought that file system technology had no more excitement to offer, you should reconsider your opinion, and let this book wet your appetite.

The historical perspective offered by the author not only gives a compelling insight in the evolution of UNIX and the manner which this has been influenced by many parties—companies, academic institutions, and individuals—it also gives the reader an understanding of why things work the way they do, rather than just how they work.

By also covering a wide range of UNIX variants and file system types, and discussing implementation issues in-depth, this book will appeal to a broad audience. I highly recommend it to anyone with an interest in UNIX and its history, students of Operating Systems and File Systems, UNIX system administrators, and experienced engineers who want to move into file system development or just broaden their knowledge. Expect this to become a reference work for UNIX developers and system administrators.

Fred van den Bosch

Executive Vice President and Chief Technology Officer
VERITAS Software Corporation

Introduction

Welcome to *UNIX Filesystems—Evolution, Design, and Implementation*, the first book that is solely dedicated to UNIX internals from a filesystem perspective.

Much has been written about the different UNIX and UNIX-like kernels since Maurice Bach's book *The Design of the UNIX Operating System* [BACH86] first appeared in 1986. At that time, he documented the internals of System V Release 2 (SVR2). However, much had already happened in the UNIX world when SVR2 appeared. The earliest documented kernel was 6th Edition as described in John Lions' work *Lions' Commentary on UNIX 6th Edition—with Source Code* [LION96], which was an underground work until its publication in 1996. In addition to these two books, there have also been a number of others that have described the different UNIX kernel versions.

When writing about operating system internals, there are many different topics to cover from process management to virtual memory management, from device drivers to networking, and hardware management to filesystems. One could fill a book on each of these areas and, in the case of networking and device drivers, specialized books have in fact appeared over the last decade.

Filesystems are a subject of great interest to many although they have typically been poorly documented. This is where this book comes into play.

This book covers the history of UNIX describing how filesystems were implemented in the early research editions of UNIX up to today's highly scalable enterprise class UNIX systems. All of the major changes in the history of UNIX that pertain to filesystems are covered along with a view of how some of the more well known filesystems are implemented.

Not forgetting the user interface to filesystems, the book also presents the file and filesystem-level system call and library-level APIs that programmers expect to see. By providing this context it is easier to understand the services that filesystems are expected to provide and therefore why they are implemented the way they are.

Wherever possible, this book provides practical examples, either through programmatic means or through analysis. To provide a more practical edge to the material presented, the book provides a complete implementation of a filesystem on Linux together with instructions on how to build the kernel and filesystem, how to install it, and analyze it using appropriate kernel-level debuggers. Examples are then given for readers to experiment further.

Who Should Read This Book?

Rather than reach for the usual group of suspects—kernel engineers and operating system hobbyists—this book is written in such a way that anyone who has an interest in filesystem technology, regardless of whether they understand operating system internals or not, can read the book to gain an understanding of file and filesystem principles, operating system internals, and filesystem implementations.

This book should appeal to anyone interested in UNIX, its history, and the standards that UNIX adheres to. Anyone involved in the storage industry should also benefit from the material presented here.

Because the book has a practical edge, the material should be applicable for undergraduate degree-level computer science courses. As well as a number of examples throughout the text, which are applicable to nearly all versions of UNIX, the chapter covering Linux filesystems provides a number of areas where students can experiment.

How This Book Is Organized

Although highly technical in nature, as with all books describing operating system kernels, the goal of this book has been to follow an approach that enables readers not proficient in operating system internals to read the book.

Earlier chapters describe UNIX filesystems from a user perspective. This includes a view of UNIX from a historical perspective, application programming interfaces (APIs), and filesystem basics. This provides a base on which to understand how the UNIX kernel provides filesystem services.

Modern UNIX kernels are considerably more complex than their predecessors. Before diving into the newer kernels, an overview of 5th/6th Edition UNIX is described in order to introduce kernel concepts and how they relate to filesystems. The major changes in the kernel, most notably the introduction of vnodes in Sun's SunOS operating system, are then described together with the differences in filesystem architectures between the SVR4 variants and non-SVR4 variants.

Later chapters start to dig into filesystem internals and the features they provide. This concludes with an implementation of the original System V UNIX filesystem on Linux to demonstrate how a simple filesystem is actually implemented. This working filesystem can be used to aid students and other interested parties by allowing them to play with a real filesystem, understand the flow through the kernel, and add additional features.

The following sections describe the book's chapters in more detail.

Chapter 1: UNIX Evolution and Standardization

Because the book covers many UNIX and UNIX-like operating systems, this chapter provides a base by describing UNIX from a historical perspective. Starting with the research editions that originated in Bell Labs in the late 1960s, the chapter follows the evolution of UNIX through BSD, System V, and the many UNIX and UNIX-like variants that followed such as Linux.

The latter part of the chapter describes the various standards bodies and the standards that they have produced which govern the filesystem level interfaces provided by UNIX.

Chapter 2: File-Based Concepts

This chapter presents concepts and commands that relate to files. The different file types are described along with the commands that manipulate them. The chapter also describes the UNIX security model.

Chapter 3: User File I/O

Moving down one level, this chapter describes file access from a programmatic aspect covering the difference between library-level functions and system calls. Building on the six basic system calls to allocate files, seek, read, and write file data, the chapter then goes on to describe all of the main file related functions available in UNIX. This includes everything from file locking to asynchronous I/O to memory mapped files.

Examples are given where applicable including a simple implementation of UNIX commands such as cat, dd, and cp.

Chapter 4: The Standard I/O Library

One part of the UNIX API often used but rarely described in detail is the standard I/O library. This chapter, using the Linux standard I/O library as an example, describes how the library is implemented on top of the standard file-based system calls.

The main structures and the flow through the standard I/O library functions are described, including the various types of buffering that are employed.

Chapter 5: Filesystem-Based Concepts

This chapter concludes the user-level angle by describing the main features exported by UNIX for creation and management of filesystems.

The UNIX filesystem hierarchy is described followed by a description of disk partitioning to produce raw slices or volumes on which filesystems can then be created. The main commands used for creating, mounting and managing filesystems is then covered along with the various files that are used in mounting filesystems.

To show how the filesystem based commands are implemented, the chapter also provides a simple implementation of the commands mount, df, and fstyp.

Chapter 6: UNIX Kernel Concepts

Today's UNIX kernels are extremely complicated. Even operating systems such as Linux have become so large as to make study difficult for the novice.

By starting with 5th Edition, which had around 9,000 lines of code in the whole kernel, this chapter presents the fundamentals of the kernel from a filesystem perspective. Main concepts such as the inode cache, buffer cache, and process-related structures are covered followed by a description of how simple operations such as read() and write() flow through the kernel.

The concepts introduced in these early kernels are still as relevant today as they were when first introduced. Studying these older kernels therefore presents the ideal way to learn about the UNIX kernel.

Chapter 7: Development of the SVR4 VFS/Vnode Architecture

Arguably the most significant filesystem-related development in UNIX was the introduction of the VFS/vnode architecture. Developed by Sun Microsystems in the mid 1980s, the architecture allowed support for multiple, different filesystem types to reside in the kernel simultaneously.

This chapter follows the evolution of this architecture from its first introduction in SunOS through to SVR4 and beyond.

Chapter 8: Non-SVR4-Based Filesystem Architectures

Although the VFS/vnode architecture was mirrored in the development of many other of the UNIX variants, subtle differences crept in, and some versions of UNIX and UNIX-like operating systems adopted different approaches to solving the problems of supporting different filesystem types.

This chapter explores some of the VFS/vnode variants along with non-VFS architectures ranging from microkernel implementations to Linux.

Chapter 9: Disk-Based Filesystem Case Studies

By choosing three different filesystem implementations, the VERITAS Filesystem (VxFS), the UFS filesystem, and the Linux-based ext2/3 filesystems, this chapter explores in more detail the type of features that individual filesystems provide along with an insight into their implementation.

Chapter 10: Mapping Filesystems to Multiprocessor Systems

The UNIX implementations described in earlier chapters changed considerably with the introduction of Symmetric Multiprocessing (SMP). Because multiple threads of execution could be running within the kernel at the same time, the need to protect data structures with finer and finer grain locks became apparent.

This chapter follows the evolution of UNIX from a monolithic design through to today's highly scalable SMP environments and describes the types of locking changes that were added to filesystems to support these new architectures.

Chapter 11: Pseudo Filesystems

In addition to the traditional disk-based filesystems, there are a number of pseudo filesystems that, to the user, appear similar to other filesystems, but have no associated physical storage. Filesystems such as /proc and device filesystems such as specfs have become common across many versions of UNIX.

This chapter describes some of the more well-known pseudo filesystems. For the /proc filesystem, the chapter shows how debuggers and trace utilities can be written together with an example of how the UNIX ps command can be written.

Chapter 12: Filesystem Backup

Another area that is typically not well documented is the area of filesystem backup. This chapter describes some of the backup techniques that can be used to back up a set of files or whole filesystems, and the various archiving tools such as tar, and the dump/restore utilities. The main part of the chapter describes frozen image techniques that show how persistent and non persistent snapshot technologies can be used to obtain stable backups.

Chapter 13: Clustered and Distributed Filesystems

This chapter describes both distributed filesystems and clustered filesystems. For distributed filesystems, the chapter covers the development of NFS through its early adoption to the features that are being implemented as part of NFS v4. Other distributed filesystems such as AFS and DFS are also described.

The components required to build a clustered filesystem using Storage Area Networks (SANs) is then covered followed by a description of the various components of the VERITAS Clustered Filesystem.

Chapter 14: Developing a Filesystem for the Linux Kernel

In order to understand how filesystems are implemented and how they work, it is best to play with an existing filesystem and see how it works internally and responds to the various file-related system calls. This chapter provides an implementation of the old System V filesystem on the Linux kernel. By showing how to utilize various kernel debuggers, the chapter shows how to analyze the operation of the filesystem.

There are a number of features omitted from the filesystem that are left for the reader to complete.

Typographical Conventions

All of the program listings, UNIX commands, library functions, and system calls are displayed in a fixed-width font `as shown here`.

Many examples are shown that have required keyboard input. In such cases, all input is shown in a **`bold, fixed-width font`**. Commands entered by the superuser are prefixed with the # prompt while those commands which do not require superuser privileges are prefixed with the $ prompt.

Shown below is an example of user input:

```
$ ls -l myfile
-rw-r--r-   1 spate     fcf                    0 Feb 16 11:14 myfile
```

Accessing Manual Pages

The internet offers the opportunity to view the manual pages of all major versions of UNIX without having to locate a system of that type. Searching for manual pages, say on Solaris, will reveal a large number of Web sites that enable you to scan for manual pages, often for multiple versions of the operating system. The following Web site:

```
http://unix.about.com/library/misc/blmanpg.htm
```

contains pointers to the manual pages for most versions of UNIX and Linux.

Manual pages contain a wealth of information, and for those who wish to learn more about a specific operating system, this is an excellent place to start.

Acknowledgements

First of all I would like to thank VERITAS for allowing me to work a 4-day week for more than a year, while spending Fridays working on this book. In particular, my manager, Ashvin Kamaraju, showed considerable patience, always leaving it to my judgement to balance book time and work time. He finally gets those Fridays back!

Next I would like to thank Marianne Lent who reviewed the book from a technical perspective but also helped to make it more readable. Thanks also to Pat Carri for help on FrameMaker.

Dheer Moghe reviewed the chapter on clustered filesystems and Amit Kale was gracious enough to allow me to steal his makefiles which I used for uxfs.

Finally, I would like to thank my better half, Eleanor, for her patience over the last 18 months. It will certainly be nice for *The book* not to dominate the conversation. Well, until the next one!

UNIX Evolution and Standardization

This chapter introduces UNIX from a historical perspective, showing how the various UNIX versions have evolved over the years since the very first implementation in 1969 to the present day. The chapter also traces the history of the different attempts at standardization that have produced widely adopted standards such as POSIX and the Single UNIX Specification.

The material presented here is not intended to document all of the UNIX variants, but rather describes the early UNIX implementations along with those companies and bodies that have had a major impact on the direction and evolution of UNIX.

A Brief Walk through Time

There are numerous events in the computer industry that have occurred since UNIX started life as a small project in Bell Labs in 1969. UNIX history has been largely influenced by Bell Labs' Research Editions of UNIX, AT&T's System V UNIX, Berkeley's Software Distribution (BSD), and Sun Microsystems' SunOS and Solaris operating systems.

The following list shows the major events that have happened throughout the history of UNIX. Later sections describe some of these events in more detail.

1969. Development on UNIX starts in AT&T's Bell Labs.

1971. 1st Edition UNIX is released.

1973. 4th Edition UNIX is released. This is the first version of UNIX that had the kernel written in C.

1974. Ken Thompson and Dennis Ritchie publish their classic paper, "The UNIX Timesharing System" [RITC74].

1975. 6th Edition, also called V6 UNIX, becomes the first version of UNIX to be used outside Bell Labs. The University of California at Berkeley starts development on the *Berkeley Software Distribution* or more commonly called BSD.

1977. At this stage there were 500 sites running UNIX. Universities accounted for about 20 percent of those sites.

1979. 7th Edition UNIX was rewritten to make it more portable. Microsoft licenses 7th Edition and starts development of Xenix.

1980. Microsoft releases Xenix, a PC-based version of UNIX.

1982. AT&T's UNIX Systems Group releases System III UNIX. The Santa Cruz Operation (SCO) licenses Xenix from Microsoft.

1983. AT&T's UNIX System Development Labs release System V Release 1 UNIX.

1984. 4.2BSD is released including TCP/IP. System V Release 2 is released and the number of installations of UNIX worldwide exceeds 100,000. Digital Equipment Corporation's (DEC's) 4.2BSD-based Ultrix is released.

1986. 4.3BSD is released. 4.2BSD-based HP-UX first appears. IBM releases AIX 2 for the RT server.

1987. AT&T releases System V Release 3, which includes STREAMS, the Network File System (NFS), and the Transport Level Interface (TLI).

1989. As a joint venture between AT&T's Unix System Laboratories (USL) and Sun Microsystems, System V Release 4.0 is released.

1990. Based on SVR2 with enhancements from 4.2BSD and 4.3BSD, IBM releases AIX 3.1.

1991. Linus Torvalds announces Linux 0.0.1.

1992. USL releases System V Release 4.2 that includes the VERITAS filesystem VxFS and Volume Manager VxVM.

1993. 4.4BSD, the last release from Berkeley, is released. SVR4.2MP is released by Novell following their purchase of USL from AT&T.

1994. 4.4BSD Lite, which was free of copyrighted UNIX source code, is released.

1995. SCO buys Novell's UNIX business.

1996. The Linux 2.0 kernel is released.

1997. UnixWare 7, a merge of SVR4.2MP and SCO OpenServer, is released.

2001. SCO's UNIX business is sold to Linux distributor Caldera. The Linux 2.4 kernel emerges after many delays.

How Many Versions of UNIX Are There?

Most versions of UNIX have stemmed from System V or BSD, with many taking enhancements from both. The 1980s saw a proliferation of versions of UNIX. Although it is difficult to give an exact figure on how many versions of UNIX have actually been produced, by the late 1980s it is safe to say that there were close to 100 different UNIX variants employed throughout the world. It is no wonder why UNIX has had its critics and not surprising that attempts at standardization have proceeded for much of UNIX's history.

Developing operating systems is a costly business, however, which has resulted in consolidation throughout the mid to late 1990s. On the low end, Linux and SCO variants tend to dominate while in the mid to high-end, Sun's Solaris, Hewlett Packard's HP-UX, and IBM's AIX account for most of the market share.

As time goes by there is likely to be further consolidation at the low to mid-range of PCs, workstations, and servers with Linux clearly leading the way. UNIX is still a clear leader at the high end of the market with Sun, HP, and IBM all having enterprise level capabilities in their UNIX offerings. While it is difficult to see further consolidation at this end of the market, only time will tell.

Why Is UNIX So Successful?

Although the large number of different versions of UNIX can be considered a weakness since it raised the possibility of incompatibilities, it also demonstrates one of the great strengths of UNIX: the ease by which UNIX has been ported to a wide number of different hardware architectures and platforms, a task that was addressed very early on during development at Bell Labs.

Even though the number of versions of UNIX increased dramatically over the years, porting applications between one version and the next was still considerably easier than porting between one proprietary OS and the next. This task has been made easier by the introduction of relevant standards that nearly all of the major UNIX vendors have adopted. No other operating system can claim this level of dominance across such a wide range of platforms. The proliferation of UNIX resulted in a huge amount of development pushing UNIX way ahead of its nearest proprietary competitors.

The Early Days of UNIX

The research arm of the Bell Telephone Company, Bell Labs, had seen the need for a new computer operating system in the late 1950s. This resulted in the BESYS operating system which, although used internally, had limited distribution outside of Bell Labs. By the mid 1960s, third-generation computer equipment was emerging and the people at Bell Labs had to decide whether to create a new operating system or to adopt a third party OS. The decision was eventually made to join General Electric and MIT to create a new timesharing system called the *MULTIplexed Information and Computing Service* (MULTICS). This collaborative venture aimed to show that general purpose, multiuser operating systems were a viable solution. Based on a research operating system from MIT called the *Compatible Time Sharing System* (CTSS), the MULTICS project resulted in a wide range of new approaches. Amongst those working on MULTICS were Bell Lab researchers Ken Thomson and Dennis Ritchie, who would take many of the ideas from MULTICS and evolve them into what would become UNIX. As an example, many of the UNIX commands were based on commands of the same name in MULTICS, namely ls, cd, and pwd. Due to the high cost of development and the amount of time that it was believed MULTICS would take to complete, AT&T withdrew from the MULTICS project in 1969.

On an internal GE-645 computer at Bell Labs, the GECOS operating system was installed, which proved inadequate to many of the researchers. For many this was seen as being back at square one. This resulted in a proposal by Thompson and Ritchie to get Bell Labs to buy a new machine so they could start work on their own interactive time-sharing system. The proposal was rejected and Thompson started work on an old PDP-7. Developing initially on a GE-635, Thompson produced a primitive kernel, assembler, shell, and a few utilities (rm, cat, cp) that were then transported to the PDP-7 by paper tape. Even at this stage the new primitive OS was sufficient for all further development to proceed on the PDP-7 itself. As a pun on MULTICS, the new environment was named UNIX.

In 1970 the UNIX pioneers acquired a DEC PDP-11 that was initially diskless and had 24KB of memory. They used 12KB for the operating system, allowed a small amount of space for user programs, and the rest was used as a RAM disk. It was around this time that the first 1st Edition UNIX appeared.

The Early History of the C Language

Following the early assembler versions of UNIX, Thompson worked on a Fortran compiler that evolved to support the language B, a cut-down version of BCPL. The B compiler was provided as part of 1st Edition UNIX in 1971, and some of the first utilities were even written in B. It was Ritchie's work over the next two years that resulted in the first C compiler, which became part of 3rd Edition UNIX in 1973. Note that it would still be another 5 years before the appearance of Kernighan and Ritchie's book, *The C Programming Language* [KERN78]. Following an abortive attempt by Thompson to write part of the kernel in an early version of C which did not support structures, by 4th Edition UNIX that appeared in 1973, Thompson and Ritchie had rewritten the kernel in C.

Research Editions of UNIX

There were a total of ten research editions of UNIX from Bell Labs. Perhaps the most famous was 6th Edition UNIX which was described in John Lions' book *Lions' Commentary on UNIX 6th Edition* [LION96], which until it was published in 1996 remained an underground work. One thing that distinguished each research edition was the introduction of a new *Programmer's Reference Manual*. Following is a brief summary of the different research editions and which UNIX features they introduced:

1st Edition—1971. As well as the B compiler, 1st Edition UNIX introduced a number of well-known UNIX commands including `cat`, `chdir`, `chmod`, `chown`, `cp`, `ed`, `find`, `mkdir`, `mkfs`, `mount`, `mv`, `rm`, `rmdir`, `wc`, and `who`.

2nd Edition—1972. One amusing note on 2nd Edition was a comment in the *Programmer's Reference Manual* that the number of UNIX installations had now grown to 10!

3th Edition—1973. The UNIX C compiler (`cc`) first appeared. The kernel was still written in assembler and the number of installations had grown to 16. Pipes were also introduced.

4th Edition—1973. The kernel was rewritten in C.

5th Edition—1974. This edition appeared around the time of Thompson and Ritchie's paper "The UNIX Time Sharing System" [RITC74]. The source code was made freely available to universities for educational purposes.

6th Edition—1975. This edition, also known as V6, was the first edition widely available outside of Bell Labs. Most of the operating system by this time had been written in C.

7th Edition—1979. The first K&R (Kernighan and Ritchie) compliant C compiler made its appearance with 7th edition together with Steve Bourne's shell (`sh`). The kernel was rewritten to make it more portable to other architectures. At this time the UNIX Systems Group was created and started working on enhancing 7th Edition (on which System V UNIX would be based). Microsoft also licensed 7th Edition, which it used to develop the Xenix operating system. Note that the size of the 7th Edition kernel was only 40KB, a tiny program by today's standards.

8th Edition—1985. 8th Edition UNIX picked up some enhancements developed from 4.1BSD. This edition was used as the basis for System V Release 3.

9th Edition—1988. This edition picked up enhancements made for 4.3BSD.

10th Edition—1989. This was the last edition.

AT&T's Commercial Side of UNIX

In the late 1960s, while Bell Labs was looking for a new timesharing system, the Bell Telephone company was looking for a way to automate their telephone operations using minicomputers to switch over from their existing system of people and paper.

It was Berkley Tague, the head of the computer planning department, who, having seen the capabilities of UNIX, realized its potential and saw how it could ease their job. By 1971 Tague gained approval for the adoption of UNIX to support Bell Telephone operations. By 1973 he formed the *UNIX Support Group* (USG) which worked closely with the UNIX team from Bell Labs. During the same year, the first UNIX applications started to appear, initially involved in updating customer directory information and intercepting calls to phone numbers that had been changed. 1973 also saw the first C version of UNIX released internally together with the first *Programmer's Work Bench*, which included sccs and other tools.

Around the time of 7th Edition UNIX, USG took responsibility for UNIX and after a number of internal-only releases, System III UNIX became the first version of UNIX that was available for use outside Bell Labs.

USG later became the *UNIX System Development Laboratory* (USDL). In 1984, this group released System V Release 2 (SVR2) which was the first version of UNIX to support paging, copy-on-write semantics, shared memory, and file locking. SVR2 UNIX is described in Bach's classic book *The Design of the UNIX Operating System* [BACH86]. At this time there were about 100,000 installations of UNIX worldwide running on a whole host of different platforms and architectures. The fact that no other operating system had achieved this goal was perhaps the single greatest reason why UNIX became so popular.

Following yet another name change to *AT&T Information Systems* (ATTIS), the group released System V Release 3 (SVR3) in 1987. This included a number of enhancements:

- The File System Switch (FSS) provided an architecture under which multiple filesystems could coexist in the kernel at the same time. The FSS provided a layer by which the rest of the kernel could perform file and filesystem related operations in a filesystem independent manner through a well defined interface.

- The RFS (Remote File Sharing) filesystem provided a fully distributed, cache-coherent file system.

- The STREAMS subsystem for building networking stacks. The initial implementation of STREAMS was first introduced in 8th Edition UNIX.

- The Transport Layer Interface (TLI) for network programming.

- Shared libraries which can reduce the amount of memory used.

System V Release 3.2 was released in 1987 which involved a merge of SVR3 and Xenix, produced by Microsoft and the Santa Cruz Operation (SCO).

One of the major releases of UNIX from AT&T was System V Release 4 in conjunction with Sun Microsystems. This is described in more detail in the section *System V Release 4 and Variants* later in the chapter.

The Evolution of BSD UNIX

Following Thompson and Ritchie's paper on UNIX at the Symposium on Operating System Principles in 1974, Bob Fabry, a professor at the University of California at Berkeley wanted to get a copy to experiment with.

After buying a PDP 11/45, he received the tapes for 4th Edition UNIX which was installed in 1974. Due to disk related problems, Ken Thompson spent time dialed in over a modem debugging the system.

Following the purchase of a Vax 11/70 in 1975, Ken Thompson started a sabbatical at Berkeley during which time he brought up 6th Edition. Around this time, graduate students Bill Joy and Chuck Haley arrived and started working on the newly installed system, initially enhancing a Pascal system that Thompson had put together. The same year, they produced the ex editor and started working on the kernel following the departure of Thompson back to Bell Labs.

Following requests for the Pascal environment, Bill Joy put together the *Berkeley Software Distribution* (consider this as 1BSD) in 1977 and distributed thirty copies. Soon after, Joy wrote the vi editor, still hugely popular 25 years later.

In 1978 Joy released the second Berkeley Software Distribution which became known as 2BSD. This included an updated Pascal system, the vi editor, and termcap which could be used for driving multiple different terminal types, a must for supporting vi.

Needing more power, a Vax 11/780 was purchased and the 32/V port of UNIX, initiated at Bell Labs, was installed. Following a number of enhancements to make use of the new virtual memory capabilities of the machine, Joy started porting 2BSD to produce the third Berkeley distribution, 3BSD, which was released in 1979.

Around this time, DARPA (*Defense Advanced Research Projects Agency*) decided to standardize on UNIX in order to provide a network to link their major research centers. Based on Fabry's proposal to DARPA and the ensuing success of 3BSD, an 18 month contract was awarded to Berkeley. Fabry set up the *Computer Systems Research Group* (CSRG) to handle the contract and research. Bill Joy came on board and set to work on what would become 4BSD. Released in 1980, the new system included the Pascal compiler, job control, auto reboot, and a 1KB size filesystem. Joy then released 4.1BSD which contained numerous performance improvements to the kernel.

Following renewal of the contract by DARPA, the new project would produce what would become the *Berkeley Fast File System*, support for large virtual address spaces and better IPC mechanisms. The TCP/IP stack was integrated into BSD and a number of temporary tools were introduced on top of the networking stack. These temporary tools, namely rcp, rsh, rlogin, and rwho are a little more permanent than their original authors anticipated, still being used today.

Following Bill Joy's departure in 1982 to co-found Sun Microsystems, 4.2BSD was released in 1983. Due to the introduction of TCP/IP and the Fast File System, the number of 4.2BSD installations far exceeded System V from AT&T.

Following criticism of 4.1BSD performance, a two year period of tuning and refining produced 4.3BSD which was released in 1986. Two years later, completing the work started by Joy to divide the BSD kernel into machine dependent and machine independent layers, CSRG released the finished work under 4.3BSD-Tahoe. Further development which resulted in a rewrite of the virtual memory subsystem, based on the Mach microkernel, together with NFS, produced 4.3BSD-Reno in 1990.

BSD Networking Releases

To avoid BSD recipients having to obtain an AT&T source license while wanting to have source access to the networking components of BSD, the *Networking Release* of BSD was released in 1989. An expanded version, which involved rewriting all except six kernel files, was distributed as the Networking Release 2 in 1991. This involved a huge effort by many people.

Bill Jolitz continued the work by rewriting the remaining six kernel files to avoid AT&T copyrighted source code and porting the system to the Intel 386, resulting in 386/BSD which was distributed over the internet.

UNIX Goes to Court

Following the Net/2 release of BSD, the *Berkeley Software Design, Incorporated* (BSDI) company was formed to develop a fully supported, commercial version. The BSDI version, released in 1992, included replacements for the six kernel files, was considerably cheaper than System V UNIX from USL, and used *UNIX* as part of the telephone number in their advertisements to call for questions. This was followed by a lawsuit from AT&T, initially aiming to prevent BSDI from promoting their product as UNIX. This was then followed by an additional lawsuit that claimed that the BSDI version contained proprietary USL source code and secrets.

While the lawsuit continued, USL was purchased by Novell in 1993. Novell founder and CEO, Ray Noorda, wanted to drop the lawsuit and in 1994 an agreement was finally reached. As part of the agreement, 5 of the 18,000 files that made up the distribution were removed. With some minor changes to other files and the addition of copyright notices in an additional 70 files, the new, 4.4BSD-Lite version was released.

The NetBSD Operating System

386/BSD was extremely successful. Unfortunately Jolitz was unable to work full time and keep up with his work on 386/BSD. Frustrated with the way that development of 386/BSD was progressing, others started working on a parallel development path, taking a combination of 386BSD and Net/2 and porting it to large array of other platforms and architectures.

The FreeBSD Operating System

Following work on Jolitz's 386/BSD system, Jordan Hubbard, Rod Grimes, and Nate Williams released the *Unofficial 386BSD Patchkit* which contained a number of changes. Jolitz denounced approval of the project in 1993, which was followed by discussions between Hubbard and Walnut Creek to produce a new operating system, which they called FreeBSD. The first CDROM version of FreeBSD, version 1.0, was released in December of 1993.

Following the USL lawsuit, the base operating system was upgraded from Net/2 to 4.4BSD-Lite, which resulted in the release of FreeBSD 2.0 in November of 1994. Enhancements continue to be added with the latest stable release being FreeBSD 4.2.

FreeBSD has been relatively successful on its own ground. It was also used as the basis for Apple's Mac OS X operating system.

The OpenBSD Operating System

Following a disagreement between Theo de Raadt, who had been responsible for the SPARC port of NetBSD, and the NetBSD core team, de Raadt founded OpenBSD. The new OS started to diverge from NetBSD 1.1 in 1995 and this was followed by the first release, OpenBSD 3.0 in October of 1996. The core focus of OpenBSD was security.

Although not as portable as NetBSD, OpenBSD still runs on a wide range of machines and architectures and continues to lead the way as the most secure BSD release available.

Sun Microsystems and SunOS

Sun Microsystems was founded in 1982 by four people including current CEO Scott McNeally and BSD developer Bill Joy. In their first year they released their first workstation based on hardware developed at Stanford University and on the BSD operating system.

Sun has continued from day one to innovate and enhance UNIX. In order to provide remote file access they introduced the *Network File System* (NFS) and the VFS/vnode architecture to support it.

In 1987 Sun and AT&T joined forces to develop UNIX System V Release 4, which combined the best of SunOS and System V Release 3.2. SVR4 encompassed many of the ideas that Sun had implemented including VFS/vnodes, NFS, and their virtual memory architecture, which cleanly divides memory management into machine dependent and machine independent layers. Sun, together with IBM and HP, continues to take UNIX to the enterprise, continually enhancing their UNIX offerings while retaining compatibility at the standards level.

System V Release 4 and Variants

System V Release 4 set the standard for everyone else to follow producing an extremely feature-rich operating system that combined the best of the historical versions of UNIX with many new ideas from Sun. The following list shows some of the major enhancements that came with SVR4:

- The VFS/vnode architecture that replaced the FSS from SVR3. The VFS/vnode architecture was originally developed as part of SunOS.

- Symbolic links.

- The C and Korn Shells along with job control.

- Memory mapped files.

- The UFS filesystem derived from the BSD Fast File System. UFS became the defacto standard on most versions of UNIX. It is still the default filesystem on Solaris and is still undergoing major development. SVR4 also included the NFS filesystem. At this stage, the largely unsuccessful RFS was starting to fade.

- STREAMS-based console and TTY (teletype) management.

- Real-time scheduling and a partial implementation of kernel preemption.

Enhancements continued thereafter. SVR4.1 included Asynchronous I/O. SVR4.2 included Access Control Lists (ACLs), the VERITAS Filesystem (VxFS), and VERITAS Volume Manager (VxVM). Following this, with a major rewrite, SVR4.2MP introduced Symmetric Multiprocessing (SMP) capabilities and kernel threads.

Novell's Entry into the UNIX Market

The UnixWare 1.0 release of UNIX was released in 1992 as a joint venture between Novell and USL under the name Univel. Novell completed the acquisition of USL in 1993, and both USL and Univel were merged to form the Novell UNIX Systems Group.

UnixWare 1.0 was based on SVR4.0. This was followed by UnixWare 1.1, which was based on SVR4.2. With the introduction of UnixWare 2.0, the kernel (SVR4.2MP) had changed significantly, introducing SMP support and kernel threads.

In 1993 Novell transferred the rights to the UNIX trademark to the X/Open organization (now the Open Group). Two years later they sold their UNIX business to SCO who in turn sold a dwindling UNIX business to Caldera in 2001.

Linux and the Open Source Movement

One could argue that if readers didn't have to purchase Andrew Tanenbaum's MINIX operating system that accompanied his book *Operating Systems: Design and Implementation* [TANE87], there would be no Linux.

However, the *Free Software Foundation*, founded by Richard Stallman, had already been working for a number of years on a free version of UNIX. The compiler, utilities, and just about everything except the kernel had been written under the auspices of the GNU license which allowed the source to be freely distributed.

Linus Torvalds, a research assistant at the University of Helsinki in Finland, released Linux 0.0.1 in August of 1991, and the rest, as they say, is history. Popularity of Linux continues to grow. Although it originally took many of its ideas from Minix, Linux has been influenced by all versions of UNIX and non-UNIX systems. Linux followed in the success of UNIX by being ported to just about every hardware architecture and platform available from IBM mainframes down to hand-held organizers.

Users of Linux will find a number of components from many different authors and organizations. A Linux OS is comprised of the Linux kernel, much of the Free Software Foundation's GNU software, and a number of other free applications and utilities. There are many distributors of Linux, with the top players being Red Hat, SuSe, TurboLinux, and Caldera.

UNIX Standardization

The section *A Brief Walk through Time* earlier in the chapter showed how the different versions of UNIX came into existence through the 1980s. Although most of these versions stemmed from either System V or BSD, each OS vendor added its own enhancements, whether to increase performance or add new interfaces in response to internal or customer demands. Because application portability was crucial to the success of application developers, it soon became clear that a level of standardization was needed to prevent this divergence from going too far.

Various bodies have been responsible for driving the standardization of UNIX interfaces, whether at a command level, library, or system call level; or newer initiatives such as the Large File Summit for 64-bit file access and the Data Management Interfaces Group (DMIG) for interfaces relating to Hierarchical Storage Management. This section describes the main standards bodies, their goals, and the standards that they have produced.

IEEE and POSIX

The /usr/group organization was formed by a group of individuals in 1980 with the intention of standardizing user-level interfaces with the goal of application portability.

They reached consensus in 1984, and their work was used by the ANSI X3J11 committee, the same group who were working on standardization of the C language. As the number of versions of UNIX started to increase, divergence continued, and the /usr/group standard became less and less effective. This led to the formation of the *Portable Operating System Interface for Computing Environments* (POSIX) in 1995 which used the /usr/group standard as its base working document. As a point of interest, the name POSIX was suggested by Richard Stallman, founder of the *Free Software Foundation* (FSF).

The standard produced by this group, POSIX 1003.1-1998 became the most widely recognized standard throughout the UNIX industry and is available on many non-UNIX platforms. The initial standard was revised throughout the next three years and adopted by the Institute of Electrical and Electronics Engineers (IEEE) organization to become IEEE Std 1003.1-1990 although it is still more commonly known as POSIX.1 or simply the POSIX standard. In 1989 the /usr/group changed its name to Uniforum.

The POSIX working committees did not stop there and produced a number of other standards of which some are shown in Table 1.1.

The X/Open Group

With the same goals as the /usr/group, a number of European computer companies formed a non profit organization in 1984 called X/Open.

Although many of the players were not specifically UNIX based, application portability was still key. The first published standard from X/Open was the *X/Open Portability Guide* (XPG). The third draft of this standard, XPG3, included both POSIX 1003.1-1998 and a number of interfaces pertaining to the X Window System. The XPG3 test suite contained over 5,500 different tests that exercised system calls, library interfaces, and the C language.

The XPG4 standard was released in October of 1992. This encompassed not only POSIX.1, but also POSIX.2 and ISO C. A successful branding program was put in place so that companies could claim XPG4 compliance.

The System V Interface Definition

The UNIX System Group (USG) released the *System V Interface Definition* (SVID) version 1 with System V Release 2 in 1994. The SVID was a two-volume book that described all user accessible interfaces that were available with SVR2. SVID version 2 accompanied SVR3 in 1996.

With the introduction of SVR4 in 1989, version 3 of the SVID became available, this time a four-volume set. To accompany the SVID, USG produced SVVS, the *System V Verification Suite*, an exhaustive test suite that exercised all of the visible interfaces. Any vendors licensing System V were required to run and pass SVVS in order to use the name System V.

Since by this stage the SVID effectively encompassed the POSIX.1 standard, it was used as the main document in producing what would become the *Single UNIX Specification*.

Table 1.1 POSIX Standards

STANDARD	DESCRIPTION
1003.1	System call and library routines
1003.2	The shell and UNIX utilities
1003.3	Test methods and conformance
1003.4	Real-time interfaces

Spec 11/70 and the Single UNIX Specification

In order to combine the existing UNIX standards such as POSIX.1 and XPG4, a group was formed by Sun Microsystems, HP, IBM, Novell/USL, and the Open Software Foundation (OSF) to provide a single unified standard based on existing standards and additional features provided by the different UNIX versions. Using XPG4 as a base which already encompassed POSIX.1 and ANSI/ISO C, a collection of 1,170 APIs were specified in total, and thus the name Spec 11/70 was given to the group and the specification.

The Spec 11/70 API was delivered to X/Open in 1983 resulting in the *Single UNIX Specification*, which was published in 1994. Various names have since followed this publication including UNIX 95 and the enhanced version renamed UNIX 98.

The standard is still maintained by the *Open Group* which was formed by a merge of X/Open and OSF. The Single UNIX Specification can be viewed online at www.opengroup.org.

The main components of the Single UNIX Specification are:

System Interface Definitions (XBD). This document outlines common definitions used in the XSH and XCU documents.

System Interfaces and Headers (XSH). This document describes all programming interfaces and all header files. Most of the text provides UNIX manual style representations for each API.

Commands and Utilities (XCU). This document describes all of the commands and utilities in a UNIX manual page style format.

Networking Services. This document describes the X/Open Transport Interface (XTI), XPG4 sockets, and the IP address resolution interfaces.

X/Open Curses. This document describes X/Open version 3 *curses*.

UNIX International and OSF

The *Open Software Foundation* (OSF) was founded in 1988 by seven leading computer companies with the goal of producing an operating system together with an open and portable application environment.

As a reaction to OSF and with a consortium of over 200 vendors and users,

UNIX International (UI) was founded in 1988 centered around AT&T's SVR4 version of UNIX. The goals of the organization were to drive the direction for SVR4 although in reality, UI turned out to be more of a marketing machine with little actual output. Within a few years, UI was dissolved, and the direction of SVR4 was left to Novell/USL and then SCO.

Both OSF and UI achieved some notable successes. The big battle predicted between the two never happened in reality. Through USL, UI pushed the SVID version 3, which became the basis for the Single UNIX Specification. OSF merged with X/Open to form the *Open Group* which still maintains the Single UNIX Specification today along with other UNIX related standards.

The Data Management Interfaces Group

A small number of independent software and hardware vendors were developing Hierarchical Storage Management (HSM) solutions, which involved modifications to the base UNIX kernel (see the section *Hierarchical Storage Management* in Chapter 12 for further details). Following publication of Neil Webber's USENIX paper "Operating System Support for Portable Filesystem Extensions" [WEBB93], a group of HSM, backup, OS, and filesystem vendors formed the Data Management Interfaces Group (DMIG) with the goal of producing an interface specification that the OS/filesystem vendors would implement to prevent the constant rewrite of HSM software with each iteration of the operating system.

X/Open adopted the Data Management API (DMAPI) and renamed it XDSM (*X/Open Data Storage Management*).

The standard allows for applications to transparently migrate data from the filesystem (termed secondary storage) to tape or other offline storage devices (tertiary storage) bypassing the UNIX timestamping mechanisms and without knowledge of user-level applications. This allows HSM applications to achieve a virtual memory-like approach to storage.

The Large File Summit

32-bit operating systems imposed limits on the size of files that could be accessed due to limits imposed at various layers throughout the operating system, not least the fact that the value that could be held in a signed integer, the maximum value that could be held in a `size_t`, was limited to 2GB -1.

To provide an intermediate solution that could allow access to files greater than 2GB before the advent of 64-bit operating systems, the *Large File Summit*, a group of operating system and filesystem vendors, was formed to produce a specification that introduced a new set of data types and APIs that allowed for large file access.

Applications could access *large files*, files greater than 2GB, by either invoking 64-bit versions of the system calls or via compile time flags that switched the size of various data types. At the time of writing, much of this is now a moot point with 64-bit file access being the norm in UNIX.

Summary

This chapter highlighted the main events that show how the different versions of UNIX have evolved and where specific pieces of technology have come from. The history of UNIX could fill a book by itself. Indeed, Peter Salus' book *A Quarter Century of UNIX* [SALU96] describes UNIX history from 1969 to 1994.

Programmers wishing to follow UNIX standards should adhere to the Single UNIX Specification when striving for application compatibility across all the major versions of UNIX. Although Linux does not comply completely with the specification, most interfaces are supported. At a very minimum, the POSIX interfaces are supported by just about every operating system, UNIX and non-UNIX alike.

File-Based Concepts

To gain a full picture of the internal operation of filesystems, it is necessary to understand what the user sees, why things are presented they way they are, and what the main concepts are.

This chapter provides an introduction to basic file concepts. Users experienced in UNIX may wish to skip this chapter. Users new to UNIX and those starting to program in the UNIX environment will find these concepts useful. A basic implementation of the ls program helps to reinforce the material presented and provides an introduction to file-related libraries and system calls, a topic that will be expanded upon in the next chapter.

One peculiarity that UNIX introduced was the notion that everything in the UNIX namespace (file tree) is visible as a file and that the same operations can be applied to all file types. Thus one can open and read a directory in the same way in which a file can be opened and read. Of course, this doesn't always have the desired effect. For example, running the UNIX command cat on a directory will likely produce a screen full of unreadable characters. However, these and other simple concepts are one of the great strengths of UNIX. The following sections provide introductory material which describe file-based concepts and start to paint a picture of how these components fit together.

UNIX File Types

The two most common file types are *regular files* and *directories*. Regular files are by far the most common type of files in a UNIX system, with program source, documents, executable programs, and scripts all being stored as regular files. One could argue that executable files are a special type of regular file but their handling by the filesystem is just the same, that is, the file contains a stream of bytes that the filesystem never needs to interpret.

Directories are different however. Although they also contain a stream of bytes, filesystems interpret these bytes in a manner that allows users to see which files are present in the directory and how they are linked together from a hierarchical perspective.

There are other file types which must be considered by programmers and administrators. They are outlined here and described in more detail throughout the chapter:

Regular files. As mentioned above, regular files hold data that is not interpreted by the filesystem, such as program source and binaries, documents and scripts.

Directories. Directories are used to provide structure within a filesystem. Directories can index files of any type including other directories.

Symbolic links. A symbolic link, also called a symlink, is a means by which one file can refer to another file through use of a different name. Symbolic links can cross filesystem boundaries. Removing a symbolic link has no impact on the file it references.

Hard links. Whereas a symbolic name is simply a mapping between one file name and another with no impact on the referenced file, a hard link actually refers to the same physical storage as the file to which it references. Thus by creating a hard link, the file's *link count* is incremented. When the hard link is removed the link count is decremented. When the link count reaches zero, the file is removed. Hard links cannot cross filesystem boundaries.

Named pipes. A named pipe is a bi-directional IPC (*Inter Process Communication*) mechanism that allows unrelated processes to communicate. This differs from traditional UNIX pipes that can only be accessed by related processes.

Special files. A special file is a file that refers to a device such as a disk or tape. To access a device, the caller would open the special file and access it just like any other file.

Xenix special file. Semaphores and shared memory segments in the Xenix operating system could be managed through the UNIX namespace. A special file of zero length could be used to represent a semaphore or a shared memory segment. There were a host of Xenix specific functions available for management of these IPC mechanisms. None of the calls were part of any standard and therefore will not be discussed further.

To obtain the properties of any file type, the stat() system call can be invoked. This is called by the ls command on each file that must be displayed. The section *Basic File Properties*, a bit later in this chapter, provides a simple implementation of ls to show how this works in practice.

File Descriptors

In order to give a more practical edge to the descriptions that follow, it is necessary to provide some examples in C. Therefore, before describing the various file properties, it is necessary to show how to access them; thus, the need to introduce *file descriptors*. Consider the following example:

```
$ cat open.c
#include <sys/types.h>
#include <sys/stat.h>
#include <fcntl.h>

main()
{
    int fd;

    fd = open("/etc/passwd", O_RDONLY);
    printf("fd = %d\n", fd);
    close(fd);
}
$ make open
cc        open.c    -o open
$ ./open
fd = 3
```

To access a file's data, the file must first be opened. In this case, the open() system call is used. Looking at the manual page for open(), it shows that three header files must be included as the following excerpt shows:

```
NAME
     open open a file

SYNOPSIS
     #include <sys/types.h>
     #include <sys/stat.h>
     #include <fcntl.h>

     int open(const char *path, int oflag, ...);

DESCRIPTION
     The open() function establishes  the  connection  between  a
     file and a file descriptor. It creates an ...
```

The result of a successful open is a *file descriptor* that is a handle through which the file can then be subsequently accessed. The file descriptor is required in calls such as `read()`, `write()`, and `lseek()`. The value of the file descriptor is not important although how the value is assigned will be explained in the section *File Descriptors and the File Table* in Chapter 6. What is important is that it is used consistently. Following the `open()` call shown above, every time the `passwd` file is to be accessed by a system call or library function that requires a file descriptor, the value returned in `fd` must be used.

Note with this example and with many other short examples shown here and in other books, the use of the `close()` system call is often omitted. This is generally fine since files are automatically closed when the process exits.

Basic File Properties

Typing `ls -l` at the command prompt, users will see a whole host of properties associated with each file displayed, as shown in Figure 2.1. The main properties displayed are:

- The file type and access permissions
- The link count of the file
- The file's owner and group
- The size of the file
- The date on which the file was last modified
- The name of the file

Some of the values displayed will be obvious to most readers although there are a few peculiarities. First of all however, where does this information come from? There are two calls that the `ls` command must make to get this information. Here is a brief sketch of both:

1. For the current directory, retrieve the files that are stored in the directory.
2. For each file, obtain the properties of the file.

After this information is available, the `ls` command can simply print out the information that it receives. Shown below is an example of how the `ls` command is implemented. In summary, the system call `getdents()` will return all entries in the directory, then for each entry, `ls` will call the `stat()` system call to obtain the file properties.

Here is the interface for the `stat()` system call:

```
#include <sys/types.h>
#include <sys/stat.h>

int stat(const char *path, struct stat *buf);
```

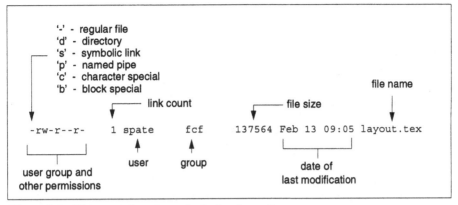

Figure 2.1 File properties shown by typing `ls -l`

Thus the caller specifies the pathname of a file for which properties are to be read and gets all of this information passed back in a `stat` structure defined as follows:

```
struct stat {
    dev_t    st_dev;        /* ID of device containing file */
    ino_t    st_ino;        /* Inode number / file serial number */
    mode_t   st_mode;       /* File mode */
    nlink_t  st_nlink;      /* Number of links to file */
    uid_t    st_uid;        /* User ID of file */
    gid_t    st_gid;        /* Group ID of file */
    dev_t    st_rdev;       /* Device ID for char/blk special file */
    off_t    st_size;       /* File size in bytes (regular file) */
    time_t   st_atime;      /* Time of last access */
    time_t   st_mtime;      /* Time of last data modification */
    time_t   st_ctime;      /* Time of last status change */
    long     st_blksize;    /* Preferred I/O block size */
    blkcnt_t st_blocks;     /* Number of 512 byte blocks allocated */
};
```

Given this information, it is relatively easy to map the fields shown here to the information displayed by the `ls` command. To help show how this works, an abbreviated version of the `ls` command is shown below. Note that this is not complete, nor is it the best way to implement the command. It does however show how to obtain information about individual files.

```
1 #include <sys/types.h>
2 #include <sys/stat.h>
3 #include <sys/dirent.h>
4 #include <sys/unistd.h>
5 #include <fcntl.h>
6 #include <unistd.h>
7 #include <errno.h>
8 #include <pwd.h>
9 #include <grp.h>
```

```
10
11 #define BUFSZ          1024
12
13 main()
14 {
15      struct dirent      *dir;
16      struct stat        st;
17      struct passwd      *pw;
18      struct group       *grp;
19      char               buf[BUFSZ], *bp, *ftime;
20      int                dfd, fd, nread;
21
22      dfd = open(".", O_RDONLY);
23      bzero(buf, BUFSZ);
24      while (nread = getdents(dfd, (struct dirent *)&buf,
25                          BUFSZ) != 0) {
26          bp = buf;
27          dir = (struct dirent *)buf;
28          do {
29              if (dir->d_reclen != 0) {
30                  stat(dir->d_name, &st);
31                  ftime = ctime(&st.st_mtime);
32                  ftime[16] = '\0'; ftime += 4;
33                  pw = getpwuid(st.st_uid);
34                  grp = getgrgid(st.st_gid);
35                  perms(st.st_mode);
36                  printf("%3d %-8s %-7s %9d %s %s\n",
37                      st.st_nlink, pw->pw_name, grp->gr_name,
38                      st.st_size, ftime, dir->d_name);
39              }
40              bp = bp + dir->d_reclen;
41              dir = (struct dirent *)(bp);
42          } while (dir->d_ino != 0);
43          bzero(buf, BUFSZ);
44      }
45 }
```

The basic loop shown here is fairly straightforward. The majority of the program deals with collecting the information obtained from stat() and putting it in a form which is more presentable to the caller.

If a directory contains a large number of entries, it may be difficult to read all entries in one call. Therefore the getdents() system call must be repeated until all entries have been read. The value returned from getdents() is the number of bytes read and not the number of directory entries. After all entries have been read, a subsequent call to getdents() will return 0.

There are numerous routines available for gathering per user and group information and for formatting different types of data. It is beyond the scope of this book to describe all of these interfaces. Using the UNIX manual pages, especially with the -k option, is often the best way to find the routines available. For example, on Solaris, running man passwd produces the man page for the

passwd command. The "SEE ALSO" section contains references to getpwnam().
The man page for getpwnam() contains information about the getpwuid()
function that is used in the above program.

As mentioned, the program shown here is far from being a complete
implementation of ls nor indeed is it without bugs. The following examples
should allow readers to experiment:

- Although it is probably a rare condition, the program could crash
  depending on the directory entries read. How could this crash occur?

- Implement the perms() function.

- Enhance the program to accept arguments including short and long
  listings and allowing the caller to specify the directory to list.

In addition to the stat() system call shown previously there are also two
additional system calls which achieve the same result:

```
#include <sys/types.h>
#include <sys/stat.h>

int lstat(const char *path, struct stat *buf);

int fstat(int fildes, struct stat *buf);
```

The only difference between stat() and lstat() is that for symbolic links,
lstat() returns information about the symbolic link whereas stat() returns
information about the file to which the symbolic link points.

The File Mode Creation Mask

There are many commands that can be used to change the properties of files.
Before describing each of these commands it is necessary to point out the file *mode
creation mask*. Consider the file created using the touch command as follows:

```
$ touch myfile
$ ls -l myfile
-rw-r--r--   1 spate     fcf              0 Feb 16 11:14 myfile
```

The first command instructs the shell to create a file if it doesn't already exist. The
shell in turn invokes the open() or creat() system call to instruct the operating
system to create the file, passing a number of properties along with the creation
request. The net effect is that a file of zero length is created.

The file is created with the owner and group IDs set to those of the caller (as
specified in /etc/passwd). The permissions of the file indicate that it is readable
and writable by the owner (rw-) and readable both by other members of the
group fcf and by everyone else.

What happens if you don't want these permissions when the file is created? Each shell supports the umask command that allows the user to change the default mask, often referred to as the file *mode creation mask*. There are actually two umask calls that take the same arguments. The first is a shell built-in variable that keeps the specified mask for the lifetime of the shell, and the second is a system binary, which is only really useful for checking the existing mask.

The current mask can be displayed in numeric or symbolic form as the two following examples show:

```
$ umask
022
$ umask -S
u=rwx,g=rx,o=rx
```

To alter the creation mask, umask is called with a three digit number for which each digit must be in the range 0 to 7. The three digits represent user, group, and owner. Each can include access for read (r=4), write (w=2), and execute (x=1).

When a file is created, the caller specifies the new mode or access permissions of the file. The umask for that process is then subtracted from the mode resulting in the permissions that will be set for the file.

As an example, consider the default umask, which for most users is 022, and a file to be created by calling the touch utility:

```
$ umask
022
$ strace touch myfile 2>&1 | grep open | grep myfile
open("myfile",
O_WRONLY_O_NONBLOCK_O_CREAT_O_NOCTTY_O_LARGEFILE, 0666) = 3
$ ls -l myfile
-rw-r--r--   1 spate    fcf            0 Apr  4 09:45 myfile
```

A umask value of 022 indicates that write access should be turned off for the group and others. The touch command then creates the file and passes a mode of 666. The resulting set of permissions will be 666 - 022 = 644, which gives the permissions -rw-r--r--.

Changing File Permissions

There are a number of commands that allow the user to change file properties. The most commonly used is the chmod utility, which takes arguments as follows:

```
chmod [ -fR ] <absolute-mode> file ...

chmod [ -fR ] <symbolic-mode-list> file ...
```

The mode to be applied gives the new or modified permissions of the file. For example, if the new permissions for a file should be `rwxr--r--`, this equates to the value `744`. For this case, `chmod` can be called with an absolute-mode argument as follows:

```
$ ls -l myfile
-rw------  1 spate      fcf             0 Mar  6 10:09 myfile
$ chmod 744 myfile
$ ls -l myfile
-rwxr--r-  1 spate      fcf             0 Mar  6 10:09 myfile*
```

To achieve the same result passing a symbolic-mode argument, `chmod` can be called as follows:

```
$ ls -l myfile
-rw------  1 spate      fcf             0 Mar  6 10:09 myfile
$ chmod u+x,a+r myfile
$ ls -l myfile
-rwxr--r-  1 spate      fcf             0 Mar  6 10:09 myfile*
```

In symbolic mode, the permissions for user, group, other, or all users can be modified by specifying u, g, o, or a. Permissions may be specified by adding (+), removing (-), or specifying directly (=), For example, another way to achieve the above change is:

```
$ ls -l myfile
-rw------  1 spate      fcf             0 Mar  6 10:09 myfile
$ chmod u=rwx,g=r,o=r myfile
$ ls -l myfile
-rwxr--r-  1 spate      fcf             0 Mar  6 10:09 myfile*
```

One last point worthy of mention is the `-R` argument which can be passed to `chmod`. With this option, `chmod` recursively descends through any directory arguments. For example:

```
$ ls -ld mydir
drwxr-xr-x  2 spate      fcf          4096 Mar 30 11:06 mydir//
$ ls -l mydir
total 0
-rw-r--r-  1 spate      fcf             0 Mar 30 11:06 fileA
-rw-r--r-  1 spate      fcf             0 Mar 30 11:06 fileB
$ chmod -R a+w mydir
$ ls -ld mydir
drwxrwxrwx  2 spate      fcf          4096 Mar 30 11:06 mydir/
$ ls -l mydir
total 0
-rw-rw-rw  1 spate      fcf             0 Mar 30 11:06 fileA
-rw-rw-rw  1 spate      fcf             0 Mar 30 11:06 fileB
```

Note that the recursive option is typically available with most commands that change file properties. Where it is not, the following invocation of find will achieve the same result:

```
$ find mydir -print | xargs chmod a+w
```

The chmod command is implemented on top of the chmod() system call. There are two calls, one that operates on a pathname and one that operates on a file descriptor as the following declarations show:

```
#include <sys/types.h>
#include <sys/stat.h>

int chmod(const char *path, mode_t mode);

int fchmod(int fildes, mode_t mode);
```

The mode argument is a bitwise OR of the fields shown in Table 2.1. Some of the flags can be combined as shown below:

S_IRWXU. This is the bitwise OR of S_IRUSR, S_IWUSR and S_IXUSR

S_IRWXG. This is the bitwise OR of S_IRGRP, S_IWGRP and S_IXGRP

S_IRWXO. This is the bitwise OR of S_IROTH, S_IWOTH and S_IXOTH

One can see from the preceding information that the chmod utility is largely a string parsing command which collects all the information required and then makes a call to chmod().

Changing File Ownership

When a file is created, the user and group IDs are set to those of the caller. Occasionally it is useful to change ownership of a file or change the group in which the file resides. Only the root user can change the ownership of a file although any user can change the file's group ID to another group in which the user resides.

There are three calls that can be used to change the file's user and group as shown below:

```
#include <sys/types.h>
#include <unistd.h>

int chown(const char *path, uid_t owner, gid_t group);
int fchown(int fd, uid_t owner, gid_t group);
int lchown(const char *path, uid_t owner, gid_t group);
```

The difference between chown() and lchown() is that the lchown() system call operates on the symbolic link specified rather than the file to which it points.

Table 2.1   Permissions Passed to chmod()

PERMISSION	DESCRIPTION
S_IRWXU	Read, write, execute/search by owner
S_IRUSR	Read permission by owner
S_IWUSR	Write permission by owner
S_IXUSR	Execute/search permission by owner
S_IRWXG	Read, write, execute/search by group
S_IRGRP	Read permission by group
S_IWGRP	Write permission by group
S_IXGRP	Execute/search permission by group
S_IRWXO	Read, write, execute/search by others
S_IROTH	Read permission by others
S_IWOTH	Write permission by others
S_IXOTH	Execute/search permission by others
S_ISUID	Set-user-ID on execution
S_ISGID	Set-group-ID on execution
S_ISVTX	On directories, set the restricted deletion flag

In addition to setting the user and group IDs of the file, it is also possible to set the effective user and effective group IDs such that if the file is executed, the caller effectively becomes the owner of the file for the duration of execution. This is a commonly used feature in UNIX. For example, the passwd command is a *setuid* binary. When the command is executed it must gain an effective user ID of root in order to change the passwd(F) file. For example:

```
$ ls -l /etc/passwd
-r--r--r-    1 root      other    157670 Mar 14 16:03 /etc/passwd
$ ls -l /usr/bin/passwd
-r-sr-sr-x  3 root      sys       99640 Oct  6  1998 /usr/bin/passwd*
```

Because the passwd file is not writable by others, changing it requires that the passwd command run as root as noted by the s shown above. When run, the process runs as root allowing the passwd file to be changed.

The setuid() and setgid() system calls enable the user and group IDs to be changed. Similarly, the seteuid() and setegid() system calls enable the effective user and effective group ID to be changed:

```
#include <unistd.h>

int setuid(uid_t uid)
int seteuid(uid_t euid)
int setgid(gid_t gid)
int setegid(gid_t egid)
```

Handling permissions checking is a task performed by the kernel.

Changing File Times

When a file is created, there are three timestamps associated with the file as shown in the stat structure earlier. These are the creation time, the time of last modification, and the time that the file was last accessed.

On occasion it is useful to change the access and modification times. One particular use is in a programming environment where a programmer wishes to force re-compilation of a module. The usual way to achieve this is to run the touch command on the file and then recompile. For example:

```
$ ls -l hello*
-rwxr-xr-x   1 spate    fcf              13397 Mar 30 11:53 hello*
-rw-r--r-    1 spate    fcf                 31 Mar 30 11:52 hello.c
$ make hello
make: 'hello' is up to date.
$ touch hello.c
$ ls -l hello.c
-rw-r--r-    1 spate    fcf                 31 Mar 30 11:55 hello.c
$ make hello
cc      hello.c   -o hello
$
```

The system calls utime() and utimes() can be used to change both the access and modification times. In some versions of UNIX, utimes() is simply implemented by calling utime().

```
#include <sys/types.h>
#include <utime.h>

int utime(const char *filename, struct utimbuf *buf);

#include <sys/time.h>

int utimes(char *filename, struct timeval *tvp);

struct utimbuf {
    time_t  actime;    /* access time */
    time_t  modtime;   /* modification time */
};

struct timeval {
```

```
    long    tv_sec;    /* seconds */
    long    tv_usec;   /* microseconds */
};
```

By running `strace`, `truss` etc., it is possible to see how a call to `touch` maps onto the `utime()` system call as follows:

```
$ strace touch myfile 2>&1 | grep utime
utime("myfile", NULL)                    = 0
```

To change just the access time of the file, the `touch` command must first determine what the modification time of the file is. In this case, the call sequence is a little different as the following example shows:

```
$ strace touch -a myfile
...
time([984680824])                        = 984680824
open("myfile",
O_WRONLY|O_NONBLOCK|O_CREAT|O_NOCTTY|O_LARGEFILE, 0666) = 3
fstat(3, st_mode=S_IFREG|0644, st_size=0, ...) = 0
close(3)                                 = 0
utime("myfile", [2001/03/15-10:27:04, 2001/03/15-10:26:23]) = 0
```

In this case, the current time is obtained through calling `time()`. The file is then opened and `fstat()` called to obtain the file's modification time. The call to `utime()` then passes the original modification time and the new access time.

Truncating and Removing Files

Removing files is something that people just take for granted in the same vein as pulling up an editor and creating a new file. However, the internal operation of truncating and removing files can be a particularly complicated operation as later chapters will show.

There are two calls that can be invoked to truncate a file:

```
#include <unistd.h>

int truncate(const char *path, off_t length);
int ftruncate(int fildes, off_t length);
```

The confusing aspect of truncation is that through the calls shown here it is possible to truncate upwards, thus increasing the size of the file! If the value of `length` is less than the current size of the file, the file size will be changed and storage above the new size can be freed. However, if the value of `length` is greater than the current size, storage will be allocated to the file, and the file size will be modified to reflect the new storage.

To remove a file, the `unlink()` system call can be invoked:

```
#include <unistd.h>

int unlink(const char *path);
```

The call is appropriately named since it does not necessarily remove the file but decrements the file's link count. If the link count reaches zero, the file is indeed removed as the following example shows:

```
$ touch myfile
$ ls -l myfile
-rw-r--r-   1 spate     fcf              0 Mar 15 11:09 myfile
$ ln myfile myfile2
$ ls -l myfile*
-rw-r--r-   2 spate     fcf              0 Mar 15 11:09 myfile
-rw-r--r-   2 spate     fcf              0 Mar 15 11:09 myfile2
$ rm myfile
$ ls -l myfile*
-rw-r--r-   1 spate     fcf              0 Mar 15 11:09 myfile2
$ rm myfile2
$ ls -l myfile*
ls: myfile*: No such file or directory
```

When myfile is created it has a link count of 1. Creation of the hard link (myfile2) increases the link count. In this case there are two directory entries (myfile and myfile2), but they point to the same file.

To remove myfile, the unlink() system call is invoked, which decrements the link count and removes the directory entry for myfile.

Directories

There are a number of routines that relate to directories. As with other simple UNIX commands, they often have a close correspondence to the system calls that they call, as shown in Table 2.2.

The arguments passed to most directory operations is dependent on where in the file hierarchy the caller is at the time of the call, together with the pathname passed to the command:

Current working directory. This is where the calling process is at the time of the call; it can be obtained through use of pwd from the shell or getcwd() from within a C program.

Absolute pathname. An absolute pathname is one that starts with the character /. Thus to get to the base filename, the full pathname starting at / must be parsed. The pathname /etc/passwd is absolute.

Relative pathname. A relative pathname does not contain / as the first character and starts from the current working directory. For example, to reach the same passwd file by specifying passwd the current working directory must be /etc.

Table 2.2 Directory Related Operations

COMMAND	SYSTEM CALL	DESCRIPTION
mkdir	mkdir()	Make a new directory
rmdir	rmdir()	Remove a directory
pwd	getcwd()	Display the current working directory
cd	chdir() fchdir()	Change directory
chroot	chroot()	Change the root directory

The following example shows how these calls can be used together:

```
$ cat dir.c
#include <sys/stat.h>
#include <sys/types.h>
#include <sys/param.h>
#include <fcntl.h>
#include <unistd.h>

main()
{
    printf("cwd = %s\n", getcwd(NULL, MAXPATHLEN));
    mkdir("mydir", S_IRWXU);
    chdir("mydir");
    printf("cwd = %s\n", getcwd(NULL, MAXPATHLEN));
    chdir("..");
    rmdir("mydir");
}
$ make dir
cc     -o dir dir.c
$ ./dir
cwd = /h/h065/spate/tmp
cwd = /h/h065/spate/tmp/mydir
```

Special Files

A *special file* is a file that has no associated storage but can be used to gain access to a device. The goal here is to be able to access a device using the same mechanisms by which regular files and directories can be accessed. Thus, callers are able to invoke open(), read(), and write() in the same way that these system calls can be used on regular files.

One noticeable difference between special files and other file types can be seen by issuing an ls command as follows:

```
$ ls -l /dev/vx/*dsk/homedg/h
brw------ 1 root   root   142,4002 Jun 5  1999 /dev/vx/dsk/homedg/h
crw------ 1 root   root   142,4002 Dec 5 21:48 /dev/vx/rdsk/homedg/h
```

In this example there are two device files denoted by the b and c as the first character displayed on each line. This letter indicates the type of device that this file represents. Block devices are represented by the letter b while character devices are represented by the letter c. For block devices, data is accessed in fixed-size blocks while for character devices data can be accessed in multiple different sized blocks ranging from a single character upwards.

Device special files are created with the mknod command as follows:

```
mknod name b major minor
mknod name c major minor
```

For example, to create the above two files, execute the following commands:

```
# mknod /dev/vx/dsk/homedg/h b 142 4002
# mknod /dev/vx/rdsk/homedg/h c 142 4002
```

The major number is used to point to the device driver that controls the device, while the minor number is a private field used by the device driver.

The mknod command is built on top of the mknod() system call:

```
#include <sys/stat.h>

int mknod(const char *path, mode_t mode, dev_t dev);
```

The mode argument specifies the type of file to be created, which can be one of the following:

S_IFIFO. FIFO special file (named pipe).

S_IFCHR. Character special file.

S_IFDIR. Directory file.

S_IFBLK. Block special file.

S_IFREG. Regular file.

The file access permissions are also passed in through the mode argument. The permissions are constructed from a bitwise OR for which the values are the same as for the chmod() system call as outlined in the section *Changing File Permissions* earlier in this chapter.

Symbolic Links and Hard Links

Symbolic links and hard links can be created using the ln command, which in turn maps onto the link() and symlink() system calls. Both prototypes are shown below:

```
#include <unistd.h>

int link(const char *existing, const char *new);
int symlink(const char *name1, const char *name2);
```

The section *Truncating and Removing Files* earlier in this chapter describes hard links and showed the effects that link() and unlink() have on the underlying file. Symbolic links are managed in a very different manner by the filesystem as the following example shows:

```
$ echo "Hello world" > myfile
$ ls -l myfile
-rw-r--r-   1 spate     fcf             12 Mar 15 12:17 myfile
$ cat myfile
Hello world
$ strace ln -s myfile mysymlink 2>&1 | grep link
execve("/bin/ln", ["ln", "-s", "myfile",
"mysymlink"], [/* 39 vars */]) = 0
lstat("mysymlink", 0xbffff660) = -1 ENOENT (No such file/directory)
symlink("myfile", "mysymlink") = 0
$ ls -l my*
-rw-r--r-   1 spate     fcf    12 Mar 15 12:17 myfile
lrwxrwxrwx  1 spate     fcf     6 Mar 15 12:18 mysymlink -> myfile
$ cat mysymlink
Hello world
$ rm myfile
$ cat mysymlink
cat: mysymlink: No such file or directory
```

The ln command checks to see if a file called mysymlink already exists and then calls symlink() to create the symbolic link. There are two things to notice here. First of all, after the symbolic link is created, the link count of myfile does not change. Secondly, the size of mysymlink is 6 bytes, which is the length of the string myfile.

Because creating a symbolic link does not change the file it points to in any way, after myfile is removed, mysymlink does not point to anything as the example shows.

Named Pipes

Although Inter Process Communication is beyond the scope of a book on filesystems, since *named pipes* are stored in the filesystem as a separate file type, they should be given some mention here.

A named pipe is a means by which unrelated processes can communicate. A simple example will show how this all works:

```
$ mkfifo mypipe
$ ls -l mypipe
prw-r--r-   1 spate     fcf                 0 Mar 13 11:29 mypipe
$ echo "Hello world" > mypipe &
[1] 2010
$ cat < mypipe
Hello world
[1]+  Done                     echo "Hello world" >mypipe
```

The mkfifo command makes use of the mknod() system call.

The filesystem records the fact that the file is a named pipe. However, it has no storage associated with it and other than responding to an open request, the filesystem plays no role on the IPC mechanisms of the pipe. Pipes themselves traditionally used storage in the filesystem for temporarily storing the data.

Summary

It is difficult to provide an introductory chapter on file-based concepts without digging into too much detail. The chapter provided many of the basic functions available to view files, return their properties and change these properties.

To better understand how the main UNIX commands are implemented and how they interact with the filesystem, the GNU *fileutils* package provides excellent documentation, which can be found online at:

    www.gnu.org/manual/fileutils/html_mono/fileutils.html

and the source for these utilities can be found at:

    ftp://alpha.gnu.org/gnu/fetish

CHAPTER

3

User File I/O

Building on the principles introduced in the last chapter, this chapter describes the major file-related programmatic interfaces (at a C level) including basic file access system calls, memory mapped files, asynchronous I/O, and sparse files.

To reinforce the material, examples are provided wherever possible. Such examples include simple implementations of various UNIX commands including cat, cp, and dd.

The previous chapter described many of the basic file concepts. This chapter goes one step further and describes the different interfaces that can be called to access files. Most of the APIs described here are at the system call level. Library calls typically map directly to system calls so are not addressed in any detail here.

The material presented here is important for understanding the overall implementation of filesystems in UNIX. By understanding the user-level interfaces that need to be supported, the implementation of filesystems within the kernel is easier to grasp.

Library Functions versus System Calls

System calls are functions that transfer control from the user process to the operating system kernel. Functions such as read() and write() are system calls. The process invokes them with the appropriate arguments, control transfers to the kernel where the system call is executed, results are passed back to the calling process, and finally, control is passed back to the user process.

Library functions typically provide a richer set of features. For example, the fread() library function reads a number of elements of data of specified size from a file. While presenting this formatted data to the user, internally it will call the read() system call to actually read data from the file.

Library functions are implemented on top of system calls. The decision whether to use system calls or library functions is largely dependent on the application being written. Applications wishing to have much more control over how they perform I/O in order to optimize for performance may well invoke system calls directly. If an application writer wishes to use many of the features that are available at the library level, this could save a fair amount of programming effort. System calls can consume more time than invoking library functions because they involve transferring control of the process from user mode to kernel mode. However, the implementation of different library functions may not meet the needs of the particular application. In other words, whether to use library functions or systems calls is not an obvious choice because it very much depends on the application being written.

Which Header Files to Use?

The UNIX header files are an excellent source of information to understand user-level programming and also kernel-level data structures. Most of the header files that are needed for user level programming can be found under /usr/include and /usr/include/sys.

The header files that are needed are shown in the manual page of the library function or system call to be used. For example, using the stat() system call requires the following two header files:

```
#include <sys/types.h>
#include <sys/stat.h>

int stat(const char path, struct stat buf);
```

The stat.h header file defines the stat structure. The types.h header file defines the types of each of the fields in the stat structure.

Header files that reside in /usr/include are used purely by applications. Those header files that reside in /usr/include/sys are also used by the kernel. Using stat() as an example, a reference to the stat structure is passed from the user process to the kernel, the kernel fills in the fields of the structure and then returns. Thus, in many circumstances, both user processes and the kernel need to understand the same structures and data types.

The Six Basic File Operations

Most file creation and file I/O needs can be met by the six basic system calls shown in Table 3.1. This section uses these commands to show a basic implementation of the UNIX `cat` command, which is one of the easiest of the UNIX commands to implement.

However, before giving its implementation, it is necessary to describe the terms *standard input, standard output,* and *standard error.* As described in the section *File Descriptors* in Chapter 2, the first file that is opened by a user process is assigned a file descriptor value of 3. When the new process is created, it typically inherits the first three file descriptors from its parent. These file descriptors (0, 1, and 2) have a special meaning to routines in the C runtime library and refer to the standard input, standard output, and standard error of the process respectively. When using library routines, a *file stream* is specified that determines where data is to be read from or written to. Some functions such as `printf()` write to standard output by default. For other routines such as `fprintf()`, the file stream must be specified. For standard output, `stdout` may be used and for standard error, `stderr` may be used. Similarly, when using routines that require an input stream, `stdin` may be used. Chapter 5 describes the implementation of the standard I/O library. For now simply consider them as a layer on top of file descriptors.

When directly invoking system calls, which requires file descriptors, the constants `STDIN_FILENO`, `STDOUT_FILENO`, and `STDERR_FILENO` may be used. These values are defined in `unistd.h` as follows:

```
#define STDIN_FILENO    0
#define STDOUT_FILENO   1
#define STDERR_FILENO   2
```

Looking at the implementation of the `cat` command, the program must be able to use standard input, output, and error to handle invocations such as:

```
$ cat              # read from standard input
$ cat file         # read from 'file'
$ cat file > file2 # redirect standard output
```

Thus there is a small amount parsing to be performed before the program knows which file to read from and which file to write to. The program source is shown below:

```
1 #include <sys/types.h>
2 #include <sys/stat.h>
3 #include <fcntl.h>
4 #include <unistd.h>
5
6 #define BUFSZ        512
7
8 main(int argc, char argv)
9 {
```

Table 3.1   The Six Basic System Calls Needed for File I/O

SYSTEM CALL	FUNCTION
open()	Open an existing file or create a new file
creat()	Create a new file
close()	Close an already open file
lseek()	Seek to a specified position in the file
read()	Read data from the file from the current position
write()	Write data starting at the current position

```
10      char    buf[BUFSZ];
11      int     ifd, ofd, nread;
12
13      get_fds(argc, argv, &ifd, &ofd);
14      while ((nread = read(ifd, buf, BUFSZ)) != 0) {
15          write(ofd, buf, nread);
16      }
17 }
```

As previously mentioned, there is actually very little work to do in the main program. The get_fds() function, which is not shown here, is responsible for assigning the appropriate file descriptors to ifd and ofd based on the following input:

```
$ mycat
ifd = STDIN_FILENO
ofd = STDOUT_FILENO

$ mycat file
ifd = open(file, O_RDONLY)
ofd = STDOUT_FILENO

$ mycat > file
ifd = STDIN_FILENO
ofd = open(file, O_WRONLY | O_CREAT)

$ mycat fileA > fileB
ifd = open(fileA, O_RDONLY)
ofd = open(fileB, O_WRONLY | O_CREAT)
```

The following examples show the program running:

```
$ mycat > testfile
Hello world
$ mycat testfile
Hello world
$ mycat testfile > testfile2
```

```
$ mycat testfile2
Hello world
$ mycat
Hello
Hello
world
world
```

To modify the program, one exercise to try is to implement the get_fds() function. Some additional exercises to try are:

1. Number all output lines (cat -n). Parse the input strings to detect the -n.

2. Print all tabs as ^I and place a $ character at the end of each line (cat -ET).

The previous program reads the whole file and writes out its contents. Commands such as dd allow the caller to seek to a specified block in the input file and output a specified number of blocks.

Reading sequentially from the start of the file in order to get to the part which the user specified would be particularly inefficient. The lseek() system call allows the file pointer to be modified, thus allowing random access to the file. The declaration for lseek() is as follows:

```
#include <sys/types.h>
#include <unistd.h>

off_t lseek(int fildes, off_t offset, int whence);
```

The offset and whence arguments dictate where the file pointer should be positioned:

- If whence is SEEK_SET the file pointer is set to offset bytes.

- If whence is SEEK_CUR the file pointer is set to its current location plus offset.

- If whence is SEEK_END the file pointer is set to the size of the file plus offset.

When a file is first opened, the file pointer is set to 0 indicating that the first byte read will be at an offset of 0 bytes from the start of the file. Each time data is read, the file pointer is incremented by the amount of data read such that the next read will start from the offset in the file referenced by the updated pointer. For example, if the first read of a file is for 1024 bytes, the file pointer for the next read will be set to 0 + 1024 = 1024. Reading another 1024 bytes will start from byte offset 1024. After that read the file pointer will be set to 1024 + 1024 = 2048 and so on.

By seeking throughout the input and output files, it is possible to see how the dd command can be implemented. As with many UNIX commands, most of the work is done in parsing the command line to determine the input and output files, the starting position to read, the block size for reading, and so on. The example below shows how lseek() is used to seek to a specified starting offset within the input file. In this example, all data read is written to standard output:

```
 1 #include <sys/types.h>
 2 #include <sys/stat.h>
 3 #include <fcntl.h>
 4 #include <unistd.h>
 5
 6 #define BUFSZ    512
 7
 8 main(int argc, char argv)
 9 {
10          char     *buf;
11          int      fd, nread;
12          off_t    offset;
13          size_t   iosize;
14
15          if (argc != 4) {
16                  printf("usage: mydd filename offset size\n");
17          }
18          fd = open(argv[1], O_RDONLY);
19          if (fd < 0) {
20                  printf("unable to open file\n");
21                  exit(1);
22          }
23          offset = (off_t)atol(argv[2]);
24          buf = (char *)malloc(argv[3]);
25          lseek(fd, offset, SEEK_SET);
26          nread = read(fd, buf, iosize);
27          write(STDOUT_FILENO, buf, nread);
28 }
```

Using a large file as an example, try different offsets and sizes and determine the effect on performance. Also try multiple runs of the program. Some of the effects seen may not be as expected. The section *Data and Attribute Caching,* a bit later in this chapter, discusses some of these effects.

Duplicate File Descriptors

The section *File Descriptors,* in Chapter 2, introduced the concept of file descriptors. Typically a file descriptor is returned in response to an open() or creat() system call. The dup() system call allows a user to duplicate an existing open file descriptor.

```
#include <unistd.h>

int dup(int fildes);
```

There are a number of uses for dup() that are really beyond the scope of this book. However, the shell often uses dup() when connecting the input and output streams of processes via pipes.

Seeking and I/O Combined

The pread() and pwrite() system calls combine the effects of lseek() and read() (or write()) into a single system call. This provides some improvement in performance although the net effect will only really be visible in an application that has a very I/O intensive workload. However, both interfaces are supported by the Single UNIX Specification and should be accessible in most UNIX environments. The definition of these interfaces is as follows:

```
#include <unistd.h>

ssize_t pread(int fildes, void buf, size_t nbyte, off_t offset);
ssize_t pwrite(int fildes, const void buf, size_t nbyte,
            off_t offset);
```

The example below continues on from the dd program described earlier and shows the use of combining the lseek() with read() and write() calls:

```
 1 #include <sys/types.h>
 2 #include <sys/stat.h>
 3 #include <fcntl.h>
 4 #include <unistd.h>
 5
 6 main(int argc, char argv)
 7 {
 8         char    *buf;
 9         int     ifd, ofd, nread;
10         off_t   inoffset, outoffset;
11         size_t  insize, outsize;
12
13         if (argc != 7) {
14                 printf("usage: mydd infilename in_offset"
15                         " in_size outfilename out_offset"
16                         " out_size\n");
17         }
18         ifd = open(argv[1], O_RDONLY);
19         if (ifd < 0) {
20                 printf("unable to open %s\n", argv[1]);
21                 exit(1);
22         }
23         ofd = open(argv[4], O_WRONLY);
24         if (ofd < 0) {
25                 printf("unable to open %s\n", argv[4]);
26                 exit(1);
27         }
28         inoffset = (off_t)atol(argv[2]);
```

```
29              insize = (size_t)atol(argv[3]);
30              outoffset = (off_t)atol(argv[5]);
31              outsize = (size_t)atol(argv[6]);
32              buf = (char *)malloc(insize);
33              if (insize < outsize)
34                      outsize = insize;
35
36              nread = pread(ifd, buf, insize, inoffset);
37              pwrite(ofd, buf,
38                      (nread < outsize) ? nread : outsize, outoffset);
39 }
```

The simple example below shows how the program is run:

```
$ cat fileA
0123456789
$ cat fileB
----------
$ mydd2 fileA 2 4 fileB 4 3
$ cat fileA
0123456789
$ cat fileB
----234---
```

To indicate how the performance may be improved through the use of pread() and pwrite() the I/O loop was repeated 1 million times and a call was made to time() to determine how many seconds it took to execute the loop between this and the earlier example.

For the pread()/pwrite() combination the average time to complete the I/O loop was 25 seconds while for the lseek()/read() and lseek()/write() combinations the average time was 35 seconds, which shows a considerable difference.

This test shows the advantage of pread() and pwrite() in its best form. In general though, if an lseek() is immediately followed by a read() or write(), the two calls should be combined.

Data and Attribute Caching

There are a number of flags that can be passed to open() that control various aspects of the I/O. Also, some filesystems support additional but non standard methods for improving I/O performance.

Firstly, there are three options, supported under the Single UNIX Specification, that can be passed to open() that have an impact on subsequent I/O operations. When a write takes place, there are two items of data that must be written to disk, namely the file data and the file's inode. An *inode* is the object stored on disk that describes the file, including the properties seen by calling stat() together with a block map of all data blocks associated with the file.

The three options that are supported from a standards perspective are:

O_SYNC. For all types of writes, whether allocation is required or not, the data and any meta-data updates are committed to disk before the write returns. For reads, the access time stamp will be updated before the read returns.

O_DSYNC. When a write occurs, the data will be committed to disk before the write returns but the file's meta-data may not be written to disk at this stage. This will result in better I/O throughput because, if implemented efficiently by the filesystem, the number of inode updates will be minimized, effectively halving the number of writes. Typically, if the write results in an allocation to the file (a write over a hole or beyond the end of the file) the meta-data is also written to disk. However, if the write does not involve an allocation, the timestamps will typically not be written synchronously.

O_RSYNC. If both the O_RSYNC and O_DSYNC flags are set, the read returns after the data has been read and the file attributes have been updated on disk, with the exception of file timestamps that may be written later. If there are any writes pending that cover the range of data to be read, these writes are committed before the read returns.

If both the O_RSYNC and O_SYNC flags are set, the behavior is identical to that of setting O_RSYNC and O_DSYNC except that all file attributes changed by the read operation (including all time attributes) must also be committed to disk before the read returns.

Which option to choose is dependent on the application. For I/O intensive applications where timestamps updates are not particularly important, there can be a significant performance boost by using O_DSYNC in place of O_SYNC.

VxFS Caching Advisories

Some filesystems provide non standard means of improving I/O performance by offering additional features. For example, the VERITAS filesystem, VxFS, provides the noatime mount option that disables access time updates; this is usually fine for most application environments.

The following example shows the effect that selecting O_SYNC versus O_DSYNC can have on an application:

```
#include <sys/unistd.h>
#include <sys/types.h>
#include <fcntl.h>

main(int argc, char argv[])
{
    char        buf[4096];
    int         i, fd, advisory;

    fd = open("myfile", O_WRONLY|O_DSYNC);
    for (i=0 ; i<1024 ; i++) {
       write(fd, buf, 4096);
    }
}
```

By having a program that is identical to the previous with the exception of setting O_SYNC in place of O_DSYNC, the output of the two programs is as follows:

```
# time ./sync
real  0m8.33s
user  0m0.03s
sys   0m1.92s
# time ./dsync
real  0m6.44s
user  0m0.02s
sys   0m0.69s
```

This clearly shows the increase in time when selecting O_SYNC. VxFS offers a number of other advisories that go beyond what is currently supported by the traditional UNIX standards. These options can only be accessed through use of the ioctl() system call. These advisories give an application writer more control over a number of I/O parameters:

VX_RANDOM. Filesystems try to determine the I/O pattern in order to perform read ahead to maximize performance. This advisory indicates that the I/O pattern is random and therefore read ahead should not be performed.

VX_SEQ. This advisory indicates that the file is being accessed sequentially. In this case the filesystem should maximize read ahead.

VX_DIRECT. When data is transferred to or from the user buffer and disk, a copy is first made into the kernel buffer or page cache, which is a cache of recently accessed file data. Although this cache can significantly help performance by avoiding a read of data from disk for a second access, the double copying of data has an impact on performance. The VX_DIRECT advisory avoids this double buffering by copying data directly between the user's buffer and disk.

VX_NOREUSE. If data is only to be read once, the in-kernel cache is not needed. This advisory informs the filesystem that the data does not need to be retained for subsequent access.

VX_DSYNC. This option was in existence for a number of years before the O_DSYNC mode was adopted by the UNIX standards committees. It can still be accessed on platforms where O_DSYNC is not supported.

Before showing how these caching advisories can be used it is first necessary to describe how to use the ioctl() system call. The definition of ioctl(), which is not part of any UNIX standard, differs slightly from platform to platform by requiring different header files. The basic definition is as follows:

```
#include <unistd.h>        # Solaris
#include <stropts.h>       # Solaris, AIX and HP-UX
#include <sys/ioctl.h>     # Linux

int ioctl(int fildes, int request, /* arg ... */);
```

Note that AIX does not, at the time of writing, support `ioctl()` calls on regular files. Ioctl calls may be made to VxFS regular files, but the operation is not supported generally.

The following program shows how the caching advisories are used in practice. The program takes VX_SEQ, VX_RANDOM, or VX_DIRECT as an argument and reads a 1MB file in 4096 byte chunks.

```
#include <sys/unistd.h>
#include <sys/types.h>
#include <fcntl.h>
#include "sys/fs/vx_ioctl.h"

#define MB        (1024 * 1024)

main(int argc, char argv[])
{
    char        *buf;
    int         i, fd, advisory;
    long        pagesize, pagemask;

    if (argc != 2) {
        exit(1);
    }
    if (strcmp(argv[1], "VX_SEQ") == 0) {
        advisory = VX_SEQ;
    } else if (strcmp(argv[1], "VX_RANDOM") == 0) {
        advisory = VX_RANDOM;
    } else if (strcmp(argv[1], "VX_DIRECT") == 0) {
        advisory = VX_DIRECT;
    }
    pagesize = sysconf(_SC_PAGESIZE);
    pagemask = pagesize - 1;
    buf = (char *)(malloc(2 * pagesize) & pagemask);
    buf = (char *)(((long)buf + pagesize) & ~pagemask);

    fd = open("myfile", O_RDWR);
    ioctl(fd, VX_SETCACHE, advisory);
    for (i=0 ; i<MB ; i++) {
        read(fd, buf, 4096);
    }
}
```

The program was run three times passing each of the advisories in turn. The `times` command was run to display the time to run the program and the amount of time that was spent in user and system space.

```
VX_SEQ

real      2:47.6
user         5.9
sys       2:41.4
```

```
VX_DIRECT

real      2:35.7
user         6.7
sys       2:28.7


VX_RANDOM

real      2:43.6
user         5.2
sys       2:38.1
```

Although the time difference between the runs shown here is not significant, the appropriate use of these caching advisories can have a significant impact on overall performance of large applications.

Miscellaneous Open Options

Through use of the O_NONBLOCK and O_NDELAY flags that can be passed to open(), applications can gain some additional control in the case where they may block for reads and writes.

O_EXCL. If both O_CREAT and O_EXCL are set, a call to open() fails if the file exists. If the O_CREAT option is not set, the effect of passing O_EXCL is undefined.

O_NONBLOCK / O_NDELAY. These flags can affect subsequent reads and writes. If both the O_NDELAY and O_NONBLOCK flags are set, O_NONBLOCK takes precedence. Because both options are for use with pipes, they won't be discussed further here.

File and Record Locking

If multiple processes are writing to a file at the same time, the result is non deterministic. Within the UNIX kernel, only one write to the same file may proceed at any given time. However, if multiple processes are writing to the file, the order in which they run can differ depending on many different factors. Obviously this is highly undesirable and results in a need to lock files at an application level, whether the whole file or specific sections of a file. Sections of a file are also called records, hence file and record locking.

There are numerous uses for file locking. However, looking at database file access gives an excellent example of the types of locks that applications require. For example, it is important that all users wishing to view database records are able to do so simultaneously. When updating records it is imperative that while one record is being updated, other users are still able to access other records. Finally it is imperative that records are updated in a time-ordered manner.

There are two types of locks that can be used to coordinate access to files, namely *mandatory* and *advisory* locks. With advisory locking, it is possible for cooperating processes to safely access a file in a controlled manner. Mandatory locking is somewhat of a hack and will be described later. The majority of this section will concentrate on advisory locking, sometimes called *record locking*.

Advisory Locking

There are three functions which can be used for advisory locking. These are lockf(), flock(), and fcntl(). The flock() function defined below:

```
/usr/ucb/cc [ flag ... ] file ...
#include <sys/file.h>

int flock(fd,  operation);
int fd, operation;
```

was introduced in BSD UNIX and is not supported under the Single UNIX Specification standard. It sets an advisory lock on the whole file. The lock type, specified by the operation argument, may be exclusive (LOCK_EX) or shared (LOCK_SH). By OR'ing operation with LOCK_NB, if the file is already locked, EAGAIN will be returned. The LOCK_UN operation removes the lock.

The lockf() function, which is typically implemented as a call to fcntl(), can be invoked to apply or remove an advisory lock on a segment of a file as follows:

```
#include <sys/file.h>

int lockf(int fildes, int function, off_t size);
```

To use lockf(), the file must have been opened with one of the O_WRONLY or O_RDWR flags. The size argument specifies the number of bytes to be locked, starting from the current file pointer. Thus, a call to lseek() should be made prior to calling lockf(). If the value of size is 0 the file is locked from the current offset to the end of the file.

The function argument can be one of the following:

F_LOCK. This command sets an exclusive lock on the file. If the file is already locked, the calling process will block until the previous lock is relinquished.

F_TLOCK. This performs the same function as the F_LOCK command but will not block—thus if the file is already locked, EAGAIN is returned.

F_ULOCK. This command unlocks a segment of the file.

F_TEST. This command is used to test whether a lock exists for the specified segment. If there is no lock for the segment, 0 is returned, otherwise -1 is returned, and errno is set to EACCES.

If the segment to be locked contains a previous locked segment, in whole or part, the result will be a new, single locked segment. Similarly, if F_ULOCK is specified, the segment of the file to be unlocked may be a subset of a previously locked segment or may cover more than one previously locked segment. If size is 0, the file is unlocked from the current file offset to the end of the file. If the segment to be unlocked is a subset of a previously locked segment, the result will be one or two smaller locked segments.

It is possible to reach deadlock if two processes make a request to lock segments of a file owned by each other. The kernel is able to detect this and, if the condition would occur, EDEADLK is returned.

Note as mentioned above that flock() is typically implemented on top of the fcntl() system call, for which there are three commands that can be passed to manage record locking. Recall the interface for fcntl():

```
#include <sys/types.h>
#include <unistd.h>
#include <fcntl.h>

int fcntl(int fildes, int cmd, ...);
```

All commands operate on the flock structure that is passed as the third argument:

```
struct flock {
    short    l_type;      /* F_RDLCK, F_WRLCK or F_UNLOCK */
    short    l_whence;    /* flag for starting offset */
    off_t    l_start;     /* relative offset in bytes */
    off_t    l_len;       /* size; if 0 then until EOF */
    pid_t    l_pid;       /* process ID of lock holder */
};
```

The commands that can be passed to fcntl() are:

F_GETLK. This command returns the first lock that is covered by the flock structure specified. The information that is retrieved overwrites the fields of the structure passed.

F_SETLK. This command either sets a new lock or clears an existing lock based on the value of l_type as shown above.

F_SETLKW. This command is the same as F_SETLK with the exception that the process will block if the lock is held by another process.

Because record locking as defined by fcntl() is supported by all appropriate UNIX standards, this is the routine that should be ideally used for application portability.

The following code fragments show how advisory locking works in practice. The first program, lock, which follows, sets a writable lock on the whole of the file myfile and calls pause() to wait for a SIGUSR1 signal. After the signal arrives, a call is made to unlock the file.

```
 1 #include <sys/types.h>
 2 #include <unistd.h>
 3 #include <fcntl.h>
 4 #include <signal,h>
 5
 6 void
 7 mysig(int signo)
 8 {
 9         return;
10 }
11
12 main()
13 {
14         struct flock        lk;
15         int                 fd, err;
16
17         sigset(SIGUSR1, mysig);
18
19         fd = open("myfile", O_WRONLY);
20
21         lk.l_type = F_WRLCK;
22         lk.l_whence = SEEK_SET;
23         lk.l_start = 0;
24         lk.l_len = 0;
25         lk.l_pid = getpid();
26
27         err = fcntl(fd, F_SETLK, &lk);
28         printf("lock: File is locked\n");
29         pause();
30         lk.l_type = F_UNLCK;
31         err = fcntl(fd, F_SETLK, &lk);
32         printf("lock: File is unlocked\n");
33 }
```

Note that the process ID of this process is placed in l_pid so that anyone requesting information about the lock will be able to determine how to identify this process.

The next program (mycat1) is a modified version of the cat program that will only display the file if there are no write locks held on the file. If a lock is detected, the program loops up to 5 times waiting for the lock to be released. Because the lock will still be held by the lock program, mycat1 will extract the process ID from the flock structure returned by fcntl() and post a SIGUSR1 signal. This is handled by the lock program which then unlocks the file.

```
 1 #include <sys/types.h>
 2 #include <sys/stat.h>
 3 #include <fcntl.h>
 4 #include <unistd.h>
 5 #include <signal.h>
 6
 7 pid_t
 8 is_locked(int fd)
 9 {
```

```
10              struct flock    lk;
11
12              lk.l_type = F_RDLCK;
13              lk.l_whence = SEEK_SET;
14              lk.l_start = 0;
15              lk.l_len = 0;
16              lk.l_pid = 0;
17
18              fcntl(fd, F_GETLK, &lk);
19              return (lk.l_type == F_UNLCK) ? 0 : lk.l_pid;
20 }
21
22 main()
23 {
24              struct flock    lk;
25              int             i, fd, err;
26              pid_t           pid;
27
28              fd = open("myfile", O_RDONLY);
29
30              for (i = 0 ; i < 5 ; i++) {
31                      if ((pid = is_locked(fd)) == 0) {
32                              catfile(fd);
33                              exit(0);
34                      } else {
35                              printf("mycatl: File is locked ...\n");
36                              sleep(1);
37                      }
38              }
39              kill(pid, SIGUSR1);
40              while ((pid = is_locked(fd)) != 0) {
41                      printf("mycatl: Waiting for lock release\n");
42                      sleep(1);
43              }
44              catfile(fd);
45 }
```

Note the use of fcntl() in the mycatl program. If no lock exists on the file that would interfere with the lock requested (in this case the program is asking for a read lock on the whole file), the l_type field is set to F_UNLCK. When the program is run, the following can be seen:

```
$ cat myfile
Hello world
$ lock&
[1] 2448
lock: File is locked
$ mycatl
mycatl: File is locked ...
mycatl: File is locked ...
mycatl: File is locked ...
mycatl: File is locked ...
mycatl: File is locked ...
mycatl: Waiting for lock release
```

```
lock: File is unlocked
Hello world
[1]+  Exit 23                ./lock
```

The following example shows where advisory locking fails to become effective if processes are not cooperating:

```
$ lock&
[1] 2494
lock: File is locked
$ cat myfile
Hello world
$ rm myfile
$ jobs
[1]+  Running               ./lock &
```

In this case, although the file has a segment lock, a non-cooperating process can still access the file, thus the real cat program can display the file and the file can also be removed! Note that removing a file involves calling the unlink() system call. The file is not actually removed until the last close. In this case the lock program still has the file open. The file will actually be removed once the lock program exits.

Mandatory Locking

As the previous example shows, if all processes accessing the same file do not cooperate through the use of advisory locks, unpredictable results can occur. Mandatory locking provides file locking between non-cooperating processes. Unfortunately, the implementation, which arrived with SVR3, leaves something to be desired.

Mandatory locking can be enabled on a file if the set group ID bit is switched on and the group execute bit is switched off—a combination that together does not otherwise make any sense. Thus if the following were executed on a system that supports mandatory locking:

```
$ lock&
[1] 12096
lock: File is locked
$ cat myfile              # The cat program blocks here
```

the cat program will block until the lock is relinquished. Note that mandatory locking is not supported by the major UNIX standards so further details will not be described here.

File Control Operations

The fcntl() system call is designed to provide file control functions for open files. The definition was shown in a previous section, *File and Record Locking*, earlier in the chapter. It is repeated below:

```
#include <sys/types.h>
#include <unistd.h>
#include <fcntl.h>

int fcntl(int fildes, int cmd, ...);
```

The file descriptor refers to a previously opened file and the cmd argument is one of the commands shown below:

F_DUPFD. This command returns a new file descriptor that is the lowest numbered file descriptor available (and is not already open). The file descriptor returned will be greater than or equal to the third argument. The new file descriptor refers to the same open file as the original file descriptor and shares any locks. The FD_CLOEXEC (see F_SETFD below) flag associated with the new file descriptor is cleared to keep the file open across calls to one of the exec functions.

F_GETFD. This command returns the flags associated with the specified file descriptor. This is a little bit of a misnomer because there has only ever been one flag, the FD_CLOEXEC flag that indicates that the file should be closed following a successful call to exec().

F_SETFD. This command sets the FD_CLOEXEC flag.

F_GETFL. This command returns the file status flags and file access modes for fildes. The file access modes can be extracted from the return value using the mask O_ACCMODE. The flags are O_RDONLY, O_WRONLY and O_RDWR.

The file status flags, as described in the sections *Data and Attribute Caching* and *Miscellaneous Open Options*, earlier in this chapter, can be either O_APPEND, O_SYNC, O_DSYNC, O_RSYNC, or O_NONBLOCK.

F_SETFL. This command sets the file status flags for the specified file descriptor.

F_GETLK. This command retrieves information about an advisory lock. See the section *File and Record Locking*, earlier in this chapter, for further information.

F_SETLK. This command clears or sets an advisory lock. See the section *File and Record Locking*, earlier in this chapter, for further information.

F_SETLKW. This command also clears or sets an advisory lock. See the section *File and Record Locking*, earlier in this chapter, for further information.

Vectored Reads and Writes

If the data that a process reads from a file in a single read needs to placed in different areas of memory, this would typically involve more than one call to read(). However, the readv() system call can be used to perform a single read from the file but copy the data to the multiple memory locations, which can cut down on system call overhead and therefore increase performance in environments where there is a lot of I/O activity. When writing to files the writev() system call can be used.

Here are the definitions for both functions:

```
#include <sys/uio.h>

ssize_t readv(int fildes, const struct iovec iov, int iovcnt);
ssize_t writev(int fildes, const struct iovec iov, int iovcnt);
```

Note that although multiple I/Os can be combined, they must all be contiguous within the file.

```
struct uio {
    void    *iov_base;   /* Address in memory of buffer for r/w */
    size_t  iov_len;     /* Size of the above buffer in memory */
}
```

Figure 3.1 shows how the transfer of data occurs for a read operation. The shading on the areas of the file and the address space show where the data will be placed after the read has completed.

The following program corresponds to the example shown in Figure 3.1:

```
 1 #include <sys/uio.h>
 2 #include <unistd.h>
 3 #include <fcntl.h>
 4
 5 main()
 6 {
 7         struct iovec    uiop[3];
 8         void            *addr1, *addr2, *addr3;
 9         int             fd, nbytes;
10
11         addr1 = (void *)malloc(4096);
12         addr2 = (void *)malloc(4096);
13         addr3 = (void *)malloc(4096);
14
15         uiop[0].iov_base = addr1;  uiop[0].iov_len = 512;
16         uiop[1].iov_base = addr2;  uiop[1].iov_len = 512;
17         uiop[2].iov_base = addr3;  uiop[2].iov_len = 1024;
18
19         fd = open("myfile", O_RDONLY);
20         nbytes = readv(fd, uiop, 3);
21         printf("number of bytes read = %d\n", nbytes);
22 {
```

Note that readv() returns the number of bytes read. When this program runs, the result is 2048 bytes, the total number of bytes obtained by adding the three individual iovec structures.

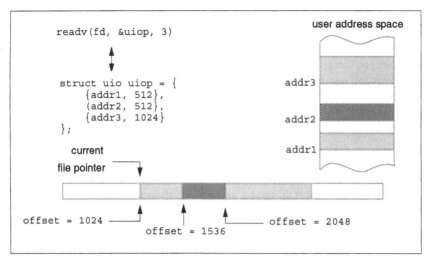

Figure 3.1   Using `readv()` to perform multiple read operations.

```
$ readv
number of bytes read = 2048
```

Asynchronous I/O

By issuing an I/O asynchronously, an application can continue with other work rather than waiting for the I/O to complete. There have been numerous different implementations of asynchronous I/O (commonly referred to as async I/O) over the years. This section will describe the interfaces as supported by the Single UNIX Specification.

As an example of where async I/O is commonly used, consider the Oracle database writer process (DBWR), one of the main Oracle processes; its role is to manage the Oracle buffer cache, a user-level cache of database blocks. This involves responding to read requests and writing dirty (modified) buffers to disk.

In an active database, the work of DBWR is complicated by the fact that it is constantly writing dirty buffers to disk in order to allow new blocks to be read. Oracle employs two methods to help alleviate some of the performance bottlenecks. First, it supports multiple DBWR processes (called DBWR slave processes); the second option, which greatly improves throughput, is through use of async I/O. If I/O operations are being performed asynchronously, the DBWR processes can be doing other work, whether flushing more buffers to disk, reading data from disk, or other internal functions.

All of the Single UNIX Specification async I/O operations center around an I/O control block defined by the `aiocb` structure as follows:

```
struct aiocb {
    int             aio_fildes;     /* file descriptor */
    off_t           aio_offset;     /* file offset */
    volatile void   *aio_buf;       /* location of buffer */
    size_t          aio_nbytes;     /* length of transfer */
    int             aio_reqprio;    /* request priority offset */
    struct sigevent aio_sigevent;    /* signal number and value */
    int             aio_lio_opcode; /* operation to be performed */
};
```

The fields of the `aiocb` structure will be described throughout this section as the various interfaces are described. The first interface to describe is `aio_read()`:

```
cc  [ flag... ] file... -lrt [ library... ]
#include <aio.h>
int aio_read(struct aiocb aiocbp);
```

The `aio_read()` function will read `aiocbp->aio_nbytes` from the file associated with file descriptor `aiocbp->aio_fildes` into the buffer referenced by `aiocbp->aio_buf`. The call returns when the I/O has been initiated. Note that the requested operation takes place at the offset in the file specified by the `aio_offset` field.

Similarly, to perform an asynchronous write operation, the function to call is `aio_write()` which is defined as follows:

```
cc  [ flag... ] file... -lrt [ library... ]
#include <aio.h>

int aio_write(struct aiocb aiocbp);
```

and the fields in the aio control block used to initiate the write are the same as for an async read.

In order to retrieve the status of a pending I/O, there are two interfaces that can be used. One involves the posting of a signal and will be described later; the other involves the use of the `aio_return()` function as follows:

```
#include <aio.h>

ssize_t aio_return(struct aiocb aiocbp);
```

The aio control block that was passed to `aio_read()` should be passed to `aio_return()`. The result will either be the same as if a call to `read()` or `write()` had been made or, if the operation is still in progress, the result is undefined.

The following example shows some interesting properties of an asynchronous write:

```
1 #include <aio.h>
2 #include <time.h>
3 #include <errno.h>
```

```
 4
 5  #define FILESZ            (1024 * 1024 * 64)
 6
 7  main()
 8  {
 9          struct aiocb     aio;
10          void             *buf;
11          time_t           time1, time2;
12          int              err, cnt = 0;
13
14          buf = (void *)malloc(FILESZ);
15          aio.aio_fildes = open("/dev/vx/rdsk/fs1", O_WRONLY);
16          aio.aio_buf = buf;
17          aio.aio_offset = 0;
18          aio.aio_nbytes = FILESZ;
19          aio.aio_reqprio = 0;
20
21          time(&time1);
22          err = aio_write(&aio);
23          while ((err = aio_error(&aio)) == EINPROGRESS) {
24                  sleep(1);
25          }
26          time(&time2);
27          printf("The I/O took %d seconds\n", time2 - time1);
28  }
```

The program uses the raw device /dev/vx/rdsk/fs1 to write a single 64MB
buffer. The aio_error() call:

```
cc  [ flag... ] file... -lrt [ library... ]
#include <aio.h>

int aio_error(const struct aiocb aiocbp);
```

can be called to determine whether the I/O has completed, is still in progress, or
whether an error occurred. The return value from aio_error() will either
correspond to the return value from read(), write(), or will be EINPROGRESS
if the I/O is still pending. Note when the program is run:

```
# aiowrite
The I/O took 7 seconds
```

Thus if the process had issued a write through use of the write() system call, it
would wait for 7 seconds before being able to do anything else. Through the use
of async I/O the process is able to continue processing and then find out the
status of the async I/O at a later date.

For async I/O operations that are still pending, the aio_cancel() function
can be used to cancel the operation:

```
cc  [ flag... ] file... -lrt [ library... ]
#include <aio.h>

int aio_cancel(int fildes, struct aiocb aiocbp);
```

The `filedes` argument refers to the open file on which a previously made async I/O, as specified by `aiocbp`, was issued. If `aiocbp` is `NULL`, all pending async I/O operations are canceled. Note that it is not always possible to cancel an async I/O. In many cases, the I/O will be queued at the driver level before the call from `aio_read()` or `aio_write()` returns.

As an example, following the above call to `aio_write()`, this code is inserted:

```
err = aio_cancel(aio.aio_fildes, &aio);
switch (err) {
   case AIO_CANCELED:
      errstr = "AIO_CANCELED";
      break;

   case AIO_NOTCANCELED:
      errstr = "AIO_NOTCANCELED";
      break;

   case AIO_ALLDONE:
      errstr = "AIO_ALLDONE";
      break;
   default:
      errstr = "Call failed";
}
printf("Error value returned %s\n", errstr);
```

and when the program is run, the following error value is returned:

```
Error value returned AIO_CANCELED
```

In this case, the I/O operation was canceled. Consider the same program but instead of issuing a 64MB write, a small 512 byte I/O is issued:

```
Error value returned AIO_NOTCANCELED
```

In this case, the I/O was already in progress, so the kernel was unable to prevent it from completing.

As mentioned above, the Oracle DBWR process will likely issue multiple I/Os simultaneously and wait for them to complete at a later time. Multiple `read()` and `write()` system calls can be combined through the use of `readv()` and `write()` to help cut down on system call overhead. For async I/O, the `lio_listio()` function achieves the same result:

```
#include <aio.h>

int lio_listio(int mode, struct aiocb const list[], int nent,
            struct sigevent sig);
```

The mode argument can be one of `LIO_WAIT` in which the requesting process will block in the kernel until all I/O operations have completed or `LIO_NOWAIT` in which case the kernel returns control to the user as soon as the I/Os have been queued. The list argument is an array of nent aiocb structures. Note that for each aiocb structure, the aio_lio_opcode field must be set to either LIO_READ for a read operation, LIO_WRITE for a write operation, or LIO_NOP in which case the entry will be ignored.

If the mode flag is LIO_NOWAIT, the sig argument specifies the signal that should be posted to the process once the I/O has completed.

The following example uses lio_listio() to issue two async writes to different parts of the file. Once the I/O has completed, the signal handler aiohdlr() will be invoked; this displays the time that it took for both writes to complete.

```
 1 #include <aio.h>
 2 #include <time.h>
 3 #include <errno.h>
 4 #include <signal.h>
 5
 6 #define FILESZ          (1024 * 1024 * 64)
 7 time_t                  time1, time2;
 8
 9 void
10 aiohdlr(int signo)
11 {
12          time(&time2);
13          printf("Time for write was %d seconds\n", time2 - time1);
14 }
15
16 main()
17 {
18          struct sigevent    mysig;
19          struct aiocb       *laio[2];
20          struct aiocb       aio1, aio2;
21          void               *buf;
22          char               errstr;
23          int                fd;
24
25          buf = (void *)malloc(FILESZ);
26          fd = open("/dev/vx/rdsk/fs1", O_WRONLY);
27
28          aio1.aio_fildes = fd;
29          aio1.aio_lio_opcode = LIO_WRITE;
30          aio1.aio_buf = buf;
31          aio1.aio_offset = 0;
32          aio1.aio_nbytes = FILESZ;
33          aio1.aio_reqprio = 0;
34          laio[0] = &aio1;
35
36          aio2.aio_fildes = fd;
37          aio2.aio_lio_opcode = LIO_WRITE;
38          aio2.aio_buf = buf;
39          aio2.aio_offset = FILESZ;
40          aio2.aio_nbytes = FILESZ;
41          aio2.aio_reqprio = 0;
42          laio[1] = &aio2;
```

```
43
44          sigset(SIGUSR1, aiohdlr);
45          mysig.sigev_signo = SIGUSR1;
46          mysig.sigev_notify = SIGEV_SIGNAL;
47          mysig.sigev_value.sival_ptr = (void *)laio;
48
49          time(&time1);
50          lio_listio(LIO_NOWAIT, laio, 2, &mysig);
51          pause();
52 }
```

The call to lio_listio() specifies that the program should not wait and that a signal should be posted to the process after all I/Os have completed. Although not described here, it is possible to use real-time signals through which information can be passed back to the signal handler to determine which async I/O has completed. This is particularly important when there are multiple simultaneous calls to lio_listio(). Bill Gallmeister's book *Posix.4: Programming for the Real World* [GALL95] describes how to use real-time signals.

When the program is run the following is observed:

```
# listio
Time for write was 12 seconds
```

which clearly shows the amount of time that this process could have been performing other work rather than waiting for the I/O to complete.

Memory Mapped Files

In addition to reading and writing files through the use of read() and write(), UNIX supports the ability to *map* a file into the process' address space and read and write to the file through memory accesses. This allows unrelated processes to access files with either shared or private mappings. Mapped files are also used by the operating system for executable files.

The mmap() system call allows a process to establish a mapping to an already open file:

```
#include <sys/mman.h>

void mmap(void addr, size_t len, int prot, int flags,
          int fildes, off_t off);
```

The file is mapped from an offset of off bytes within the file for len bytes. Note that the offset must be on a page size boundary. Thus, if the page size of the system is 4KB, the offset must be 0, 4096, 8192 and so on. The size of the mapping does not need to be a multiple of the page size although the kernel will round the request up to the nearest page size boundary. For example, if off is set to 0 and size is set to 2048, on systems with a 4KB page size, the mapping established will actually be for 4KB.

Figure 3.2 shows the relationship between the pages in the user's address space and how they relate to the file being mapped. The page size of the underlying hardware platform can be determined by making a call to sysconf() as follows:

```
#include <unistd.h>

main()
{
    printf("PAGESIZE = %d\n", sysconf(_SC_PAGESIZE));
}
```

Typically the page size will be 4KB or 8KB. For example, as expected, when the program is run on an x86 processor, the following is reported:

```
# ./sysconf
PAGESIZE = 4096
```

while for Sparc 9 based hardware:

```
# ./sysconf
PAGESIZE = 8192
```

Although it is possible for the application to specify the address to which the file should be mapped, it is recommended that the addr field be set to 0 so that the system has the freedom to choose which address the mapping will start from. The operating system dynamic linker places parts of the executable program in various memory locations. The amount of memory used differs from one process to the next. Thus, an application should never rely on locating data at the same place in memory even within the same operating system and hardware architecture. The address at which the mapping is established is returned if the call to mmap() is successful, otherwise 0 is returned.

Note that after the file has been mapped it can be closed and still accessed through the mapping.

Before describing the other parameters, here is a very simple example showing the basics of mmap():

```
 1 #include <sys/types.h>
 2 #include <sys/stat.h>
 3 #include <sys/mman.h>
 4 #include <fcntl.h>
 5 #include <unistd.h>
 6
 7 #define MAPSZ        4096
 8
 9 main()
10 {
11         char       *addr, c;
12         int        fd;
```

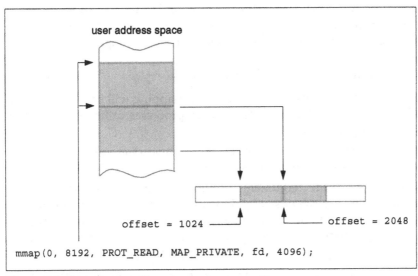

Figure 3.2 Mapping two file pages using mmap().

```
13
14              fd = open("/etc/passwd", O_RDONLY);
15              addr = (char *)mmap(NULL, MAPSZ,
16                                  PROT_READ, MAP_SHARED, fd, 0);
17              close(fd);
18              for (;;) {
19                      c = *addr;
20                      putchar(c);
21                      addr++;
22                      if (c == '\n') {
23                              exit(0);
24                      }
25              }
26 }
```

The /etc/passwd file is opened and a call to mmap() is made to map the first MAPSZ bytes of the file. A file offset of 0 is passed. The PROT_READ and MAP_SHARED arguments describe the type of mapping and how it relates to other processes that map the same file. The prot argument (in this case PROT_READ) can be one of the following:

PROT_READ. The data can be read.

PROT_WRITE. The data can be written.

PROT_EXEC. The data can be executed.

PROT_NONE. The data cannot be accessed.

Note that the different access types can be combined. For example, to specify read and write access a combination of (PROT_READ | PROT_WRITE) may be specified. By specifying PROT_EXEC it is possible for application writers to produce their own dynamic library mechanisms. The PROT_NONE argument can be used for user level memory management by preventing access to certain parts of memory at certain times. Note that PROT_NONE cannot be used in conjunction with any other flags.

The flags argument can be one of the following:

MAP_SHARED. Any changes made through the mapping will be reflected back to the mapped file and are visible by other processes calling mmap() and specifying MAP_SHARED.

MAP_PRIVATE. Any changes made through the mapping are private to this process and are not reflected back to the file.

MAP_FIXED. The addr argument should be interpreted exactly. This argument will be typically used by dynamic linkers to ensure that program text and data are laid out in the same place in memory for each process. If MAP_FIXED is specified and the area specified in the mapping covers an already existing mapping, the initial mapping is first unmapped.

Note that in some versions of UNIX, the flags have been enhanced to include operations that are not covered by the Single UNIX Specification. For example, on the Solaris operating system, the MAP_NORESERVE flag indicates that swap space should not be reserved. This avoids unnecessary wastage of virtual memory and is especially useful when mappings are read-only. Note, however, that this flag is not portable to other versions of UNIX.

To give a more concrete example of the use of mmap(), an abbreviated implementation of the cp utility is given. This is how some versions of UNIX actually implement cp.

```
 1 #include <sys/types.h>
 2 #include <sys/stat.h>
 3 #include <sys/mman.h>
 4 #include <fcntl.h>
 5 #include <unistd.h>
 6
 7 #define MAPSZ           4096
 8
 9 main(int argc, char argv)
10 {
11          struct stat    st;
12          size_t         iosz;
13          off_t          off = 0;
14          void           *addr;
15          int            ifd, ofd;
16
17          if (argc != 3) {
18                  printf("Usage: mycp srcfile destfile\n");
19                  exit(1);
20          }
21          if ((ifd = open(argv[1], O_RDONLY)) < 0) {
22                  printf("Failed to open %s\n", argv[1]);
23          }
```

```
24              if ((ofd = open(argv[2],
25                  O_WRONLY|O_CREAT|O_TRUNC, 0777)) < 0) {
26                      printf("Failed to open %s\n", argv[2]);
27              }
28              fstat(ifd, &st);
29              if (st.st_size < MAPSZ) {
30                      addr = mmap(NULL, st.st_size,
31                              PROT_READ, MAP_SHARED, ifd, 0);
32                      printf("Mapping entire file\n");
33                      close(ifd);
34                      write(ofd, (char *)addr, st.st_size);
35              } else {
36                      printf("Mapping file by MAPSZ chunks\n");
37                      while (off <= st.st_size) {
38                              addr = mmap(NULL, MAPSZ, PROT_READ,
39                                      MAP_SHARED, ifd, off);
40                              if (MAPSZ < (st.st_size - off)) {
41                                      iosz = MAPSZ;
42                              } else {
43                                      iosz = st.st_size - off;
44                              }
45                              write(ofd, (char *)addr, iosz);
46                              off += MAPSZ;
47                      }
48              }
49 }
```

The file to be copied is opened and the file to copy to is created on lines 21-27. The fstat() system call is invoked on line 28 to determine the size of the file to be copied. The first call to mmap() attempts to map the whole file (line 30) for files of size less then MAPSZ. If this is successful, a single call to write() can be issued to write the contents of the mapping to the output file.

If the attempt at mapping the whole file fails, the program loops (lines 37-47) mapping sections of the file and writing them to the file to be copied.

Note that in the example here, MAP_PRIVATE could be used in place of MAP_SHARED since the file was only being read. Here is an example of the program running:

```
$ cp mycp.c fileA
$ mycp fileA fileB
Mapping entire file
$ diff fileA fileB
$ cp mycp fileA
$ mycp fileA fileB
Mapping file by MAPSZ chunks
$ diff fileA fileB
```

Note that if the file is to be mapped in chunks, we keep making repeated calls to mmap(). This is an extremely inefficient use of memory because each call to mmap() will establish a new mapping without first tearing down the old mapping. Eventually the process will either exceed its virtual memory quota or run out of address space if the file to be copied is very large. For example, here is a run of a modified version of the program that displays the addresses returned by mmap():

```
$ dd if=/dev/zero of=20kfile bs=4096 count=5
5+0 records in
5+0 records out
$ mycp_profile 20kfile newfile
Mapping file by MAPSZ chunks
map addr = 0x40019000
map addr = 0x4001a000
map addr = 0x4001b000
map addr = 0x4001c000
map addr = 0x4001d000
map addr = 0x4001e000
```

The different addresses show that each call to mmap() establishes a mapping at a new address. To alleviate this problem, the munmap() system call can be used to unmap a previously established mapping:

```
#include <sys/mman.h>

int munmap(void *addr, size_t len);
```

Thus, using the example above and adding the following line:

```
munmap(addr, iosz);
```

after line 46, the mapping established will be unmapped, freeing up both the user's virtual address space and associated physical pages. Thus, running the program again and displaying the addresses returned by calling mmap() shows:

```
$ mycp2 20kfile newfile
Mapping file by MAPSZ chunks
map addr = 0x40019000
map addr = 0x40019000
map addr = 0x40019000
map addr = 0x40019000
map addr = 0x40019000
map addr = 0x40019000
```

The program determines whether to map the whole file based on the value of MAPSZ and the size of the file. One way to modify the program would be to attempt to map the whole file regardless of size and only switch to mapping in segments if the file is too large, causing the call to mmap() to fail.

After a mapping is established with a specific set of access protections, it may be desirable to change these protections over time. The mprotect() system call allows the protections to be changed:

```
#include <sys/mman.h>

int mprotect(void *addr, size_t len, int prot);
```

The `prot` argument can be one of `PROT_READ`, `PROT_WRITE`, `PROT_EXEC`, `PROT_NONE`, or a valid combination of the flags as described above. Note that the range of the mapping specified by a call to `mprotect()` does not have to cover the entire range of the mapping established by a previous call to `mmap()`. The kernel will perform some rounding to ensure that `len` is rounded up to the next multiple of the page size.

The other system call that is of importance with respect to memory mapped files is `msync()`, which allows modifications to the mapping to be flushed to the underlying file:

```
#include <sys/mman.h>

int msync(void *addr, size_t len, int flags);
```

Again, the range specified by the combination of `addr` and `len` does not need to cover the entire range of the mapping. The `flags` argument can be one of the following:

`MS_ASYNC`. Perform an asynchronous write of the data.

`MS_SYNC`. Perform a synchronous write of the data.

`MS_INVALIDATE`. Invalidate any cached data.

Thus, a call to `mmap()` followed by modification of the data followed by a call to `msync()` specifying the `MS_SYNC` flag is similar to a call to `write()` following a call to `open()` and specifying the `O_SYNC` flag. By specifying the `MS_ASYNC` flag, this is loosely synonymous to opening a file without the `O_SYNC` flag. However, calling `msync()` with the `MS_ASYNC` flag is likely to initiate the I/O while writing to a file without specifying `O_SYNC` or `O_DSYNC` could result in data sitting in the system page or buffer cache for some time.

One unusual property of mapped files occurs when the pseudo device `/dev/zero` is mapped. As one would expect, this gives access to a contiguous set of zeroes covering any part of the mapping that is accessed. However, following a mapping of `/dev/zero`, if the process was to fork, the mapping would be visible by parent and child. If `MAP_PRIVATE` was specified on the call to `mmap()`, parent and child will share the same physical pages of the mapping until a modification is made at which time the kernel will copy the page that makes the modification private to the process which issued the write.

If `MAP_SHARED` is specified, both parent and children will share the same physical pages regardless of whether read or write operations are performed.

64-Bit File Access (LFS)

32-bit operating systems have typically used a signed long integer as the offset to files. This leads to a maximum file size of 2^{31} - 1 (2GB - 1). The amount of work to convert existing applications to use a different size type for file offsets was considered too great, and thus the *Large File Summit* was formed, a group of OS and filesystem vendors who wanted to produce a specification that could allow access to *large files*. The specification would then be included as part of the Single UNIX Specification (UNIX 95 and onwards). The specification provided the following concepts:

- The off_t data type would support one of two or more sizes as the OS and filesystem evolved to a full 64-bit solution.

- An *offset maximum* which, as part of the interface, would give the maximum offset that the OS/filesystem would allow an application to use. The offset maximum is determined through a call to open() by specifying (or not) whether the application wishes to access large files.

- When applications attempt to read parts of a file beyond their understanding of the offset maximum, the OS would return a new error code, namely EOVERFLOW.

In order to provide both an explicit means of accessing large files as well as a hidden and easily upgradable approach, there were two programmatic models. The first allowed the size of off_t to be determined during the compilation and linking process. This effectively sets the size of off_t and determines whether the standard system calls such as read() and write() will be used or whether the large file specific libraries will be used. Either way, the application continues to use read(), write(), and related system calls, and the mapping is done during the link time.

The second approach provided an explicit model whereby the size of off_t was chosen explicitly within the program. For example, on a 32-bit OS, the size of off_t would be 32 bits, and large files would need to be accessed through use of the off64_t data type. In addition, specific calls such as open64(), read64() would be required in order to access large files.

Today, the issue has largely gone away, with most operating systems supporting large files by default.

Sparse Files

Due to their somewhat rare usage, *sparse files* are often not well understood and a cause of confusion. For example, the VxFS filesystem up to version 3.5 allowed a maximum filesystem size of 1TB but a maximum file size of 2TB. How can a single file be larger than the filesystem in which it resides?

A *sparse file* is simply a file that contains one or more *holes*. This statement itself is probably the reason for the confusion. A hole is a gap within the file for which there are no allocated data blocks. For example, a file could contain a 1KB data block followed by a 1KB hole followed by another 1KB data block. The size of the file would be 3KB but there are only two blocks allocated. When reading over a hole, zeroes will be returned.

The following example shows how this works in practice. First of all, a 20MB filesystem is created and mounted:

```
# mkfs -F vxfs /dev/vx/rdsk/rootdg/vol2 20m
version 4 layout
40960 sectors, 20480 blocks of size 1024, log size 1024 blocks
unlimited inodes, largefiles not supported
20480 data blocks, 19384 free data blocks
1 allocation units of 32768 blocks, 32768 data blocks
last allocation unit has 20480 data blocks
# mount -F vxfs /dev/vx/dsk/rootdg/vol2 /mnt2
```

and the following program, which is used to create a new file, seeks to an offset of 64MB and then writes a single byte:

```
#include <sys/types.h>
#include <fcntl.h>
#include <unistd.h>

#define IOSZ      (1024 * 1024 *64)

main()
{
    int     fd;

    fd = open("/mnt2/newfile", O_CREAT | O_WRONLY, 0666);
    lseek(fd, IOSZ, SEEK_SET);
    write(fd, "a", 1);
}
```

The following shows the result when the program is run:

```
# ./lf
# ls -l /mnt2
total 2
drwxr-xr-x   2 root      root            96 Jun 13 08:25 lost+found/
-rw-r--r     1 root      other     67108865 Jun 13 08:28 newfile
# df -k | grep mnt2
/dev/vx/dsk/rootdg/vol2   20480     1110    18167     6%    /mnt2
```

And thus, the filesystem which is only 20MB in size contains a file which is 64MB. Note that, although the file size is 64MB, the actual space consumed is very low. The 6 percent usage, as displayed by running df, shows that the filesystem is mostly empty.

To help understand how sparse files can be useful, consider how storage is allocated to a file in a hypothetical filesystem. For this example, consider a filesystem that allocates storage to files in 1KB chunks and consider the interaction between the user and the filesystem as follows:

User	Filesystem
create()	Create a new file
write(1k of 'a's)	Allocate a new 1k block for range 0 to 1023 bytes
write(1k of 'b's)	Allocate a new 1k block for range 1024 to 2047 bytes
close()	Close the file

In this example, following the close() call, the file has a size of 2048 bytes. The data written to the file is stored in two 1k blocks. Now, consider the example below:

User	Filesystem
create()	Create a new file
lseek(to 1k)	No effect on the file
write(1k of 'b's)	Allocate a new 1k block for range 1024 to 2047 bytes
close()	Close the file

The chain of events here also results in a file of size 2048 bytes. However, by seeking to a part of the file that doesn't exist and writing, the allocation occurs at the position in the file as specified by the file pointer. Thus, a single 1KB block is allocated to the file. The two different allocations are shown in Figure 3.3.

Note that although filesystems will differ in their individual implementations, each file will contain a block map mapping the blocks that are allocated to the file and at which offsets. Thus, in Figure 3.3, the hole is explicitly marked.

So what use are sparse files and what happens if the file is read? All UNIX standards dictate that if a file contains a hole and data is read from a portion of a file containing a hole, zeroes must be returned. Thus when reading the sparse file above, we will see the same result as for a file created as follows:

User	Filesystem
create()	Create a new file
write(1k of 0s)	Allocate a new 1k block for range 1023 to 2047 bytes
write(1k of 'b's)	Allocate a new 1k block for range 1024 to 2047 bytes
close()	Close the file

Not all filesystems implement sparse files and, as the examples above show, from a programmatic perspective, the holes in the file are not actually visible. The main benefit comes from the amount of storage that is saved. Thus, if an application wishes to create a file for which large parts of the file contain zeroes, this is a useful way to save on storage and potentially gain on performance by avoiding unnecessary I/Os.

The following program shows the example described above:

```
1 #include <sys/types.h>
2 #include <fcntl.h>
3 #include <unistd.h>
```

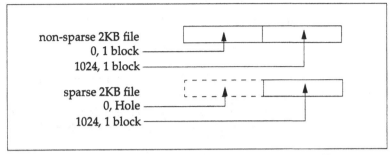

Figure 3.3 Allocation of storage for sparse and non-sparse files.

```
4
5 main()
6 {
7          char     buf[1024];
8          int      fd;
9
10         memset(buf, 'a', 1024);
11         fd = open("newfile", O_RDWR|O_CREAT|O_TRUNC, 0777);
12         lseek(fd, 1024, SEEK_SET);
13         write(fd, buf, 1024);
14 }
```

When the program is run the contents are displayed as shown below. Note the zeroes for the first 1KB as expected.

```
$ od -c newfile
0000000 \0 \0 \0 \0 \0 \0 \0 \0 \0 \0 \0 \0 \0 \0 \0 \0
*
0002000  a  a  a  a  a  a  a  a  a  a  a  a  a  a  a  a
*
0004000
```

If a write were to occur within the first 1KB of the file, the filesystem would have to allocate a 1KB block even if the size of the write is less than 1KB. For example, by modifying the program as follows:

```
memset(buf, 'b', 512);
fd = open("newfile", O_RDWR);
lseek(fd, 256, SEEK_SET);
write(fd, buf, 512);
```

and then running it on the previously created file, the resulting contents are:

```
$ od -c newfile
0000000 \0 \0 \0 \0 \0 \0 \0 \0 \0 \0 \0 \0 \0 \0 \0 \0
*
0000400  b  b  b  b  b  b  b  b  b  b  b  b  b  b  b  b
*
0001400 \0 \0 \0 \0 \0 \0 \0 \0 \0 \0 \0 \0 \0 \0 \0 \0
```

```
*
0002000   a a a a a a a a a a a a a a a a
*
0004000
```

Therefore in addition to allocating a new 1KB block, the filesystem must zero fill those parts of the block outside of the range of the write.

The following example shows how this works on a VxFS filesystem. A new file is created. The program then seeks to byte offset 8192 and writes 1024 bytes.

```
#include <sys/types.h>
#include <fcntl.h>
#include <unistd.h>

main()
{
    int      fd;
    char     buf[1024];

    fd = open("myfile", O_CREAT | O_WRONLY, 0666);
    lseek(fd, 8192, SEEK_SET);
    write(fd, buf, 1024);
}
```

In the output shown below, the program is run, the size of the new file is displayed, and the inode number of the file is obtained:

```
# ./sparse
# ls -l myfile
-rw-r--r 1 root        other          9216 Jun 13 08:37 myfile
# ls -i myfile
6 myfile
```

The VxFS `fsdb` command can show which blocks are assigned to the file. The inode corresponding to the file created is displayed:

```
# umount /mnt2
# fsdb -F vxfs /dev/vx/rdsk/rootdg/vol2
# > 6i
inode structure at 0x00000431.0200
type IFREG mode 100644  nlink 1  uid 0  gid 1  size 9216
atime 992447379 122128   (Wed Jun 13 08:49:39 2001)
mtime 992447379 132127   (Wed Jun 13 08:49:39 2001)
ctime 992447379 132127   (Wed Jun 13 08:49:39 2001)
aflags 0 orgtype 1 eopflags 0 eopdata 0
fixextsize/fsindex 0   rdev/reserve/dotdot/matchino 0
blocks 1   gen 844791719   version 0 13   iattrino 0
de:       0 1096    0     0     0     0     0     0     0     0
des:      8    1    0     0     0     0     0     0     0     0
ie:       0    0
ies:      0
```

The de field refers to a direct extent (filesystem block) and the des field is the extent size. For this file the first extent starts at block 0 and is 8 blocks (8KB) in size. VxFS uses block 0 to represent a hole (note that block 0 is never actually used). The next extent starts at block 1096 and is 1KB in length. Thus, although the file is 9KB in size, it has only one 1KB block allocated to it.

Summary

This chapter provided an introduction to file I/O based system calls. It is important to grasp these concepts before trying to understand how filesystems are implemented. By understanding what the user expects, it is easier to see how certain features are implemented and what the kernel and individual filesystems are trying to achieve.

Whenever programming on UNIX, it is always a good idea to follow appropriate standards to allow programs to be portable across multiple versions of UNIX. The commercial versions of UNIX typically support the Single UNIX Specification standard although this is not fully adopted in Linux and BSD. At the very least, all versions of UNIX will support the POSIX.1 standard.

The Standard I/O Library

Many users require functionality above and beyond what is provided by the basic file access system calls. The standard I/O library, which is part of the ANSI C standard, provides this extra level of functionality, avoiding the need for duplication in many applications.

There are many books that describe the calls provided by the standard I/O library (stdio). This chapter offers a different approach by describing the implementation of the Linux standard I/O library showing the main structures, how they support the functions available, and how the library calls map onto the system call layer of UNIX.

The needs of the application will dictate whether the standard I/O library will be used as opposed to basic file-based system calls. If extra functionality is required and performance is not paramount, the standard I/O library, with its rich set of functions, will typically meet the needs of most programmers. If performance is key and more control is required over the execution of I/O, understanding how the filesystem performs I/O and bypassing the standard I/O library is typically a better choice.

Rather than describing the myriad of stdio functions available, which are well documented elsewhere, this chapter provides an overview of how the standard I/O library is implemented. For further details on the interfaces available, see Richard Steven's book *Advanced Programming in the UNIX Programming Environment* [STEV92] or consult the Single UNIX Specification.

The FILE Structure

Where system calls such as open() and dup() return a file descriptor through which the file can be accessed, the stdio library operates on a FILE structure, or *file stream* as it is often called. This is basically a character buffer that holds enough information to record the current read and write file pointers and some other ancillary information. On Linux, the IO_FILE structure from which the FILE structure is defined is shown below. Note that not all of the structure is shown here.

```
struct _IO_FILE {
   char *_IO_read_ptr;    /* Current read pointer */
   char *_IO_read_end;    /* End of get area. */
   char *_IO_read_base;   /* Start of putback and get area. */
   char *_IO_write_base;  /* Start of put area. */
   char *_IO_write_ptr;   /* Current put pointer. */
   char *_IO_write_end;   /* End of put area. */
   char *_IO_buf_base;    /* Start of reserve area. */
   char *_IO_buf_end;     /* End of reserve area. */
   int   _fileno;
   int   _blksize;
};

typedef struct _IO_FILE FILE;
```

Each of the structure fields will be analyzed in more detail throughout the chapter. However, first consider a call to the open() and read() system calls:

```
fd = open("/etc/passwd", O_RDONLY);
read(fd, buf, 1024);
```

When accessing a file through the stdio library routines, a FILE structure will be allocated and associated with the file descriptor fd, and all I/O will operate through a single buffer. For the _IO_FILE structure shown above, _fileno is used to store the file descriptor that is used on subsequent calls to read() or write(), and _IO_buf_base represents the buffer through which the data will pass.

Standard Input, Output, and Error

The standard input, output, and error for a process can be referenced by the file descriptors STDIN_FILENO, STDOUT_FILENO, and STDERR_FILENO. To use the stdio library routines on either of these files, their corresponding file streams stdin, stdout, and stderr can also be used. Here are the definitions of all three:

```
extern FILE *stdin;
extern FILE *stdout;
extern FILE *stderr;
```

All three file streams can be accessed without opening them in the same way that the corresponding file descriptor values can be accessed without an explicit call to open().

There are some standard I/O library routines that operate on the standard input and output streams explicitly. For example, a call to printf() uses stdin by default whereas a call to fprintf() requires the caller to specify a file stream. Similarly, a call to getchar() operates on stdin while a call to getc() requires the file stream to be passed. The declaration of getchar() could simply be:

```
#define getchar()    getc(stdin)
```

Opening and Closing a Stream

The fopen() and fclose() library routines can be called to open and close a file stream:

```
#include <stdio.h>

FILE *fopen(const char *filename, const char *mode);
int  fclose(FILE *stream);
```

The mode argument points to a string that starts with one of the following sequences. Note that these sequences are part of the ANSI C standard.

r, rb. Open the file for reading.

w, wb. Truncate the file to zero length or, if the file does not exist, create a new file and open it for writing.

a, ab. Append to the file. If the file does not exist, it is first created.

r+, rb+, r+b. Open the file for update (reading and writing).

w+, wb+, w+b. Truncate the file to zero length or, if the file does not exist, create a new file and open it for update (reading and writing).

a+, ab+, a+b. Append to the file. If the file does not exist it is created and opened for update (reading and writing). Writing will start at the end of file.

Internally, the standard I/O library will map these flags onto the corresponding flags to be passed to the open() system call. For example, r will map to O_RDONLY, r+ will map to O_RDWR and so on. The process followed when opening a stream is shown in Figure 4.1.

The following example shows the effects of some of the library routines on the FILE structure:

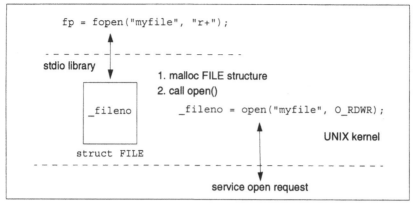

Figure 4.1   Opening a file through the stdio library.

```
1 #include <stdio.h>
2
3 main()
4 {
5         FILE    *fp1, *fp2;
6         char    c;
7
8         fp1 = fopen("/etc/passwd", "r");
9         fp2 = fopen("/etc/mtab", "r");
10         printf("address of fp1      = 0x%x\n", fp1);
11         printf("  fp1->_fileno      = 0x%x\n", fp1->_fileno);
12         printf("address of fp2      = 0x%x\n", fp2);
13         printf("  fp2->_fileno      = 0x%x\n\n", fp2->_fileno);
14
15         c = getc(fp1);
16         c = getc(fp2);
17         printf("  fp1->_IO_buf_base = 0x%x\n",
18                 fp1->_IO_buf_base);
19         printf("  fp1->_IO_buf_end  = 0x%x\n",
20                 fp1->_IO_buf_end);
21         printf("  fp2->_IO_buf_base = 0x%x\n",
22                 fp2->_IO_buf_base);
23         printf("  fp2->_IO_buf_end  = 0x%x\n",
24                 fp2->_IO_buf_end);
25 }
```

Note that, even following a call to fopen(), the library will not allocate space to the I/O buffer unless the user actually requests data to be read or written. Thus, the value of _IO_buf_base will initially be NULL. In order for a buffer to be allocated in the program here, a call is made to getc() in the above example, which will allocate the buffer and read data from the file into the newly allocated buffer.

```
$ fpopen
Address of fp1       = 0x8049860
```

```
fp1->_fileno            = 0x3
Address of fp2          = 0x80499d0
fp2->_fileno            = 0x4

fp1->_IO_buf_base       = 0x40019000
fp1->_IO_buf_end        = 0x4001a000
fp2->_IO_buf_base       = 0x4001a000
fp2->_IO_buf_end        = 0x4001b000
```

Note that one can see the corresponding system calls that the library will make by running strace, truss etc.

```
$ strace fpopen 2>&1 | grep open
open("/etc/passwd", O_RDONLY)           = 3
open("/etc/mtab", O_RDONLY)             = 4
$ strace fpopen 2>&1 | grep read
read(3, "root:x:0:0:root:/root:/bin/bash\n"..., 4096) = 827
read(4, "/dev/hda6 / ext2 rw 0 0 none /pr"..., 4096) = 157
```

Note that despite the program's request to read only a single character from each file stream, the stdio library attempted to read 4KB from each file. Any subsequent calls to getc() do not require another call to read() until all characters in the buffer have been read.

There are two additional calls that can be invoked to open a file stream, namely fdopen() and freopen():

```
#include <stdio.h>

FILE *fdopen (int fildes, const char *mode);
FILE *freopen (const char *filename,
               const char *mode, FILE *stream);
```

The fdopen() function can be used to associate an already existing file stream with a file descriptor. This function is typically used in conjunction with functions that only return a file descriptor such as dup(), pipe(), and fcntl().

The freopen() function opens the file whose name is pointed to by filename and associates the stream pointed to by stream with it. The original stream (if it exists) is first closed. This is typically used to associate a file with one of the predefined streams, standard input, output, or error. For example, if the caller wishes to use functions such as printf() that operate on standard output by default, but also wants to use a different file stream for standard output, this function achieves the desired effect.

Standard I/O Library Buffering

The stdio library buffers data with the goal of minimizing the number of calls to the read() and write() system calls. There are three different types of buffering used:

Fully (block) buffered. As characters are written to the stream, they are buffered up to the point where the buffer is full. At this stage, the data is written to the file referenced by the stream. Similarly, reads will result in a whole buffer of data being read if possible.

Line buffered. As characters are written to a stream, they are buffered up until the point where a newline character is written. At this point the line of data including the newline character is written to the file referenced by the stream. Similarly for reading, characters are read up to the point where a newline character is found.

Unbuffered. When an output stream is unbuffered, any data that is written to the stream is immediately written to the file to which the stream is associated.

The ANSI C standard dictates that standard input and output should be fully buffered while standard error should be unbuffered. Typically, standard input and output are set so that they are line buffered for terminal devices and fully buffered otherwise.

The `setbuf()` and `setvbuf()` functions can be used to change the buffering characteristics of a stream as shown:

```
#include <stdio.h>

void setbuf(FILE *stream, char *buf);
int setvbuf(FILE *stream, char *buf, int type, size_t size);
```

The `setbuf()` function must be called after the stream is opened but before any I/O to the stream is initiated. The buffer specified by the `buf` argument is used in place of the buffer that the stdio library would use. This allows the caller to optimize the number of calls to `read()` and `write()` based on the needs of the application.

The `setvbuf()` function can be called at any stage to alter the buffering characteristics of the stream. The `type` argument can be one of `_IONBF` (unbuffered), `_IOLBF` (line buffered), or `_IOFBF` (fully buffered). The buffer specified by the `buf` argument must be at least `size` bytes. Prior to the next I/O, this buffer will replace the buffer currently in use for the stream if one has already been allocated. If `buf` is NULL, only the buffering mode will be changed.

Whether full or line buffering is used, the `fflush()` function can be used to force all of the buffered data to the file referenced by the stream as shown:

```
#include <stdio.h>

int fflush(FILE *stream);
```

Note that all output streams can be flushed by setting `stream` to NULL. One further point worthy of mention concerns termination of a process. Any streams that are currently open are flushed and closed before the process exits.

Reading and Writing to/from a Stream

There are numerous stdio functions for reading and writing. This section describes some of the functions available and shows a different implementation of the cp program using various buffering options. The program shown below demonstrates the effects on the FILE structure by reading a single character using the getc() function:

```
 1 #include <stdio.h>
 2
 3 main()
 4 {
 5         FILE    *fp;
 6         char    c;
 7
 8         fp = fopen("/etc/passwd", "r");
 9         printf("address of fp       = 0x%x\n", fp);
10         printf("  fp->_fileno       = 0x%x\n", fp->_fileno);
11         printf("  fp->_IO_buf_base  = 0x%x\n", fp->_IO_buf_base);
12         printf("  fp->_IO_read_ptr  = 0x%x\n", fp->_IO_read_ptr);
13
14         c = getc(fp);
15         printf(" fp->_IO_buf_base = 0x%x (size = %d)\n",
16                 fp->_IO_buf_base,
17                 fp->_IO_buf_end fp->_IO_buf_base);
18         printf(" fp->_IO_read_ptr = 0x%x\n", fp->_IO_read_ptr);
19         c = getc(fp);
20         printf(" fp->_IO_read_ptr = 0x%x\n", fp->_IO_read_ptr);
21 }
```

Note as shown in the output below, the buffer is not allocated until the first I/O is initiated. The default size of the buffer allocated is 4KB. With successive calls to getc(), the read pointer is incremented to reference the next byte to read within the buffer. Figure 4.2 shows the steps that the stdio library goes through to read the data.

```
$ fpinfo
Address of fp      = 0x8049818
fp->_fileno        = 0x3
fp->_IO_buf_base = 0x0
fp->_IO_read_ptr = 0x0
fp->_IO_buf_base = 0x40019000  (size = 4096)
fp->_IO_read_ptr = 0x40019001
fp->_IO_read_ptr = 0x40019002
```

By running strace on Linux, it is possible to see how the library reads the data following the first call to getc(). Note that only those lines that reference the /etc/passwd file are displayed here:

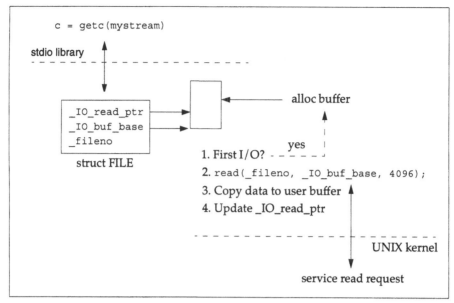

Figure 4.2 Reading a file through the standard I/O library.

```
$ strace fpinfo
...

open("/etc/passwd", O_RDONLY) = 3
...
fstat(3, st_mode=S_IFREG_0644, st_size=788, ...) = 0
...
read(3, "root:x:0:0:root:/root:/bin/bash\n"..., 4096) = 788
```

The call to fopen() results in a call to open() and the file descriptor returned is
stored in fp->_fileno as shown above. Note that although the program only
asked for a single character (line 14), the standard I/O library issued a 4KB read
to fill up the buffer. The next call to getc() did not require any further data to be
read from the file. Note that when the end of the file is reached, a subsequent call
to getc() will return EOL.

The following example provides a simple cp program showing the effects of
using fully buffered, line buffered, and unbuffered I/O. The buffering option is
passed as an argument. The file to copy from and the file to copy to are hard
coded into the program for this example.

```
1 #include <time.h>
2 #include <stdio.h>
3
4 main(int argc, char **argv)
5 {
6          time_t   time1, time2;
```

```
7          FILE     *ifp, *ofp;
8          int      mode;
9          char     c, ibuf[16384], obuf[16384];
10
11         if (strcmp(argv[1], "_IONBF") == 0) {
12                 mode = _IONBF;
13         } else if (strcmp(argv[1], "_IOLBF") == 0) {
14                 mode = _IOLBF;
15         } else {
16                 mode = _IOFBF;
17         }
18
19         ifp = fopen("infile", "r");
20         ofp = fopen("outfile", "w");
21
22         setvbuf(ifp, ibuf, mode, 16384);
23         setvbuf(ofp, obuf, mode, 16384);
24
25         time(&time1);
26         while ((c = fgetc(ifp)) != EOF) {
27                 fputc(c, ofp);
28         }
29         time(&time2);
30         fprintf(stderr, "Time for %s was %d seconds\n", argv[1],
31                 time2 - time1);
32 }
```

The input file has 68,000 lines of 80 characters each. When the program is run with the different buffering options, the following results are observed:

```
$ ls -l infile
-rw-r--r-   1 spate     fcf          5508000 Jun 29 15:38 infile
$ wc -l infile
68000 infile
$ ./fpcp _IONBF
Time for _IONBF was 35 seconds
$ ./fpcp _IOLBF
Time for _IOLBF was 3 seconds
$ ./fpcp _IOFBF
Time for _IOFBF was 2 seconds
```

The reason for such a huge difference in performance can be seen by the number of system calls that each option results in. For unbuffered I/O, each call to getc() or putc() produces a system call to read() or write(). All together, there are 68,000 reads and 68,000 writes! The system call pattern seen for unbuffered is as follows:

```
...
open("infile", O_RDONLY)                    = 3
open("outfile", O_WRONLY|O_CREAT|O_TRUNC, 0666) = 4
time([994093607])                           = 994093607
read(3, "0", 1)                             = 1
```

```
write(4, "0", 1)                                    = 1
read(3, "1", 1)                                     = 1
write(4, "1", 1)                                    = 1
...
```

For line buffered, the number of system calls is reduced dramatically as the system call pattern below shows. Note that data is still read in buffer-sized chunks.

```
...
open("infile", O_RDONLY)                            = 3
open("outfile", O_WRONLY|O_CREAT|O_TRUNC, 0666)     = 4
time([994093688])                                   = 994093688
read(3, "012345678901234567890123456789012"..., 16384) = 16384
write(4, "012345678901234567890123456789012"..., 81)   = 81
write(4, "012345678901234567890123456789012"..., 81)   = 81
write(4, "012345678901234567890123456789012"..., 81)   = 81
...
```

For the fully buffered case, all data is read and written in buffer size (16384 bytes) chunks, reducing the number of system calls further as the following output shows:

```
open("infile", O_RDONLY)                            = 3
open("outfile", O_WRONLY|O_CREAT|O_TRUNC, 0666)     = 4
read(3, "678901234567890123456789012345667"..., 4096) = 4096
write(4, "012345678901234567890123456789012"..., 4096) = 4096
read(3, "123456789012345678901234567890012"..., 4096) = 4096
write(4, "678901234567890123456789012345667"..., 4096) = 4096
```

Seeking through the Stream

Just as the lseek() system call can be used to set the file pointer in preparation for a subsequent read or write, the fseek() library function can be called to set the file pointer for the stream such that the next read or write will start from that offset.

```
#include <stdio.h>

int fseek(FILE *stream, long int offset, int whence);
```

The offset and whence arguments are identical to those supported by the lseek() system call. The following example shows the effect of calling fseek() on the file stream:

```
1 #include <stdio.h>
2
3 main()
4 {
```

```
5          FILE        *fp;
6          char        c;
7
8          fp = fopen("infile", "r");
9          printf("address of fp       = 0x%x\n", fp);
10         printf("  fp->_IO_buf_base = 0x%x\n", fp->_IO_buf_base);
11         printf("  fp->_IO_read_ptr = 0x%x\n", fp->_IO_read_ptr);
12
13         c = getc(fp);
14         printf("  fp->_IO_read_ptr = 0x%x\n", fp->_IO_read_ptr);
15         fseek(fp, 8192, SEEK_SET);
16         printf("  fp->_IO_read_ptr = 0x%x\n", fp->_IO_read_ptr);
17         c = getc(fp);
18         printf("  fp->_IO_read_ptr = 0x%x\n", fp->_IO_read_ptr);
19 }
```

By calling getc(), a 4KB read is used to fill up the buffer pointed to by _IO_buf_base. Because only a single character is returned by getc(), the read pointer is only advanced by one. The call to fseek() modifies the read pointer as shown below:

```
$ fpseek
Address of fp     = 0x80497e0
fp->_IO_buf_base = 0x0
fp->_IO_read_ptr = 0x0
fp->_IO_read_ptr = 0x40019001
fp->_IO_read_ptr = 0x40019000
fp->_IO_read_ptr = 0x40019001
```

Note that no data needs to be read for the second call to getc(). Here are the relevant system calls:

```
open("infile", O_RDONLY)                    = 3
fstat64(1, st_mode=S_IFCHR_0620, st_rdev=makedev(136, 0), ...) = 0
read(3, "01234567890123456789012345678901"..., 4096) = 4096
write(1, ...)                               # display _IO_read_ptr
_llseek(3, 8192, [8192], SEEK_SET)          = 0
write(1, ...)                               # display _IO_read_ptr
read(3, "12345678901234567890123456789012"..., 4096) = 4096
write(1, ...)                               # display _IO_read_ptr
```

The first call to getc() results in the call to read(). Seeking through the stream results in a call to lseek(), which also resets the read pointer. The second call to getc() then involves another call to read data from the file.

There are four other functions available that relate to the file position within the stream, namely:

```
#include <stdio.h>

long ftell( FILE *stream);
void rewind( FILE *stream);
int fgetpos( FILE *stream, fpos_t *pos);
int fsetpos( FILE *stream, fpos_t *pos);
```

The ftell() function returns the current file position. In the preceding example following the call to fseek(), a call to ftell() would return 8192. The rewind() function is simply the equivalent of calling:

```
fseek(stream, 0, SEEK_SET)
```

The fgetpos() and fsetpos() functions are equivalent to ftell() and fseek() (with SEEK_SET passed), but store the current file pointer in the argument referenced by pos.

Summary

There are numerous functions provided by the standard I/O library that often reduce the work of an application writer. By aiming to minimize the number of system calls, performance of some applications may be considerably improved. Buffering offers a great deal of flexibility to the application programmer by allowing finer control over how I/O is actually performed.

This chapter highlighted how the standard I/O library is implemented but stops short of describing all of the functions that are available. Richard Steven's book *Advanced Programming in the UNIX Environment* [STEV92] provides more details from a programming perspective. Herbert Schildt's book *The Annotated ANSI C Standard* [SCHI93] provides detailed information on the stdio library as supported by the ANSI C standard.

Filesystem-Based Concepts

The UNIX filesystem hierarchy contains a number of different filesystem types including disk-based filesystems such as VxFS and UFS and also pseudo filesystems such as procfs and tmpfs. This chapter describes concepts that relate to filesystems as a whole such as disk partitioning, mounting and unmounting of filesystems, and the main commands that operate on filesystems such as mkfs, mount, fsck, and df.

What's in a Filesystem?

At one time, filesystems were either disk based in which all files in the filesystem were held on a physical disk, or were RAM based. In the latter case, the filesystem only survived until the system was rebooted. However, the concepts and implementation are the same for both. Over the last 10 to 15 years a number of pseudo filesystems have been introduced, which to the user look like filesystems, but for which the implementation is considerably different due to the fact that they have no physical storage. Pseudo filesystems will be presented in more detail in Chapter 11. This chapter is primarily concerned with disk-based filesystems.

A UNIX filesystem is a collection of files and directories that has the following properties:

- It has a root directory (/) that contains other files and directories. Most disk-based filesystems will also contain a lost+found directory where orphaned files are stored when recovered following a system crash.

- Each file or directory is uniquely identified by its name, the directory in which it resides, and a unique identifier, typically called an *inode*.

- By convention, the root directory has an inode number of 2 and the lost+found directory has an inode number of 3. Inode numbers 0 and 1 are not used. File inode numbers can be seen by specifying the -i option to ls.

- It is self contained. There are no dependencies between one filesystem and any other.

A filesystem must be in a *clean* state before it can be mounted. If the system crashes, the filesystem is said to be *dirty*. In this case, operations may have been only partially completed before the crash and therefore the filesystem structure may no longer be intact. In such a case, the filesystem check program fsck must be run on the filesystem to check for any inconsistencies and repair any that it finds. Running fsck returns the filesystem to its clean state. The section *Repairing Damaged Filesystems*, later in this chapter, describes the fsck program in more detail.

The Filesystem Hierarchy

There are many different types of files in a complete UNIX operating system. These files, together with user home directories, are stored in a hierarchical tree structure that allows files of similar types to be grouped together. Although the UNIX directory hierarchy has changed over the years, the structure today still largely reflects the filesystem hierarchy developed for early System V and BSD variants.

For both root and normal UNIX users, the PATH shell variable is set up during login to ensure that the appropriate paths are accessible from which to run commands. Because some directories contain commands that are used for administrative purposes, the path for root is typically different from that of normal users. For example, on Linux the path for a root and non root user may be:

```
# echo $PATH
/usr/sbin:/sbin:/bin:/usr/bin:/usr/local/bin:/usr/bin/X11:/root/bin
$ echo $PATH
/home/spate/bin:/usr/bin:/bin:/usr/bin/X11:/usr/local/bin:
        /home/spate/office52/program
```

The following list shows the main UNIX directories and the type of files that reside in each directory. Note that this structure is not strictly followed among the different UNIX variants but there is a great deal of commonality among all of them.

/usr. This is the main location of binaries for both user and administrative purposes.

/usr/bin. This directory contains user binaries.

/usr/sbin. Binaries that are required for system administration purposes are stored here. This directory is not typically on a normal user's path. On some versions of UNIX, some of the system binaries are stored in /sbin.

/usr/local. This directory is used for locally installed software that is typically separate from the OS. The binaries are typically stored in /usr/local/bin.

/usr/share. This directory contains architecture-dependent files including ASCII help files. The UNIX manual pages are typically stored in /usr/share/man.

/usr/lib. Dynamic and shared libraries are stored here.

/usr/ucb. For non-BSD systems, this directory contains binaries that originated in BSD.

/usr/include. User header files are stored here. Header files used by the kernel are stored in /usr/include/sys.

/usr/src. The UNIX kernel source code was once held in this directory although this hasn't been the case for a long time, Linux excepted.

/bin. Has been a symlink to /usr/bin for quite some time.

/dev. All of the accessible device files are stored here.

/etc. Holds configuration files and binaries which may need to be run before other filesystems are mounted. This includes many startup scripts and configuration files which are needed when the system bootstraps.

/var. System log files are stored here. Many of the log files are stored in /var/log.

/var/adm. UNIX accounting files and system login files are stored here.

/var/preserve. This directory is used by the vi and ex editors for storing backup files.

/var/tmp. Used for user temporary files.

/var/spool. This directory is used for UNIX commands that provide spooling services such as uucp, printing, and the cron command.

/home. User home directories are typically stored here. This may be /usr/home on some systems. Older versions of UNIX and BSD often store user home directories under /u.

/tmp. This directory is used for temporary files. Files residing in this directory will not necessarily be there after the next reboot.

/opt. Used for optional packages and binaries. Third-party software vendors store their packages in this directory.

When the operating system is installed, there are typically a number of filesystems created. The root filesystem contains the basic set of commands, scripts, configuration files, and utilities that are needed to bootstrap the system. The remaining files are held in separate filesystems that are visible after the system bootstraps and system administrative commands are available.

For example, shown below are some of the mounted filesystems for an active Solaris system:

```
/proc on /proc read/write/setuid
/ on /dev/dsk/c1t0d0s0 read/write/setuid
/dev/fd on fd read/write/setuid
/var/tmp on /dev/vx/dsk/sysdg/vartmp read/write/setuid/tmplog
/tmp on /dev/vx/dsk/sysdg/tmp read/write/setuid/tmplog
/opt on /dev/vx/dsk/sysdg/opt read/write/setuid/tmplog
/usr/local on /dev/vx/dsk/sysdg/local read/write/setuid/tmplog
/var/adm/log on /dev/vx/dsk/sysdg/varlog read/write/setuid/tmplog
/home on /dev/vx/dsk/homedg/home read/write/setuid/tmplog
```

During installation of the operating system, there is typically a great deal of flexibility allowed so that system administrators can tailor the number and size of filesystems to their specific needs. The basic goal is to separate those filesystems that need to grow from the root filesystem, which must remain stable. If the root filesystem becomes full, the system becomes unusable.

Disks, Slices, Partitions, and Volumes

Each hard disk is typically split into a number of separate, different sized units called *partitions* or *slices*. Note that is not the same as a partition in PC terminology. Each disk contains some form of partition table, called a VTOC (Volume Table Of Contents) in SVR4 terminology, which describes where the slices start and what their size is. Each slice may then be used to store bootstrap information, a filesystem, swap space, or be left as a *raw partition* for database access or other use.

Disks can be managed using a number of utilities. For example, on Solaris and many SVR4 derivatives, the prtvtoc and fmthard utilities can be used to edit the VTOC to divide the disk into a number of slices. When there are many disks, this hand editing of disk partitions becomes tedious and very error prone.

For example, here is the output of running the prtvtoc command on a root disk on Solaris:

```
# prtvtoc /dev/rdsk/c0t0d0s0
* /dev/rdsk/c0t0d0s0 partition map
```

```
 *
 * Dimensions:
 *      512 bytes/sector
 *      135 sectors/track
 *       16 tracks/cylinder
 *     2160 sectors/cylinder
 *     3882 cylinders
 *     3880 accessible cylinders
 *
 * Flags:
 *    1: unmountable
 *   10: read-only
 *
 *                              First     Sector     Last
 * Partition  Tag   Flags      Sector      Count    Sector    Mount Dir
         0     2    00              0     788400    788399    /
         1     3    01         788400    1049760   1838159
         2     5    00              0    8380800   8380799
         4     0    00        1838160    4194720   6032879    /usr
         6     4    00        6032880    2347920   8380799    /opt
```

The partition tag is used to identify each slice such that c0t0d0s0 is the slice that holds the root filesystem, c0t0d0s4 is the slice that holds the /usr filesystem, and so on.

The following example shows partitioning of an IDE-based, root Linux disk. Although the naming scheme differs, the concepts are similar to those shown previously.

```
# fdisk /dev/hda

Command (m for help): p

Disk /dev/hda: 240 heads, 63 sectors, 2584 cylinders
Units = cylinders of 15120 * 512 bytes

Device     Boot    Start      End     Blocks   Id   System
/dev/hda1    *          1        3      22648+  83   Linux
/dev/hda2             556      630     567000    6   FAT16
/dev/hda3               4       12      68040   82   Linux swap
/dev/hda4             649     2584   14636160    f   Win95 Ext'd (LBA)
/dev/hda5            1204     2584   10440328+   b   Win95 FAT32
/dev/hda6             649     1203    4195737   83   Linux
```

Logical volume managers provide a much easier way to manage disks and create new slices (called *logical volumes*). The volume manager takes ownership of the disks and gives out space as requested. Volumes can be simple, in which case the volume simply looks like a basic raw disk slice, or they can be mirrored or striped. For example, the following command can be used with the VERITAS Volume Manager, VxVM, to create a new simple volume:

```
# vxassist make myvol 10g
# vxprint myvol
```

```
Disk group: rootdg

TY NAME          ASSOC       KSTATE    LENGTH    PLOFFS    STATE
v  myvol         fsgen       ENABLED   20971520            ACTIVE
pl myvol-01      myvol       ENABLED   20973600            ACTIVE
sd disk12-01     myvol-01    ENABLED   8378640   0         -
sd disk02-01     myvol-01    ENABLED   8378640   8378640   -
sd disk03-01     myvol-01    ENABLED   4216320   16757280  -
```

VxVM created the new volume, called myvol, from existing free space. In this case, the 1GB volume was created from three separate, contiguous chunks of disk space that together can be accessed like a single raw partition.

Raw and Block Devices

With each disk slice or logical volume there are two methods by which they can be accessed, either through the raw (character) interface or through the block interface. The following are examples of character devices:

```
# ls -l /dev/vx/rdsk/myvol
crw------  1 root    root      86,  8 Jul  9 21:36 /dev/vx/rdsk/myvol
# ls -lL /dev/rdsk/c0t0d0s0
crw------  1 root    sys      136,  0 Apr 20 09:51 /dev/rdsk/c0t0d0s0
```

while the following are examples of block devices:

```
# ls -l /dev/vx/dsk/myvol
brw------  1 root    root      86,  8 Jul  9 21:11 /dev/vx/dsk/myvol
# ls -lL /dev/dsk/c0t0d0s0
brw------  1 root    sys      136,  0 Apr 20 09:51 /dev/dsk/c0t0d0s0
```

Note that both can be distinguished by the first character displayed (b or c) or through the location of the device file. Typically, raw devices are accessed through /dev/rdsk while block devices are accessed through /dev/dsk. When accessing the block device, data is read and written through the system buffer cache. Although the buffers that describe these data blocks are freed once used, they remain in the buffer cache until they get reused. Data accessed through the raw or character interface is not read through the buffer cache. Thus, mixing the two can result in stale data in the buffer cache, which can cause problems.

All filesystem commands, with the exception of the mount command, should therefore use the raw/character interface to avoid this potential caching problem.

Filesystem Switchout Commands

Many of the commands that apply to filesystems may require filesystem specific processing. For example, when creating a new filesystem, each different filesystem may support a wide range of options. Although some of these options will be common to most filesystems, many may not be.

To support a variety of command options, many of the filesystem-related commands are divided into generic and filesystem dependent components. For example, the generic mkfs command that will be described in the next section, is invoked as follows:

```
# mkfs -F vxfs -o ...
```

The -F option (-t on Linux) is used to specify the filesystem type. The -o option is used to specify filesystem-specific options. The first task to be performed by mkfs is to do a preliminary sanity check on the arguments passed. After this has been done, the next job is to locate and call the filesystem specific mkfs function.

Take for example the call to mkfs as follows:

```
# mkfs -F nofs /dev/vx/rdsk/myvol
mkfs: FSType nofs not installed in the kernel
```

Because there is no filesystem type of nofs, the generic mkfs command is unable to locate the nofs version of mkfs. To see how the search is made for the filesystem specific mkfs command, consider the following:

```
# truss -o /tmp/truss.out mkfs -F nofs /dev/vx/rdsk/myvol
mkfs: FSType nofs not installed in the kernel
# grep nofs /tmp/truss.out
execve("/usr/lib/fs/nofs/mkfs", 0x000225C0, 0xFFBEFDA8) Err#2 ENOENT
execve("/etc/fs/nofs/mkfs", 0x000225C0, 0xFFBEFDA8) Err#2 ENOENT
sysfs(GETFSIND, "nofs") Err#22 EINVAL
```

In this case, the generic mkfs command assumes that commands for the nofs filesystem will be located in one of the two directories shown above. In this case, the files don't exist. As a finally sanity check, a call is made to sysfs() to see if there actually is a filesystem type called nofs.

Consider the location of the generic and filesystem-specific fstyp commands in Solaris:

```
# which fstyp
/usr/sbin/fstyp
# ls /usr/lib/fs
autofs/    fd/        lofs/      nfs/       proc/      udfs/      vxfs/
cachefs/   hsfs/      mntfs/     pcfs/      tmpfs/     ufs/
# ls /usr/lib/fs/ufs/fstyp
/usr/lib/fs/ufs/fstyp
# ls /usr/lib/fs/vxfs/fstyp
/usr/lib/fs/vxfs/fstyp
```

Using this knowledge it is very straightforward to write a version of the generic fstyp command as follows:

```
 1 #include <sys/fstyp.h>
 2 #include <sys/fsid.h>
 3 #include <unistd.h>
 4
 5 main(int argc, char **argv)
 6 {
 7         char    cmd[256];
 8
 9         if (argc != 4 && (strcmp(argv[1], "-F") != 0)) {
10                 printf("usage: myfstyp -F fs-type\n");
11                 exit(1);
12         }
13         sprintf(cmd, "/usr/lib/fs/%s/fstyp", argv[2]);
14         if (execl(cmd, argv[2], argv[3], NULL) < 0) {
15                 printf("Failed to find fstyp command for %s\n",
16                         argv[2]);
17         }
18         if (sysfs(GETFSTYP, argv[2]) < 0) {
19                 printf("Filesystem type %s  doesn't exist\n",
20                         argv[2]);
21         }
22 }
```

This version requires that the filesystem type to search for is specified. If it is located in the appropriate place, the command is executed. If not, a check is made to see if the filesystem type exists as the following run of the program shows:

```
# myfstyp -F vxfs /dev/vx/rdsk/myvol
vxfs
# myfstyp -F nofs /dev/vx/rdsk/myvol
Failed to find fstyp command for nofs
Filesystem type "nofs" doesn't exist
```

Creating New Filesystems

Filesystems can be created on raw partitions or logical volumes. For example, in the prtvtoc output shown above, the root (/) filesystem was created on the raw disk slice /dev/rdsk/c0t0d0s0 and the /usr filesystem was created on the raw disk slice /dev/rdsk/c0t0d0s4.

The mkfs command is most commonly used to create a new filesystem, although on some platforms the newfs command provides a more friendly interface and calls mkfs internally. The type of filesystem to create is passed to mkfs as an argument. For example, to create a VxFS filesystem, this would be achieved by invoking mkfs -F vxfs on most UNIX platforms. On Linux, the call would be mkfs -t vxfs.

The filesystem type is passed as an argument to the generic mkfs command (-F or -t). This is then used to locate the switchout command by searching well-known locations as shown above. The following two examples show how to create a VxFS filesystem. In the first example, the size of the filesystem to create is passed as an argument. In the second example, the size is omitted, in which case VxFS determines the size of the device and creates a filesystem of that size.

```
# mkfs -F vxfs /dev/vx/rdsk/vol1 25g
version 4 layout
52428800 sectors, 6553600 blocks of size 4096,
log size 256 blocks unlimited inodes, largefiles not supported
6553600 data blocks, 6552864 free data blocks
200 allocation units of 32768 blocks, 32768 data blocks

# mkfs -F vxfs /dev/vx/rdsk/vol1
version 4 layout
54525952 sectors, 6815744 blocks of size 4096,
log size 256 blocks unlimited inodes, largefiles not supported
6815744 data blocks, 6814992 free data blocks
208 allocation units of 32768 blocks, 32768 data blocks
```

The following example shows how to create a UFS filesystem. Note that although the output is different, the method of invoking mkfs is similar for both VxFS and UFS.

```
# mkfs -F ufs /dev/vx/rdsk/vol1 54525952
/dev/vx/rdsk/vol1: 54525952 sectors in 106496 cylinders of
    16 tracks, 32 sectors
26624.0MB in 6656 cyl groups (16 c/g, 4.00MB/g, 1920 i/g)
super-block backups (for fsck -F ufs -o b=#) at:
  32, 8256, 16480, 24704, 32928, 41152, 49376, 57600, 65824,
  74048, 82272, 90496, 98720, 106944, 115168, 123392, 131104,
  139328, 147552, 155776, 164000,
  ...
  54419584, 54427808, 54436032, 54444256, 54452480, 54460704,
  54468928, 54477152, 54485376, 54493600, 54501824, 54510048,
```

The time taken to create a filesystem differs from one filesystem type to another. This is due to how the filesystems lay out their structures on disk. In the example above, it took UFS 23 minutes to create a 25GB filesystem, while for VxFS it took only half a second. Chapter 9 describes the implementation of various filesystems and shows how this large difference in filesystem creation time can occur.

Additional arguments can be passed to mkfs through use of the -o option, for example:

```
# mkfs -F vxfs -obsize=8192,largefiles /dev/vx/rdsk/myvol
    version 4 layout
    20971520 sectors, 1310720 blocks of size 8192,
    log size 128 blocks
    unlimited inodes, largefiles not supported
    1310720 data blocks, 1310512 free data blocks
    40 allocation units of 32768 blocks, 32768 data blocks
```

For arguments specified using the -o option, the generic mkfs command will pass the arguments through to the filesystem specific mkfs command without trying to interpret them.

Mounting and Unmounting Filesystems

The root filesystem is mounted by the kernel during system startup. Each filesystem can be mounted on any directory in the root filesystem, except /. A mount point is simply a directory. When a filesystem is mounted on that directory, the previous contents of the directory are hidden for the duration of the mount, as shown in Figure 5.1.

In order to mount a filesystem, the filesystem type, the device (slice or logical volume), and the mount point must be passed to the mount command. In the example below, a VxFS filesystem is mounted on /mnt1. Running the mount command by itself shows all the filesystems that are currently mounted, along with their mount options:

```
# mount -F vxfs /dev/vx/dsk/vol1 /mnt1
# mount | grep mnt1
/mnt1 on /dev/vx/dsk/vol1 read/write/setuid/delaylog/
        nolargefiles/ioerror=mwdisable/dev=1580006
        on Tue Jul  3 09:40:27 2002
```

Note that the mount shows default mount options as well as options that were explicitly requested. On Linux, the -t option is used to specify the filesystem type so the command would be invoked with mount -t vxfs.

As with mkfs, the mount command is a switchout command. The generic mount runs first and locates the filesystem-specific command to run, as the following output shows. Note the use of the access() system call. There are a number of well-known locations for which the filesystem-dependent mount command can be located.

```
1379: execve("/usr/sbin/mount", 0xFFBEFD8C, 0xFFBEFDA4)  argc = 5
. . .
1379: access("/usr/lib/fs/vxfs/mount", 0) Err#2 ENOENT
1379: execve("/etc/fs/vxfs/mount", 0xFFBEFCEC, 0xFFBEFDA4)  argc = 3
. . .
1379: mount("/dev/vx/dsk/vol1", "/mnt1", MS_DATA|MS_OPTIONSTR,
        "vxfs", 0xFFBEFBF4, 12) = 0
. . .
```

When a filesystem is mounted, an entry is added to the *mount table*, which is a file held in /etc that records all filesystems mounted, the devices on which they reside, the mount points on which they're mounted, and a list of options that were passed to mount or which the filesystem chose as defaults.

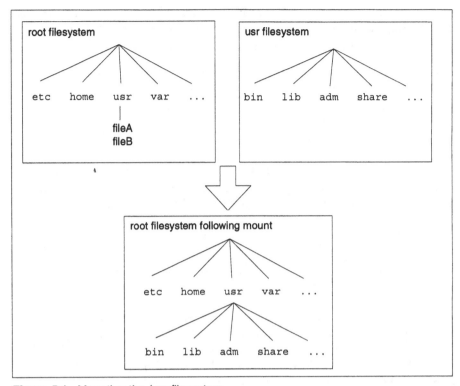

Figure 5.1 Mounting the /usr filesystem.

The actual name chosen for the mount table differs across different versions of UNIX. On all System V variants, it is called `mnttab`, while on Linux and BSD variants it is called `mtab`.

Shown below are the first few lines of `/etc/mnttab` on Solaris followed by the contents of a `/etc/mtab` on Linux:

```
# head -6 /etc/mnttab
/proc /proc proc rw,suid,dev=2f80000 995582515
/dev/dsk/c1t0d0s0 / ufs rw,suid,dev=1d80000,largefiles 995582515
fd /dev/fd fd rw,suid,dev=3080000 995582515
/dev/dsk/c1t1d0s0 /space1 ufs ro,largefiles,dev=1d80018 995582760
/dev/dsk/c1t2d0s0 /rootcopy ufs ro,largefiles,dev=1d80010
     995582760
/dev/vx/dsk/sysdg/vartmp /var/tmp vxfs rw,tmplog,suid,nolargefiles
     995582793

# cat /etc/mtab
/dev/hda6 / ext2 rw 0 0
none /proc proc rw 0 0
usbdevfs /proc/bus/usb usbdevfs rw 0 0
/dev/hda1 /boot ext2 rw 0 0
none /dev/pts devpts rw,gid=5,mode=620 0 0
```

All versions of UNIX provide a set of routines for manipulating the mount table, either for adding entries, removing entries, or simply reading them. Listed below are two of the functions that are most commonly available:

```
#include <stdio.h>
#include <sys/mnttab.h>

int getmntent(FILE *fp, struct mnttab *mp);

int putmntent(FILE *iop, struct mnttab *mp);
```

The getmntent(L) function is used to read entries from the mount table while putmntent(L) can be used to remove entries. Both functions operate on the mnttab structure, which will contain at least the following members:

```
char    *mnt_special;   /* The device on which the fs resides */
char    *mnt_mountp;    /* The mount point */
char    *mnt_fstype;    /* The filesystem type */
char    *mnt_mntopts;   /* Mount options */
char    *mnt_time;      /* The time of the mount */
```

Using the getmntent(L) library routine, it is very straightforward to write a simple version of the mount command that, when run with no arguments, displays the mounted filesystems by reading entries from the mount table. The program, which is shown below, simply involves opening the mount table and then making repeated calls to getmntent(L) to read all entries.

```
 1 #include <stdio.h>
 2 #include <sys/mnttab.h>
 3
 4 main()
 5 {
 6          struct mnttab       mt;
 7          FILE                *fp;
 8
 9          fp = fopen("/etc/mnttab", "r");
10
11          printf("%-15s%-10s%-30s\n",
12                  "mount point", "fstype", "device");
13          while ((getmntent(fp, &mt)) != -1) {
14                  printf("%-15s%-10s%-30s\n", mt.mnt_mountp,
15                          mt.mnt_fstype, mt.mnt_special);
16          }
17 }
```

Each time getmntent(L) is called, it returns the next entry in the file. Once all entries have been read, -1 is returned. Here is an example of the program running:

```
$ mymount | head -7
/proc           proc        /proc
```

```
    /                    ufs       /dev/dsk/c1t0d0s0
    /dev/fd              fd        fd
    /space1              ufs       /dev/dsk/c1t1d0s0
    /var/tmp             vxfs      /dev/vx/dsk/sysdg/vartmp
    /tmp                 vxfs      /dev/vx/dsk/sysdg/tmp
```

On Linux, the format of the mount table is slightly different and the getmntent(L) function operates on a mntent structure. Other than minor differences with field names, the following program is almost identical to the one shown above:

```
 1 #include <stdio.h>
 2 #include <mntent.h>
 3
 4 main()
 5 {
 6         struct mntent    *mt;
 7         FILE             *fp;
 8
 9         fp = fopen("/etc/mtab", "r");
10
11         printf("%-15s%-10s%-30s\n",
12                 "mount point", "fstype", "device");
13         while ((mt = getmntent(fp)) != NULL) {
14                 printf("%-15s%-10s%-30s\n", mt->mnt_dir,
15                         mt->mnt_type, mt->mnt_fsname);
16         }
17 }
```

Following is the output when the program runs:

```
$ lmount
mount point      fstype      device
/                ext2        /dev/hda6
/proc            proc        none
/proc/bus/usb    usbdevfs    usbdevfs
/boot            ext2        /dev/hda1
/dev/pts         devpts      none
/mnt1            vxfs        /dev/vx/dsk/myvol
```

To unmount a filesystem either the mount point or the device can be passed to the umount command, as the following examples show:

```
# umount /mnt1
# mount | grep mnt1
# mount -F vxfs /dev/vx/dsk/vol1 /mnt1
# mount | grep mnt1
/mnt1 on /dev/vx/dsk/vol1 read/write/setuid/delaylog/ ...
# umount /dev/vx/dsk/vol1
# mount | grep mnt1
```

After each invocation of umount, the entry is removed from the mount table.

Mount and Umount System Call Handling

As the preceding examples showed, the mount and umount commands result in
a call to the mount() and umount() system calls respectively.

```
#include <sys/types.h>
#include <sys/mount.h>

int mount(const char *spec, const char *dir, int  mflag,  /*
char *fstype, const char *dataptr, int datalen */ ...);

#include <sys/mount.h>

int umount(const char *file);
```

Usually there should never be a direct need to invoke either the mount() or
umount() system calls. Although many of the arguments are self explanatory,
the handling of per-filesystem options, as pointed to by dataptr, is not typically
published and often changes. If applications have a need to mount and unmount
filesystems, the system(L) library function is recommended as a better choice.

Mounting Filesystems Automatically

As shown in the next section, after filesystems are created, it is typically left to the
system to mount them during bootstrap. The virtual filesystem table, called
/etc/vfstab on System V variants and /etc/fstab on BSD variants,
contains all the necessary information about each filesystem to be mounted.

This file is partially created during installation of the operating system. When
new filesystems are created, the system administrator will add new entries
ensuring that all the appropriate fields are entered correctly. Shown below is an
example of the vfstab file on Solaris:

```
# cat /etc/vfstab
...
fd                                      /dev/fd     fd    - no   -
/proc                                   /proc       proc  - no   -
/dev/dsk/c0t0d0s0   /dev/rdsk/c0t0d0s0  /           ufs   1 no   -
/dev/dsk/c0t0d0s6   /dev/rdsk/c0t0d0s6  /usr        ufs   1 no   -
/dev/dsk/c0t0d0s4   /dev/rdsk/c0t0d0s4  /c          ufs   2 yes  -
...
```

Here the fields are separated by spaces or tabs. The first field shows the block
device (passed to mount), the second field shows the raw device (passed to
fsck), the third field specifies the mount point, and the fourth specifies the
filesystem type. The remaining three fields specify the order in which the
filesystems will be checked, whether they should be mounted during bootstrap,
and what options should be passed to the mount command.

Here is an example of a Linux fstab table:

```
# cat /etc/fstab
LABEL=/              /              ext2      defaults            1 1
LABEL=/boot          /boot          ext2      defaults            1 2
/dev/cdrom           /mnt/cdrom     iso9660   noauto,owner,ro     0 0
/dev/fd0             /mnt/floppy    auto      noauto,owner        0 0
none                 /proc          proc      defaults            0 0
none                 /dev/pts       devpts    gid=5,mode=620      0 0
/dev/hda3            swap           swap      defaults            0 0
/SWAP                swap           swap      defaults            0 0
```

The first four fields describe the device, mount point, filesystem type, and options to be passed to mount. The fifth field is related to the dump command and records which filesystems need to be backed up. The sixth field is used by the fsck program to determine the order in which filesystems should be checked during bootstrap.

Mounting Filesystems During Bootstrap

Once filesystems are created and entries placed in /etc/vfstab, or equivalent, there is seldom need for administrator intervention. This file is accessed during system startup to mount all filesystems before the system is accessible to most applications and users.

When the operating system bootstraps, the kernel is read from a well-known location of disk and then goes through basic initialization tasks. One of these tasks is to mount the root filesystem. This is typically the only filesystem that is mounted until the system rc scripts start running.

The init program is spawned by the kernel as the first process (process ID of 1). By consulting the inittab(F) file, it determines which commands and scripts it needs to run to bring the system up further. This sequence of events can differ between one system and another. For System V-based systems, the rc scripts are located in /etc/rcX.d where X corresponds to the run level at which init is running.

Following are a few lines from the inittab(F) file:

```
$ head -9 inittab
ap::sysinit:/sbin/autopush -f /etc/iu.ap
ap::sysinit:/sbin/soconfig -f /etc/sock2path
fs::sysinit:/sbin/rcS sysinit
is:3:initdefault:
p3:s1234:powerfail:/usr/sbin/shutdown -y -i5 -g0
sS:s:wait:/sbin/rcS
s0:0:wait:/sbin/rc0
s1:1:respawn:/sbin/rc1
s2:23:wait:/sbin/rc2
```

Of particular interest is the last line. The system goes multiuser at init state 2. This is achieved by running the rc2 script which in turn runs all of the scripts found in /etc/rc2.d. Of particular interest is the script S01MOUNTFSYS. This is the script that is responsible for ensuring that all filesystems are checked for consistency and mounted as appropriate. The `mountall` script is responsible for actually mounting all of the filesystems.

The layout of files and scripts used on non-System V variants differs, but the concepts are the same.

Repairing Damaged Filesystems

A filesystem can typically be in one of two states, either clean or dirty. To mount a filesystem it must be *clean*, which means that it is structurally intact. When filesystems are mounted read/write, they are marked dirty to indicate that there is activity on the filesystem. Operations may be pending on the filesystem during a system crash, which could leave the filesystem with structural damage. In this case it can be dangerous to mount the filesystem without knowing the extent of the damage. Thus, to return the filesystem to a clean state, a filesystem-specific check program called `fsck` must be run to repair any damage that might exist.

For example, consider the following call to `mount` after a system crash:

```
# mount -F vxfs /dev/vx/dsk/vol1 /mnt1
UX:vxfs mount: ERROR: /dev/vx/dsk/vol1 is corrupted. needs checking
```

The filesystem is marked dirty and therefore the mount fails. Before it can be mounted again, the VxFS `fsck` program must be run as follows:

```
# fsck -F vxfs /dev/vx/rdsk/vol1
log replay in progress
replay complete marking super-block as CLEAN
```

VxFS is a transaction-based filesystem in which structural changes made to the filesystem are first written to the filesystem log. By replaying the transactions in the log, the filesystem returns to its clean state.

Most UNIX filesystems are not transaction-based, and therefore the whole filesystem must be checked for consistency. In the example below, a full `fsck` is performed on a UFS filesystem to show the type of checks that will be performed. UFS on most versions of UNIX is not transaction-based although Sun has added journaling support to its version of UFS.

```
# fsck -F ufs -y /dev/vx/rdsk/myvol
** /dev/vx/dsk/myvol
** Last Mounted on /mnt1
** Phase 1 Check Blocks and Sizes
** Phase 2 Check Pathnames
** Phase 3 Check Connectivity
** Phase 4 Check Reference Counts
** Phase 5 Check Cyl groups
61 files, 13 used, 468449 free (41 frags, 58551 blocks,  0
                              .0% fragmentation)
```

Running fsck is typically a non-interactive task performed during system initialization. Interacting with fsck is not something that system administrators will typically need to do. Recording the output of fsck is always a good idea in case fsck fails to clean the filesystem and support is needed by filesystem vendors and/or developers.

The Filesystem Debugger

When things go wrong with filesystems, it is necessary to debug them in the same way that it is necessary to debug other applications. Most UNIX filesystems have shipped with the filesystem debugger, fsdb, which can be used for that purpose.

It is with good reason that fsdb is one of the least commonly used of the UNIX commands. In order to use fsdb effectively, knowledge of the filesystem structure on disk is vital, as well as knowledge of how to use the filesystem specific version of fsdb. Note that one version of fsdb does not necessarily bear any resemblance to another.

In general, fsdb should be left well alone. Because it is possible to damage the filesystem beyond repair, its use should be left for filesystem developers and support engineers only.

Per Filesystem Statistics

In the same way that the stat() system call can be called to obtain per-file related information, the statvfs() system call can be invoked to obtain per-filesystem information. Note that this information will differ for each different mounted filesystem so that the information obtained for, say, one VxFS filesystem, will not necessarily be the same for other VxFS filesystems.

```
#include <sys/types.h>
#include <sys/statvfs.h>

int statvfs(const char *path, struct statvfs *buf);
int fstatvfs(int fildes, struct statvfs *buf);
```

Both functions operate on the statvfs structure, which contains a number of filesystem-specific fields including the following:

```
u_long      f_bsize;       /* file system block size */
u_long      f_frsize;      /* fundamental filesystem block
                              (size if supported) */
fsblkcnt_t f_blocks;       /* total # of blocks on file system
                              in units of f_frsize */
fsblkcnt_t f_bfree;        /* total # of free blocks */
fsblkcnt_t f_bavail;       /* # of free blocks avail to
                              non-super-user */
fsfilcnt_t f_files;        /* total # of file nodes (inodes) */
```

```
fsfilcnt_t f_ffree;               /* total # of free file nodes */
fsfilcnt_t f_favail;              /* # of inodes avail to non-suser*/
u_long     f_fsid;                /* file system id (dev for now) */
char       f_basetype[FSTYPSZ];   /* fs name null-terminated */
u_long     f_flag;                /* bit mask of flags */
u_long     f_namemax;             /* maximum file name length */
char       f_fstr[32];            /* file system specific string */
```

The statvfs(L) function is not available on Linux. In its place is the
statfs(L) function that operates on the statfs structure. The fields of this
structure are very similar to the statvfs structure, and therefore implementing
commands such as df require very little modification if written for a system
complying with the Single UNIX Specification.

The following program provides a simple implementation of the df command
by invoking statvfs(L) to obtain per filesystem statistics as well as locating
the entry in the /etc/vfstab file:

```
 1 #include <stdio.h>
 2 #include <sys/types.h>
 3 #include <sys/statvfs.h>
 4 #include <sys/mnttab.h>
 5
 6 #define Kb              (stv.f_frsize / 1024)
 7
 8 main(int argc, char **argv)
 9 {
10        struct mnttab    mt, mtp;
11        struct statvfs   stv;
12        int              blocks, used, avail, capacity;
13        FILE             *fp;
14
15        statvfs(argv[1], &stv);
16
17        fp = fopen("/etc/mnttab", "r");
18        memset(&mtp, 0, sizeof(struct mnttab));
19        mtp.mnt_mountp = argv[1];
20        getmntany(fp, &mt, &mtp);
21
22        blocks = stv.f_blocks * Kb;
23        used = (stv.f_blocks - stv.f_bfree) * Kb;
24        avail = stv.f_bfree * Kb;
25        capacity = ((double)used / (double)blocks) * 100;
26        printf("Filesystem          kbytes  used "
27                "avail capacity  Mounted on\n");
28        printf("%-22s%-7d%8d%8d    %2d%%      %s\n",
29            mt.mnt_special, blocks, used, avail,
30            capacity, argv[1]);
31 }
```

In the output shown next, the df command is run first followed by output from
the example program:

```
$ df -k /h
Filesystem                    kbytes    used    avail capacity  Mounted on
/dev/vx/dsk/homedg/h        7145728 5926881 1200824    84%        /h
$ mydf /h
Filesystem                    kbytes    used    avail capacity  Mounted on
/dev/vx/dsk/homedg/h        7145728 5926881 1218847    82%        /h
```

In practice, there is a lot of formatting work needed by df due to the different sizes of device names, mount paths, and the additional information displayed about each filesystem.

Note that the preceding program has no error checking. As an exercise, enhance the program to add error checking. On Linux the program needs modification to access the /etc/mtab file and to use the statfs(L) function. The program can be enhanced further to display all entries on the mount table as well as accept some of the other options that df provides.

User and Group Quotas

Although there may be multiple users of a filesystem, it is possible for a single user to consume all of the space within the filesystem. User and group quotas provide the mechanisms by which the amount of space used by a single user or all users within a specific group can be limited to a value defined by the administrator.

Quotas are based on the number of files used and the number of blocks. Some filesystems have a limited number of inodes available. Even though the amount of space consumed by a user may be small, it is still possible to consume all of the files in the filesystem even though most of the free space is still available.

Quotas operate around two limits that allow the user to take some action if the amount of space or number of disk blocks start to exceed the administrator defined limits:

Soft Limit. If the user exceeds the limit defined, there is a grace period that allows the user to free up some space. The quota can be exceeded during this time. However, after the time period has expired, no more files or data blocks may be allocated.

Hard Limit. When the hard limit is reached, regardless of the grace period, no further files or blocks can be allocated.

The grace period is set on a per-filesystem basis. For the VxFS filesystem, the default is seven days. The soft limit allows for users running applications that may create a lot of temporary files that only exist for the duration of the application. If the soft limit is exceeded, no action is taken. After the application exits, the temporary files are removed, and the amount of files and/or disk blocks goes back under the soft limit once more. Another circumstance when the soft limit is exceeded occurs when allocating space to a file. If files are written to sequentially, some filesystems, such as VxFS, allocate large extents (contiguous data blocks) to try to keep file data in one place. When the file is closed, the portion of the extent unused is freed.

In order for user quotas to work, there must be a file called quotas in the root directory of the filesystem. Similarly, for group quotas, the quotas.grp file must be present. Both of these files are used by the administrator to set quota limits for users and/or groups. If both user and group quotas are used, the amount of space allocated to a user is the lower of the two limits.

There are a number of commands to administer quotas. Those shown here are provided by VxFS. UFS provides a similar set of commands. Each command can take a -u or -g option to administer user and group quotas respectively.

vxedquota. This command can be used to edit the quota limits for users and groups.

vxrepquota. This command provides a summary of the quota limits together with disk usage.

vxquot. This command displays file ownership and usage summaries.

vxquota. This command can be used to view quota limits and usage.

vxquotaon. This command turns on quotas for a specified VxFS filesystem.

vxquotaoff. This command turns off quotas for the specified filesystem.

Quota checks are performed when the filesystem is mounted. This involves reading all inodes on disk and calculating usage for each user and group if needed.

Summary

This chapter described the main concepts applicable to filesystems as a whole, how they are created and mounted, and how they are repaired if damaged by a system crash or other means. Although the format of some of the mount tables differs between one system and the next, the location of the files differ only slightly, and the principles apply across all systems.

In general, unless administrating a UNIX-based machine, many of the commands here will not be used by the average UNIX user. However, having a view of how filesystems are managed helps gain a much better understanding of filesystems overall.

CHAPTER 6

UNIX Kernel Concepts

This chapter covers the earlier versions of UNIX up to 7th Edition and describes the main kernel concepts, with particular reference to the kernel structures related to filesystem activity and how the main file access-based system calls were implemented.

The structures, kernel subsystems, and flow of control through the research edition UNIX kernels are still largely intact after more than 25 years of development. Thus, the simple approaches described in this chapter are definitely a prerequisite to understanding the more complex UNIX implementations found today.

5th to 7th Edition Internals

From the mid 1980s onwards, there have been a number of changes in the UNIX kernel that resulted in the mainstream kernels diverging in their implementation. For the first fifteen years of UNIX development, there wasn't a huge difference in the way many kernel subsystems were implemented, and therefore understanding the principles behind these earlier UNIX versions will help readers understand how the newer kernels have changed.

The earliest documented version of UNIX was 6th Edition, which can be seen in John Lions' book *Lions' Commentary on UNIX 6th Edition—with source code* [LION96]. It is now also possible to download free versions of UNIX from 5th Edition onwards. The kernel source base is very small by today's standards. With less than 8,000 lines of code for the whole kernel, it is easily possible to gain an excellent understanding of how the kernel worked. Even the small amounts of assembler code do not need significant study to determine their operation.

This chapter concentrates on kernel principles from a filesystem perspective. Before describing the newer UNIX implementations, it is first necessary to explain some fundamental UNIX concepts. Much of the description here centers around the period covering 5th to 7th Edition UNIX, which generally covers the first ten years of UNIX development. Note that the goal here is to avoid swamping the reader with details; therefore, little knowledge of UNIX kernel internals is required in order to read through the material with relative ease.

Note that at this early stage, UNIX was a uniprocessor-based kernel. It would be another 10 years before mainstream multiprocessor-based UNIX versions first started to appear.

The UNIX Filesystem

Before describing how the different kernel structures work together, it is first necessary to describe how the original UNIX filesystem was stored on disk. Figure 6.1 shows the layout of various filesystem building blocks. The first (512 byte) block was unused. The second block (block 1) held the *superblock,* a structure that holds information about the filesystem as a whole such as the number of blocks in the filesystem, the number of *inodes* (files), and the number of free inodes and data blocks. Each file in the filesystem was represented by a unique inode that contained fields such as:

i_mode. This field specifies whether the file is a directory (IFDIR), a block special file (IFBLK), or a character special file (IFCHR). Note that if one of the above modes was not set, the file was assumed to be a regular file. This would later be replaced by an explicit flag, IFREG.

i_nlink. This field recorded the number of hard links to the file. When this field reaches zero, the inode is freed.

i_uid. The file's user ID.

i_gid. The file's group ID.

i_size. The file size in bytes.

i_addr. This field holds block addresses on disk where the file's data blocks are held.

i_mtime. The time the file was last modified.

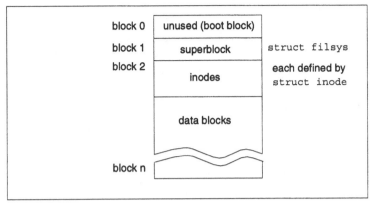

Figure 6.1   The on-disk layout of the first UNIX filesystem.

i_atime. The time that the file was last accessed.

The i_addr field was an array of 8 pointers. Each pointer could reference a single disk block, giving 512 bytes of storage or could reference what is called an indirect block. Each indirect block contained 32 pointers, each of which could point to a 512 byte block of storage or a double indirect block. Double indirects point to indirect data blocks. Figure 6.2 shows the two extremes whereby data blocks are accessed directly from the inode or from double indirects.

In the first example, the inode directly references two data blocks. The file size in this case will be between 513 and 1024 bytes in size. If the size of the file is less than 512 bytes, only a single data block is needed. Elements 2 to 7 of the i_addr[] array will be NULL in this case.

The second example shows the maximum possible file size. Each element of i_addr[] references an indirect block. Each indirect block points to 32 double indirect blocks, and each double indirect block points to 32 data blocks. This gives a maximum file size of 32 * 32 * 32 = 32,768 data blocks.

Filesystem-Related Kernel Structures

This section describes the main structures used in the UNIX kernel that are related to file access, from the file descriptor level down to issuing read and write calls to the disk driver.

User Mode and Kernel Mode

Each UNIX process is separated both from other processes and from the kernel through hardware-protection mechanisms. Thus, one process is unable to access the address space of another and is unable to either read from or

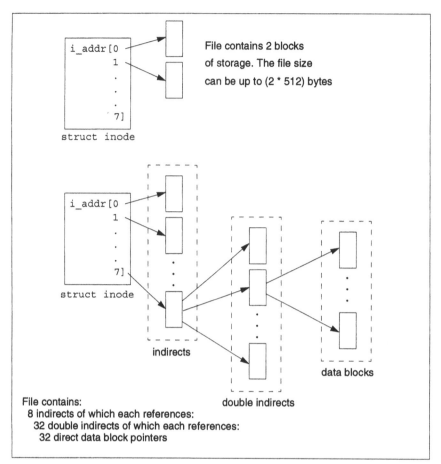

Figure 6.2   File storage through the use of indirect data blocks.

write to the kernel data structures.

When a process is running it can either be in user mode or kernel mode. When in user mode it runs on its own stack and executes instructions from the application binary or one of the libraries that it may be linked with. In order to execute a system call, the process transfers to kernel mode by issuing a special hardware instruction. When in the kernel, all arguments related to the system call are copied into the kernel's address space. Execution proceeds on a separate kernel stack. A *context switch* (a switch to another user process) can take place prior to returning to the user process if the *timeslice* of that process has been exceeded or if the process goes to sleep (for example, while waiting for an I/O operation).

The mechanisms for transferring control between user and kernel mode are dependent on the hardware architecture.

UNIX Process-Related Structures

Information about each process is divided between two different kernel structures. The proc structure is always present in memory, while the user structure holds information that is only needed when the process is running. Thus, when a process is not running and is eligible to be *swapped out*, all structures related to the process other than the proc structure may be written to the swap device. Needless to say, the proc structure must record information about where on the swap device the other process-related structures are located.

The proc structure does not record information related to file access. However the user structure contains a number of important file-access-related fields, namely:

u_cdir. The inode of the current working directory is stored here. This is used during pathname resolution when a user specifies a relative pathname.

u_uid/u_gid. The process user ID and group ID used for permissions checking for file-access-based system calls. Similarly, u_euid and u_egid hold the effective user and group IDs.

u_ofile. This array holds the process file descriptors. This is described in more detail later.

u_arg. An array of system call arguments set up during the transition from user to kernel mode when invoking a system call.

u_base. This field holds the address of a user space buffer in which to read data from or write data to when processing a system call such as read() or write().

u_count. The number of bytes to read or write is held here. It is decremented during the I/O operation and the result can be passed back to the user.

u_offset. This field records the offset within the file for the current read or write operation.

u_error. When processing a system call, this field is set if an error is encountered. The value of u_error is then passed back to the user when the system call returns.

There are other fields which have significance to file-access-based calls. However, these fields became redundant over the years and to avoid bloating this section, they won't be described further.

Users familiar with the chroot() system call and later versions of UNIX may have been wondering why there is no u_rdir to hold the current, per-process root director—at this stage in UNIX development, chroot() had not been implemented.

File Descriptors and the File Table

The section *File Descriptors*, in Chapter 2, described how file descriptors are returned from system calls such as open(). The u_ofile[] array in the user structure is indexed by the file descriptor number to locate a pointer to a file structure.

In earlier versions of UNIX, the size of the u_ofile[] array was hard coded and had NOFILE elements. Because the stdin, stdout, and stderr file descriptors occupied slots 0, 1, and 2 within the array, the first file descriptor returned in response to an open() system call would be 3. For the early versions of UNIX, NOFILE was set at 15. This would then make its way to 20 by the time that 7th Edition appeared.

The file structure contains more information about how the file was opened and where the current file pointer is positioned within the file for reading or writing. It contained the following members:

f_flag. This flag was set based on how the file was opened. If open for reading it was set to FREAD, and if open for writing it was set to FWRITE.

f_count. Each file structure had a reference count. This field is further described below.

f_inode. After a file is opened, the inode is read in from disk and stored in an in-core inode structure. This field points to the in-core inode.

f_offset. This field records the offset within the file when reading or writing. Initially it will be zero and will be incremented by each subsequent read or write or modified by lseek().

The file structure contains a reference count. Calls such as dup() result in a new file descriptor being allocated that points to the same file table entry as the original file descriptor. Before dup() returns, the f_count field is incremented.

Although gaining access to a running 5th Edition UNIX system is a little difficult 27 years after it first appeared, it is still possible to show how these concepts work in practice on more modern versions of UNIX. Take for example the following program running on Sun's Solaris version 8:

```
#include <fcntl.h>

main()
{
    int     fd1, fd2;

    fd1 = open("/etc/passwd", O_RDONLY);
    fd2 = dup(fd1);
    printf("fd1 = %d, fd2 = %d\n", fd1, fd2);
    pause();
}
```

The crash program can be used to analyze various kernel structures. In this case, it is possible to run the preceding program, locate the process with crash, and then display the corresponding user and file structures.

First of all, the program is run in the background, which displays file descriptor values of 3 and 4 as expected. The crash utility is then run and the proc command is used in conjunction with grep to locate the process in question as shown here:

```
# ./mydup&
[1] 1422
fd1 = 3, fd2 = 4
# crash
dumpfile = /dev/mem, namelist = /dev/ksyms, outfile = stdout
> proc | grep mydup
37 s  1422  1389  1422  1389     0  46 mydup           load
```

The process occupies slot 37 (consider this as an array of proc structures). The slot number can be passed to the user command that displays the user area corresponding to the process. Not all of the structure is shown here although it easy to see some relevant information about the process including the list of file descriptors. Note that file descriptor values 0, 1, and 2 all point to the same file table entry. Also, because a call was made to dup() in the program, entries 3 and 4 in the array point to the same file table entry.

```
> user 37
PER PROCESS USER AREA FOR PROCESS 37
PROCESS MISC:
command: mydup, psargs: ./mydup
start: Sat Jul 28 08:50:16 2001
mem: 90, type: exec su-user
vnode of current directory: 300019b5468
OPEN FILES, FLAGS, AND THREAD REFCNT:
[0]: F 30000adad68, 0, 0 [1]: F 30000adad68, 0, 0
[2]: F 30000adad68, 0, 0 [3]: F 30000adb078, 0, 0
[4]: F 30000adb078, 0, 0
...
```

Finally, the file command can be used to display the file table entry corresponding to these file descriptors. Note that the reference count is now 2, the offset is 0 because no data has been read and the flags hold FREAD as indicated by the read flag displayed.

```
> file 30000adb078
ADDRESS      RCNT    TYPE/ADDR           OFFSET    FLAGS
30000adb078   2      UFS /30000aafe30        0     read
```

With the exception that this file structure points to a *vnode* as opposed to the old in-core inode, the main structure has remained remarkably intact for UNIX's 30+ year history.

The Inode Cache

Each file is represented on disk by an inode. When a file is opened, the inode must be retrieved from disk. Operations such as the `stat()` system call retrieve much of the information they require from the `inode` structure.

The inode must remain in memory for the duration of the open and is typically written back to disk if any operations require changes to the inode structure. For example, consider writing 512 bytes of data at the end of the file that has an existing size of 512 bytes and therefore one block allocated (referenced by `i_addr[0]`). This will involve changing `i_size` to 1024 bytes, allocating a new block to the file, and setting `i_addr[1]` to point to this newly allocated block. These changes will be written back to disk.

After the file has been closed and there are no further processes holding the file open, the in-core inode can be freed.

If the inode were always freed on close, however, it would need to be read in again from disk each time the file is opened. This is very costly, especially considering that some inodes are accessed frequently such as the inodes for /, /usr, and /usr/bin. To prevent this from happening, inodes are retained in an *inode cache* even when the inode is no longer in use. Obviously if new inodes need to be read in from disk, these unused, cached inodes will need to be reallocated.

Figure 6.3 shows the linkage between file descriptors and inodes. The top process shows that by calling `dup()`, a new file descriptor is allocated resulting in `fdb` and `fdc` both pointing to the same file table entry. The file table entry then points to the inode for /etc/passwd.

For the bottom process, the open of /etc/passwd results in allocation of both a new file descriptor and file table entry. The file table entry points to the same in-core copy of the inode for this file as referenced by the top process. To handle these multiple references, the `i_count` field is used. Each time a file is opened, `i_count` is incremented and subsequently decremented on each close. Note that the inode cannot be released from the inode cache until after the last close.

The Buffer Cache

Devices were and still are accessed by the device ID and block number. Device IDs are constructed from the device *major number* and *minor number*. The major number has traditionally been nothing more than an entry into an array of vectors pointing to device driver entry points. Block special files are accessed through the `bdevsw[]` array while character special files are accessed through the `cdevsw[]` array. Both arrays were traditionally hard coded into the kernel. Filesystems access the disk through the block driver interface for which the disk driver exports a *strategy* function that is called by the filesystem.

Each driver, through its exported strategy function, accepts a `buf` structure

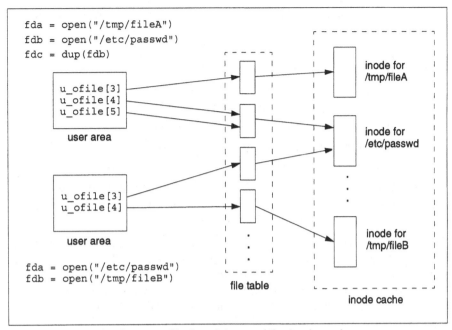

```
fda = open("/tmp/fileA")
fdb = open("/etc/passwd")
fdc = dup(fdb)
```

u_ofile[3]
u_ofile[4]
u_ofile[5]

user area

u_ofile[3]
u_ofile[4]

user area

```
fda = open("/etc/passwd")
fdb = open("/tmp/fileB")
```

file table

inode for
/tmp/fileA

inode for
/etc/passwd

inode for
/tmp/fileB

inode cache

Figure 6.3   Mapping between file descriptors and the inode cache.

that contains all the necessary information required to perform the I/O. The buf structure has actually changed very little over the years. Around 5th Edition it contained the following fields:

```
int         b_flags;
struct buf *b_forw;
struct buf *b_back;
struct buf *av_forw;
struct buf *av_back;
int         b_dev;
char       *b_addr;
char       *b_blkno;
char        b_error;
char       *b_resid;
```

The b_forw and b_back fields can be used by the device driver to chain related buffers together. After I/O is complete and the buffer is freed, the av_forw and av_back fields are used to hold the buffer on the free list. Note that buffers on the free list retain their identity until reused and thus act as a cache of recently accessed blocks. The b_dev and b_blkno fields are used to associate the buffer with a particular device and block number, while the b_addr field points to an in-core buffer that holds the data read or to be written. The b_wcount, b_error, and b_resid fields are used during I/O and will be described in the section *Putting It All Together* later in this chapter.

The b_flags field contains information about the state of the buffer. Some of the possible flags are shown below:

B_WRITE. A call to the driver will cause the buffer contents to be written to block b_blkno within the device specified by b_dev.

B_READ. A call to the driver will read the block specified by b_blkno and b_dev into the buffer data block referenced by b_addr.

B_DONE. I/O has completed and the data may be used.

B_ERROR. An error occurred while reading or writing.

B_BUSY. The buffer is currently in use.

B_WANTED. This field is set to indicate that another process wishes to use this buffer. After the I/O is complete and the buffer is relinquished, the kernel will wake up the waiting process.

When the kernel bootstraps, it initializes an array of NBUF buffers to comprise the buffer cache. Each buffer is linked together through the av_forw and av_back fields and headed by the bfreelist pointer.

The two main interfaces exported by the buffer cache are bread() and bwrite() for reading and writing respectively. Both function declarations are shown below:

```
struct buf *
bread(int dev, int blkno)

void
bwrite(struct buf *bp);
```

Considering bread() first, it must make a call to getblk() to search for a buffer in the cache that matches the same device ID and block number. If the buffer is not in the cache, getblk() takes the first buffer from the free list, sets its identity to that of the device (dev) and block number (blkno), and returns it.

When bread() retrieves a buffer from getblk(), it checks to see if the B_DONE flag is set. If this is the case, the buffer contents are valid and the buffer can be returned. If B_DONE is not set, the block must be read from disk. In this case a call is made to the disk driver strategy routine followed by a call to iowait() to sleep until the data has been read

One final point worthy of mention at this stage is that the driver strategy interface is asynchronous. After the I/O has been queued, the device driver returns. Performing I/O is a time-consuming operation, so the rest of the system could be doing something else while the I/O is in progress. In the case shown above, a call is made to iowait(), which causes the current process to sleep until the I/O is complete. The asynchronous nature of the strategy function allowed *read ahead* to be implemented whereby the kernel could start an asynchronous read of the next block of the file so that the data may already be in memory when the process requests it. The data requested is read, but before returning to the user with the data, a strategy call is made to read the next block without a subsequent call to `iowait()`.

To perform a write, a call is made to `bwrite()`, which simply needs to invoke the two line sequence previously shown.

After the caller has finished with the buffer, a call is made to `brelse()`, which takes the buffer and places it at the back of the freelist. This ensures that the oldest free buffer will be reassigned first.

Mounting Filesystems

The section *The UNIX Filesystem*, earlier in this chapter, showed how filesystems were laid out on disk with the superblock occupying block 1 of the disk slice. Mounted filesystems were held in a linked list of `mount` structures, one per filesystem with a maximum of `NMOUNT` mounted filesystems. Each mount structure has three elements, namely:

- `m_dev`. This field holds the device ID of the disk slice and can be used in a simple check to prevent a second mount of the same filesystem.

- `m_buf`. This field points to the superblock (`struct filsys`), which is read from disk during a mount operation.

- `m_inodp`. This field references the inode for the directory onto which this filesystem is mounted. This is further explained in the section *Pathname Resolution* later in this chapter.

The root filesystem is mounted early on during kernel initialization. This involved a very simple code sequence that relied on the root device being hard coded into the kernel. The block containing the superblock of the root filesystem is read into memory by calling `bread()`; then the first `mount` structure is initialized to point to the buffer.

Any subsequent mounts needed to come in through the `mount()` system call. The first task to perform would be to walk through the list of existing `mount` structures checking `m_dev` against the device passed to `mount()`. If the filesystem is mounted already, `EBUSY` is returned; otherwise another mount structure is allocated for the new mounted filesystem.

System Call Handling

Arguments passed to system calls are placed on the user stack prior to invoking a hardware instruction that then transfers the calling process from user mode to kernel mode. Once inside the kernel, any system call handler needs to be able to access the arguments, because the process may sleep awaiting some resource, resulting in a context switch, the kernel needs to copy these arguments into the kernel address space.

The sysent[] array specifies all of the system calls available, including the number of arguments.

By executing a hardware trap instruction, control is passed from user space to the kernel and the kernel trap() function runs to determine the system call to be processed. The C library function linked with the user program stores a unique value on the user stack corresponding to the system call. The kernel uses this value to locate the entry in sysent[] to understand how many arguments are being passed.

For a read() or write() system call, the arguments are accessible as follows:

```
fd = u.u_ar0[R0]
u_base  = u.u_arg[0]
u_count = u.u_arg[1]
```

This is a little strange because the first and subsequent arguments are accessed in a different manner. This is partly due to the hardware on which 5th Edition UNIX was based and partly due to the method that the original authors chose to handle traps.

If any error is detected during system call handling, u_error is set to record the error found. For example, if an attempt is made to mount an already mounted filesystem, the mount system call handler will set u_error to EBUSY. As part of completing the system call, trap() will set up the r0 register to contain the error code, that is then accessible as the return value of the system call once control is passed back to user space.

For further details on system call handling in early versions of UNIX, [LION96] should be consulted. Steve Pate's book *UNIX Internals—A Practical Approach* [PATE96] describes in detail how system calls are implemented at an assembly language level in System V Release 3 on the Intel x86 architecture.

Pathname Resolution

System calls often specify a pathname that must be resolved to an inode before the system call can continue. For example, in response to:

```
fd = open("/etc/passwd", O_RDONLY);
```

the kernel must ensure that /etc is a directory and that passwd is a file within the /etc directory.

Where to start the search depends on whether the pathname specified is absolute or relative. If it is an absolute pathname, the search starts from rootdir, a pointer to the root inode in the root filesystem that is initialized during kernel bootstrap. If the pathname is relative, the search starts from u_cdir, the inode of the current working directory. Thus, one can see that changing a directory involves resolving a pathname to a base directory component and then setting u_cdir to reference the inode for that directory.

The routine that performs pathname resolution is called namei(). It uses fields in the user area as do many other kernel functions. Much of the work of namei() involves parsing the pathname to be able to work on one component at a time. Consider, at a high level, the sequence of events that must take place to resolve /etc/passwd.

```
        if (absolute pathname) {
            dip = rootdir
        } else {
            dip = u.u_cdir
        }
  loop:
        name = next component
        scan dip for name / inode number
        iput(dip)
        dip = iget() to read in inode
        if last component {
            return dip
        } else {
            goto loop
        }
```

This is an oversimplification but it illustrates the steps that must be performed. The routines iget() and iput() are responsible for retrieving an inode and releasing an inode respectively. A call to iget() scans the inode cache before reading the inode from disk. Either way, the returned inode will have its hold count (i_count) increased. A call to iput() decrements i_count and, if it reaches 0, the inode can be placed on the free list.

To facilitate crossing mount points, fields in the mount and inode structures are used. The m_inodp field of the mount structure points to the directory inode on which the filesystem is mounted allowing the kernel to perform a ".." traversal over a mount point. The inode that is mounted on has the IMOUNT flag set that allows the kernel to go over a mount point.

Putting It All Together

In order to describe how all of the above subsystems work together, this section will follow a call to open() on /etc/passwd followed by the read() and close() system calls.

Figure 6.4 shows the main structures involved in actually performing the read. It is useful to have this figure in mind while reading through the following sections.

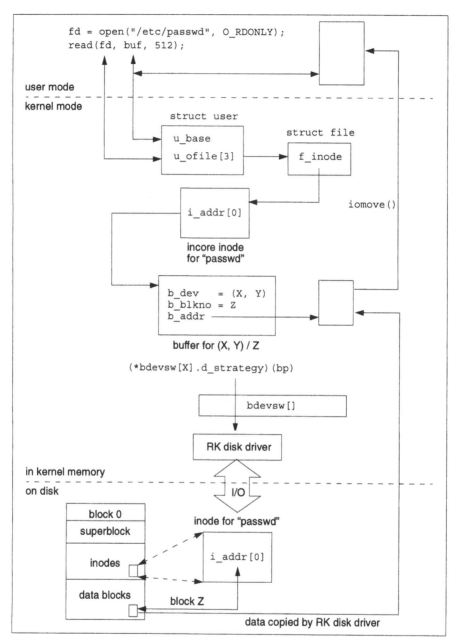

Figure 6.4   Kernel structures used when reading from a file.

Opening a File

The open() system call is handled by the open() kernel function. Its first task is to call namei() to resolve the pathname passed to open(). Assuming the pathname is valid, the inode for `passwd` is returned. A call to `open1()` is then made passing the open mode. The split between `open()` and `open1()` allows the `open()` and `creat()` system calls to share much of the same code.

First of all, `open1()` must call `access()` to ensure that the process can access the file according to ownership and the mode passed to `open()`. If all is fine, a call to `falloc()` is made to allocate a file table entry. Internally this invokes `ufalloc()` to allocate a file descriptor from `u_ofile[]`. The newly allocated file descriptor will be set to point to the newly allocated file table entry. Before returning from `open1()`, the linkage between the file table entry and the inode for `passwd` is established as was shown in Figure 6.3.

Reading the File

The `read()` and `write()` systems calls are handled by kernel functions of the same name. Both make a call to `rdwr()` passing FREAD or FWRITE. The role of `rdwr()` is fairly straightforward in that it sets up the appropriate fields in the user area to correspond to the arguments passed to the system call and invokes either `readi()` or `writei()` to read from or write to the file. The following pseudo code shows the steps taken for this initialization. Note that some of the error checking has been removed to simplify the steps taken.

```
get file pointer from user area
set u_base to u.u_arg[0]; /* user supplied buffer */
set u_count to u.u_arg[1]; /* number of bytes to read/write */
if (reading) {
    readi(fp->f_inode);
} else {
    writei(fp->f_inode);
}
```

The internals of `readi()` are fairly straightforward and involve making repeated calls to `bmap()` to obtain the disk block address from the file offset. The `bmap()` function takes a logical block number within the file and returns the physical block number on disk. This is used as an argument to `bread()`, which reads in the appropriate block from disk. The `uiomove()` function then transfers data to the buffer specified in the call to `read()`, which is held in `u_base`. This also increments `u_base` and decrements `u_count` so that the loop will terminate after all the data has been transferred.

If any errors are encountered during the actual I/O, the `b_flags` field of the `buf` structure will be set to B_ERROR and additional error information may be stored in `b_error`. In response to an I/O error, the `u_error` field of the user structure will be set to either EIO or ENXIO.

The `b_resid` field is used to record how many bytes out of a request size of u_count were not transferred. Both fields are used to notify the calling process of how many bytes were actually read or written.

Closing the File

The close() system call is handled by the close() kernel function. It performs little work other than obtaining the file table entry by calling getf(), zeroing the appropriate entry in u_ofile[], and then calling closef(). Note that because a previous call to dup() may have been made, the reference count of the file table entry must be checked before it can be freed. If the reference count (f_count) is 1, the entry can be removed and a call to closei() is made to free the inode. If the value of f_count is greater than 1, it is decremented and the work of close() is complete.

To release a hold on an inode, iput() is invoked. The additional work performed by closei() allows a device driver close call to be made if the file to be closed is a device.

As with closef(), iput() checks the reference count of the inode (i_count). If it is greater than 1, it is decremented, and there is no further work to do. If the count has reached 1, this is the only hold on the file so the inode can be released. One additional check that is made is to see if the hard link count of the inode has reached 0. This implies that an unlink() system call was invoked while the file was still open. If this is the case, the inode can be freed on disk.

Summary

This chapter concentrated on the structures introduced in the early UNIX versions, which should provide readers with a basic grounding in UNIX kernel principles, particularly as they apply to how filesystems and files are accessed. It says something for the design of the original versions of UNIX that many UNIX based kernels still bear a great deal of similarity to the original versions developed over 30 years ago.

Lions' book *Lions' Commentary on UNIX 6th Edition* [LION96] provides a unique view of how 6th Edition UNIX was implemented and lists the complete kernel source code. For additional browsing, the source code is available online for download.

For a more concrete explanation of some of the algorithms and more details on the kernel in general, Bach's book *The Design of the UNIX Operating System* [BACH86] provides an excellent overview of System V Release 2. Pate's book *UNIX Internals—A Practical Approach* [PATE96] describes a System V Release 3 variant. The UNIX versions described in both books bear most resemblance to the earlier UNIX research editions.

Development of the SVR4 VFS/Vnode Architecture

The development of the *File System Switch* (FSS) architecture in SVR3, the Sun VFS/vnode architecture in SunOS, and then the merge between the two to produce SVR4, substantially changed the way that filesystems were accessed and implemented. During this period, the number of filesystem types increased dramatically, including the introduction of commercial filesystems such as VxFS that allowed UNIX to move toward the enterprise computing market.

SVR4 also introduced a number of other important concepts pertinent to filesystems, such as tying file system access with memory mapped files, the DNLC (Directory Name Lookup Cache), and a separation between the traditional buffer cache and the page cache, which also changed the way that I/O was performed.

This chapter follows the developments that led up to the implementation of SVR4, which is still the basis of Sun's Solaris operating system and also freely available under the auspices of Caldera's OpenUNIX.

The Need for Change

The research editions of UNIX had a single filesystem type, as described in Chapter 6. The tight coupling between the kernel and the filesystem worked well at this stage because there was only one filesystem type and the kernel was *single threaded*, which means that only one process could be running in the kernel at the same time.

Before long, the need to add new filesystem types—including non-UNIX filesystems—resulted in a shift away from the old style filesystem implementation to a newer, cleaner architecture that clearly separated the different physical filesystem implementations from those parts of the kernel that dealt with file and filesystem access.

Pre-SVR3 Kernels

With the exception of Lions' book on 6th Edition UNIX [LION96], no other UNIX kernels were documented in any detail until the arrival of System V Release 2 that was the basis for Bach's book *The Design of the UNIX Operating System* [BACH86]. In his book, Bach describes the on-disk layout to be almost identical to that of the earlier versions of UNIX.

There was little change between the research editions of UNIX and SVR2 to warrant describing the SVR2 filesystem architecture in detail. Around this time, most of the work on filesystem evolution was taking place at the University of Berkeley to produce the BSD Fast File System which would, in time, become UFS.

The File System Switch

Introduced with System V Release 3.0, the *File System Switch* (FSS) architecture introduced a framework under which multiple different filesystem types could coexist in parallel.

The FSS was poorly documented and the source code for SVR3-based derivatives is not publicly available. [PATE96] describes in detail how the FSS was implemented. Note that the version of SVR3 described in that book contained a significant number of kernel changes (made by SCO) and therefore differed substantially from the original SVR3 implementation. This section highlights the main features of the FSS architecture.

As with earlier UNIX versions, SVR3 kept the mapping between file descriptors in the user area to the file table to in-core inodes. One of the main goals of SVR3 was to provide a framework under which multiple different filesystem types could coexist at the same time. Thus each time a call is made to mount, the caller could specify the filesystem type. Because the FSS could support multiple different filesystem types, the traditional UNIX filesystem needed to be named so it could be identified when calling the mount command. Thus, it became known as the s5 (System V) filesystem. Throughout the USL-based development of System V through to the various SVR4 derivatives, little development would occur on s5. SCO completely restructured their s5-based filesystem over the years and added a number of new features.

The boundary between the filesystem-independent layer of the kernel and the filesystem-dependent layer occurred mainly through a new implementation of the in-core inode. Each filesystem type could potentially have a very different on-disk representation of a file. Newer diskless filesystems such as NFS and RFS had different, non-disk-based structures once again. Thus, the new inode contained fields that were generic to all filesystem types such as user and group IDs and file size, as well as the ability to reference data that was filesystem-specific. Additional fields used to construct the FSS interface were:

i_fsptr. This field points to data that is private to the filesystem and that is not visible to the rest of the kernel. For disk-based filesystems this field would typically point to a copy of the disk inode.

i_fstyp. This field identifies the filesystem type.

i_mntdev. This field points to the mount structure of the filesystem to which this inode belongs.

i_mton. This field is used during pathname traversal. If the directory referenced by this inode is mounted on, this field points to the mount structure for the filesystem that covers this directory.

i_fstypp. This field points to a vector of filesystem functions that are called by the filesystem-independent layer.

The set of filesystem-specific operations is defined by the fstypsw structure. An array of the same name holds an fstypsw structure for each possible filesystem. The elements of the structure, and thus the functions that the kernel can call into the filesystem with, are shown in Table 7.1.

When a file is opened for access, the i_fstypp field is set to point to the fstypsw[] entry for that filesystem type. In order to invoke a filesystem-specific function, the kernel performs a level of indirection through a macro that accesses the appropriate function. For example, consider the definition of FS_READI() that is invoked to read data from a file:

```
#define FS_READI(ip)  (*fstypsw[(ip)->i_fstyp].fs_readi)(ip)
```

All filesystems must follow the same calling conventions such that they all understand how arguments will be passed. In the case of FS_READI(), the arguments of interest will be held in u_base and u_count. Before returning to the filesystem-independent layer, u_error will be set to indicate whether an error occurred and u_resid will contain a count of any bytes that could not be read or written.

Mounting Filesystems

The method of mounting filesystems in SVR3 changed because each filesystem's superblock could be different and in the case of NFS and RFS, there was no superblock per se. The list of mounted filesystems was moved into an array of mount structures that contained the following elements:

Table 7.1   File System Switch Functions

FSS OPERATION	DESCRIPTION
fs_init	Each filesystem can specify a function that is called during kernel initialization allowing the filesystem to perform any initialization tasks prior to the first `mount` call
fs_iread	Read the inode (during pathname resolution)
fs_iput	Release the inode
fs_iupdat	Update the inode timestamps
fs_readi	Called to read data from a file
fs_writei	Called to write data to a file
fs_itrunc	Truncate a file
fs_statf	Return file information required by `stat()`
fs_namei	Called during pathname traversal
fs_mount	Called to mount a filesystem
fs_umount	Called to unmount a filesystem
fs_getinode	Allocate a file for a pipe
fs_openi	Call the device open routine
fs_closei	Call the device close routine
fs_update	Sync the superblock to disk
fs_statfs	Used by `statfs()` and `ustat()`
fs_access	Check access permissions
fs_getdents	Read directory entries
fs_allocmap	Build a block list map for demand paging
fs_freemap	Frees the demand paging block list map
fs_readmap	Read a page using the block list map
fs_setattr	Set file attributes
fs_notify	Notify the filesystem when file attributes change
fs_fcntl	Handle the `fcntl()` system call
fs_fsinfo	Return filesystem-specific information
fs_ioctl	Called in response to a `ioctl()` system call

m_flags. Because this is an array of mount structures, this field was used to indicate which elements were in use. For filesystems that were mounted, m_flags indicates whether the filesystem was also mounted read-only.

m_fstyp. This field specified the filesystem type.

m_bsize. The logical block size of the filesystem is held here. Each filesystem could typically support multiple different block sizes as the unit of allocation to a file.

m_dev. The device on which the filesystem resides.

m_bufp. A pointer to a buffer containing the superblock.

m_inodp. With the exception of the root filesystem, this field points to the inode on which the filesystem is mounted. This is used during pathname traversal.

m_mountp. This field points to the root inode for this filesystem.

m_name. The file system name.

Figure 7.1 shows the main structures used in the FSS architecture. There are a number of observations worthy of mention:

- The structures shown are independent of filesystem type. The mount and inode structures abstract information about the filesystems and files that they represent in a generic manner. Only when operations go through the FSS do they become filesystem-dependent. This separation allows the FSS to support very different filesystem types, from the traditional s5 filesystem to DOS to diskless filesystems such as NFS and RFS.

- Although not shown here, the mapping between file descriptors, the user area, the file table, and the inode cache remained as is from earlier versions of UNIX.

- The Virtual Memory (VM) subsystem makes calls through the FSS to obtain a *block map* for executable files. This is to support demand paging. When a process runs, the pages of the program text are *faulted in* from the executable file as needed. The VM makes a call to FS_ALLOCMAP() to obtain this mapping. Following this call, it can invoke the FS_READMAP() function to read the data from the file when handling a page fault.

- There is no clean separation between file-based and filesystem-based operations. All functions exported by the filesystem are held in the same fstypsw structure.

The FSS was a big step away from the traditional single filesystem-based UNIX kernel. With the exception of SCO, which retained an SVR3-based kernel for many years after the introduction of SVR3, the FSS was short lived, being replaced by the better Sun VFS/vnode interface introduced in SVR4.

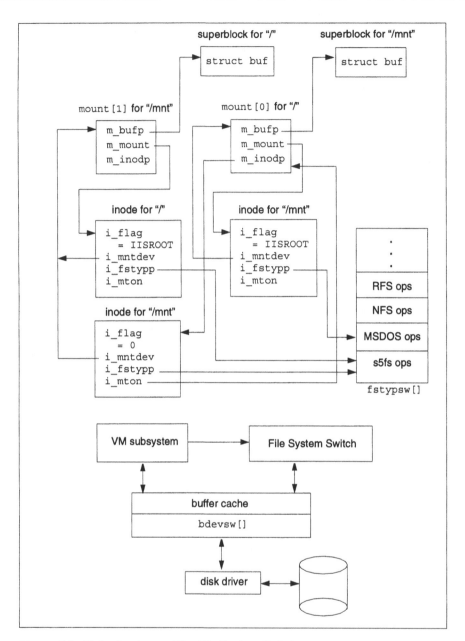

Figure 7.1   Main structures of the File System Switch.

The Sun VFS/Vnode Architecture

Developed on Sun Microsystem's SunOS operating system, the world first came to know about vnodes through Steve Kleiman's often-quoted Usenix paper

"Vnodes: An Architecture for Multiple File System Types in Sun UNIX" [KLEI86]. The paper stated four design goals for the new filesystem architecture:

- The filesystem implementation should be clearly split into a filesystem independent and filesystem-dependent layer. The interface between the two should be well defined.

- It should support local disk filesystems such as the 4.2BSD Fast File System (FSS), non-UNIX like filesystems such as MS-DOS, stateless filesystems such as NFS, and stateful filesystems such as RFS.

- It should be able to support the server side of remote filesystems such as NFS and RFS.

- Filesystem operations across the interface should be atomic such that several operations do not need to be encompassed by locks.

One of the major implementation goals was to remove the need for global data, allowing the interfaces to be re-entrant. Thus, the previous style of storing filesystem-related data in the user area, such as u_base and u_count, needed to be removed. The setting of u_error on error also needed removing and the new interfaces should explicitly return an error value.

The main components of the Sun VFS architecture are shown in Figure 7.2. These components will be described throughout the following sections.

The architecture actually has two sets of interfaces between the filesystem-independent and filesystem-dependent layers of the kernel. The VFS interface was accessed through a set of *vfsops* while the vnode interface was accessed through a set of *vnops* (also called *vnodeops*). The vfsops operate on a filesystem while vnodeops operate on individual files.

Because the architecture encompassed non-UNIX- and non disk-based filesystems, the in-core inode that had been prevalent as the memory-based representation of a file over the previous 15 years was no longer adequate. A new type, the *vnode* was introduced. This simple structure contained all that was needed by the filesystem-independent layer while allowing individual filesystems to hold a reference to a private data structure; in the case of the disk-based filesystems this may be an inode, for NFS, an rnode, and so on.

The fields of the vnode structure were:

v_flag. The VROOT flag indicates that the vnode is the root directory of a filesystem, VNOMAP indicates that the file cannot be memory mapped, VNOSWAP indicates that the file cannot be used as a swap device, VNOMOUNT indicates that the file cannot be mounted on, and VISSWAP indicates that the file is part of a virtual swap device.

v_count. Similar to the old i_count inode field, this field is a reference count corresponding to the number of open references to the file.

v_shlockc. This field counts the number of shared locks on the vnode.

v_exlockc. This field counts the number of exclusive locks on the vnode.

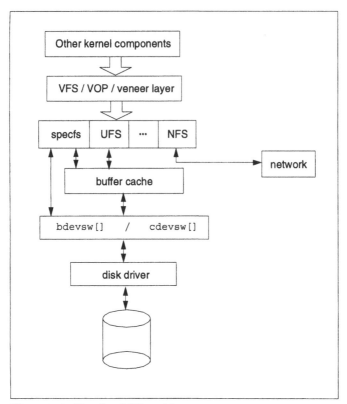

Figure 7.2 The Sun VFS architecture.

v_vfsmountedhere. If a filesystem is mounted on the directory referenced by this vnode, this field points to the vfs structure of the mounted filesystem. This field is used during pathname traversal to cross filesystem mount points.

v_op. The vnode operations associated with this file type are referenced through this pointer.

v_vfsp. This field points to the vfs structure for this filesystem.

v_type. This field specifies the type of file that the vnode represents. It can be set to VREG (regular file), VDIR (directory), VBLK (block special file), VCHR (character special file), VLNK (symbolic link), VFIFO (named pipe), or VXNAM (Xenix special file).

v_data. This field can be used by the filesystem to reference private data such as a copy of the on-disk inode.

There is nothing in the vnode that is UNIX specific or even pertains to a local filesystem. Of course not all filesystems support all UNIX file types. For example, the DOS filesystem doesn't support symbolic links. However, filesystems in the

VFS/vnode architecture are not required to support all vnode operations. For those operations not supported, the appropriate field of the vnodeops vector will be set to fs_nosys, which simply returns ENOSYS.

The uio Structure

One way of meeting the goals of avoiding user area references was to package all I/O-related information into a uio structure that would be passed across the vnode interface. This structure contained the following elements:

uio_iov. A pointer to an array of iovec structures each specifying a base user address and a byte count.

uio_iovcnt. The number of iovec structures.

uio_offset. The offset within the file that the read or write will start from.

uio_segflg. This field indicates whether the request is from a user process (user space) or a kernel subsystem (kernel space). This field is required by the kernel copy routines.

uio_resid. The residual count following the I/O.

Because the kernel was now supporting filesystems such as NFS, for which requests come over the network into the kernel, the need to remove user area access was imperative. By creating a uio structure, it is easy for NFS to then make a call to the underlying filesystem.

The uio structure also provides the means by which the readv() and writev() system calls can be implemented. Instead of making multiple calls into the filesystem for each I/O, several iovec structures can be passed in at the same time.

The VFS Layer

The list of mounted filesystems is maintained as a linked list of vfs structures. As with the vnode structure, this structure must be filesystem independent. The vfs_data field can be used to point to any filesystem-dependent data structure, for example, the superblock.

Similar to the File System Switch method of using macros to access filesystem-specific operations, the vfsops layer utilizes a similar approach. Each filesystem provides a vfsops structure that contains a list of functions applicable to the filesystem. This structure can be accessed from the vfs_op field of the vfs structure. The set of operations available is:

vfs_mount. The filesystem type is passed to the mount command using the -F option. This is then passed through the mount() system call and is used to locate the vfsops structure for the filesystem in question. This function can be called to mount the filesystem.

vfs_unmount. This function is called to unmount a filesystem.

vfs_root. This function returns the root vnode for this filesystem and is called during pathname resolution.

vfs_statfs. This function returns filesystem-specific information in response to the statfs() system call. This is used by commands such as df.

vfs_sync. This function flushes file data and filesystem structural data to disk, which provides a level of *filesystem hardening* by minimizing data loss in the event of a system crash.

vfs_fid. This function is used by NFS to construct a file handle for a specified vnode.

vfs_vget. This function is used by NFS to convert a file handle returned by a previous call to vfs_fid into a vnode on which further operations can be performed.

The Vnode Operations Layer

All operations that can be applied to a file are held in the vnode operations vector defined by the vnodeops structure. The functions from this vector follow:

vop_open. This function is only applicable to device special files, files in the namespace that represent hardware devices. It is called once the vnode has been returned from a prior call to vop_lookup.

vop_close. This function is only applicable to device special files. It is called once the vnode has been returned from a prior call to vop_lookup.

vop_rdwr. Called to read from or write to a file. The information about the I/O is passed through the uio structure.

vop_ioctl. This call invokes an ioctl on the file, a function that can be passed to device drivers.

vop_select. This vnodeop implements select().

vop_getattr. Called in response to system calls such as stat(), this vnodeop fills in a vattr structure, which can be returned to the caller via the stat structure.

vop_setattr. Also using the vattr structure, this vnodeop allows the caller to set various file attributes such as the file size, mode, user ID, group ID, and file times.

vop_access. This vnodeop allows the caller to check the file for read, write, and execute permissions. A cred structure that is passed to this function holds the credentials of the caller.

vop_lookup. This function replaces part of the old namei() implementation. It takes a directory vnode and a component name and returns the vnode for the component within the directory.

vop_create. This function creates a new file in the specified directory vnode. The file properties are passed in a vattr structure.

vop_remove. This function removes a directory entry.

vop_link. This function implements the link() system call.

vop_rename. This function implements the rename() system call.

vop_mkdir. This function implements the mkdir() system call.

vop_rmdir. This function implements the rmdir() system call.

vop_readdir. This function reads directory entries from the specified directory vnode. It is called in response to the getdents() system call.

vop_symlink. This function implements the symlink() system call.

vop_readlink. This function reads the contents of the symbolic link.

vop_fsync. This function flushes any modified file data in memory to disk. It is called in response to an fsync() system call.

vop_inactive. This function is called when the filesystem-independent layer of the kernel releases its last hold on the vnode. The filesystem can then free the vnode.

vop_bmap. This function is used for demand paging so that the virtual memory (VM) subsystem can map logical file offsets to physical disk offsets.

vop_strategy. This vnodeop is used by the VM and buffer cache layers to read blocks of a file into memory following a previous call to vop_bmap().

vop_bread. This function reads a logical block from the specified vnode and returns a buffer from the buffer cache that references the data.

vop_brelse. This function releases the buffer returned by a previous call to vop_bread.

If a filesystem does not support some of these interfaces, the appropriate entry in the vnodeops vector should be set to fs_nosys(), which, when called, will return ENOSYS. The set of vnode operations are accessed through the v_op field of the vnode using macros as the following definition shows:

```
#define VOP_INACTIVE(vp, cr) \
    (*(vp)->v_op->vop_inactive)(vp, cr)
```

Pathname Traversal

Pathname traversal differs from the File System Switch method due to differences in the structures and operations provided at the VFS layer. Consider the example shown in Figure 7.3 and consider the following two scenarios:

1. A user types "cd /mnt" to move into the mnt directory.

2. A user is in the directory /mnt and types "cd .." to move up one level.

In the first case, the pathname is absolute, so a search will start from the root directory vnode. This is obtained by following rootvfs to the first vfs structure and invoking the vfs_root function. This returns the root vnode for the root filesystem (this is typically cached to avoid repeating this set of steps). A scan is

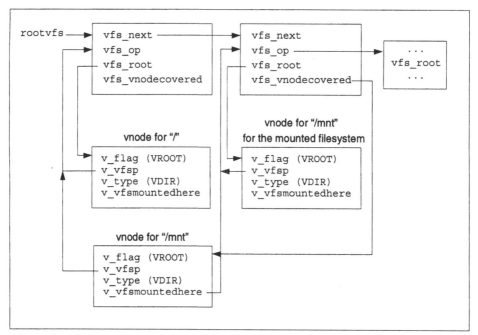

Figure 7.3 Pathname traversal in the Sun VFS/vnode architecture.

then made of the root directory to locate the mnt directory. Because the vfs_mountedhere field is set, the kernel follows this link to locate the vfs structure for the mounted filesystem through which it invokes the vfs_root function for that filesystem. Pathname traversal is now complete so the u_cdir field of the user area is set to point to the vnode for /mnt to be used in subsequent pathname operations.

In the second case, the user is already in the root directory of the filesystem mounted on /mnt (the v_flag field of the vnode is set to VROOT). The kernel locates the *mounted on* vnode through the vfs_vnodecovered field. Because this directory (/mnt in the root directory) is not currently visible to users (it is hidden by the mounted filesystem), the kernel must then move up a level to the root directory. This is achieved by obtaining the vnode referenced by ".." in the /mnt directory of the root filesystem.

Once again, the u_cdir field of the user area will be updated to reflect the new current working directory.

The Veneer Layer

To provide more coherent access to files through the vnode interface, the implementation provided a number of functions that other parts of the kernel could invoke. The set of functions is:

vn_open. Open a file based on its file name, performing appropriate permission checking first.

vn_close. Close the file given by the specified vnode.

vn_rdwr. This function constructs a uio structure and then calls the vop_rdwr() function to read from or write to the file.

vn_create. Creates a file based on the specified name, performing appropriate permission checking first.

vn_remove. Remove a file given the pathname.

vn_link. Create a hard link.

vn_rename. Rename a file based on specified pathnames.

VN_HOLD. This macro increments the vnode reference count.

VN_RELE. This macro decrements the vnode reference count. If this is the last reference, the vop_inactive() vnode operation is called.

The veneer layer avoids duplication throughout the rest of the kernel by providing a simple, well-defined interface that kernel subsystems can use to access filesystems.

Where to Go from Here?

The Sun VFS/vnode interface was a huge success. Its merger with the File System Switch and the SunOS virtual memory subsystem provided the basis for the SVR4 VFS/vnode architecture. There were a large number of other UNIX vendors who implemented the Sun VFS/vnode architecture. With the exception of the read and write paths, the different implementations were remarkably similar to the original Sun VFS/vnode implementation.

The SVR4 VFS/Vnode Architecture

System V Release 4 was the result of a merge between SVR3 and Sun Microsystems' SunOS. One of the goals of both Sun and AT&T was to merge the Sun VFS/vnode interface with AT&T's File System Switch.

The new VFS architecture, which has remained largely unchanged for over 15 years, introduced and brought together a number of new ideas, and provided a clean separation between different subsystems in the kernel. One of the fundamental changes was eliminating the tight coupling between the filesystem and the VM subsystem which, although elegant in design, was particularly complicated resulting in a great deal of difficulty when implementing new filesystem types.

Changes to File Descriptor Management

A file descriptor had previously been an index into the u_ofile[] array. Because this array was of fixed size, the number of files that a process could have open was bound by the size of the array. Because most processes do not open a lot of files, simply increasing the size of the array is a waste of space, given the large number of processes that may be present on the system.

With the introduction of SVR4, file descriptors were allocated dynamically up to a fixed but tunable limit. The u_ofile[] array was removed and replaced by two new fields, u_nofiles, which specified the number of file descriptors that the process can currently access, and u_flist, a structure of type ufchunk that contains an array of NFPCHUNK (which is 24) pointers to file table entries. After all entries have been used, a new ufchunk structure is allocated, as shown in Figure 7.4.

The uf_pofile[] array holds file descriptor flags as set by invoking the fcntl() system call.

The maximum number of file descriptors is constrained by a per-process limit defined by the rlimit structure in the user area.

There are a number of per-process limits within the u_rlimit[] array. The u_rlimit[RLIMIT_NOFILE] entry defines both a soft and hard file descriptor limit. Allocation of file descriptors will fail once the soft limit is reached. The setrlimit() system call can be invoked to increase the soft limit up to that of the hard limit, but not beyond. The hard limit can be raised, but only by root.

The Virtual Filesystem Switch Table

Built dynamically during kernel compilation, the *virtual file system switch table*, underpinned by the vfssw[] array, contains an entry for each filesystem that can reside in the kernel. Each entry in the array is defined by a vfssw structure as shown below:

```
struct vfssw {
    char            *vsw_name;
    int             (*vsw_init)();
    struct vfsops   *vsw_vfsops;
}
```

The vsw_name is the name of the filesystem (as passed to mount -F). The vsw_init() function is called during kernel initialization, allowing the filesystem to perform any initialization it may require before a first call to mount().

Operations that are applicable to the filesystem as opposed to individual files are held in both the vsw_vfsops field of the vfssw structure and subsequently in the vfs_ops field of the vfs structure.

The fields of the vfs structure are shown below:

vfs_mount. This function is called to mount a filesystem.

vfs_unmount. This function is called to unmount a filesystem.

vfs_root. This function returns the root vnode for the filesystem. This is used during pathname traversal.

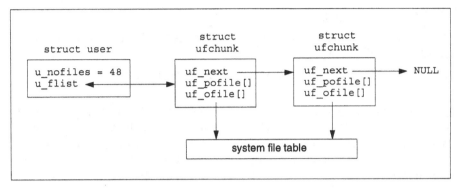

Figure 7.4 SVR4 file descriptor allocation.

vfs_statvfs. This function is called to obtain per-filesystem-related statistics. The df command will invoke the statvfs() system call on filesystems it wishes to report information about. Within the kernel, statvfs() is implemented by invoking the statvfs vfsop.

vfs_sync. There are two methods of *syncing* data to the filesystem in SVR4, namely a call to the sync command and internal kernel calls invoked by the *fsflush* kernel thread. The aim behind fsflush invoking vfs_sync is to flush any modified file data to disk on a periodic basis in a similar way to which the bdflush daemon would flush dirty (modified) buffers to disk. This still does not prevent the need for performing a fsck after a system crash but does help *harden* the system by minimizing data loss.

vfs_vget. This function is used by NFS to return a vnode given a specified file handle.

vfs_mountroot. This entry only exists for filesystems that can be mounted as the root filesystem. This may appear to be a strange operation. However, in the first version of SVR4, the s5 and UFS filesystems could be mounted as root filesystems and the root filesystem type could be specified during UNIX installation. Again, this gives a clear, well defined interface between the rest of the kernel and individual filesystems.

There are only a few minor differences between the vfsops provided in SVR4 and those introduced with the VFS/vnode interface in SunOS. The vfs structure with SVR4 contained all of the original Sun vfs fields and introduced a few others including vfs_dev, which allowed a quick and easy scan to see if a filesystem was already mounted, and the vfs_fstype field, which is used to index the vfssw[] array to specify the filesystem type.

Changes to the Vnode Structure and VOP Layer

The vnode structure had some subtle differences. The v_shlockc and v_exlockc fields were removed and replaced by additional vnode interfaces to handle locking. The other fields introduced in the original vnode structure remained and the following fields were added:

v_stream. If the file opened references a STREAMS device, the vnode field
points to the STREAM head.

v_filocks. This field references any file and record locks that are held on
the file.

v_pages. I/O changed substantially in SVR4 with all data being read and
written through pages in the *page cache* as opposed to the buffer cache,
which was now only used for meta-data (inodes, directories, etc.). All pages
in-core that are part of a file are linked to the vnode and referenced through
this field.

The vnodeops vector itself underwent more change. The vop_bmap(), the
vop_bread(), vop_brelse(), and vop_strategy() functions were
removed as part of changes to the read and write paths. The vop_rdwr() and
vop_select() functions were also removed. There were a number of new
functions added as follows:

vop_read. The vop_rdwr function was split into separate read and write
vnodeops. This function is called in response to a read() system call.

vop_write. The vop_rdwr function was split into separate read and write
vnodeops. This function is called in response to a write() system call.

vop_setfl. This function is called in response to an fcntl() system call
where the F_SETFL (set file status flags) flag is specified. This allows the
filesystem to validate any flags passed.

vop_fid. This function was previously a VFS-level function in the Sun
VFS/vnode architecture. It is used to generate a unique file handle from
which NFS can later reference the file.

vop_rwlock. Locking was moved under the vnode interface, and filesystems
implemented locking in a manner that was appropriate to their own internal
implementation. Initially the file was locked for both read and write access.
Later SVR4 implementations changed the interface to pass one of two flags,
namely LOCK_SHARED or LOCK_EXCL. This allowed for a single writer but
multiple readers.

vop_rwunlock. All vop_rwlock invocations should be followed by a
subsequent vop_rwunlock call.

vop_seek. When specifying an offset to lseek(), this function is called to
determine whether the filesystem deems the offset to be appropriate. With
sparse files, seeking beyond the end of file and writing is a valid UNIX
operation, but not all filesystems may support sparse files. This vnode
operation allows the filesystem to reject such lseek() calls.

vop_cmp. This function compares two specified vnodes. This is used in the
area of pathname resolution.

vop_frlock. This function is called to implement file and record locking.

vop_space. The fcntl() system call has an option, F_FREESP, which allows the caller to free space within a file. Most filesystems only implement freeing of space at the end of the file making this interface identical to truncate().

vop_realvp. Some filesystems, for example, specfs, present a vnode and hide the underlying vnode, in this case, the vnode representing the device. A call to VOP_REALVP() is made by filesystems when performing a link() system call to ensure that the link goes to the underlying file and not the specfs file, that has no physical representation on disk.

vop_getpage. This function is used to read pages of data from the file in response to a page fault.

vop_putpage. This function is used to flush a modified page of file data to disk.

vop_map. This function is used for implementing memory mapped files.

vop_addmap. This function adds a mapping.

vop_delmap. This function deletes a mapping.

vop_poll. This function is used for implementing the poll() system call.

vop_pathconf. This function is used to implement the pathconf() and fpathconf() system calls. Filesystem-specific information can be returned, such as the maximum number of links to a file and the maximum file size.

The vnode operations are accessed through the use of macros that reference the appropriate function by indirection through the vnode v_op field. For example, here is the definition of the VOP_LOOKUP() macro:

```
#define VOP_LOOKUP(vp,cp,vpp,pnp,f,rdir,cr) \
    (*(vp)->v_op->vop_lookup)(vp,cp,vpp,pnp,f,rdir,cr)
```

The filesystem-independent layer of the kernel will only access the filesystem through macros. Obtaining a vnode is performed as part of an open() or creat() system call or by the kernel invoking one of the veneer layer functions when kernel subsystems wish to access files directly. To demonstrate the mapping between file descriptors, memory mapped files, and vnodes, consider the following example:

```
 1 #include <sys/types.h>
 2 #include <sys/stat.h>
 3 #include <sys/mman.h>
 4 #include <fcntl.h>
 5 #include <unistd.h>
 6
 7 #define MAPSZ          4096
 8
 9 main()
10 {
11         char          *addr, c;
12         int           fd1, fd2;
```

```
13
14              fd1 = open("/etc/passwd", O_RDONLY);
15              fd2 = dup(fd1);
16              addr = (char *)mmap(NULL, MAPSZ, PROT_READ,
17                                  MAP_SHARED, fd1, 0);
18              close(fd1);
19              c = *addr;
20              pause();
21 }
```

A file is opened and then dup() is called to duplicate the file descriptor. The file is then mapped followed by a close of the first file descriptor. By accessing the address of the mapping, data can be read from the file.

The following examples, using crash and adb on Solaris, show the main structures involved and scan for the data read, which should be attached to the vnode through the v_pages field. First of all, the program is run and crash is used to locate the process:

```
# ./vnode&
# crash
dumpfile = /dev/mem, namelist = /dev/ksyms, outfile = stdout
> p | grep vnode
35 s  4365  4343  4365  4343      0  46 vnode             load
> u 35
PER PROCESS USER AREA FOR PROCESS 35
PROCESS MISC:
command: vnode, psargs: ./vnode
start: Fri Aug 24 10:55:32 2001
mem: b0, type: exec
vnode of current directory: 30000881ab0
OPEN FILES, FLAGS, AND THREAD REFCNT:
[0]: F 30000adaa90, 0, 0 [1]: F 30000adaa90, 0, 0
[2]: F 30000adaa90, 0, 0 [4]: F 30000adac50, 0, 0
...
```

The p (proc) command displays the process table. The output is piped to grep to locate the process. By running the u (user) command and passing the process slot as an argument, the file descriptors for this process are displayed. The first file descriptor allocated (3) was closed and the second (4) retained as shown above.

The entries shown reference file table slots. Using the file command, the entry for file descriptor number 4 is displayed followed by the vnode that it references:

```
> file 30000adac50
ADDRESS     RCNT     TYPE/ADDR           OFFSET    FLAGS
30000adac50  1       UFS /30000aafe30       0      read
> vnode -l 30000aafe30
VCNT VFSMNTED    VFSP     STREAMP VTYPE  RDEV        VDATA       VFILOCKS
VFLAG
   3         0 104440b0         0     f        30000aafda0        0        -
```

```
mutex v_lock: owner 0 waiters 0
Condition variable v_cv: 0
```

The file table entry points to a vnode that is then displayed using the vnode command. Unfortunately the v_pages field is not displayed by crash. Looking at the header file that corresponds to this release of Solaris, it is possible to see where in the structure the v_pages field resides. For example, consider the surrounding fields:

```
...
struct vfs      *v_vfsp;        /* ptr to containing VFS */
struct stdata   *v_stream;      /* associated stream */
struct page     *v_pages;       /* vnode pages list */
enum vtype      v_type;         /* vnode type */
...
```

The v_vfsp and v_type fields are displayed above so by dumping the area of memory starting at the vnode address, it is possible to display the value of v_pages. This is shown below:

```
> od -x 30000aafe30 8
30000aafe30:  000000000000  cafe00000003  000000000000  0000104669e8
30000aafe50:  0000104440b0  000000000000  0000106fbe80  0001baddcafe
```

There is no way to display page structures in crash, so the Solaris adb command is used as follows:

```
# adb -k
physmem 3ac5
106fbe80$<page
106fbe80:       vnode               hash                vpnext
            30000aafe30         1073cb00            106fbe80
106fbe98:       vpprev              next                prev
            106fbe80            106fbe80            106fbe80
106fbeb0:       offset              selock              lckcnt
            0                   0                   0
106fbebe:       cowcnt              cv                  io_cv
            0                   0                   0
106fbec4:  iolock_state         fsdata              state
            0                   0                   0
```

Note that the offset field shows a value of 0 that corresponds to the offset within the file that the program issues the mmap() call for.

Pathname Traversal

The implementation of namei() started to become incredibly complex in some versions of UNIX as more and more functionality was added to a UNIX kernel implementation that was really inadequate to support it. [PATE96] shows how namei() was implemented in SCO OpenServer, a derivative of SVR3 for which namei() became overly complicated. With the addition of new vnodeops, pathname traversal in SVR4 became greatly simplified.

Because one of the goals of the original Sun VFS/vnode architecture was to support non-UNIX filesystems, it is not possible to pass a full pathname to the filesystem and ask it to resolve it to a vnode. Non-UNIX filesystems may not recognize the "/" character as a pathname component separator, DOS being a prime example. Thus, pathnames are resolved one component at a time.

The lookupname() function replaced the old namei() function found in earlier versions of UNIX. This takes a pathname structure and returns a vnode (if the pathname is valid). Internally, lookupname() allocates a pathname structure and calls lookuppn() to actually perform the necessary parsing and component lookup. The steps performed by lookuppn() are as follows:

```
if (absolute_pathname) {
    dirvp = rootdir
} else {
    dirvp = u.u_cdir
}

do {
    name = extract string from pathname
    newvp = VOP_LOOKUP(dirvp, name, ...)
    if not last component {
        dirvp = newvp
    }
} until basename of pathname reached

return newvp
```

This is a fairly simple task to perform. Obviously, users can add all sorts of character combinations, and "." and ".." in the specified pathname, so there is a lot of string manipulation to perform which complicates the work of lookuppn().

The Directory Name Lookup Cache

The section *The Inode Cache* in Chapter 6 described how the inode cache provided a means by which to store inodes that were no longer being used. This helped speed up access during pathname traversal if an inode corresponding to a component in the pathname was still present in the cache.

Introduced initially in 4.2BSD and then in SVR4, the *directory name lookup cache* (DNLC) provides an easy and fast way to get from a pathname to a vnode. For example, in the old inode cache method, parsing the pathname /usr/lib/fs/vxfs/bin/mkfs would involve working on each component of the pathname one at a time. The inode cache merely saved going to disk during processing of iget(), not to say that this isn't a significant performance enhancement. However it still involved a directory scan to locate the appropriate inode number. With the DNLC, a search may be made by the name component alone. If the entry is cached, the vnode is returned. At hit rates over 90 percent, this results in a significant performance enhancement.

The DNLC is a cache of ncache structures linked on an LRU (Least Recently Used) list. The main elements of the structure are shown below and the linkage between elements of the DNLC is shown in Figure 7.5.

name. The pathname stored.

namelen. The length of the pathname.

vp. This field points to the corresponding vnode.

dvp. The credentials of the file's owner.

The ncache structures are hashed to improve lookups. This alleviates the need for unnecessary string comparisons. To access an entry in the DNLC, a hash value is calculated from the filename and parent vnode pointer. The appropriate entry in the nc_hash[] array is accessed, through which the cache can be searched. There are a number of DNLC-provided functions that are called by both the filesystem and the kernel.

dnlc_enter. This function is called by the filesystem to add an entry to the DNLC. This is typically called during pathname resolution on a successful VOP_LOOKUP() call. It is also called when a new file is created or after other operations which involve introducing a new file to the namespace such as creation of hard and symbolic links, renaming of files, and creation of directories.

dnlc_lookup. This function is typically called by the filesystem during pathname resolution. Because pathnames are resolved one entry at a time, the parent directory vnode is passed in addition to the file name to search for. If the entry exists, the corresponding vnode is returned, otherwise NULL is returned.

dnlc_remove. Renaming of files and removal of files are functions for which the entry in the DNLC must be removed.

dnlc_purge_vp. This function can be called to remove all entries in the cache that reference the specified vnode.

dnlc_purge_vfsp. When a filesystem is to be unmounted, this function is called to remove all entries that have vnodes associated with the filesystem that is being unmounted.

dnlc_purge1. This function removes a single entry from the DNLC. SVR4 does not provide a centralized inode cache as found in earlier versions of UNIX. Any caching of inodes or other filesystem-specific data is the responsibility of the filesystem. This function was originally implemented to handle the case where an inode that was no longer in use has been removed from the inode cache.

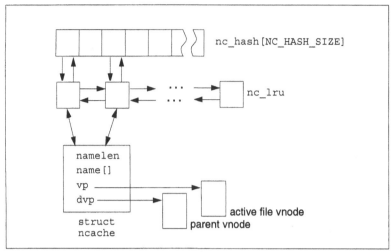

Figure 7.5   Structures used to manage the DNLC.

As mentioned previously, there should be a hit rate of greater than 90 percent in the DNLC; otherwise it should be tuned appropriately. The size of the DNLC is determined by the tunable `ncsize` and is typically based on the maximum number of processes and the maximum number of users.

Filesystem and Virtual Memory Interactions

With the inclusion of the SunOS VM subsystem in SVR4, and the integration between the filesystem and the Virtual Memory (VM) subsystem, the SVR4 VFS architecture radically changed the way that I/O took place. The buffer cache changed in usage and a tight coupling between VM and filesystems together with *page-based I/O* involved changes throughout the whole kernel from filesystems to the VM to individual disk drivers.

Consider the old style of file I/O that took place in UNIX up to and including SVR3. The filesystem made calls into the buffer cache to read and write file data. For demand paging, the File System Switch architecture provided filesystem interfaces to aid demand paging of executable files, although all file data was still read and written through the buffer cache.

This was still largely intact when the Sun VFS/vnode architecture was introduced. However, in addition to their VFS/vnode implementation, Sun Microsystems introduced a radically new Virtual Memory subsystem that was, in large part, to become the new SVR4 VM.

The following sections describe the main components and features of the SVR4 VM together with how file I/O takes place. For a description of the SunOS implementation, consult the Usenix paper "Virtual Memory Architecture in SunOS" [GING87].

An Overview of the SVR4 VM Subsystem

The memory image of each user process is defined by an as (address space) structure that references a number of *segments* underpinned by the seg structure. Consider a typical user process. The address space of the process will include separate segments for text, data, and stack, in addition to various libraries, shared memory, and memory-mapped files as shown pictorially in Figure 7.6.

The seg structure defines the boundaries covering each segment. This includes the base address in memory together with the size of the segment.

There are a number of different segment types. Each segment type has an array of segment-related functions in the same way that each vnode has an array of vnode functions. In the case of a page fault, the kernel will call the fault() function for the specified segment causing the segment handler to respond by reading in the appropriate data from disk. When a process is forked, the dup() function is called for each segment and so on.

For those segments such as process text and data that are backed by a file, the *segvn* segment type is used. Each segvn segment has associated private, per-segment data that is accessed through the s_data field of the seg structure. This particular structure, segvn_data, contains information about the segment as well as the underlying file. For example, segvn segment operations need to know whether the segment is read-only, read/write, or whether it has execute access so that it can respond accordingly to a page fault. As well as referencing the vnode backing the segment, the offset at which the segment is mapped to the file must be known. As a hypothetical example, consider the case where user text is held at an offset of 0x4000 from the start of the executable file. If a page fault occurs within the text segment at the address s_base + 0x2000, the segment page fault handler knows that the data must be read from the file at an offset of 0x4000 + 0x2000 = 0x6000.

After a user process starts executing, there will typically be no physical pages of data backing these segments. Thus, the first instruction that the process executes will generate a page fault within the segment covering the instruction. The kernel page fault handler must first determine in which segment the fault occurred. This is achieved using the list of segments referenced by the process as structure together with the base address and the size of each segment. If the address that generated the page fault does not fall within the boundaries of any of the process segments, the process will be posted a SIGSEGV, which will typically result in the process dumping core.

To show how these structures are used in practice, consider the following invocation of the sleep(1) program:

```
$ /usr/bin/sleep 100000&
```

Using crash, the process can be located and the list of segments can be displayed as follows:

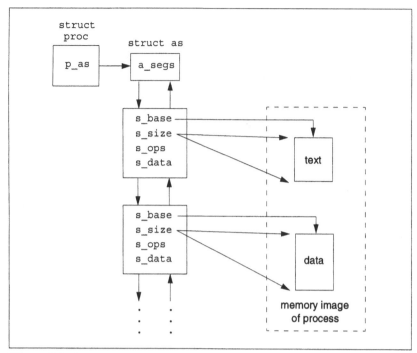

Figure 7.6   Structures used to manage the process address space.

```
# crash
dumpfile = /dev/mem, namelist = /dev/ksyms, outfile = stdout
> p | grep sleep
32 s  7719  7694  7719  7694     0  46 sleep         load
> as -f 32
PROC          PAGLCK   CLGAP  VBITS HAT         HRM          RSS
  SEGLST      LOCK            SEGS       SIZE      LREP TAIL      NSEGS
  32          0        0      0x0   0x4f958     0x0
0xb10070    0x7fffefa0  0xb5aa50    950272  0      0xb3ccc0      14
BASE        SIZE    OPS           DATA
0x   10000    8192 segvn_ops   0x30000aa46b0
0x   20000    8192 segvn_ops   0x30000bfa448
0x   22000    8192 segvn_ops   0x30000b670f8
0xff280000 679936 segvn_ops   0x30000aa4e40
0xff336000  24576 segvn_ops   0x30000b67c50
0xff33c000   8192 segvn_ops   0x30000bfb260
0xff360000  16384 segvn_ops   0x30000bfac88
0xff372000  16384 segvn_ops   0x30000bface0
0xff380000  16384 segvn_ops   0x30001af3f48
0xff3a0000   8192 segvn_ops   0x30000b677d8
0xff3b0000   8192 segvn_ops   0x30000b239d8
0xff3c0000 131072 segvn_ops   0x30000b4c5e0
0xff3e0000   8192 segvn_ops   0x30000b668b8
0xffbee000   8192 segvn_ops   0x30000bfad38
```

There are 14 different segment types used to construct the address space, all of which are segvn type segments. Looking at the highlighted segment, the segvn private data structure associated with this segment can be displayed within adb as follows:

```
0x30000aa4e40$<segvn
30000aa4e40:          lock
30000aa4e40:          wwwh
0
30000aa4e48:     pageprot          prot          maxprot
                        0           015              017
30000aa4e4b:         type        offset               vp
                       02             0      30000749c58
30000aa4e60:  anon_index           amp            vpage
                        0             0                0
30000aa4e78:         cred        swresv           advice
              30000429b68             0                0
```

The vnode representing the file backing this segment together with the offset within the file are displayed. The vnode and inode commands can be used to display both the vnode and the underlying UFS inode:

```
30000749c58$<vnode
30000749c60:             flag        refcnt          vfsmnt
                         1000            63               0
30000749c70:               op          vfsp          stream
                  ufs_vnodeops      104440b0               0
30000749c88:            pages          type            rdev
                      107495e0             1               0
30000749ca0:             data       filocks        shrlocks
             30000749bc8             0             0
...
30000749bc8$<inode
...
30000749ce0:           number        diroff                    ufsvfs
                        50909             0               3000016ee18
...
```

Finally, the following library is displayed whose inode number matches the inode displayed above.

```
# ls -i /usr/lib/libc.so.1
50909 /usr/lib/libc.so.1
```

An interesting exercise to try is to run some of the programs presented in the book, particularly those that use memory-mapped files, map the segments displayed back to the specific file on disk, and note the file offsets and size of the segments in question.

The segvn segment type is of most interest to filesystem writers. Other segments include seg_u for managing user areas, *seg_kmem* for use by the kernel virtual memory allocator, and *seg_dev*, which is used to enable applications to memory-map devices.

The kernel address space is managed in a similar manner to the user address space in that it has its own address space structure referenced by the kernel variable k_as. This points to a number of different segments, one of which represents the SVR4 *page cache* that is described later in this chapter.

Anonymous Memory

When a process starts executing, the data section may be modified and therefore, once read from the file, loses its file association thereafter. All such segvn segments contain a reference to the original file where the data must be read from but also contain a reference to a set of *anonymous pages*.

Every anonymous page has reserved space on the swap device. If memory becomes low and anonymous pages need to be paged out, they can be written to the swap device and read back into memory at a later date. Anonymous pages are described by the anon structure, which contains a reference count as well as a pointer to the actual page. It also points to an entry within an si_anon[] array for which there is one per swap device. The location within this array determines the location on the swap device where the page of memory will be paged to if necessary. This is shown pictorially in Figure 7.7.

File I/O through the SVR4 VFS Layer

SVR4 implemented what is commonly called the *page cache* through which all file data is read and written. This is actually a somewhat vague term because the page cache differs substantially from the fixed size caches of the buffer cache, DNLC, and other types of caches.

The page cache is composed of two parts, a segment underpinned by the *seg_map* segment driver and a list of free pages that can be used for any purpose. Thus, after a page of file data leaves the cache, it is added to the list of free pages. While the page is on the free list, it still retains its identity so that if the kernel wishes to locate the same data prior to the page being reused, the page is removed from the free list and the data does not need to be re-read from disk. The main structures used in constructing the page cache are shown in Figure 7.8.

The segmap structure is part of the kernel address space and is underpinned by the segmap_data structure that describes the properties of the segment. The size of the segment is tunable and is split into MAXBSIZE (8KB) chunks where each 8KB chunk represents an 8KB window into a file. Each chunk is referenced by an smap structure that contains a pointer to a vnode for the file and the offset within the file. Thus, whereas the buffer cache references file data by device and block number, the page cache references file data by vnode pointer and file offset.

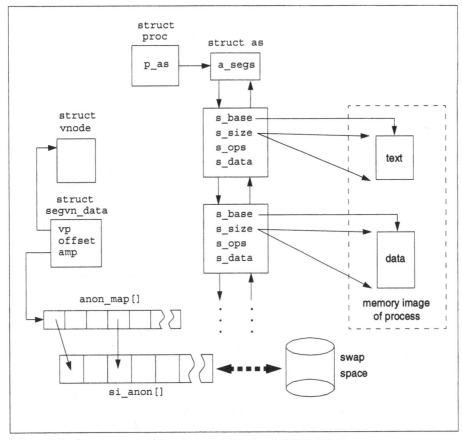

Figure 7.7 Structures used to manage anonymous memory.

Two VM functions provide the basis for performing I/O in the new SVR4 model. The first function, shown below, is used in a similar manner to getblk() to essentially return a new entry in the page cache or return a previously cached entry:

```
addr_t
segmap_getmap(struct seg *seg, vnode_t *vp, uint_t *offset);
```

The seg argument is always segkmap. The remaining two arguments are the vnode and the offset within the vnode where the data is to be read from or written to. The offset must be in 8KB multiples from the start of the file.

The address returned from segmap_getmap() is a kernel virtual address within the segmap segment range s_base to s_base + s_size. When the page cache is first initialized, the first call to segmap_getmap() will result in the first smap structure being used. The sm_vp and sm_off fields are updated to hold the vnode and offset passed in, and the virtual address corresponding to this entry is returned. After all slots in the segmap window have been used, the

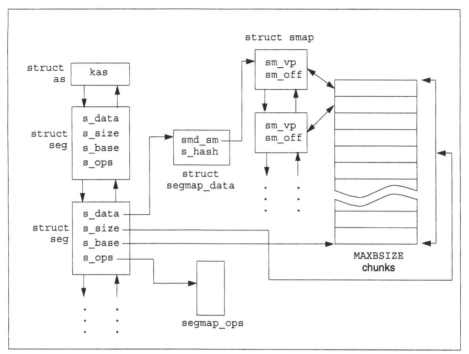

Figure 7.8   Main structures used in constructing the SVR4 page cache.

segmap driver must reuse one of the existing slots. This works in a similar manner to the buffer cache where older buffers are reused when no free buffers are available. After a slot is reallocated, the pages backing that slot are placed on the free list. Thus, the page cache essentially works at two levels with the page free list also acting as a cache.

The segmap_release() function, shown below, works in a similar way to brelse() by allowing the entry to be reused:

```
int
segmap_release(struct seg *seg, addr_t addr, u_int flags)
```

This is where the major difference between SVR4 and other UNIX kernels comes into play. The virtual address returned by segmap_getmap() will not have any associated physical pages on the first call with a specific vnode and offset. Consider the following code fragment, which is used by the filesystem to read from an offset of 8KB within a file and read 1024 bytes:

```
kaddr = segmap_getmap(segkmap, vp, 8192);
uiomove(kaddr, 1024, UIO_READ, uiop);
segmap_release(segkmap, kaddr, SM_FREE);
```

The uiomove() function is called to copy bytes from one address to another. Because there are no physical pages backing kaddr, a page fault will occur.

Because the kernel address space, referenced by kas, contains a linked list of segments each with a defined start and end address, it is easy for the page fault handling code to determine which segment fault handler to call to satisfy the page fault. In this case the s_fault() function provided with the segmap driver will be called as follows:

```
segkmap->s_ops->fault(seg, addr, ssize, type, rw);
```

By using the s_base and addr arguments passed to the fault handler, the appropriate vnode can be located from the corresponding smap structure. A call is then made to the filesystem's VOP_GETPAGE() function, which must allocate the appropriate pages and read the data from disk before returning. After this is all complete, the page fault is satisfied and the uiomove() function continues.

A pictorial view of the steps taken when reading a file through the VxFS filesystem is shown in Figure 7.9.

To write to a file, the same procedure is followed up to the point where segmap_release() is called. The flags argument determines what happens to the pages once the segment is released. The values that flags can take are:

SM_WRITE. The pages should be written, via VOP_PUTPAGE(), to the file once the segment is released.

SM_ASYNC. The pages should be written asynchronously.

SM_FREE. The pages should be freed.

SM_INVAL. The pages should be invalidated.

SM_DONTNEED. The filesystem has no need to access these pages again.

If no flags are specified, the call to VOP_PUTPAGE() will not occur. This is the default behavior when reading from a file.

Memory-Mapped File Support in SVR4

A call to mmap() will result in a new *segvn* segment being attached to the calling process' address space. A call will be made to the filesystem VOP_MAP() function, which performs some level of validation before calling the map_addr() function to actually initialize the process address space with the new segment.

Page faults on the mapping result in a very similar set of steps to page faults on the segmap segment. The segvn fault handler is called with the process address space structure and virtual address. Attached to the private data of this segment will be the vnode, the offset within the file that was requested of mmap(), and a set of permissions to indicate the type of mapping.

In the simple case of a memory read access, the segvn driver will call VOP_GETPAGE() to read in the requested page from the file. Again, the filesystem will allocate the page and read in the contents from disk.

In the following program, /etc/passwd is mapped. The following text then shows how to display the segments for this process and from there show the segvn segment for the mapped region and show how it points back to the passwd

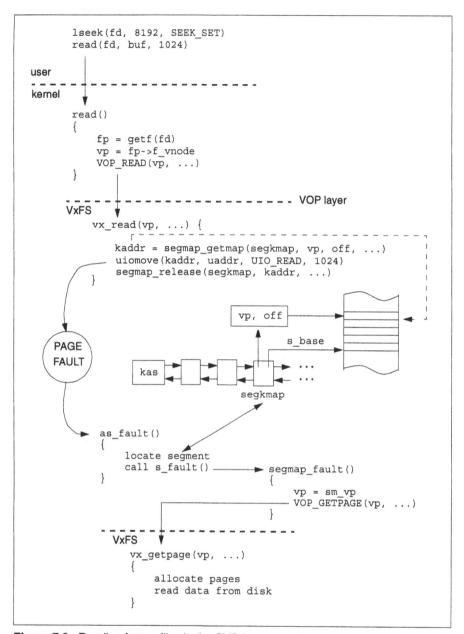

Figure 7.9 Reading from a file via the SVR4 page cache.

file so that data can be read and written as appropriate. The program is very straightforward, mapping an 8KB chunk of the file from a file offset of 0.

```
1 #include <sys/types.h>
2 #include <sys/stat.h>
3 #include <sys/mman.h>
```

```
 4 #include <fcntl.h>
 5 #include <unistd.h>
 6
 7 #define MAPSZ                4096
 8
 9 main()
10 {
11          char          *addr, c;
12          int           fd;
13
14          fd = open("/etc/passwd", O_RDONLY);
15          addr = (char *)mmap(NULL, MAPSZ,
16                              PROT_READ, MAP_SHARED, fd, 0);
17          printf("addr = 0x%x\n", addr);
18          c = *addr;
19          pause();
20 }
```

After running the program, it can be located with crash as follows. Using the program slot, the as (address space) for the process is then displayed.

```
# mydup&
addr = 0xff390000
# crash
> p | grep mydup
38 s  4836  4800  4836  4800      0  46 map              load
> p -f 38
PROC TABLE SIZE = 1882
SLOT ST  PID  PPID  PGID   SID   UID PRI   NAME        FLAGS
  38  s 4836  4800  4836  4800     0  46    map         load
Session: sid: 4800, ctty: vnode(30001031448) maj(24) min(1)
Process Credentials: uid: 0, gid: 1, real uid: 0, real gid: 1
as: 300005d8ff8
...
```

From within adb the address space can be displayed by invoking the as macro. This shows a pointer to the list of segments corresponding to this process. In this case there are 12 segments. The seglist macro then displays each segment in the list. In this case, only the segment corresponding to the mapped file is displayed. This is located by looking at the base address of the segment that corresponds to the address returned from mmap(), which is displayed above.

```
300005d8ff8$<as
...
300005d9040:       segs           size             tail
30000b5a2a8        e0000      30000b5a190
300005d9058:       nsegs          lrep             hilevel
                      12             0                   0

...
30000b5a2a8$<seglist
...
30000b11f80:       base           size             as
ff390000           2000       300005d8ff8
```

```
30000b11f98:          next              prev              ops
30000b5a4a0    30000b5b8c0        segvn_ops
30000b11fb0:          data
               30000b4d138
. . .
```

Note that in addition to the base address, the size of the segment corresponds to the size of the mapping requested, in this case 8KB. The data field points to private segment-specific data. This can be displayed using the segvn macro as follows:

```
30000b4d138$<segvn
. . .
30000b4d143:          type            offset                 vp
                        01                 0         30000aafe30
. . .
```

Of most interest here, the vp field points to the vnode from which this segment is backed. The offset field gives the offset within the file which, as specified to mmap(), is 0.

The remaining two macro calls display the vnode referenced previously and the UFS inode corresponding to the vnode.

```
30000aafe30$<vnode
30000aafe38:          flag            refcnt            vfsmnt
                        0                 3                 0
30000aafe48:          op              vfsp             stream
               ufs_vnodeops         104440b0                 0
30000aafe60:          pages           type              rdev
               106fbe80                1                 0
30000aafe78:          data          filocks          shrlocks
               30000aafda0                0                 0
30000aafda0$<inode
. . .
30000aafeb8:          number         diroff            ufsvfs
                    129222                0         3000016ee18
. . .
```

As a check, the inode number is displayed and also displayed below:

```
# ls -i /etc/passwd
   129222 /etc/passwd
```

Flushing Dirty Pages to Disk

There are a number of cases where modified pages need to be written to disk. This may result from the pager finding pages to steal, an explicit call to msync(), or when a process exits and modified pages within a mapping need to be written back to disk. The VOP_PUTPAGE() vnode operation is called to write a single page back to disk.

The single page approach may not be ideal for filesystems such as VxFS that can have multipage extents. The same also holds true for any filesystem where the block size is greater than the page size. Rather than flush a single dirty page to disk, it is preferable to flush a range of pages. For VxFS this may cover all dirty pages within the extent that may be in memory. The VM subsystem provides a number of routines for manipulating lists of pages. For example, the function pvn_getdirty_range() can be called to gather all dirty pages in the specified range. All pages within this range are gathered together in a linked list and passed to a filesystem-specified routine, that can then proceed to write the page list to disk.

Page-Based I/O

Prior to SVR4, all I/O went through the buffer cache. Each buffer pointed to a kernel virtual address where the data could be transferred to and from. With the change to a page-based model for file I/O in SVR4, the filesystem deals with pages for file data I/O and may wish to perform I/O to more than one page at a time. For example, as described in the previous section, a call back into the filesystem from pvn_getdirty_range() passes a linked list of page structures. However, these pages do not typically have associated kernel virtual addresses. To avoid an unnecessary use of kernel virtual address space and an increased cost in time to map these pages, the buffer cache subsystem as well as the underlying device drivers were modified to accept a list of pages. In this case, the b_pages field is set to point to the linked list of pages and the B_PAGES field must be set.

At the stage that the filesystem wishes to perform I/O, it will typically have a linked list of pages into which data needs to be read or from which data needs to be written. To prevent duplication across filesystems, the kernel provides a function, pageio_setup(), which allocates a buf structure, attaches the list of pages to b_pages, and initializes the b_flags to include B_PAGES. This is used by the driver the indicate that page I/O is being performed and that b_pages should be used and not b_addr. Note that this buffer is not part of the buffer cache.

The I/O is actually performed by calling the driver *strategy* function. If the filesystem needs to wait for the I/O completion, it must call biowait(), passing the buf structure as an argument. After the I/O is complete, a call to pageio_done() will free the buffer, leaving the page list intact.

Adoption of the SVR4 Vnode Interface

Although many OS vendors implemented the VFS/vnode architecture within the framework of their UNIX implementations, the SVR4 style of page I/O, while elegant and efficient in usage of the underlying memory, failed to gain widespread adoption. In part this was due to the closed nature in which SVR4 was developed because the implementation was not initially documented. An additional reason was due to the amount of change that was needed both to the VM subsystem as well as every filesystem supported.

Summary

The period between development of both SVR3 and SunOS and the transition to SVR4 saw a substantial investment in both the filesystem framework within the kernel and the development of individual filesystems. The VFS/vnode architecture has proved to be immensely popular and has been ported in one way or another to most versions of UNIX. For further details of SVR4.0, Goodheart and Cox's book *The Magic Garden Explained: The Internals of System V Release 4, An Open Systems Design* [GOOD94] provides a detailed account of SVR4 kernel internals. For details on the File System Switch (FSS) architecture, Pate's book *UNIX Internals—A Practical Approach* [PATE96] is one of the few references.

Non-SVR4-Based Filesystem Architectures

Previous chapters have centered around the main evolutionary path that UNIX took from the early research editions through to System V Release 4, which involved the last major enhancements to the UNIX filesystem architecture.

While many different UNIX and UNIX-like vendors adopted the Sun VFS/vnode interface to one degree or another, their implementations differed in many other areas, most notably in how file I/O takes place. Some of the microkernel implementations offered new approaches to supporting UNIX-based filesystems.

This chapter describes the major different UNIX and UNIX-like operating systems from a filesystem perspective, showing the similarities and differences to the pre-VFS and post-VFS/vnode implementations.

The BSD Filesystem Architecture

The first version of BSD UNIX, introduced in 1978, was based on 6th Edition UNIX. Almost from day one, subtle differences between the two code bases started to appear. However, with 3BSD, introduced in 1980 and based on 7th Edition, one can still see very similar code paths between 3BSD and 7th Edition UNIX, which was described in Chapter 6. Therefore, understanding the kernel paths in the earlier research editions will help in understanding the paths through the earlier BSD versions.

The source of all of the BSD kernels is now available on a single CD set, distributed under the auspices of the ancient UNIX source code license that was introduced to allow the research editions to become accessible to anyone. At the time of writing, Kirk McKusick, one of the BSD contributors, is distributing the CDs. For further information, see www.mckusick.com.

The three the most significant contributions that the Berkeley team made in the area of filesystems were quotas, the directory name lookup cache (DNLC), and the introduction of the *Berkeley Fast File System* (FFS), which would eventually be renamed UFS (UNIX File System). This was first documented in [MCKU84] and is described in more detail in Chapter 9.

UFS first made its appearance in later versions of 4.1BSD. Note, however, that it did not appear as an additional filesystem but as a replacement for the old research edition filesystem because, at that stage, the kernel had no means of supporting multiple different filesystem types.

Around the time of 4.3BSD, traces of the old UNIX filesystem had disappeared. The filesystem disk layout was that of early UFS, which was considerably more complex than its predecessor. The in-core `file` structure still pointed to an in-core inode but this was changed to include a copy of the disk-based portion of the UFS inode when the file was opened. The implementation of `namei()` also became more complex with the introduction of the *name cache* (DNLC).

File I/O in 4.3BSD

To illustrate some of the areas where BSD UNIX differed from the research editions, consider the case of file I/O. At this stage, the BSD implementation had already started to move away from the use of user area fields to hold information pertaining to the read or write operation and introduced the `uio` and `iovec` structures as described in the section *The uio Structure* in Chapter 7.

Another difference was the introduction of a function vector, which was accessed through the `file` structure and referenced the following functions:

fo_rw. This function is called when performing a read or write operation. For reading and writing to/from files, this field pointed to the `ino_rw()` function.

fo_ioctl. Called to handle the `ioctl(S)` system call. For file access, the `ino_ioctl()` function was called.

fo_select. Called to handle the `select(S)` system call. For file access, the `ino_select()` function was called.

fo_close. Called to handle the `close(S)` system call. For file access, the `ino_close()` function was called.

By supporting multiple operation vectors, this allowed applications to access sockets (a channel for communicating over networks) in the same way that regular files were accessed.

For reading from and writing to regular files, ino_rw() calls rwip(), which performs most of the work by calling bmap() to map an offset to a block on disk and then calling into the buffer cache to actually read the data. The bmap() function actually returns two blocks, namely the requested block, which was read synchronously, and the next block in the file for which an asynchronous read was initiated. This allows for read ahead in order to improve performance.

Although the bmap() function is called directly from rwip(), the separation of filesystem-specific code was starting to appear, paving the way for what would eventually be an architecture that would support multiple filesystem types.

The BSD buffer cache is not significantly different from other buffer cache implementations described elsewhere in the book and therefore does not warrant further description here.

Filename Caching in 4.3BSD

Two name caching mechanisms were introduced in BSD UNIX. Firstly, namei() was enhanced to allow for faster scans of a directory when the process was scanning the directory sequentially. This could be proved to have a significant effect given the right benchmark. However, it proved to be useful in only a small number of practical cases.

More significant was the introduction of a new name cache that held recent name-to-inode lookups. This cache, which was adopted in SVR4 as the *Directory Name Lookup Cache* (DNLC), contained entries that mapped a file name and device number to a pointer to an in-core inode. The BSD name cache used a *softhold* mechanism whereby inodes referenced by entries in the cache did not require the inode i_count field to be incremented. This avoided limiting the size of the cache to the size of the inode table. To handle the case where inodes were not in the inode cache but were still held in the name cache and were subsequently unlinked and reused, inodes were assigned a *capability,* a field, that was incremented each time the inode was reused. If a cache hit were to find the previous instantiation of the inode, the capabilities would not match and the name cache entry would be removed.

Both caches combined were hugely successful, resulting in the name cache being implemented on just about every UNIX implementation that followed. As documented in [KARE86], on a 12-hour period for a range of machines with between 500,000 and 1,000,000 name lookups, the combined cache hit of the two caches was 85 percent.

The Introduction of Vnodes in BSD UNIX

[KARE86] described the rationale for the introduction of a variant of the Sun VFS/vnode interface in Berkeley UNIX, together with the areas where the interface would differ from the original Sun implementation. The study compared Sun's VFS/vnode architecture with the File System Switch (FSS) from

AT&T and the GFS architecture from Digital.

The implementation that followed closely matched the Sun VFS architecture with the exception of pathname resolution where they retained their existing namei() and name cache implementation. Many of the VFS-level structures and interfaces were very similar. Before describing the differences, it is first necessary to describe the modifications made to namei().

The original namei() implementation used fields in the user area that were set up prior to the kernel calling namei(). The BSD model was modified to pass all such arguments in a nameidata structure that was the sole argument to the namei() function. The fields of the nameidata structure are as follows:

```
struct nameidata {
    caddr_t        ni_dirp;      /* pathname pointer */
    enum uio_seg   ni_seg;       /* location of pathname */
    short          ni_nameiop;   /* operation to perform */
    struct vnode   *ni_cdir;     /* current working directory */
    struct vnode   *ni_rdir;     /* root directory */
    struct ucred   *ni_cred;     /* caller credentials */
    caddr_t        ni_pnbuf;     /* pathname buffer */
    char           *ni_ptr;      /* cur loc in pathname */
    int            ni_pathlen;   /* remaining chars in pathname */
    short          ni_more;      /* more left to translate? */
    short          ni_loopcnt;   /* count of symlinks found */
    struct vnode   *nivp;        /* vnode of result */
    struct vnode   *nidvp;       /* vnode of parent directory */
}
```

The BSD namei() function started from a base directory, either the root directory for absolute pathnames or the current working directory for relative pathnames. This base directory inode was stored in ni_cdir, and the pathname to parse, in ni_dirp.

The operation to perform was held in the ni_nameiop field and could be one of the following:

LOOKUP. Only perform a lookup operation.

CREATE. Prepare for file creation.

DELETE. Prepare for file deletion.

WANTPARENT. Also return the parent directory vnode.

NOCACHE. Do not leave the name in the name cache.

FOLLOW. Follow symbolic links.

NOFOLLOW. Do not follow symbolic links.

The LOOKUP operation is identical to the Sun VFS VOP_LOOKUP() operation. The CREATE and DELETE operations are called prior to vnodeop functions such as VOP_CREATE(), VOP_UNLINK(), and VOP_MKNOD(). Because not all of these operations are followed by the intended vnode operation, the kernel may invoke the VOP_ABORTOP() function.

VFS and Vnode Structure Differences

Most structures introduced in the Sun VFS architecture also found their way into BSD UNIX with very few modifications. The vfs structure added vfs_bsize, the optimal filesystem block size, although this was rarely used.

The statfs structure was enhanced to add f_bsize and information about where the filesystem was mounted. The vnode structure gained the v_text field, which was used for executable files.

A few additional vnode operations were added:

vn_mknod. Handles the mknod(S) system call.

vn_read. Handles the read(S) system call.

vn_write. Handles the write(S) system call.

vn_seek. Called in response to an lseek(S) system call.

vn_abortop. This function is called when a previous namei() call specified CREATE or DELETE but the operation is not to be carried out.

vn_lock. The filesystem independent layer typically calls VOP_LOCK() to lock a file prior to a subsequent vnode operation.

vn_unlock. This vnode operation unlocks a vnode previously locked with a call to VOP_LOCK().

Reading and writing to files was handled by invoking the VOP_READ() and VOP_WRITE() vnode operations. Both functions are surrounded by calls to VOP_LOCK() and VOP_UNLOCK() vnode operations. The actual reading and writing of regular files was handled by the UFS functions ufs_read() and ufs_write() functions that mapped onto buffer cache functions.

Digital UNIX / True64 UNIX

Digital UNIX, formerly called DEC OSF/1, is a microkernel-based implementation of UNIX utilizing the Mach microkernel and the BSD 4.3/4.4 versions of UNIX. For further details on microkernel-based UNIX implementations, see the section *Microkernel Support for UNIX Filesystems*, later in this chapter. With the merger between Compaq and Digital, the name of the operating system was changed to True64 UNIX. True64 now contains a considerable rewrite of many of the components of the OSF/1 kernel and differs substantially from the UNIX emulation on Mach, described in the section *The Mach Microkernel* later in this chapter.

From a filesystem perspective, True64 UNIX supports a large number of filesystems including UFS, NFS, procfs, and AdvFS (Advanced File System), a transaction-based filesystem that provides many features.

The True64 UNIX filesystem architecture was derived from the 4.3BSD Reno release but has, over the last several years, been modified to include a number of new features.

Steven Hancock's book *True64 UNIX File System Administration Guide* [HANC01] is an excellent source of information on the True64 filesystem architecture and individual filesystem implementations. The following sections provide a brief highlight of the main features.

Like most other versions of UNIX, True64 employs the same structures related to file access, namely file descriptors pointing to the system-wide file table whose entries point to vnodes.

The per-process file table is stored in the process utask structure which is similar to the traditional user area. This employs two limits, a soft limit and hard limit, which determine the number of open files that a process may have open at any one time. These limits are governed by the setrlimit(S) system call.

The file structure is similar to its BSD counterpart, employing the operations vector to allow access to files and sockets.

Although based on the 4.3BSD Reno VFS, the True64 UNIX VFS has undergone substantial modifications. The vnode structure has been significantly modified to include a large number of fields in addition to the original BSD vnode structure. Unlike the SVR4 vnode, which has a v_data field pointing to a filesystem-independent structure, the True64 vnode is a single structure that contains the filesystem-independent structure whose type is identified by the v_tag field (VT_UFS, VT_NFS etc).

Two fields of the vnode reference the pages that have been read into core and possibly modified. The v_cleanblkhd field points to a list of buffers for pages that have not been modified, while the v_dirtyblkhd field references a list of dirty buffers.

The vnode operations vector is not too dissimilar from the BSD equivalent. Pathname lookup is performed by a similar namei() implementation that results in the need for the VOP_ABORTOP() vnode operation. In addition to providing a number of vnode operations to handle access control lists (ACLs), also called *property lists*, there are a number of interfaces for supporting file access, namely:

VOP_BMAP(). This function maps a file offset to a filesystem block on disk.

VOP_STRATEGY(). Called to read or write to/from a file.

VOP_PGRD(). This function reads a specified page.

VOP_PGWR(). This function writes a specified page.

VOP_BREAD(). This function reads through the buffer cache.

VOP_BRELSE(). Releases a buffer.

True64 UNIX employed a new buffer cache that unified the old style buffer cache with the system page cache, allowing full coherency between regular file access and memory-mapped files. Each unified buffer cache buffer references physical pages in memory. The traditional buffer cache remains, but it now caches only filesystem meta-data (inodes and other structural components).

The AIX Filesystem Architecture

AIX first appeared in 1985 running on the IBM RT machine, which was IBM's first RISC-based workstation. AIX version 2 was enhanced to support TCP/IP and NFS. This was followed by a port to the PS/2 in 1989. In the same year, AIX was ported to the 370 series of mainframes and the following year saw the introduction of the RISC System/6000 with AIX version 3. AIX version 3.2, which is the most publicly documented version of AIX, as seen in David Kelly's book *AIX/6000 Internals and Architecture* [KELL96], was released in 1992. The following text describes features of AIX from the 3.2 release with information on how filesystems perform I/O on the 5.x kernel series.

Although originally based on SVR2, AIX has undergone a major rewrite adding features from other versions of UNIX including SVR4. AIX also has features not found in any other versions of UNIX, such as a pageable kernel, an area that has resulted in considerable complexity within the kernel, in particular the virtual memory subsystem.

The Filesystem-Independent Layer of AIX

As with other earlier versions of UNIX, file descriptors are held in a fixed size array within the user area for each process. Similarly, each file descriptor entry points to an entry in the system file table. Although the file table entries contained all of the fields of other versions of UNIX including referencing a vnode, each entry also pointed to a filops structure that contained all of the operations that could be applied to the open file in question. This is similar to BSD such that regular files and sockets can be accessed by the same set of system calls.

This is where the differences started to appear. Although AIX supported vnodes referenced by the file structure, each vnode pointed to an in-core inode that had an embedded gnode structure. With the exception of the gnode, the inode structure was very similar to earlier UNIX in-core inodes, containing such fields as:

i_forw / i_back. Forward and backward pointers used for a hash queue when the inode is in use.

i_next / i_prev. Forward and backward pointers used when the inode is on the free list.

i_dev. The device that holds the filesystem on which the file resides.

i_number. The disk inode number. When a file is opened, the inode cache is scanned using the i_dev and i_number fields.

i_count. A reference count holding the number of opens against the file.

i_locks. Used to serialize updates to the inode.

i_gnode. This field points to the gnode.

i_dinode. After a file is opened, the disk inode is read from disk into memory and stored at this position within the incore inode.

Unlike the SVR4 page cache where all files effectively share the virtual address window implemented by the segmap driver, in AIX each open file has its own 256MB cache backed by a *file segment*. This virtual window may be backed by pages from the file that can be accessed on a future reference.

The gnode structure contains a number of fields including a reference to the underlying file segment:

g_type. This field specifies the type of file to which the gnode belongs, such as a regular file, directory, and so on.

g_seg. This *segment ID* is used to reference the file segment that contains cached pages for the file.

g_vnode. This field references the vnode for this file.

g_filocks. For record locks, there is a linked list of filock structures referenced by this field.

g_data. This field points to the in-core inode corresponding to this file.

Each segment is represented by a *Segment Control Block* that is held in the segment information table as shown in Figure 8.1.

When a process wishes to read from or write to a file, data is accessed through a set of functions that operate on the file segment.

File Access in AIX

The vnode entry points in AIX are similar to other VFS/vnode architectures with the exception of reading from and writing to files. The entry point to handle the read(S) and write(S) system calls is vn_rdwr_attr() through which a uio structure is passed that gives details on the read or write to perform.

This is where the differences really start. There is no direct equivalent of the vn_getpage / vn_putpage entry points as seen in the SVR4 VFS. In their place, the filesystem registers a strategy routine that is called to handle page faults and flushing of file data. To register a routine, the vm_mounte() function is called with the strategy routine passed as an argument. Typically this routine is asynchronous, although later versions of AIX support the ability to have a blocking strategy routine, a feature added for VxFS support.

As mentioned in the section *The Filesystem-Independent Layer of AIX*, earlier in this chapter, each file is mapped by a file segment that represents a 256MB window into the file. To allocate this segment, vms_create() is called and, on last close of a file, the routine vms_cache_destroy() is invoked to remove the segment. Typically, file segments are created on either a first read or write.

After a file segment is allocated, the tasks performed for reading and writing are similar to those of the SVR4 page cache in that the filesystem loops, making

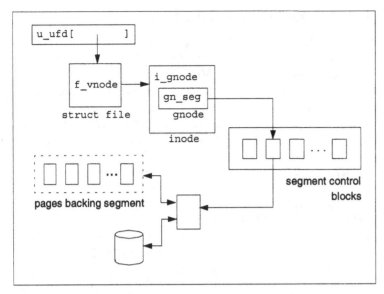

Figure 8.1   Main file-related structures in AIX.

calls to vm_uiomove() to copy data to or from the file segment. On first access, a page fault will occur resulting in a call to the filesystem's strategy routine. The arguments to this function are shown below using the VxFS entry point as an example:

```
void
vx_mm_thrpgio(struct buf *buflist, vx_u32_t vmm_flags, int path)
```

The arguments shown do not by themselves give enough information about the file. Additional work is required in order to determine the file from which data should be read or written. Note that the file can be accessed through the b_vp field of the buf structure. From here the segment can be obtained. To actually perform I/O, multiple calls may be needed to the devstrat() function, which takes a single buf structure.

The HP-UX VFS Architecture

HP-UX has a long and varied history. Although originally derived from System III UNIX, the HP-UX 1.0 release, which appeared in 1986, was largely based on SVR2. Since that time, many enhancements have been added to HP-UX from SVR3, SVR4, and Berkeley versions of UNIX. At the time of writing, HP-UX is still undergoing a number of new enhancements to make it more scalable and provide cleaner interfaces between various kernel components.

The HP-UX Filesystem-Independent Layer

HP-UX maintains the mapping between file descriptors in the user area through the system file table to a vnode, as with other VFS/vnode architectures. File descriptors are allocated dynamically as with SVR4.

The file structure is similar to its BSD counterpart in that it also includes a vector of functions so that the user can access the filesystem and sockets using the same set of file-related system calls. The operations exported through the file table are fo_rw(), fo_ioctl(), fo_select(), and fo_close().

The HP-UX VFS/Vnode Layer

Readers familiar with the SVR4 VFS/vnode architecture will find many similarities with the HP-UX implementation of vnodes.

The vfs structure, while providing some additional fields, retains most of the original fields of the original Sun implementation as documented in [KLEI86]. The VFS operations more resemble the SVR4 interfaces but also provide additional interfaces for quota management and enabling the filesystem to export a freeze/thaw capability.

The vnode structure differs in that it maintains a linked list of all clean (v_cleanblkhd) and dirty (v_dirtyblkhd) buffers associated with the file. This is somewhat similar to the v_pages in the SVR4 vnode structure although SVR4 does not provide an easy way to determine which pages are clean and which are dirty without walking the list of pages. Management of these lists is described in the next section. The vnode also provides a mapping to entries in the DNLC.

Structures used to pass data across the vnode interface are similar to their Sun/SVR4 VFS/vnode counterparts. Data for reading and writing is passed through a uio structure with each I/O being defined by an iovec structure. Similarly, for operations that set and retrieve file attributes, the vattr structure is used.

The set of vnode operations has changed substantially since the VFS/vnode architecture was introduced in HP-UX. One can see similarities between the HP-UX and BSD VFS/vnode interfaces.

File I/O in HP-UX

HP-UX provides support for memory-mapped files. File I/O still goes through the buffer cache, but there is no guarantee of data consistency between the page cache and buffer cache. The interfaces exported by the filesystem and through the vnode interface are shown in Figure 8.2.

Each filesystem provides a vop_rdwr() interface through which the kernel enters the filesystem to perform I/O, passing the I/O specification through a uio structure. Considering a read(S) system call for now, the filesystem will work through the user request calling into the buffer cache to request the appropriate

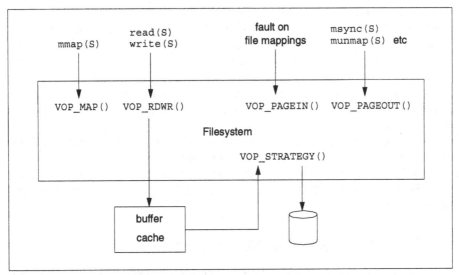

Figure 8.2 Filesystem / kernel interactions for file I/O in HP-UX.

buffer. Note that the user request will be broken down into multiple calls into the buffer cache depending on the size of the request, the block size of the filesystem, and the way in which the data is laid out on disk.

After entering the buffer cache as part of the read operation, after a valid buffer has been obtained, it is added to the v_cleanblkhd field of the vnode. Having easy access to the list of valid buffers associated with the vnode enables the filesystem to perform an initial fast scan when performing read operations to determine if the buffer is already valid.

Similarly for writes, the filesystem makes repeated calls into the buffer cache to locate the appropriate buffer into which the user data is copied. Whether the buffer is moved to the clean or dirty list of the vnode depends on the type of write being performed. For delayed writes (without the O_SYNC flag) the buffer can be placed on the dirty list and flushed at a later date.

For memory-mapped files, the VOP_MAP() function is called for the filesystem to validate before calling into the virtual memory (VM) subsystem to establish the mapping. Page faults that occur on the mapping result in a call back into the filesystem through the VOP_PAGEIN() vnode operation. To flush dirty pages to disk whether through the msync(S) system call, tearing down a mapping, or as a result of paging, the VOP_PAEGOUT() vnode operation is called.

Filesystem Support in Minix

The Minix operating system, compatible with UNIX V7 at the system call level, was written by Andrew Tanenbaum and described in his book *Operating Systems, Design and Implementation* [TANE87]. As a lecturer in operating systems for 15 years, he found it difficult to teach operating system concepts without any hands-on access to the source code. Because UNIX source code was not freely available, he wrote his own version, which although compatible at the system call level, worked very differently inside. The source code was listed in the book, but a charge was still made to obtain it. One could argue that if the source to Minix were freely available, Linux may never have been written. The source for Minix is now freely available across the Internet and is still a good, small kernel worthy of study.

Because Minix was used as a teaching tool, one of the goals was to allow students to work on development of various parts of the system. One way of achieving this was to move the Minix filesystem out of the kernel and into user space. This was a model that was also adopted by many of the microkernel implementations.

Minix Filesystem-Related Structures

Minix is logically divided into four layers. The lowest layer deals with process management, the second layer is for I/O tasks (device drivers), the third for server processes, and the top layer for user-level processes. The process management layer and the I/O tasks run together within the kernel address space. The server process layer handles memory management and filesystem support. Communication between the kernel, the filesystem, and the memory manager is performed through message passing.

There is no single `proc` structure in Minix as there is with UNIX and no `user` structure. Information that pertains to a process is described by three main structures that are divided between the kernel, the memory manager, and the file manager. For example, consider the implementation of `fork(S)`, as shown in Figure 8.3.

System calls are implemented by sending messages to the appropriate subsystem. Some can be implemented by the kernel alone, others by the memory manager, and others by the file manager. In the case of `fork(S)`, a message needs to be sent to the memory manager. Because the user process runs in user mode, it must still execute a hardware trap instruction to take it into the kernel. However, the system call handler in the kernel performs very little work other than sending the requested message to the right server, in this case the memory manager.

Each process is described by the `proc`, `mproc`, and `fproc` structures. Thus to handle `fork(S)` work must be performed by the memory manager, kernel, and file manager to initialize the new structures for the process. All file-related information is stored in the `fproc` structure, which includes the following:

`fp_workdir`. Current working directory

`fp_rootdir`. Current root directory.

`fp_filp`. The file descriptors for this process.

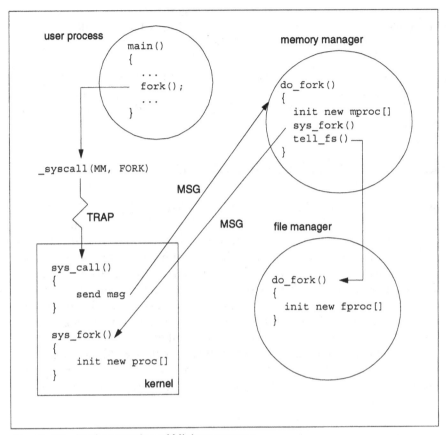

Figure 8.3 Implementation of Minix processes.

The file descriptor array contains pointers to filp structures that are very similar to the UNIX file structure. They contain a reference count, a set of flags, the current file offset for reading and writing, and a pointer to the inode for the file.

File I/O in Minix

In Minix, all file I/O and meta-data goes through the buffer cache. All buffers are held on a doubly linked list in order of access, with the least recently used buffers at the front of the list. All buffers are accessed through a hash table to speed buffer lookup operations. The two main interfaces to the buffer cache are through the get_block() and put_block() routines, which obtain and release buf structures respectively.

If a buffer is valid and within the cache, get_block() returns it; otherwise the data must be read from disk by calling the rw_block() function, which does little else other than calling dev_io().

Because all devices are managed by the device manager, dev_io() must send a message to the device manager in order to actually perform the I/O.

Reading from or writing to a file in Minix bears resemblance to its UNIX counterpart. Note, however, when first developed, Minix had a single filesystem and therefore much of the filesystem internals were spread throughout the read/write code paths.

Anyone familiar with UNIX internals will find many similarities in the Minix kernel. At the time it was written, the kernel was only 12,649 lines of code and is therefore still a good base to study UNIX-like principles and see how a kernel can be written in a modular fashion.

Pre-2.4 Linux Filesystem Support

The Linux community named their filesystem architecture the *Virtual File System Switch*, or Linux VFS which is a little of a misnomer because it was substantially different from the Sun VFS/vnode architecture and the SVR4 VFS architecture that preceded it. However, as with all POSIX-compliant, UNIX-like operating systems, there are many similarities between Linux and other UNIX variants.

The following sections describe the earlier implementations of Linux prior to the 2.4 kernel released, generally around the 1.2 timeframe. Later on, the differences introduced with the 2.4 kernel are highlighted with a particular emphasis on the style of I/O, which changed substantially.

For further details on the earlier Linux kernels see [BECK96]. For details on Linux filesystems, [BAR01] contains information about the filesystem architecture as well as details about some of the newer filesystem types supported on Linux.

Per-Process Linux Filesystem Structures

The main structures used in construction of the Linux VFS are shown in Figure 8.4 and are described in detail below.

Linux processes are defined by the `task_struct` structure, which contains information used for filesystem-related operations as well as the list of open file descriptors. The file-related fields are as follows:

```
unsigned short  umask;
struct inode    *root;
struct inode    *pwd;
```

The umask field is used in response to calls to set the umask. The root and pwd fields hold the root and current working directory fields to be used in pathname resolution.

The fields related to file descriptors are:

```
struct file     *filp[NR_OPEN];
fd_set          close_on_exec;
```

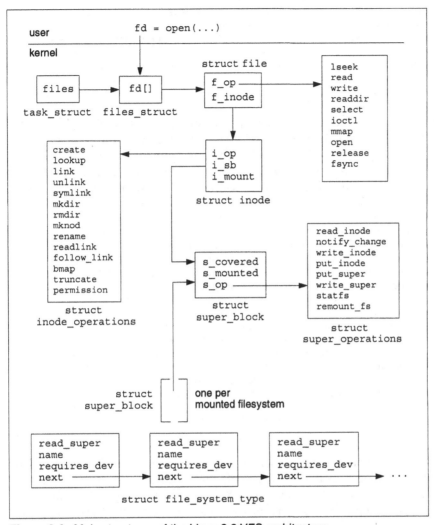

Figure 8.4 Main structures of the Linux 2.2 VFS architecture.

As with other UNIX implementations, file descriptors are used to index into a per-process array that contains pointers to the system file table. The `close_on_exec` field holds a bitmask describing all file descriptors that should be closed across an `exec(S)` system call.

The Linux File Table

The file table is very similar to other UNIX implementations although there are a few subtle differences. The main fields are shown here:

```
struct file {
    mode_t                  f_mode;     /* Access type */
```

```
    loff_t                  f_pos;      /* Current file pointer */
    unsigned short          f_flags;    /* Open flags */
    unsigned short          f_count;    /* Reference count (dup(S)) */
    struct inode            *f_inode;   /* Pointer to in-core inode */
    struct file_operations  *f_op;      /* Functions that can be */
                                        /* applied to this file */
};
```

The first five fields contain the usual type of file table information. The f_op field is a little different in that it describes the set of operations that can be invoked on this particular file. This is somewhat similar to the set of vnode operations. In Linux however, these functions are split into a number of different vectors and operate at different levels within the VFS framework. The set of file_operations is:

```
struct file_operations {
    int (*lseek)   (struct inode *, struct file *, off_t, int);
    int (*read)    (struct inode *, struct file *, char *, int);
    int (*write)   (struct inode *, struct file *, char *, int);
    int (*readdir) (struct inode *, struct file *,
                        struct dirent *, int);
    int (*select)  (struct inode *, struct file *,
                        int, select_table *);
    int (*ioctl)   (struct inode *, struct file *,
                        unsigned int, unsigned long);
    int (*mmap)    (struct inode *, struct file *, unsigned long,
                        size_t, int, unsigned long);
    int (*open)    (struct inode *, struct file *);
    int (*release) (struct inode *, struct file *);
    int (*fsync)   (struct inode *, struct file *);
};
```

Most of the functions here perform as expected. However, there are a few noticeable differences between some of these functions and their UNIX counterparts, or in some case, lack of UNIX counterpart. The ioctl() function, which typically refers to device drivers, can be interpreted at the VFS layer above the filesystem. This is primarily used to handle close-on-exec and the setting or clearing of certain flags.

The release() function, which is used for device driver management, is called when the file structure is no longer being used.

The Linux Inode Cache

Linux has a centralized inode cache as with earlier versions of UNIX. This is underpinned by the inode structure, and all inodes are held on a linked list headed by the first_inode kernel variable. The major fields of the inode together with any unusual fields are shown as follows:

```
struct inode {
    unsigned long           i_ino;      /* Inode number */
```

```
    atomic_t                    i_count;    /* Reference count */
    kdev_t                      i_dev;      /* Filesystem device */
    umode_t                     i_mode;     /* Type/access rights */
    nlink_t                     i_nlink;    /* # of hard links */
    uid_t                       i_uid;      /* User ID */
    gid_t                       i_gid;      /* Group ID */
    kdev_t                      i_rdev;     /* For device files */
    loff_t                      i_size;     /* File size */
    time_t                      i_atime;    /* Access time */
    time_t                      i_mtime;    /* Modification time */
    time_t                      i_ctime;    /* Creation time */
    unsigned long               i_blksize;  /* Fs block size */
    unsigned long               i_blocks;   /* # of blocks in file */
    struct inode_operations     *i_op;      /* Inode operations */
    struct super_block          *i_sb;      /* Superblock/mount */
    struct vm_area_struct        *i_mmap;    /* Mapped file areas */
    unsigned char               i_update;   /* Is inode current? */
    union {                                 /* One per fs type! */
        struct minix_inode_info minix_i;
        struct ext2_inode_info  ext2_i;
        ...
        void                    *generic_ip;
    } u;
};
```

Most of the fields listed here are self explanatory and common in meaning across most UNIX and UNIX-like operating systems. Note that the style of holding private, per-filesystem data is a little cumbersome. Instead of having a single pointer to per-filesystem data, the u element at the end of the structure contains a union of all possible private filesystem data structures. Note that for filesystem types that are not part of the distributed Linux kernel, the generic_ip field can be used instead.

Associated with each inode is a set of operations that can be performed on the file as follows:

```
struct inode_operations {
    struct file_operations *default_file_ops;
    int (*create)           (struct inode *, const char *, ...);
    int (*lookup)           (struct inode *, const char *, ...);
    int (*link)             (struct inode *, struct inode *, ...);
    int (*unlink)           (struct inode *, const char *, ...);
    int (*symlink)          (struct inode *, const char *, ...);
    int (*mkdir)            (struct inode *, const char *, ...);
    int (*rmdir)            (struct inode *, const char *, ...);
    int (*mknod)            (struct inode *, const char *, ...);
    int (*rename)           (struct inode *, const char *, ...);
    int (*readlink)         (struct inode *, char *,int);
    int (*follow_link)      (struct inode *, struct inode *, ...);
    int (*bmap)             (struct inode *, int);
    void (*truncate)        (struct inode *);
    int (*permission)       (struct inode *, int);
};
```

As with the file_operations structure, the functionality provided by most functions is obvious. The bmap() function is used for memory-mapped file support to map file blocks into the user address space.

The permission() function checks to ensure that the caller has the right access permissions.

Pathname Resolution

As shown in Figure 8.4, there are fields in the super_block and the inode structures that are used during pathname resolution, namely:

   s_mounted. This field points to the root inode of the filesystem and is accessed when moving from one filesystem over a mount point to another.

   s_covered. Points to the inode on which the filesystem is mounted and can therefore be used to handle "..".

   i_mount. If a file is mounted on, this field points to the root inode of the filesystem that is mounted.

Files are opened by calling the open_namei() function. Similar to its counterparts namei() and lookupname() found in pre-SVR4 and SVR4 kernels, this function parses the pathname, starting at either the root or pwd fields of the task_struct depending on whether the pathname is relative or absolute. A number of functions from the inode_operations and super_operations vectors are used to resolve the pathname. The lookup() function is called to obtain an inode. If the inode represents a symbolic link, the follow_link() inode operation is invoked to return the target inode. Internally, both functions may result in a call to the filesystem-independent iget() function, which results in a call to the super_operations function read_inode() to actually bring the inode in-core.

The Linux Directory Cache

The Linux directory cache, more commonly known as the *dcache*, originated in the ext2 filesystem before making its way into the filesystem-independent layer of the VFS. The dir_cache_entry structure, shown below, is the main component of the dcache; it holds a single *<name, inode pointer>* pair.

```
struct dir_cache_entry {
    struct hash_list            h;
    unsigned long               dev;
    unsigned long               dir;
    unsigned long               version;
    unsigned long               ino;
    unsigned char               name_len;
    char                        name[DCACHE_NAME_LEN];
    struct dir_cache_entry      **lru_head;
    struct dir_cache_entry      *next_lru, prev_lru;
};
```

The cache consists of an array of dir_cache_entry structures. The array, dcache[], has CACHE_SIZE doubly linked elements. There also exist HASH_QUEUES, hash queues accessible through the queue_tail[] and queue_head[] arrays.

Two functions, which follow, can be called to add an entry to the cache and perform a cache lookup.

```
void dcache_add(unsigned short dev, unsigned long dir,
            const char * name, int len, unsigned long ino)

int dcache_lookup(unsigned short dev, unsigned long dir,
            const char * name, int len)
```

The cache entries are hashed based on the dev and dir fields with dir being the inode of the directory in which the file resides. After a hash queue is found, the find_name() function is called to walk down the list of elements and see if the entry exists by performing a strncmp() between the name passed as an argument to dcache_lookup() and the name field of the dir_cache_entry structure.

The cache has changed throughout the development of Linux. For details of the dcache available in the 2.4 kernel series, see the section *The Linux 2.4 Directory Cache* later in this chapter.

The Linux Buffer Cache and File I/O

Linux employs a buffer cache for reading and writing blocks of data to and from disk. The I/O subsystem in Linux is somewhat restrictive in that all I/O must be of the same size. It can be changed, but once set, this size must be adhered to by any filesystem performing I/O.

Buffer cache buffers are described in the buffer_head structure, which is shown below:

```
struct buffer_head {
    char                *b_data;        /* pointer to data block */
    unsigned long       b_size;         /* block size */
    unsigned long       b_blocknr;      /* block number */
    dev_t               b_dev;          /* device (0 = free) */
    unsigned short      b_count;        /* users using this block */
    unsigned char       b_uptodate;     /* is block valid? */
    unsigned char       b_dirt;         /* 0-clean,1-dirty */
    unsigned char       b_lock;         /* 0-ok, 1-locked */
    unsigned char       b_req;          /* 0 if buffer invalidated */
    struct wait_queue   *b_wait;        /* buffer wait queue */
    struct buffer_head  *b_prev;        /* hash-queue linked list */
    struct buffer_head  *b_next;
    struct buffer_head  *b_prev_free;   /* buffer linked list */
    struct buffer_head  *b_next_free;
    struct buffer_head  *b_this_page;   /* buffers in one page */
    struct buffer_head  *b_reqnext;     /* request queue */
};
```

Unlike UNIX, there are no flags in the buffer structure. In its place, the b_uptodate and b_dirt fields indicate whether the buffer contents are valid and whether the buffer is dirty (needs writing to disk).

Dirty buffers are periodically flushed to disk by the *update* process or the bdflush kernel thread. The section *The 2.4 Linux Buffer Cache,* later in this chapter, describes how bdflush works.

Valid buffers are hashed by device and block number and held on a doubly linked list using the b_next and b_pref fields of the buffer_head structure.

Users can call getblk() and brelse() to obtain a valid buffer and release it after they have finished with it. Because the buffer is already linked on the appropriate hash queue, brelse() does little other than check to see if anyone is waiting for the buffer and issue the appropriate wake-up call.

I/O is performed by calling the ll_rw_block() function, which is implemented above the device driver layer. If the I/O is required to be synchronous, the calling thread will issue a call to wait_on_buffer(), which will result in the thread sleeping until the I/O is completed.

Linux file I/O in the earlier versions of the kernel followed the older style UNIX model of reading and writing all file data through the buffer cache. The implementation is not too different from the buffer cache-based systems described in earlier chapters and so it won't be described further here.

Linux from the 2.4 Kernel Series

The Linux 2.4 series of kernels substantially changes the way that filesystems are implemented. Some of the more visible changes are:

- File data goes through the Linux page cache rather than directly through the buffer cache. There is still a tight relationship between the buffer cache and page cache, however.

- The dcache is tightly integrated with the other filesystem-independent structures such that every open file has an entry in the dcache and each dentry (which replaces the old dir_cache_entry structure) is referenced from the file structure.

- There has been substantial rework of the various operations vectors and the introduction of a number of functions more akin to the SVR4 page cache style vnodeops.

- A large rework of the SMP-based locking scheme results in finer grain kernel locks and therefore better SMP performance.

The migration towards the page cache for file I/O actually started prior to the 2.4 kernel series, with file data being read through the page cache while still retaining a close relationship with the buffer cache.

There is enough similarity between the Linux 2.4 kernels and the SVR4 style of I/O that it is possible to port SVR4 filesystems over to Linux and retain much of the SVR4 page cache-based I/O paths, as demonstrated by the port of VxFS to Linux for which the I/O path uses very similar code.

Main Structures Used in the 2.4.x Kernel Series

The main structures of the VFS have remained largely intact as shown in Figure 8.5. One major change was the tight integration between the dcache (which itself has largely been rewritten) and the inode cache. Each open file has a dentry (which replaces the old dir_cache_entry structure) referenced from the file structure, and each dentry is underpinned by an in-core inode structure.

The file_operations structure gained an extra two functions. The check_media_change() function is used with block devices that support changeable media such as CD drives. This allows the VFS layer to check for media changes and therefore determine whether the filesystem should be remounted to recognize the new media. The revalidate() function is used following a media change to restore consistency of the block device.

The inode_operations structure gained an extra three functions. The readpage() and writepage() functions were introduced to provide a means for the memory management subsystem to read and write pages of data. The smap() function is used to support swapping to regular files.

There was no change to the super_operations structure. There were additional changes at the higher layers of the kernel. The fs_struct structure was introduced that included dentry structures for the root and current working directories. This is referenced from the task_struct structure. The files_struct continued to hold the file descriptor array.

The Linux 2.4 Directory Cache

The dentry structure, shown below, is used to represent an entry in the 2.4 dcache. This is referenced by the f_dentry field of the file structure.

```
struct dentry {
    atomic_t                    d_count;
    unsigned int                d_flags;
    struct inode                *d_inode;      /* inode for this entry */
    struct dentry               *d_parent;     /* parent directory */
    struct list_head            d_hash;        /* lookup hash list */
    struct list_head            d_lru;         /* d_count = 0 LRU list */
    struct list_head            d_child;       /* child of parent list */
    struct list_head            d_subdirs;     /* our children */
    struct list_head            d_alias;       /* inode alias list */
    int                         d_mounted;
    struct qstr                 d_name;
    struct dentry_operations    *d_op;
    struct super_block          *d_sb;         /* root of dentry tree */
    unsigned long               d_vfs_flags;
    void                        *d_fsdata;     /* fs-specific data */
    unsigned char               d_iname[DNAME_INLINE_LEN];
};
```

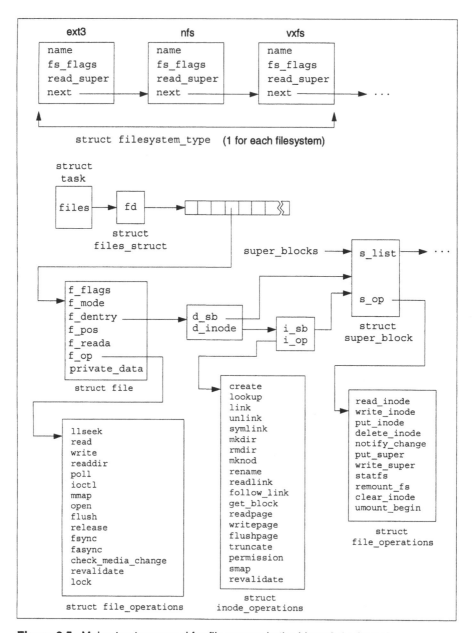

Figure 8.5 Main structures used for file access in the Linux 2.4.x kernel.

Each dentry has a pointer to the parent dentry (d_parent) as well as a list of child dentry structures (d_child).

The dentry_operations structure defines a set of dentry operations, which are invoked by the kernel. Note, that filesystems can provide their own vector if they wish to change the default behavior. The set of operations is:

d_revalidate. This function is called during pathname resolution to determine whether the dentry is still valid. If no longer valid, d_put is invoked to remove the entry.

d_hash. This function can be supplied by the filesystem if it has an unusual naming scheme. This is typically used by filesystems that are not native to UNIX.

d_compare. This function is used to compare file names.

d_delete. This function is called when d_count reaches zero. This happens when no one is using the dentry but the entry is still in the cache.

d_release. This function is called prior to a dentry being deallocated.

d_iput. This allows filesystems to provide their own version of iput().

To better understand the interactions between the dcache and the rest of the kernel, the following sections describe some of the common file operations.

Opening Files in Linux

The sys_open() function is the entry point in the kernel for handling the open(S) system call. This calls get_unused_fd() to allocate a new file descriptor and then calls filp_open(), which in turn calls open_namei() to obtain a dentry for the file. If successful, dentry_open() is called to initialize a new file structure, perform the appropriate linkage, and set up the file structure.

The first step is to perform the usual pathname resolution functions. link_path_walk() performs most of the work in this regard. This initially involves setting up a nameidata structure, which contains the dentry of the directory from which to start the search (either the root directory or the pwd field from the fs_struct if the pathname is relative). From this dentry, the inode (d_inode) gives the starting point for the search.

There are two possibilities here as the following code fragment shows:

```
dentry = cached_lookup(nd->dentry, &this, LOOKUP_CONTINUE);
if (!dentry) {
    dentry = real_lookup(nd->dentry, &this, LOOKUP_CONTINUE);
}
```

Note that the argument is the pathname component that is currently being worked on. The cached_lookup() function calls d_lookup() to perform the lookup in the dcache. If an entry is found and the filesystem has provided its own d_revalidate function, this is where it is called from. The work performed by d_lookup() is fairly straightforward in that it locates the appropriate hash queue, walks this list, and tries to locate the appropriate entry.

If the entry is not in the cache, the real_lookup() function is invoked. Taking the inode of the parent and locating the inode_operations vector, the lookup() function is invoked to read in the inode from disk. Generally this will involve a call out of the filesystem to iget(), which might find the inode in the inode cache; if the inode is not already cached, a new inode must be allocated and a call is made back into the filesystem to read the inode through the super_operations function read_inode(). The final job of iget() is to call d_add() to add the new entry to the dcache.

Closing Files in Linux

The sys_close() function is the entry point into the kernel for handling the close(S) system call. After locating the appropriate file structure, the filp_close() function is called; this invokes the flush() function in the file_operations vector to write dirty data to disk and then calls fput() to release the file structure. This involves decrementing f_count. If the count does not reach zero the work is complete (a previous call to dup(S) was made). If this is the last reference, a call to the release() function in the file_operations vector is made to let the filesystem perform any last-close operations it may wish to make.

A call to dput() is then made. If this is the last hold on the dentry, iput() is called to release the inode from the cache. The put_inode() function from the super_operations vector is then called.

The 2.4 Linux Buffer Cache

The buffer cache underwent a number of changes from the earlier implementations. Although it retained most of the earlier fields, there were a number of new fields that were introduced. Following is the complete structure:

```
struct buffer_head {
    struct buffer_head *b_next;       /* Hash queue list */
    unsigned long      b_blocknr;     /* block number */
    unsigned short     b_size;        /* block size */
    unsigned short     b_list;        /* List this buffer is on */
    kdev_t             b_dev;         /* device (B_FREE = free) */
    atomic_t           b_count;       /* users using this block */
    kdev_t             b_rdev;        /* Real device */
    unsigned long      b_state;       /* buffer state bitmap */
    unsigned long      b_flushtime;   /* Time when (dirty) buffer */
                                      /* should be written */
    struct buffer_head *b_next_free;  /* lru/free list linkage */
    struct buffer_head *b_prev_free;  /* linked list of buffers */
    struct buffer_head *b_this_page;  /* list of buffers in page */
    struct buffer_head *b_reqnext;    /* request queue */

    struct buffer_head **b_pprev;     /* linked list of hash-queue */
    char               *b_data;       /* pointer to data block */
    struct page        *b_page;       /* page this bh is mapped to */
    void (*b_end_io)(struct buffer_head *bh, int uptodate);
    void               *b_private;    /* reserved for b_end_io */

    unsigned long      b_rsector;     /* buffer location on disk */
```

```
        wait_queue_head_t    b_wait;
        struct inode *       b_inode;
        struct list_head     b_inode_buffers;/* inode dirty buffers */
    };
```

The b_end_io field allows the user of the buffer to specify a completion routine that is invoked when the I/O is completed. The b_private field can be used to store filesystem-specific data.

Because the size of all I/O operations must be of fixed size as defined by a call to set_blocksize(), performing I/O to satisfy page faults becomes a little messy if the I/O block size is less than the page size. To alleviate this problem, a page may be mapped by multiple buffers that must be passed to ll_rw_block() in order to perform the I/O. It is quite likely, but not guaranteed, that these buffers will be coalesced by the device driver layer if they are adjacent on disk.

The b_state flag was introduced to hold the many different flags that buffers can now be marked with. The set of flags is:

BH_Uptodate. Set to 1 if the buffer contains valid data.

BH_Dirty. Set to 1 if the buffer is dirty.

BH_Lock. Set to 1 if the buffer is locked.

BH_Req. Set to 0 if the buffer has been invalidated.

BH_Mapped. Set to 1 if the buffer has a disk mapping.

BH_New. Set to 1 if the buffer is new and not yet written out.

BH_Async. Set to 1 if the buffer is under end_buffer_io_async I/O.

BH_Wait_IO. Set to 1 if the kernel should write out this buffer.

BH_launder. Set to 1 if the kernel should throttle on this buffer.

The b_inode_buffers field allows filesystems to keep a linked list of modified buffers. For operations that require dirty data to be synced to disk, the new buffer cache provides routines to sync these buffers to disk. As with other buffer caches, Linux employs a daemon whose responsibility is to flush dirty buffers to disk on a regular basis. There are a number of parameters that can be changed to control the frequency of flushing. For details, see the bdflush(8) man page.

File I/O in the 2.4 Linux Kernel

The following sections describe the I/O paths in the 2.4 Linux kernel series, showing how data is read from and written to regular files through the page cache. For a much more detailed view of how filesystems work in Linux see Chapter 14.

Reading through the Linux Page Cache

Although Linux does not provide interfaces identical to the segmap style page cache interfaces of SVR4, the paths to perform a file read, as shown in Figure Figure 8.6, appear at a high level very similar in functionality to the VFS/vnode interfaces.

The `sys_read()` function is executed in response to a `read(S)` system call. After obtaining the `file` structure from the file descriptor, the `read()` function of the `file_operations` vector is called. Many filesystems simply set this function to `generic_file_read()`. If the page covering the range of bytes to read is already in the cache, the data can be simply copied into the user buffer. If the page is not present, it must be allocated and the filesystem is called, through the `inode_operations` function `readpage()`, to read the page of data from disk.

The `block_read_full_page()` is typically called by many filesystems to satisfy the `readpage()` operation. This function is responsible for allocating the appropriate number of buffer heads to perform the I/O, making repeated calls into the filesystem to get the appropriate block maps.

Writing through the Linux Page Cache

The main flow through the kernel for handling the `write(S)` system call is similar to handling a `read(S)` system call. As with reading, many file systems set the `write()`, function of their `file_operations` vector to `generic_file_write()`, which is called by `sys_write()` in response to a `write(S)` system call. Most of the work performed involves looping on a page-by-page basis with each page either being found in the cache or being created. For each page, data is copied from the user buffer into the page, and `write_one_page()` is called to write the page to disk.

Microkernel Support for UNIX Filesystems

Throughout the 1980s and early 1990s there was a great deal of interest in microkernel technology. As the name suggests, microkernels do not by themselves offer the full features of UNIX or other operating systems but export a set of features and interfaces that allow construction of new services, for example, emulation of UNIX at a system call level. Microkernels do however provide the capability of allowing a clean interface between various components of the OS, paving the way for distributed operating systems or customization of OS services provided.

This section provides an overview of Chorus and Mach, the two most popular microkernel technologies, and describes how each supports and performs file I/O. For an overview of SVR4 running on the Chorus microkernel, refer to the section *The Chorus Microkernel*, a bit later in this chapter.

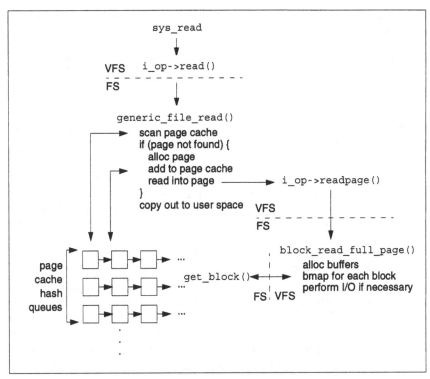

Figure 8.6   Reading through the Linux page cache.

High-Level Microkernel Concepts

Both Mach and Chorus provide a basic microkernel that exports the following main characteristics:

- The ability to define an execution environment, for example, the construction of a UNIX process. In Chorus, this is the *actor* and in Mach, the *task*. Each defines an address space, one or more threads of execution, and the means to communicate with other actors/tasks through IPC (*Inter-Process Communication*). Actors/tasks can reside in user or kernel space.

    The Chorus actor is divided into a number of *regions*, each a virtual address range backed by a *segment* that is managed by a *mapper*. The segment is often the representation of secondary storage, such as a file. For example, one can think of a mapped file being represented by a region in the process address space. The region is a window into a segment (the file), and page faults are handled by calls to the segment mapper, which will request data from the filesystem.

The Mach task is divided into a number of *VM Objects* that typically map secondary storage handled by an *external pager*.

■ Each actor/task may contain multiple threads of execution. A traditional UNIX process would be defined as an actor/task with a single thread. Threads in one actor/task communicate with threads in other actors/tasks by sending messages to ports.

■ Hardware access is managed a little differently between Chorus and Mach. The only device that Chorus knows about is the clock. By providing interfaces to dynamically connect interrupt handlers and trap handlers, devices can be managed outside of the microkernel.

Mach on the other hand exports two interfaces, `device_read()` and `device_write()`, which allow access to device drivers that are embedded within the microkernel.

Both provide the mechanisms by which binary compatibility with other operating systems can be achieved. On Chorus, supervisor actors (those residing in the kernel address space) can attach trap handlers. Mach provides the mechanisms by which a task can redirect a trap back into the user task that made the trap. This is discussed in more detail later.

Using the services provided by both Chorus and Mach it is possible to construct a binary-compatible UNIX kernel. The basic implementation of such and the methods by which files are read and written are the subject of the next two sections.

The Chorus Microkernel

The main components of an SVR4-based UNIX implementation on top of Chorus are shown in Figure 8.7. This is how SVR4 was implemented. Note however, it is entirely possible to implement UNIX as a single actor.

There are a number of supervisor actors implementing SVR4 UNIX. Those that comprise the majority of the UNIX kernel are:

Process Manager (PM). All UNIX process management tasks are handled here. This includes the equivalent of the `proc` structure, file descriptor management, and so on. The PM acts as the system call handler in that it handles traps that occur through users executing a system call.

Object Manager (OM). The Object Manager, also called the File Manager, is responsible for the majority of file related operations and implements the main UNIX filesystems. The OM acts as a mapper for UNIX file access.

STREAMS Manager (STM). As well as managing STREAMS devices such as pipes, TTYs, networking, and named pipes, the STM also implements part of the NFS protocol.

Communication between UNIX actors is achieved through message passing. Actors can either reside in a single node or be distributed across different nodes.

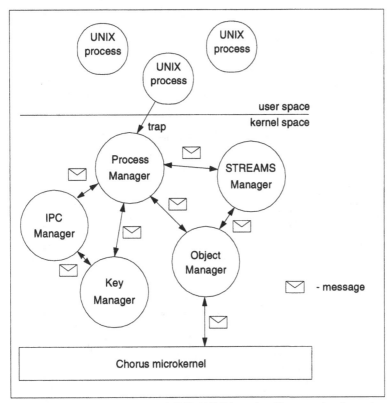

Figure 8.7   Implementation of SVR4 UNIX on the Chorus microkernel.

Handling Read Operations in Chorus

Figure 8.8 shows the steps taken to handle a file read in a Chorus-based SVR4 system. The PM provides a trap handler in order to be called when a UNIX process executes the appropriate hardware instruction to generate a trap for a system call. For each process there is state similar to the proc and user structures of UNIX. From here, the file descriptor can be used to locate the *capability* (identifier) of the segment underpinning the file. All the PM needs to do is make an sgRead() call to enter the microkernel.

Associated with each segment is a cache of pages. If the page covering the range of the read is in the cache there is no work to do other than copy the data to the user buffer. If the page is not present, the microkernel must send a message to the mapper associated with this segment. In this case, the mapper is located inside the OM. A call must then be made through the VFS/vnode layer as in a traditional SVR4-based UNIX operating system to request the data from the filesystem.

Although one can see similarities between the Chorus model and the traditional UNIX model, there are some fundamental differences. Firstly, the filesystem only gets to know about the read operation if there is a cache miss

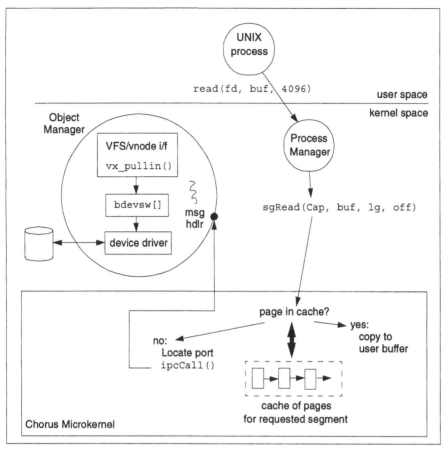

Figure 8.8   Handling read operations in the Chorus microkernel.

within the microkernel. This prevents the filesystem from understanding the I/O pattern and therefore using its own rules to determine read ahead policies. Secondly, this Chorus implementation of SVR4 required changes to the vnode interfaces to export a `pullIn()` operation to support page fault handling. This involved replacing the `getpage()` operation in SVR4-based filesystems. Note that buffer cache and device access within the OM closely mirror their equivalent subsystems in UNIX.

Handling Write Operations in Chorus

Write handling in Chorus is similar to handling read operations. The microkernel exports an `sgWrite()` operation allowing the PM to write to the segment. The main difference between reading and writing occurs when a file is extended or a write over a hole occurs. Both operations are handled by the microkernel requesting a page for read/write access from the mapper. As part of handling the `pullIn()` operation, the filesystem must allocate the appropriate backing store.

The final operation is for the PM to change its understanding of the file size.

As with the getpage() operation of SVR4, the vnode interface in Chorus was extended such that filesystems must export a pushOut() operation allowing the microkernel to flush dirty pages to disk.

The Mach Microkernel

UNIX processes are implemented in a Mach-based UNIX system as a single threaded task. There are three main components that come into play when emulating UNIX as shown in Figure 8.9.

Each UNIX process includes an emulation library linked in to the address space of the process. When the process wishes to execute a system call it issues the appropriate trap instruction, which results in the process entering the microkernel. This is managed by a trap emulator, which redirects the request to the emulation library within the process. Most of the UNIX emulation is handled by the UNIX server task although the emulation library can handle some simple system calls using information that is shared between each UNIX process and the UNIX server task. This information includes per-process related information that allows the emulation library to handle system calls such as getpid(S), getuid(S), and getrlimit(S).

The UNIX server has a number of threads that can respond to requests from a number of different UNIX processes. The UNIX server task is where most of the UNIX kernel code is based. The inode pager thread works in a similar manner to the Chorus mapper threads by responding to page-in and page-out requests from the microkernel. This is a particularly important concept in Mach UNIX emulation because all file I/O is performed through mappings that reside within the UNIX process.

Handling Read Operations in Mach

Each file that is opened by a UNIX process results in a 64KB mapping of the file. This mapping window can be moved throughout the file in response to a request from within the UNIX emulation library. If there are multiple readers or writers, the various mappings are protected through the use of a token-based scheme.

When a read(S) system call is executed, the microkernel redirects the call back into the emulation library. If the area of the file requested is already covered by the mapping and this process has a valid token, all there is to do is copy the data to the user buffer and return. Much of the difficulty in the Mach scheme results from token management and the fact that the emulation library is not protected from the user process in any way; the process can overwrite any part of the data area of the library it wishes. To acquire the token, the emulation library must communicate with the UNIX server task that in turn will communicate with other UNIX process tasks.

In addition to token management, the UNIX server task implements appropriate UNIX filesystem access, including the handling of page faults that occur on the mapping. On first access to a file mapping in the emulation library,

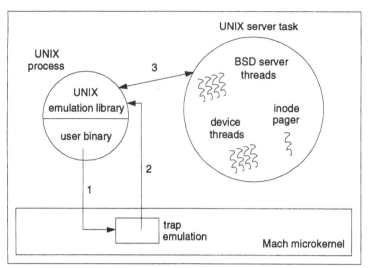

Figure 8.9 Emulating UNIX using the Mach microkernel.

the microkernel will send a `memory_object_data_request()` to the external pager responsible for backing the object. The inode pager must read the data from the filesystem in order to satisfy the request. The Mach file I/O paths are shown in Figure 8.10.

Handling Write Operations in Mach

The paths followed to implement the `write(S)` system call are almost identical to the paths followed for `read(S)`. As with Chorus, the interesting areas surround extending files and writing over holes.

For a write fault on a page not within the current mapping or a write that involves either extending the file or filling a hole, the inode pager will return `memory_object_data_unavailable`, which results in the microkernel returning a zero-filled page. If the file size is extended, the emulation library updates its understanding of the new size. At this stage there is no update to the on-disk structure that would make it difficult to implement transaction-based filesystems.

The actual changes to the disk representation of the file occur when the token is recalled, when the mapping is changed, or when the microkernel needs to flush dirty pages and sends a request to the inode pager. By revoking a token that resulted from either a hole write or a file extension, the UNIX server will invoke a `memory_object_lock_request`, which results in the kernel pushing the modified pages to disk through the inode pager. It is only when pages are written to disk that the UNIX server allocates disk blocks.

What Happened to Microkernel Technology?

During the early 1990s it seemed to be only a matter of time before all the

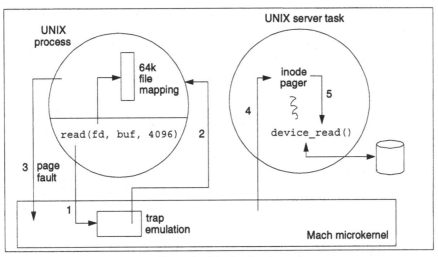

Figure 8.10   Reading from a file in the Mach microkernel.

monolithic UNIX implementations would be replaced by microkernel-based implementations. Mach was the basis of the OSF (Open Software Foundation) kernel and Chorus was employed by a number of UNIX vendors. The only UNIX vendor using microkernel technology as the core of its UNIX based operating system is Digital (now Compaq), which used OSF/1. The GNU Hurd also uses Mach as its base. Chorus has been used for a number of different projects within Sun Microsystems.

Resistance to change is always a factor to consider when moving support from one operating system to another. The cost of replacing one OS technology with another for no perceived gain in user functionality is certainly another. As UNIX evolved, moving the monolithic source base to a microkernel-based implementation was a costly project. Porting filesystems is expensive and the amount of code reuse was not as high as it could have been. The original attempts at *serverization* of UNIX were certainly one of the main reasons why the porting efforts were so high. On Chorus, replacing the multiple different actors with a single UNIX actor, together with emulation of certain SVR4 features such as the segmap driver, would have made Chorus a more appealing solution.

Having said all of that, microkernels have their place in various niche markets, but some large opportunities were missed to really capitalize on the technology.

There is a wide range of documentation available on both the Chorus and Mach microkernels. For a single paper that describes microkernels, their UNIX emulation, and how file I/O works, see [ARMA92].

Summary

In the 1980s and early 1990s, there was a lot of consolidation around the Sun VFS/vnode interface with many of the commercial UNIX vendors adopting the interface to some degree. This architecture has still remained largely intact with only a few changes over the last decade.

The Linux kernel has seen a huge amount of change over the last few years with the VFS layer still in a state of flux. This is one of the few operating systems that still shows a huge amount of new development and has by far the largest number of filesystems supported.

By looking at the different filesystem architectures, one can see a large degree of similarity among them all. After the basic concepts have been grasped, locating the structures that pertain to filesystem implementations and following the code paths to get a high level overview of how filesystems are implemented is a relatively straightforward task. Therefore, readers new to operating systems are recommended to follow the earlier, more compact implementations first.

Disk-Based Filesystem Case Studies

This chapter describes the implementation of three different filesystems: the VERITAS Filesystem, VxFS, has also been ported to many versions of UNIX and has been the most successful of the "commercially" available filesystems; the UFS filesystem, first introduced in BSD UNIX as the *Fast File System*, has been ported to most versions of UNIX; with the proliferation of Linux systems, the ext2 filesystem and its successor ext3 are widely known and have been documented extensively.

The VERITAS Filesystem

Development on the VERITAS filesystem, VxFS, started in the late 1980s with the first implementation for SVR4.0. Over the past decade, VxFS has grown to be the single most commercially successful filesystem for UNIX, with ports to many versions of UNIX, Linux, and microkernel-based UNIX implementations. At the time of writing, VERITAS directly supports Solaris, HP-UX, AIX, and Linux as its core platforms.

VxFS, a journaling, extent-based filesystem, is also one of the most feature-rich filesystems available and one of the most scalable and performant. This is the result of many years of development over many platforms from single CPU machines to 64-way enterprise-class SMP machines. As such, VxFS has been designed to automatically tune itself to the underlying platform and system resources.

VxFS Feature Overview

The following sections highlight the main features available with VxFS. At the time of writing, this covers VxFS version 3.5. Later chapters describe some of these features in more detail.

Extent-Based Allocation

Most traditional UNIX filesystems are block based such that each time data is allocated to a file, the blocks allocated correspond to the filesystem block size. If the block size is 4KB, a 16KB file will have four blocks. With the traditional scheme of mapping blocks from the inode, a large file quickly goes into indirect blocks, double indirects, and even triple indirects. There are two main problems with this approach, which results in a degradation in performance:

1. Blocks allocated to the file are unlikely to be contiguous on disk. Accessing the file therefore may result in a significant amount of disk head movement.

2. When reading data from anything other than the first few blocks, a number of reads must be issued to locate indirect, double, or triple indirect blocks that reference the block that needs to be accessed.

VxFS is an *extent-based* filesystem. Regardless of the block size chosen for a VxFS filesystem, which can be 1KB, 2KB, 4KB, or 8KB, data can be allocated in larger contiguous blocks called *extents*. The minimum size of an extent is identical to the filesystem block size. However, a file can have a single extent up to the maximum size of a file.

To give an example of how this works in practice, consider the following program, which creates a file and issues a series of 512-byte writes:

```
#include <sys/types.h>
#include <sys/stat.h>
#include <fcntl.h>

main()
{
        char    buf[512];
        int     i, fd;

        fd = open("testfile", O_CREAT|O_WRONLY, 0777);
        for (i=0 ; i<100 ; i++) {
                write(fd, buf, 512);
        }
}
```

Taking a new VxFS filesystem with a block size of 1KB and running the above program, the result will be a file with the following extents, shown from within fsdb, as follows:

```
> 5i
inode structure at 0x00000449.0100
type IFREG mode 100755  nlink 1  uid 0  gid 1  size 102400
atime 1017289300 420007  (Wed Mar 27 20:21:40 2002)
mtime 1017289300 430106  (Wed Mar 27 20:21:40 2002)
ctime 1017289300 430106  (Wed Mar 27 20:21:40 2002)
aflags 0 orgtype 1 eopflags 0 eopdata 0
fixextsize/fsindex 0  rdev/reserve/dotdot/matchino 0
blocks 100  gen 285552327  version 0 33  iattrino 0
de:  1304 1116     0    0    0    0    0    0    0    0
des:   96    4     0    0    0    0    0    0    0    0
ie:    0    0
ies:   0
```

The "5i" command displays inode number 5. The extents allocated to this file are highlighted. Note that this is almost the ideal case. There are two extents starting at block numbers 1304 and 1116 respectively. The des field indicates the size of each extent in filesystem block-size chunks. Thus the first 96 blocks of the file are contiguous followed by an extent of 4 contiguous blocks.

If a new file needs creating of a particular size, a single call can be made by using the setext command to allocate the file with a single contiguous extent. This is shown in the next section.

VxFS Extent Attributes

The default algorithms used to allocate extents to a file are based on the I/O pattern. For example, if a file is created and the file is written to sequentially, the first extent allocated will be a power of two greater than the size of the write. The extents allocated after this first write increase in size as the sequential writes continue to be issued. By allocating larger and larger extents in this manner, an attempt is made to ensure that as many blocks as possible are contiguous on disk. If a file is closed and the last write occupies only a small amount of a large extent, the extent is shortened and the remaining space returned to the free pool.

When creating a new file, if the size of the file is known prior to creation, the file extents may be pre-allocated. This can be achieved using the setext command or by use of the VX_SETEXT ioctl. The example below shows how a 100MB file is created using setext:

```
# > myfile
# setext -e 1024 -r 1024 -f chgsize myfile
# ls -l myfile
-rw-r--r--  1 root     other    1048576 Mar 29 13:36 myfile
```

The -e argument specifies a fixed extent size to be used for all allocations to this file. The -r field preallocates space to the file. Because the extent size is specified as 1024 blocks and a request has been made to preallocate 1024 blocks, this should result in a single extent of 1024 blocks being allocated. The -f option specifies that the reservation should be made immediately. The following output from fsdb shows the inode allocated and the extent allocated to this file.

```
# fsdb -F vxfs /dev/vx/rdsk/fs1
> 4i
inode structure at 0x00000449.0000
type IFREG mode 100644  nlink 1  uid 0  gid 1  size 1048576
atime 1017437793 230001  (Fri Mar 29 13:36:33 2002)
mtime 1017437793 230001  (Fri Mar 29 13:36:33 2002)
ctime 1017437805 125000  (Fri Mar 29 13:36:45 2002)
aflags 0 orgtype 1 eopflags 0 eopdata 0
fixextsize/fsindex 1024  rdev/reserve/dotdot/matchino 1024
blocks 1024  gen 391  version 0 7  iattrino 0
de:  2048    0    0    0    0    0    0    0    0    0
des: 1024    0    0    0    0    0    0    0    0    0
ie:    0    0
ies:   0
```

In this case, the file has a single direct extent (de) starting at block address 2048. This extent is 1024 blocks in size (des). The reserve field in the inode is also set to 1024 blocks. If this file were to be truncated, the size in the inode would be changed but the file would retain the number of blocks stored in the reservation.

Following the preceding example, if the extent size were set to 512 blocks and the setext call made as follows:

```
# > myfile
# setext -e 512 -r 1024 -f chgsize myfile
```

then the minimum size of an extent added to myfile will be 512 blocks. Where possible, the filesystem will attempt to allocate contiguous extents. If successful, the extents will be coalesced to create a single extent. Thus, in the above example, even though one would expect to see two extents of 512 blocks allocated to the file, a single extent is quite likely to be seen from within fsdb.

There are other extent attributes that can be set on a file as shown below:

- -f align. With this attribute, extents allocated to a file should be aligned on extent size boundaries where the extent size is specified using the -e option.
- -f chgsize. This attribute is used to change the size of the file.
- -f contig. This attribute indicates that any reservation should be allocated contiguously.
- -f noreserve. This option limits the size of the file. Once the space preallocated to the file has been used, the file cannot be further extended.
- -f trim. If a file has been given a specific reservation and the file size is less than the reservation, once the file is closed, the reservation is trimmed to the size of the file.

The following example shows how reservation works in conjunction with the trim option. This also shows the getext command, which can be used to display a file's extent attributes.

```
# dd if=/dev/zero of=8k bs=8192 count=1
1+0 records in
1+0 records out
# ls -l 8k
-rw-r--r--    1 root      other        8192 Mar 29 15:46 8k
# > myfile
# setext -e 512 -r 1024 -f trim myfile
# getext myfile
myfile:          Bsize 1024  Reserve    1024  Extent Size     512
# cat 8k >> myfile
# ls -l
total 2064
-rw-r--r--    1 root      other        8192 Mar 29 15:46 8k
drwxr-xr-x    2 root      root           96 Mar 29 15:46 lost+found
-rw-r--r--    1 root      other        8192 Mar 29 15:46 myfile
```

An 8KB file is created (for the purpose of copying only) and myfile is then created with an extent size of 512 blocks and a reservation of 1024 blocks. The trim option is also set. 8KB of data is then written to the file. The extent allocated to the file is shown below:

```
> 5i
inode structure at 0x00000449.0100
type IFREG mode 100644  nlink 1  uid 0  gid 1  size 8192
atime 1017445593 220000  (Fri Mar 29 15:46:33 2002)
mtime 1017445616 410003  (Fri Mar 29 15:46:56 2002)
ctime 1017445616 410003  (Fri Mar 29 15:46:56 2002)
aflags 0 orgtype 1 eopflags 0 eopdata 0
fixextsize/fsindex 512   rdev/reserve/dotdot/matchino 8
blocks 512   gen 1176   version 0 9   iattrino 0
de:  2048    0    0    0    0    0    0    0    0    0
des:  512    0    0    0    0    0    0    0    0    0
ie:    0    0
ies:   0
```

Although only 8KB was written to the file, the minimum extent size is 512 blocks, so a 512-block extent is allocated. Note that the reservation has been set to 8 blocks (8KB in this case) due to the trim option. If the file were truncated to zero, it would still retain 8 blocks as marked by the reservation.

Caching Advisories

Through use of the VX_SETCACHE ioctl, VxFS allows a number of different caching advisories to be set on a file that controls the manner in which I/O takes place. The advisories, which allow for direct I/O, unbuffered I/O, and data synchronous I/O are described in the section *Data and Attribute Caching* in Chapter 3.

In addition to these advisories, VxFS also implements *discovered direct I/O*. This is similar to direct I/O but is performed without user intervention. For I/O operations of specific sizes, determined by VxFS, the I/O is performed as a direct I/O, assuming the buffer and I/O size meet certain alignment requirements.

User and Group Quotas

VxFS supports both user and group quotas allowing limits to be set on both the number of files allocated and the number of blocks used. For both types of quotas, the following two limits apply:

Hard limit. This limit cannot be exceeded under any circumstance. Attempts to allocate more files or blocks will fail.

Soft limit. This limit can be exceeded temporarily for a specified time limit after which it defaults to seven days. After the time limit has expired, no further allocations can be made.

For more details on VxFS quotas, see the section *User and Group Quotas* in Chapter 5.

Filesystem Snapshots / Checkpoints

VxFS supports a number of different snapshot mechanisms, both persistent and non persistent, across system reboots or mount operations. Chapter 12 describes these mechanisms in more detail.

Panic Free and I/O Error Handling Policies

Unusual in filesystem code, there is no explicit call within VxFS to panic the filesystem. If errors are detected, such as an I/O error, VxFS disables access to specific filesystem structures while still allowing access to other structures on disk. For example, when reading an inode, VxFS performs validation of the inode to ensure that the structure is intact. If the inode fails validation, it is marked bad and a flag is set to perform a full fsck. However, access can continue to the rest of the filesystem. The same is also true when reading other filesystem structures.

This policy became problematic with the introduction of fiber channel in which the vulnerability of such a hardware configuration became relatively commonplace. Over time, cables were accidently unplugged, resulting in temporary I/O errors causing VxFS to mark inodes bad. This resulted in a full fsck to repair the damaged filesystem.

The I/O error-handling policies were modified to allow for this case and also to give administrators more flexibility on how they wished to handle I/O errors. The options are chosen by setting the ioerror option of the VxFS mount command to one of the following:

disable. If this option is selected, VxFS will disable the file system after detecting an I/O error. The file system can then be safely unmounted allowing the problem causing the error to be corrected. Typically, after the problem has been repaired, a fsck replay should be sufficient to make the filesystem structurally sound, at which point the file system can be mounted again. The disable option should be selected in environments where the underlying storage is redundant, such as with RAID-5 or mirrored (RAID-1) disks.

nodisable. If selected, when VxFS detects an I/O error it will contain the error and continue running. This policy is close to the traditional VxFS error handling model in which access to certain structures is prevented but the system continues to run. With this option, errors detected while reading inode meta-data will result in the inode being marked bad.

wdisable | mwdisable. By specifying either the wdisable (write disable) option or mwdisable (metadata-write disable) option, the file system is disabled or degraded as shown in Table 9.1. The wdisable or mwdisable options should be used in environments where read errors are more likely to persist than write errors, such as when using non redundant storage.

The mwdisable option is the default I/O error-handling option.

For file data read and write errors, VxFS sets the VX_DATAIOERR flag in the superblock. For metadata read errors, VxFS sets the VX_FULLFSCK flag. For metadata write errors, VxFS sets the VX_FULLFSCK and VX_METAIOERR flags and may mark associated metadata as bad on disk. VxFS then prints the appropriate error messages to the console.

If the VX_DATAIOERR or VX_METAIOERR flags are written to the superblock, a warning message is displayed when running fsck. If the VX_FULLFSCK flag is set, VxFS forces a full fsck to be performed.

VxFS Clustered Filesystem

As well as being a host based filesystem, VxFS is also a clustered filesystem. This aspect of VxFS is further described in Chapter 13.

The VxFS Disk Layouts

The VxFS disk layout has evolved over time to meet the needs of increasing file and filesystem sizes. The disk layout geometry has changed considerably over the years as new features and new policies have been added to VxFS.

There have been 5 different VxFS filesystem layouts. The first disk layout resembled UFS in many aspects while latter layouts are substantially different. The following sections describe the version 1 and version 5 disk layouts. The version 5 disk layout supports filesystem sizes up to 32TB and file sizes up to 2TB.

Table 9.1 VxFS I/O Error Handling Policies

POLICY OPTION	FILE READ	FILE WRITE	META-DATA READ	META-DATA WRITE
disable	disable	disable	disable	disable
nodisable	degrade	degrade	degrade	degrade
wdisable	degrade	disable	degrade	disable
mwdisable	degrade	degrade	degrade	disable

VxFS Disk Layout Version 1

The first VxFS disk layout, as shown in Figure 9.1, has three main sections. At the start of the disk slice containing the filesystem is a fixed amount of unused space that is used to store OS bootstrap routines.

The disk layout is divided into three main components:

Super block. The *super block* contains fundamental size information, a summary of available resources, and references to other places on disk where additional structural information can be found. Although there are multiple copies of the superblock in case of filesystem damage, the *initial* superblock can always be found at a well-known location. On UnixWare, it can be found at an offset of 1024 bytes from the start of the filesystem, while on Solaris, HP-UX, AIX, and Linux, it is located at byte offset 8192.

Intent log. The *intent log* contains a record of current file system activity. When a change to the filesystem is to be made that will alter the structural integrity of the filesystem, the pending change is first written to the intent log. In the event of a system failure, the operations in the log are either replayed or nullified to return the file system to a consistent state. To aid understanding, one can think of the entries in the intent log as a set of pre and post images of the modified part of the filesystem, allowing the transition from the old to new structure to be performed idempotently. Replaying the log multiple times therefore produces the same effect each time. For further details of how the intent log is used, see the section *VxFS Journaling*, later in this chapter.

Allocation units. An *allocation unit* (AU) is roughly equivalent to a UFS *cylinder group*. On disk layout version 1, each AU contains a pool of inodes and data blocks together with inode and extent bitmaps and extent summaries.

The intent log immediately follows the superblock and the first allocation unit immediately follows the log. Each allocation unit is the same size (which is determined at mkfs time) with the exception of the last AU, which may contain fewer blocks depending on the overall size of the disk slice on which the filesystem resides.

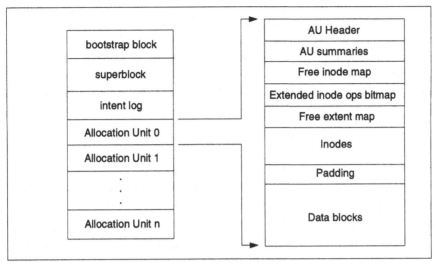

Figure 9.1 The VxFS version 1 disk layout.

Because the size of the AU is fixed at mkfs time in version 1, this results in a limitation on the size of other fundamental filesystem structures, not least, the number of inodes and the maximum extent size that can be allocated to a file.

The earlier VxFS mkfs command supported an array of options to align specific structures to various disk block boundaries. Because data is not uniformly stored on disk anymore, these parameters are not necessarily valid today.

For details on the inode extended operations map, see the section *Extended Operations*, later in this chapter.

VxFS Disk Layout Version 5

The first couple of VxFS disk layouts had a number of inherent problems. First, the fixed nature of allocation units required AU data to be written on AU boundaries across the whole disk. For large filesystems, this is a time-consuming task resulting in lengthy mkfs times. The fixed number of inodes causes two problems. First, if a filesystem contains many small files, it is possible to run out of inodes even though the utilization of disk space may be quite low. On the other hand, if only a small number of large files are required, a large amount of space could be wasted by holding unused inodes.

The other problem concerns the use of filesystems to hold database files. To gain optimal performance, databases are best stored as files with a single, large extent. If the extents need to be broken up across AU boundaries, the database files could run into indirects or double indirects, impacting performance.

The newer VxFS disk layouts solved all of these problems by storing all of the filesystem structural information in files that could grow on demand.

The newer VxFS layouts also introduced the concept of filesets, a term coined from DCE DFS (*Distributed File System*) work initiated under the auspices of the

Open Software Foundation. In the DCE model, the notion of a filesystem changes somewhat: a disk slice or volume contains an *aggregate* of filesets. Each fileset looks to the user like a filesystem—it has a root inode, lost+found directory, and a hierarchy of directories and files just like any other filesystem. Each fileset is independently mountable.

Much of this work was originally done in VxFS to support DCE DFS but has been extended in a number of ways as discussed in Chapter 12.

When creating a VxFS filesystem, two filesets are created: the *primary fileset* which is mounted in response to the mount command and the *structural fileset* which contains all the filesystem metadata. Each fileset has its own inode list, itself stored as a file. The primary fileset inode list file contains all the user directories, regular files, and so on. The structural fileset inode list file contains a number of files including:

Object location table (OLT). The OLT is referenced by the superblock. It is used when a filesystem is mounted; it contains references to structures needed to mount the filesystem.

Label file. This file holds the superblock and its replicas.

Fileset header file. Each fileset is described by an entry in the fileset header file. Each entry contains information such as the number of inodes allocated to the fileset, the inode number of the fileset's inode list file, and the inode numbers of other relevant files. To see how filesets are used to construct persistent snapshots, see the section *How Storage Checkpoints are Implemented* in Chapter 12.

Inode list file. This file, one per fileset, contains all of the inodes allocated to a fileset.

Inode allocation unit file (IAU). This file, again one per fileset, is used to manage inodes. It includes the free inode bitmap, summary information, and extended operations information.

Log file. The intent log is stored in this file.

Extent AU state file. This file indicates which AUs have been either allocated or expanded. This is described later in the chapter.

Extent AU summary file. This file summarizes the allocation of extents.

Free extent map. This file is a bitmap of free and allocated extents.

Figure 9.2 shows how some of these structures are used when mounting the filesystem. Because the filesystem information is stored in files, the filesystem needs to know how to access these structural files. Thus, various structures are used to help bootstrap this process. In order to mount a filesystem, VxFS needs to locate the root inode for the primary fileset. Following are some of the steps taken to achieve this:

1. The superblock is located by seeking 8KB into the device.

2. From the superblock, the OLT can be located; the OLT contains information about where the first few extents of the structural inode list file are located.

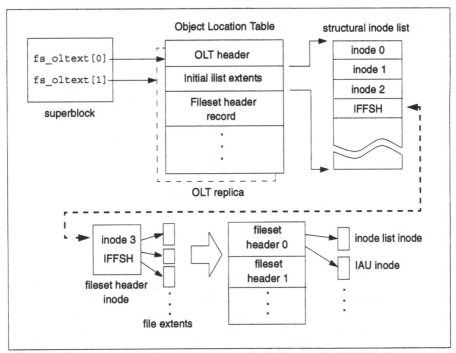

Figure 9.2 Locating structural information when mounting a VxFS filesystem.

It also contains information such as the inode number of the fileset header file that contains all the appropriate information about each fileset. Using the inode number of the primary fileset, the inode is located for the fileset header file. This file contains a record for each fileset, including the inode numbers of the inode list file, the IAU file (for allocating inodes), and so on.

3. After the entry for the primary fileset is located, all of the information necessary to mount the fileset is accessible.

Because all of the structural information about the filesystem is stored in files, the minimal amount of information is initially allocated. For example, only 32 inodes are allocated when the filesystem is created. To increase the number of inodes, the inode list file is extended in conjunction with the inode allocation unit (inode free bitmaps, etc.). Also, extent maps and summaries are only created when needed.

The notion of allocation units changed with the newer disk layouts. The filesystem is divided into fixed size AUs, each of 32KB blocks. AU 0 starts at block 0 within the filesystem. The AU state file contains 2 bits per AU, which indicate whether the AU is being used and if so, whether it has been *expanded*. When expanded, extent bitmaps and summaries are allocated to map the AU. Note however, that if a single 32KB block allocation is required, the AU state file is updated to indicate that the AU is in use but the bitmaps do not need to be created. The mapping between the structures used to manage AUs and extent maps is shown in Figure 9.3 which demonstrates the simplicity of storing

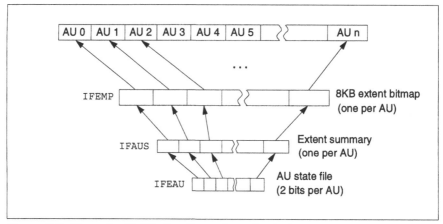

Figure 9.3   Managing VxFS allocation units and extent maps.

meta-data within a file itself.

When a filesystem is first created, only one or two AUs are initially used. This is specified in the AU state file and the corresponding extent summaries and bitmaps are expanded to reflect this. However, because none of the other AUs are used, the summaries and bitmaps are not allocated. As new files are allocated, more and more AUs are used. To make use of an unused AU, the state file is updated, and the summary and bitmap files are extended and updated with the appropriate summary and bitmap information.

This is why initial allocation of a VxFS filesystem is constant no matter what the size of the filesystem being created.

Creating VxFS Filesystems

The VxFS mkfs command has changed substantially over the years. Earlier disk layouts had a layout similar to UFS and therefore had numerous parameters that could be passed to mkfs to control alignment of filesystem structures.

If no size is passed to mkfs, VxFS will query the device on which the filesystem will be made and create a filesystem that will fill the device as follows:

```
# mkfs -F vxfs /dev/vx/rdsk/fs1
    version 4 layout
    204800 sectors, 102400 blocks of size 1024, log size 1024 blocks
    unlimited inodes, largefiles not supported
    102400 data blocks, 101280 free data blocks
    4 allocation units of 32768 blocks, 32768 data blocks
    last allocation unit has 4096 data blocks
```

The size of the filesystem can also be specified either in terms of sectors or by specifying a suffix of k (kilobytes), m (megabytes), or g (gigabytes). For example, to create a 100MByte filesystem, mkfs is run as follows:

```
# mkfs -F vxfs /dev/vx/rdsk/fs1 100m
```

For quite some time, VxFS has allocated inodes on demand, unlike many other UNIX filesystems that allocate a fixed number of inodes when the filesystem is created. VxFS does not initially create many inodes but will grow the inode list file as required. Thus, it is possible to either have a filesystem with a few very large files, a filesystem with many small files, or a combination of both.

By default, VxFS will choose a block size of 1024 bytes regardless of the filesystem size. This has been shown to be most effective in a wide range of environments. However, the block size can be 1KB, 2KB, 4KB, or 8KB. The `bsize` option can be used to override the default.

The VxFS intent log size is calculated automatically based on the size of the filesystem. This can be overridden during `mkfs` as shown in the section *VxFS Journaling* a little later in this chapter.

Forced Unmount

VxFS supports the ability to forcibly unmount a filesystem even when it is busy. This is particularly important in high-availability clustered environments where monitoring software has detected a failure and decides to switch over to a new host. The filesystem must be unmounted on the old host, then the new host runs a replay `fsck`, and mounts the filesystem. On the original host, it is highly likely that there will still be processes using files in the filesystem and therefore, a typical umount call will fail with EBUSY. Thus, the filesystem must be forcibly unmounted.

The following example shows how an unmount can be forced:

```
# mount | grep mnt2
/mnt2 on /dev/vx/dsk/fs1
read/write/delaylog/setuid/nolargefiles/ioerror=mwdisable on Fri Apr  5
21:54:09 2002
# cd /mnt2
# sleep 60000&
[1] 20507
# cd /
# umount /mnt2
vxfs umount: /mnt2 cannot unmount: Device busy
# umount -o force /mnt2
# jobs
[1] +  Running                 sleep 60000&
```

Very few UNIX operating systems support a switchable umount command. Solaris supports the `force` flag. For other operating systems, the VxFS-specific umount command must be invoked directly.

VxFS Journaling

When the system crashes, filesystems are typically damaged structurally. This results in a need to run the `fsck` utility to repair filesystem structures that may have been corrupted. Filesystems or other areas of the kernel that issue I/O can never be sure that the I/Os will be complete in the event of a crash. Each disk drive has a unit of I/O that is guaranteed to be atomic (writes of this size either succeed or fail—a drive can never write less than this amount). This is usually 512 bytes or 1024 bytes on some platforms. However, most structural filesystem operations require updates to multiple parts of the filesystem so this atomic I/O size guarantee is insufficient.

Consider the case of file creation. This involves the following operations:

1. Allocate a new inode. This involves flipping a bit in a bitmap to indicate that the inode is in use. It may also involve updating summary information.

2. Initialize the inode.

3. Update the directory inode in which the new file belongs. The timestamps of the directory inode are updated and the new file is added to the directory.

This type of operation involves updating a number of structures that are contained in a number of different blocks throughout the filesystem. If the system fails after writing some of the above data to disk but before completing the operation, the filesystem will be structurally incomplete. The role of fsck is to detect and repair any such inconsistencies resulting from a crash. For example, if the inode is allocated and initialized but not yet linked to the directory, the inode is *orphaned* and will therefore be removed by fsck or placed in lost+found.

The amount of time taken by fsck is proportional to the amount of meta-data in the filesystem and therefore typically dependent on the number of files that exist. In a world that is moving toward multi-terabyte filesystems with up to a billion files, the amount of time taken to perform fsck is unacceptable, taking many tens of hours to complete.

To solve this problem, journaling filesystems are written in such a manner that operations either succeed or fail. Either way, the filesystem should be structurally sound at all times.

VxFS solves this problem by performing all such updates as *transactions*. A transaction is a record of one or more changes to the filesystem. These changes are first written to the *intent log*, a circular buffer located within the filesystem, before they are written to their specific locations on disk. In the above example, all of the operations that comprise the file allocation are captured in a transaction. In the event of a system crash, VxFS fsck replays the contents of the intent log to complete any pending transactions. All such records in the log are idempotent such that they can be replayed an infinite number of times with the same result. This ensures that log replay can be restarted if the system crashes while the log itself is being replayed.

To help understand how transactions are written to the log, consider the example of creating a new file as follows:

```
# mount -F vxfs /dev/vx/dsk/fs1 /mnt
# > /mnt/newfile
# umount /mnt
```

The VxFS `fsdb` utility provides the command `fmtlog`, which displays the contents of the intent log in a human readable format. Shown below is an extract of the log showing the *sub functions* corresponding to the transaction that was used to create the file. Those parts of the text marked *Sub function* have been added to help annotate the output.

```
# fsdb -F vxfs /dev/vx/rdsk/fs1
> fmtlog
...
Sub function 1
00000800: id 363  func 1  ser 0  lser 3  len 292
Inode Modification  fset 999  ilist 0  dev/bno 0/1096  ino 2  osize 0
New Inode Contents:
type IFDIR mode 40755  nlink 3  uid 0  gid 0  size 6144
atime 1017451755 890011  (Fri Mar 29 17:29:15 2002)
mtime 1017451926 809999  (Fri Mar 29 17:32:06 2002)
ctime 1017451926 809999  (Fri Mar 29 17:32:06 2002)
aflags 0 orgtype 1 eopflags 0 eopdata 0
fixextsize/fsindex 0  rdev/reserve/dotdot/matchino 2
blocks 6  gen 9130  version 0 326  iattrino 0
de: 1125    0    0    0    0    0    0    0    0    0
des:   6    0    0    0    0    0    0    0    0    0
ie:    0    0
ies:   0
Sub function 2
00000940: id 363  func 5  ser 1  lser 3  len 40
free inode map changes  fset 999  ilist 0  aun 0
  map dev/bno 0/38  ausum dev/bno 0/37
        op alloc  ino 326
Sub function 3
00000980: id 363  func 1  ser 2  lser 3  len 292
Inode Modification  fset 999  ilist 0  dev/bno 0/1417  ino 326  osize 0
New Inode Contents:
type IFREG mode 100644  nlink 1  uid 0  gid 1  size 0
atime 1017451926 810000  (Fri Mar 29 17:32:06 2002)
mtime 1017451926 810000  (Fri Mar 29 17:32:06 2002)
ctime 1017451926 810000  (Fri Mar 29 17:32:06 2002)
aflags 0 orgtype 1 eopflags 0 eopdata 0
fixextsize/fsindex 0  rdev/reserve/dotdot/matchino 0
blocks 0  gen 1761727895  version 0 1  iattrino 0
de: 0 0 0 0 0 0 0 0 0
des: 0 0 0 0 0 0 0 0 0
ie: 0 0
ies: 0
Sub function 4
00000ae0: id 363  func 2  ser 3  lser 3  len 57
directory fset 999  ilist 0  inode 2  bno 1130  blen 1024  boff 116
previous  d_ino 325  d_reclen 924  d_namlen 6  d_hashnext 0000
added   d_ino 326  d_reclen 908  d_namlen 7  d_hashnext 0000
                n e w f i l e
```

The set of sub functions is as follows:

1. Update the link count and timestamps of the root directory in which the new file resides.

2. Update the inode bitmap to show that the inode has been allocated.

3. Initialize the new inode.

4. Update the directory block to add the entry for the new file.

Replaying the Intent Log

When a transaction is written to the log, markers are placed to indicate the start and end of the transaction. In the event of a system crash, `fsck` will run and perform log replay for all *complete* transactions it finds in the log. The first task is to locate the start of the log by scanning for the lowest transaction ID.

Working from start to finish, each subfunction is *replayed*, that is, the action specified in the entry is performed idempotently. This is a crucial part of the log format. Each entry must be able to be performed multiple times such that if the system crashes during log replay, the process can start over from the beginning.

An entry in the log that had an action such as "increment the inode link count" is not idempotent. If replayed multiple times, the inode link count would be invalid. Instead, an appropriate action would be "set the inode link count to 3."

The size of the intent log is chosen when the filesystem is created. It can however, be specified directly. The maximum log size is currently 16MB.

Extended Operations

Certain operations present problems for a journaling filesystem. For example, consider the case where the `unlink()` system call is invoked for a file that has a link count of 1. After the `unlink()` system call returns, the file is considered to be deleted. However, this presents a problem if the file is still opened. In this case, the file cannot be physically removed from disk until the last close is performed on the file.

To alleviate such a problem, VxFS provides *inode extended operations*. In the case of `unlink()` the `VX_IEREMOVE` extended operation is set on the inode to indicate that it should be removed. This is a transaction in itself. Any processes wishing to open the file will be denied, but processes that already have the file open will continue as is.

In the event of a system crash, extended operations must be completed before the filesystem can be accessed. In the case of `VX_IEREMOVE`, the file will be removed from the filesystem.

Extended operations are used extensively throughout VxFS but are not visible to the user.

Online Administration

One of the failures of UNIX filesystems over the years has been the lack of administrative features that can be performed while the filesystem is still mounted. One important example is the case of a filesystem resize. Traditionally, resizing a filesystem involved the following:

1. Create a new slice or volume of the appropriate size and create a new filesystem on this volume.

2. Disable access to the old filesystem (usually through a verbal warning).

3. Copy the contents of the old filesystem to the new filesystem.

4. Mount the new filesystem on the old mount point.

This is obviously undesirable because it can result in a significant interruption of service. VxFS provides the mechanisms by which a filesystem may be resized (up or down) while the filesystem is still mounted and active.

The following example shows how this can be achieved through use of the VxFS fsadm command. First of all, a filesystem is created and mounted. The size of the filesystem is 10,000 sectors. The number of 1KB blocks is 5,000.

```
# mkfs -F vxfs /dev/vx/rdsk/fs1 10000
    version 4 layout
    10000 sectors, 5000 blocks of size 1024, log size 256 blocks
    unlimited inodes, largefiles not supported
    5000 data blocks, 4672 free data blocks
    1 allocation units of 32768 blocks, 32768 data blocks
    last allocation unit has 5000 data blocks
# mount -F vxfs /dev/vx/dsk/fs1 /mnt1
# df -k | grep mnt1
/dev/vx/dsk/fs1          5000      341     4375     8%     /mnt2
```

The df command is run to show the amount of blocks in the filesystem and the amount available. The fsadm command is then run to double the size of the filesystem as follows:

```
# fsadm -b 20000 /mnt1
UX:vxfs fsadm: INFO: /dev/vx/rdsk/fs1 is currently 10000 sectors - size
will be increased
# df -k | grep mnt1
/dev/vx/dsk/fs1         10000      341     9063     4%     /mnt2
```

Notice the increase in blocks and free space once df is re-run.

The fsadm command is then run again and the filesystem size is decreased to 15000 sectors as follows:

```
# fsadm -b 15000 /mnt1
UX:vxfs fsadm: INFO: /dev/vx/rdsk/fs1 is currently 20000 sectors - size
will be reduced
# df -k | grep mnt1
/dev/vx/dsk/fs1          7500      341     6719     5%     /mnt1
```

One point to note here is that the underlying volume must be capable of holding a larger filesystem if the filesystem size is to be increased. Using volume-management capabilities such as VxVM, a volume can be easily resized online. Increasing the size of a raw partition is particularly difficult and cumbersome since this would involve taking filesystems offline, backing them up, repartitioning the disk, and then remaking and restoring the filesystems.

Extent Reorg and Directory Defragmentation

When extents are allocated to files, an attempt is made to allocate them in the most optimal manner. Over time, though, the filesystem becomes fragmented. Small free extents are spread over the filesystem resulting in a less than optimal choice when allocating extents to new files. Many filesystems employ different techniques to try and reduce the amount of fragmentation; that can provide some measure of success. However, regardless of the technique used, fragmentation will still occur over time in all filesystems.

VxFS provides, through the fsadm utility, the mechanisms through which fragmentation can be reduced while the filesystem is still online and active. The process involves locating files that have fragmented extent maps and performing *extent reorg* on these files to make the extents contiguous wherever possible. This involves allocating new extents and copying existing data where necessary. In addition to making files contiguous, free space is consolidated allowing for better allocations in the future.

Similarly, as files are allocated and removed, directories can become fragmented over time. Directories can also be defragmented with use of the fsadm command.

Both extent reorg and directory defragmentation should be run regularly on a filesystem to ensure that the most optimal layout is achieved at all times.

VxFS Performance-Related Features

Although VxFS will tune itself to the underlying system based on available memory, number of CPUs, volume geometry, and so on, certain applications may wish to perform I/O in a very specific manner. Also, in some environments performance may be critical whereas data integrity may not be an absolute priority.

To allow for such a wide range of environments and needs, VxFS provides a large number of different performance-related features, as described in the following sections.

VxFS Mount Options

There are numerous different options that can be passed to the VxFS mount command. First of all is the option to alter the way in which the intent log is managed to allow for a trade-off between data integrity and performance. The following four options are available:

`log`. With this mode, a system call that results in a change to filesystem structural data will not return to the user until VxFS has logged the changes to disk. This has traditionally been the default mode but is now being phased out and replaced by `delaylog`.

`delaylog`. With this option, many structural changes made to the filesystem are recorded in the in-core filesystem log and written to the intent log on disk at a later time. This has the effect of improving the responsiveness of the filesystem, but data can be lost in the event of a crash.

`tmplog`. With this option, nearly all structural changes are written to the in-core log. Writing to the intent log on disk is delayed as long as possible. This gives the best all-round performance but at the risk of losing data in the event of a system crash.

`nodatainlog`. By default, for small synchronous writes, VxFS writes both the inode change and the new file data to be written to the intent log. By specifying the `nodatainlog` option, the file data is written to its appropriate place in the file while the inode change is written through the intent log.

Note that regardless of which option is chosen, if the system crashes, the filesystem is still guaranteed to be structurally intact at all times.

To maintain correct UNIX semantics, reading from a file will result in a change to the access time field of the inode. There are however, few applications that look at or have need to view the access time. Using the `noatime` mount option, updates to the inodes' access time field will be ignored unless written in conjunction with an update to the modification time.

The caching behavior of the filesystem may be altered at mount time by specifying the `mincache` or `convosync` options. With these options, the administrator has a range of choices between maximum data integrity and maximum performance, depending on the workload of the machine.

The `mincache` mode has five different suboptions, based on the caching advisories described in the section *Data and Attribute Caching* in Chapter 3. These options are:

`mincache=closesync`. This option is useful in desktop environments where the machine may be powered off without cleanly shutting down the machine. With this option, any changes to the file are flushed to disk when the file is closed. Running in this mode may introduce up to a 15 percent penalty on performance.

`mincache=dsync`. When this option is specified, data is read and written as if the `VX_DSYNC` caching advisory is set. If a write to a file results in the timestamps of the inode being modified with no changes to the block allocations, the inode update will be delayed. For extending writes or when extents are being allocated, the inode update will not be delayed.

mincache=direct. With this option, all non-synchronous requests (O_SYNC not specified) are handled as if the VX_DIRECT caching advisory had been set; that is, all requests that are aligned on correct boundaries will be performed as direct I/O. Thus, writes are guaranteed to complete before the system call returns. Note however, that because I/O is performed directly between the user buffer and the file's blocks on disk, data is not cached in the kernel. Thus, when reading the same data, a request will go to disk.

mincache=unbuffered. This option is similar to mincache=direct. With the direct option however, when a file is extended or blocks are allocated to a file, the inode is updated synchronously before the call returns. When specifying mincache=unbuffered, the inode updates are always performed asynchronously.

mincache=tmpcache. This is the most performant option. Nearly all file operations are delayed. With this option, data is not flushed to disk when a file is closed. Any writes that are in progress during a system crash may result in extents that contain garbage. However, filesystem throughput will be best with this option in most environments.

The convosync mount option is used to alter the behavior of filesystems when files are opened with O_SYNC and O_DSYNC. There are five suboptions:

convosync=closesync. With this option, any synchronous (O_SYNC) or data synchronous (O_DSYNC) writes are not performed synchronously. However, when the file is closed, any updates are flushed to disk.

convosync=delay. This option causes synchronous (O_SYNC) or data synchronous (O_DSYNC) writes to be delayed.

convosync=direct. With this option, synchronous (O_SYNC) or data synchronous (O_DSYNC) writes do not update the inode when only the timestamps are modified. Changes to the file are flushed when the file is closed.

convosync=unbuffered. This option is similar to the direct option described above except that inode updates are performed asynchronously even if the file is extended or blocks are allocated to the file. Changes to the file are flushed when the file is closed.

convosync=dsync. This option converts synchronous (O_SYNC) writes to data synchronous writes. Changes to the file are flushed when the file is closed.

One final mount option worthy of mention and useful in data security environments is blkclear. When specified, any extents allocated to a file are zeroed first, ensuring that uninitialized data never appears in a file. Of course this has an impact on performance (roughly a 10 percent hit). For desktop type environments, a combination of blkclear and mincache=closesync can be used.

VxFS Tunable I/O Parameters

There are several additional parameters that can be specified to adjust the performance of a VxFS filesystem. The `vxtunefs` command can either set or display the tunable I/O parameters of mounted file systems. With no options specified, `vxtunefs` prints the existing VxFS parameters for the specified filesystem, as shown below:

```
# vxtunefs /mnt
Filesystem i/o parameters for /mnt
read_pref_io = 65536
read_nstream = 1
read_unit_io = 65536
write_pref_io = 65536
write_nstream = 1
write_unit_io = 65536
pref_strength = 10
buf_breakup_size = 262144
discovered_direct_iosz = 262144
max_direct_iosz = 1048576
default_indir_size = 8192
qio_cache_enable = 0
write_throttle = 254080
max_diskq = 1048576
initial_extent_size = 8
max_seqio_extent_size = 2048
max_buf_data_size = 8192
hsm_write_prealloc = 0
```

`vxtunefs` operates on either a list of mount points specified on the command line or all the mounted file systems listed in the `tunefstab` file. When run on a mounted filesystem, the changes are made effective immediately. The default `tunefstab` file is `/etc/vx/tunefstab`, although this can be changed by setting the `VXTUNEFSTAB` environment variable.

If the `/etc/vx/tunefstab` file is present, the VxFS mount command invokes `vxtunefs` to set any parameters found in `/etc/vx/tunefstab` that apply to the filesystem. If the file system is built on a VERITAS Volume Manager (VxVM) volume, the VxFS-specific `mount` command interacts with VxVM to obtain default values for the tunables. It is generally best to allow VxFS and VxVM to determine the best values for most of these tunables.

Quick I/O for Databases

Databases have traditionally used raw devices on UNIX to avoid various problems inherent with storing the database in a filesystem. To alleviate these problems and offer databases the same performance with filesystems that they get with raw devices, VxFS provides a feature called *Quick I/O*. Before describing how Quick I/O works, the issues that databases face with running on filesystems is first described. Figure 9.4 provides a simplified view of how databases run on traditional UNIX filesystems. The main problem areas are as follows:

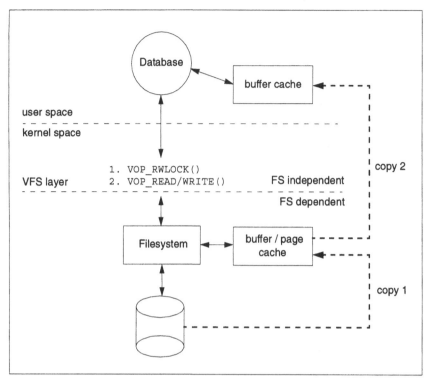

Figure 9.4   Database access through the filesystem.

■ Most database applications tend to cache data in their own user space
buffer cache. Accessing files through the filesystem results in data being
read, and therefore cached, through the traditional buffer cache or through
the system page cache. This results in double buffering of data. The
database could avoid using its own cache. However, it would then have no
control over when data is flushed from the cache.

■ The allocation of blocks to regular files can easily lead to file fragmentation,
resulting in unnecessary disk head movement when compared to running
a database on a raw volume in which all blocks are contiguous. Although
database I/O tends to take place in small I/O sizes (typically 2KB to 8KB),
the filesystem may perform a significant amount of work by continuously
mapping file offsets to block numbers. If the filesystem is unable to cache
indirect blocks, an additional overhead can be seen.

■ When writing to a regular file, the kernel enters the filesystem through the
vnode interface (or equivalent). This typically involves locking the file in
exclusive mode for a single writer and in shared mode for multiple readers.
If the UNIX API allowed for range locks, which allow sections of a file to be
locked when writing, this would alleviate the problem. However, no API

has been forthcoming. When accessing the raw device, there is no locking model enforced. In this case, databases therefore tend to implement their own locking model.

To solve these problems, databases have moved toward using *raw I/O*, which removes the filesystem locking problems and gives direct I/O between user buffers and the disk. By doing so however, administrative features provided by the filesystem are then lost.

With the *Quick I/O* feature of VxFS, these problems can be avoided through use of an alternate namespace provided by VxFS. The following example shows how this works.

First, to allocate a file for database use, the qiomkfile utility is used, which creates a file of the specified size and with a single extent as follows :

```
# qiomkfile -s 100m dbfile
# ls -al | grep dbfile
total 204800
-rw-r--r--   1 root    other    104857600 Apr 17 22:18 .dbfile
lrwxrwxrwx   1 root    other           19 Apr 17 22:18 dbfile ->
                                                 .dbfile::cdev:vxfs:
```

There are two files created. The .dbfile is a regular file that is created of the requested size. The file dbfile is a symbolic link. When this file is opened, VxFS sees the .dbfile component of the symlink together with the extension ::cdev:vxfs:, which indicates that the file must be treated in a different manner than regular files:

1. The file is opened with relaxed locking semantics, allowing both reads and writes to occur concurrently.

2. All file I/O is performed as direct I/O, assuming the request meets certain constraints such as address alignment.

When using Quick I/O with VxFS, databases can run on VxFS at the same performance as raw I/O. In addition to the performance gains, the manageability aspects of VxFS come into play, including the ability to perform a block-level incremental backup as described in Chapter 12.

External Intent Logs through QuickLog

The VxFS intent log is stored near the beginning of the disk slice or volume on which it is created. Although writes to the intent log are always sequential and therefore minimize disk head movement when reading from and writing to the log, VxFS is still operating on other areas of the filesystem, resulting in the disk heads moving to and fro between the log and the rest of the filesystem. To help minimize this disk head movement, VxFS supports the ability to move the intent log from the device holding the filesystem to a separate *QuickLog* device. In order to maximize the performance benefits, the QuickLog device should not reside on the same disk device as the filesystem.

VxFS DMAPI Support

The *Data Management Interfaces Group* specified an API (DMAPI) to be provided by filesystem and/or OS vendors, that would provide hooks to support *Hierarchical Storage Management* (HSM) applications.

An HSM application creates a *virtual filesystem* by migrating unused files to tape when the filesystem starts to become full and then migrates them back when requested. This is similar in concept to virtual memory and physical memory. The size of the filesystem can be much bigger than the actual size of the device on which it resides. A number of different policies are typically provided by HSM applications to determine the type of files to migrate and when to migrate. For example, one could implement a policy that migrates all files over 1MB that haven't been accessed in the last week when the filesystem becomes 80 percent full.

To support such applications, VxFS implements the DMAPI which provides the following features:

- The application can register for one or more events. For example, the application can be informed of every read, every write, or other events such as a mount invocation.

- The API supports a *punch hole* operation which allows the application to migrate data to tape and then punch a hole in the file to free the blocks while retaining the existing file size. After this occurs, the file is said to have a *managed region*.

- An application can perform both *invisible reads* and *invisible writes*. As part of the API, the application can both read from and write to a file without updating the file timestamps. The goal of these operations is to allow the migration to take place without the user having knowledge that the file was migrated. It also allows the HSM application to work in conjunction with a backup application. For example, if data is already migrated to tape, there is no need for a backup application to write the same data to tape.

VxFS supports a number of different HSM applications, including the VERITAS *Storage Migrator*.

The UFS Filesystem

This section explores the UFS filesystem, formerly known as the Berkeley *Fast File System* (FFS), from its roots in BSD through to today's implementation and the enhancements that have been added to the Sun Solaris UFS implementation.

UFS has been one of the most studied of the UNIX filesystems, is well understood, and has been ported to nearly every flavor of UNIX. First described in the 1984 Usenix paper "A Fast Filesystem for UNIX" [MCKU84], the decisions taken for the design of UFS have also found their way into other filesystems, including ext2 and ext3, which are described later in the chapter.

Early UFS History

In [MCKU84], the problems inherent with the original 512-byte filesystem are described. The primary motivation for change was due to poor performance experienced by applications that were starting to be developed for UNIX. The old filesystem was unable to provide high enough throughput due partly to the fact that all data was written in 512-byte blocks, which were abitrarily placed throughout the disk. Other factors that resulted in less than ideal performance were:

- Because of the small block size, anything other than small files resulted in the file going into indirects fairly quickly. Thus, more I/O was needed to access file data.

- File meta-data (inodes) and the file data were physically separate on disk and therefore could result in significant seek times. For example, [LEFF89] described how a traditional 150MB filesystem had 4MB of inodes followed by 146MB of data. When accessing files, there was always a long seek following a read of the inode before the data blocks could be read. Seek times also added to overall latency when moving from one block of data to the next, which would quite likely not be contiguous on disk.

Some early work between 3BSD and BSD4.0, which doubled the block size of the old filesystem to 1024 bytes, showed that the performance could be increased by a factor of two. The increase in block size also reduced the need for indirect data blocks for many files.

With these factors in mind, the team from Berkeley went on to design a new filesystem that would produce file access rates of many times its predecessor with less I/O and greater disk throughput.

One crucial aspect of the new design concerned the layout of data on disks, as shown in Figure 9.5. The new filesystem was divided into a number of *cylinder groups* that mapped directly to the cylindrical layout of data on disk drives at that time—note that on early disk drives, each cylinder had the same amount of data whether toward the outside of the platter or the inside. Each cylinder group contained a copy of the superblock, a fixed number of inodes, bitmaps describing free inodes and data blocks, a summary table describing data block usage, and the data blocks themselves. Each cylinder group had a fixed number of inodes. The number of inodes per cylinder group was calculated such that there was one inode created for every 2048 bytes of data. It was deemed that this should provide far more files than would actually be needed.

To help achieve some level of integrity, cylinder group meta-data was not stored in the same platter for each cylinder group. Instead, to avoid placing all of the structural filesystem data on the top platter, meta-data on the second cylinder

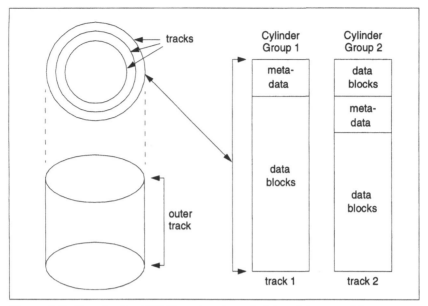

Figure 9.5 Mapping the UFS filesystem to underlying disk geometries.

group was placed on the second platter, meta-data for the third cylinder group on the third platter, and so on. With the exception of the first cylinder group, data blocks were stored both before and after the cylinder group meta-data.

Block Sizes and Fragments

Whereas the old filesystem was limited to 512-byte data blocks, the FFS allowed block sizes to be 4096 bytes at a minimum up to the limit imposed by the size of data types stored on disk. The 4096 byte block size was chosen so that files up to 2^{32} bytes in size could be accessed with only two levels of indirection. The filesystem block size was chosen when the filesystem was created and could not be changed dynamically. Of course, different filesystems could have different block sizes.

Because most files at the time the FFS was developed were less than 4096 bytes in size, file data could be stored in a single 4096 byte data block. If a file was only slightly greater than a multiple of the filesystem block size, this could result in a lot of wasted space. To help alleviate this problem, the new filesystem introduced the concept of *fragments*. In this scheme, data blocks could be split into 2, 4, or 8 fragments, the size of which is determined when the filesystem is created. If a file contained 4100 bytes, for example, the file would contain one 4096 byte data block plus a fragment of 1024 bytes to store the fraction of data remaining.

When a file is extended, a new data block or another fragment will be allocated. The policies that are followed for allocation are documented in [MCKU84] and shown as follows:

1. If there is enough space in the fragment or data block covering the end of the file, the new data is simply copied to that block or fragment.

2. If there are no fragments, the existing block is filled and new data blocks are allocated and filled until either the write has completed or there is insufficient data to fill a new block. In this case, either a block with the correct amount of fragments or a new data block will be allocated.

3. If the file contains one or more fragments and the amount of new data to write plus the amount of data in the fragments exceeds the amount of space available in a data block, a new data block is allocated and the data is copied from the fragments to the new data block, followed by the new data appended to the file. The process followed in Step 2 is then followed.

Of course, if files are extended by small amounts of data, there will be excessive copying as fragments are allocated and then deallocated and copied to a full data block.

The amount of space saved is dependent on the data block size and the fragment size. However, with a 4096-byte block size and 512-byte fragments, the amount of space lost is about the same as the old filesystem, so better throughput is gained but not at the expense of wasted space.

FFS Allocation Policies

The Berkeley team recognized that improvements were being made in disk technologies and that disks with different characteristics could be employed in a single system simultaneously. To take advantage of the different disk types and to utilize the speed of the processor on which the filesystem was running, the filesystem was adapted to the specific disk hardware and system on which it ran. This resulted in the following allocation policies:

- Data blocks for a file are allocated from within the same cylinder group wherever possible. If possible, the blocks were *rotationally well-positioned* so that when reading a file sequentially, a minimal amount of rotation was required. For example, consider the case where a file has two data blocks, the first of which is stored on track 0 on the first platter and the second of which is stored on track 0 of the second platter. After the first data block has been read and before an I/O request can be initiated on the second, the disk has rotated so that the disk heads may be one or more sectors past the sector / data just read. Thus, data for the second block is not placed in the same sector on track 0 as the first block is on track 0, but several sectors further forward on track 0. This allows for the disk to spin between the two read requests. This is known as the disk *interleave factor*.

- Related information is clustered together whenever possible. For example, the inodes for a specific directory and the files within the directory are placed within the same cylinder group. To avoid overuse of one cylinder group over another, the allocation policy for directories themselves is different. In this case, the new directory inode is allocated from another cylinder group that has a greater than average number of free inodes and the smallest number of directories.

■ File data is placed in the same cylinder group with its inode. This helps reduce the need to move the disk heads when reading an inode followed by its data blocks.

■ Large files are allocated across separate cylinder groups to avoid a single file consuming too great a percentage of a single cylinder group. Switching to a new cylinder group when allocating to a file occurs at 48KB and then at each subsequent megabyte.

For these policies to work, the filesystem has to have a certain amount of free space. Experiments showed that the scheme worked well until less than 10 percent of disk space was available. This led to a fixed amount of reserved space being set aside. After this threshold was exceeded, only the superuser could allocate from this space.

Performance Analysis of the FFS

[MCKU84] showed the results of a number of different performance runs to determine the effectiveness of the new filesystem. Some observations from these runs are as follows:

■ The inode layout policy proved to be effective. When running the `ls` command on a large directory, the number of actual disk accesses was reduced by a factor of 2 when the directory contained other directories and by a factor of 8 when the directory contained regular files.

■ The throughput of the filesystem increased dramatically. The old filesystem was only able to use 3 to 5 percent of the disk bandwidth while the FFS was able to use up to 47 percent of the disk bandwidth.

■ Both reads and writes were faster, primarily due to the larger block size. Larger block sizes also resulted in less overhead when allocating blocks.

These results are not always truly representative of real world situations, and the FFS can perform badly when fragmentation starts to occur over time. This is particularly true after the filesystem reaches about 90 percent of the available space. This is, however, generally true of all different filesystem types.

Additional Filesystem Features

The introduction of the Fast File System also saw a number of new features being added. Note that because there was no filesystem switch architecture at this time, they were initially implemented as features of UFS itself. These new features were:

Symbolic links. Prior to their introduction, only hard links were supported in the original UNIX filesystem.

Long file names. The old filesystem restricted file names to 15 characters. The FFS provided file names of arbitrary length. In the first FFS implementation, file names were initially restricted to 255 characters.

File locking. To avoid the problems of using a separate *lock file* to synchronize updates to another file, the BSD team implemented an advisory locking scheme. Locks could be shared or exclusive.

File rename. A single rename() system call was implemented. Previously, three separate system calls were required which resulted in problems following a system crash.

Quotas. The final feature added was that of support for user quotas. For further details, see the section *User and Group Quotas* in Chapter 5.

All of these features are taken for granted today and are expected to be available on most filesystems on all versions of UNIX.

What's Changed Since the Early UFS Implementation?

For quite some time, disk drives have no longer adhered to fixed-size cylinders, on the basis that more data can be stored on those tracks closer to the edge of the platter than on the inner tracks. This now makes the concept of a cylinder group somewhat of a misnomer, since the cylinder groups no longer map directly to the cylinders on the disk itself. Thus, some of the early optimizations that were present in the earlier UFS implementations no longer find use with today's disk drives and may, in certain circumstances, actually do more harm than good.

However, the locality of reference model employed by UFS still results in inodes and data being placed in close proximity and therefore is still an aid to performance.

Solaris UFS History and Enhancements

Because SunOS (the predecessor of Solaris) was based on BSD UNIX, it was one of the first commercially available operating systems to support UFS. Work has continued on development of UFS at Sun to this day.

This section analyzes the enhancements made by Sun to UFS, demonstrates how some of these features work in practice, and shows how the underlying features of the FFS, described in this chapter, are implemented in UFS today.

Making UFS Filesystems

There are still many options that can be passed to the mkfs command that relate to disk geometry. First of all though, consider the following call to mkfs to create a 100MB filesystem. Note that the size passed is specified in 512-byte sectors.

```
# mkfs -F ufs /dev/vx/rdsk/fs1 204800
/dev/vx/rdsk/fs1:204800 sectors in 400 cylinders of 16 tracks, 32 sectors
        100.0MB in 25 cyl groups (16 c/g, 4.00MB/g, 1920 i/g)
super-block backups (for fsck -F ufs -o b=#) at:
 32, 8256, 16480, 24704, 32928, 41152, 49376, 57600, 65824, 74048, 82272,
 90496, 98720, 106944, 115168, 123392, 131104, 139328, 147552, 155776,
 164000, 172224, 180448, 188672, 196896,
```

By default, mkfs determines the number of cylinder groups it chooses to make, although this can be overridden by use of the cgsize=n option. By default, the size of the filesystem is calculated by dividing the number of sectors passed to mkfs by 1GB and then multiplying by 32. For each of the 25 cylinder groups created in this filesystem, mkfs shows their location by displaying the location of the superblock that is replicated throughout the filesystem at the start of each cylinder group.

Some of the other options that can be passed to mkfs are shown below:

bsize=n. This option is used to specify the filesystem block size, which can be either 4096 or 8192 bytes.

fragsize=n. The value of n is used to specify the fragment size. For a block size of 4096, the choices are 512, 1024, 2048, or 4096. For a block size of 8192, the choices are 1024, 2048, 4096, or 8192.

free=n. This value is the amount of free space that is maintained. This is the threshold which, once exceeded, prevents anyone except root from allocating any more blocks. By default it is 10 percent. Based on the information shown in *Performance Analysis of the FFS*, a little earlier in this chapter, this value should not be decreased; otherwise, there could be an impact on performance due to the method of block and fragment allocation used in UFS.

nbpi=n. This is an unusual option in that it specifies the number of bytes per inode. This is used to determine the number of inodes in the filesystem. The filesystem size is divided by the value specified, which gives the number of inodes that are created.

Considering the nbpi option, a small filesystem is created as follows:

```
# mkfs -F ufs /dev/vx/rdsk/fs1 5120
/dev/vx/rdsk/fs1: 5120 sectors in 10 cylinders of 16 tracks, 32 sectors
        2.5MB in 1 cyl groups (16 c/g, 4.00MB/g, 1920 i/g)
super-block backups (for fsck -F ufs -o b=#) at:
 32,
```

There is one cylinder group for this filesystem. More detailed information about the filesystem can be obtained through use of the fstyp command as follows:

```
# fstyp -v /dev/vx/rdsk/fs1
ufs
magic   11954    format  dynamic time    Fri Mar  8 09:56:38 2002
sblkno  16       cblkno  24       iblkno  32       dblkno  272
```

```
sbsize   2048      cgsize   2048      cgoffset 16       cgmask  0xfffffff0
ncg      1         size     2560      blocks   2287
bsize    8192      shift    13        mask     0xffffe000
fsize    1024      shift    10        mask     0xfffffc00
frag     8         shift    3         fsbtodb  1
minfree  10%       maxbpg   2048      optim    time
maxcontig 7        rotdelay 0ms       rps      60
csaddr   272       cssize   1024      shift    9         mask    0xffffe00
ntrak    16        nsect    32        spc      512       ncyl    10
cpg      16        bpg      512       fpg      4096      ipg     1920
nindir   2048      inopb    64        nspf     2
nbfree   283       ndir     2         nifree   1916      nffree  14
cgrotor  0         fmod     0         ronly    0         logbno  0
fs_reclaim is not set
file system state is valid, fsclean is 1
blocks available in each rotational position
cylinder number 0:
...
```

This shows further information about the filesystem created, in particular the contents of the superblock. The meaning of many fields is reasonably self explanatory. The `nifree` field shows the number of inodes that are free. Note that this number of inodes is fixed as the following script demonstrates:

```
# cd /mnt
# i=1
# while [ $i -lt 1920 ] ; do ; > $i ; i=`expr $i + 1` ; done
bash: 185: No space left on device
bash: 186: No space left on device
bash: 187: No space left on device
# df -k /mnt
Filesystem            kbytes    used   avail capacity  Mounted on
/dev/vx/dsk/fs1         2287      18    2041     1%    /mnt
```

So, although the filesystem is only 1 percent full, there are no more inodes available.

Solaris UFS Mount Options

A number of new mount options that alter the behavior of the filesystem when mounted have been added to Solaris UFS over the last several years. Shown here are some of these options:

noatime. When a file is read, the inode on disk is updated to reflect the access time. This is in addition to the modification time, that is updated when the file is actually changed. Most applications tend not to be concerned about access time (atime) updates and therefore may use this option to prevent unnecessary updates to the inode on disk to improve overall performance.

forcedirectio | noforcedirectio. When a read() system call is issued, data is copied from the user buffer to a kernel buffer and then to disk. This data is cached and can therefore be used on a subsequent read without a disk access being needed. The same is also true of a write() system call. To avoid this double buffering, the forcedirectio mount option performs the I/O directly between the user buffer and the block on disk to which the file data belongs. In this case, the I/O can be performed faster than the double buffered I/O. Of course, with this scenario the data is not cached in the kernel and a subsequent read operation would involve reading the data from disk again.

logging | nologging. By specifying the logging option, the filesystem is mounted with journaling enabled, preventing the need for a full fsck in the event of a system crash. This option is described in the section *UFS Logging* later in this chapter.

Database I/O Support

The current read() / write() system call interactions between multiple processes is such that there may be multiple concurrent readers but only a single writer. As shown in the section *Quick I/O for Databases*, a little earlier in this chapter, write operations are synchronized through the VOP_RWLOCK() interface. For database and other such applications that perform their own locking, this model is highly undesirable.

With the forcedirectio mount option, the locking semantics can be relaxed when writing. In addition, direct I/O is performed between the user buffer and disk, avoiding the extra copy that is typically made when performing a read or write. By using UFS direct I/O, up to 90 percent of the performance of accessing the raw disk can be achieved.

For more information on running databases on top of filesystems, see the section *Quick I/O for Databases* a little earlier in this chapter.

UFS Snapshots

Sun implemented a snapshot mechanism with UFS whereby a consistent, point-in-time image of the filesystem can be achieved, from which a backup can be taken. The fssnap command can be used to create the snapshot. It takes a filesystem to snap and a directory into which the snapshot file is placed (a sparse file) and returns a pseudo device that can be mounted, giving access to the snapshot. Note that UFS snapshots are read-only and not persistent across a reboot. As blocks are modified in the snapped filesystem, they are first copied to the snapshot. When reading from the snapshot, either the blocks are read from the original filesystem if unchanged, or read from the snapshot if they have been overwritten in the snapped filesystem.

The following example shows how UFS snapshots are used in practice. First of all, a 100MB filesystem is created on the device fs1. This is the filesystem from which the snapshot will be taken.

```
# mkfs -F ufs /dev/vx/rdsk/fs1 204800
/dev/vx/rdsk/fs1:204800 sectors in 400 cylinders of 16 tracks, 32 sectors
```

```
        100.0MB in 25 cyl groups (16 c/g, 4.00MB/g, 1920 i/g)
super-block backups (for fsck -F ufs -o b=#) at:
 32, 8256, 16480, 24704, 32928, 41152, 49376, 57600, 65824, 74048, 82272,
 90496, 98720, 106944, 115168, 123392, 131104, 139328, 147552, 155776,
 164000, 172224, 180448, 188672, 196896,
```

The following 10MB VxFS filesystem is created in which to store the snapshot. VxFS is used to show that the snapshot device can reside on any filesystem type:

```
# mkfs -F vxfs /dev/vx/rdsk/snap1
    version 4 layout
    20480 sectors, 10240 blocks of size 1024, log size 1024 blocks
    unlimited inodes, largefiles not supported
    10240 data blocks, 9144 free data blocks
    1 allocation units of 32768 blocks, 32768 data blocks
    last allocation unit has 10240 data blocks
```

Both filesystems are mounted, and two files are created on the UFS filesystem:

```
# mount -F ufs /dev/vx/dsk/fs1 /mnt
# mount -F vxfs /dev/vx/rdsk/snap1 /snap-space
# echo "hello" > /mnt/hello
# dd if=/dev/zero of=/mnt/64m bs=65536 count=1000
1000+0 records in
1000+0 records out
# df -k
Filesystem            kbytes    used    avail capacity  Mounted on
/dev/dsk/c0t0d0s0    5121031 1653877 13315944   12%    /
/proc                      0       0        0    0%    /proc
fd                         0       0        0    0%    /dev/fd
mnttab                     0       0        0    0%    /etc/mnttab
swap                 4705240      16  4705224    1%    /var/run
swap                 4705240      16  4705224    1%    /tmp
/dev/vx/dsk/fs1        95983   64050    22335   75%    /mnt
/dev/vx/dsk/snap1     10240    1109     8568   12%    /snap-space
```

As a reference point, the df command shows the amount of space on each filesystem. Next, the fssnap command is run, which creates the snapshot and returns the pseudo device representing the snapshot:

```
# fssnap -o backing-store=/snap-space /mnt
/dev/fssnap/0
# ls -l /snap-space
total 16
drwxr-xr-x   2 root     root           96 Mar 12 19:45 lost+found
-rw------   1 root     other    98286592 Mar 12 19:48 snapshot0
```

The snapshot0 file created is a sparse file. The device returned by fssnap can now be used to mount the snapshot. The following df output shows that the snapshot mirrors the UFS filesystem created on fs1 and the size of the /snap-space filesystem is largely unchanged (showing that the snapshot0 file is sparse).

```
# mount -F ufs -o ro /dev/fssnap/0 /snap
# df -k
Filesystem           kbytes    used   avail capacity  Mounted on
/dev/dsk/c0t0d0s0   15121031 1653877 13315944   12%   /
/proc                     0       0       0    0%     /proc
fd                        0       0       0    0%     /dev/fd
mnttab                    0       0       0    0%     /etc/mnttab
swap                4705040      16 4705024    1%     /var/run
swap                4705040      16 4705024    1%     /tmp
/dev/vx/dsk/fs1        95983   64050   22335   75%    /mnt
/dev/vx/dsk/snap1      10240    1117    8560   12%    /snap-space
/dev/fssnap/0         95983   64050   22335   75%    /snap
```

The -i option to fssnap can be used to display information about the snapshot, as shown below. The *granularity* value shows the amount of data that is copied to the snapshot when blocks in the original filesystem have been overwritten.

```
# fssnap -i /mnt
Snapshot number             : 0
Block Device                : /dev/fssnap/0
Raw Device                  : /dev/rfssnap/0
Mount point                 : /mnt
Device state                : active
Backing store path          : /snap-space/snapshot0
Backing store size          : 0 KB
Maximum backing store size  : Unlimited
Snapshot create time        : Sat Mar 09 11:28:48 2002
Copy-on-write granularity   : 32 KB
```

The following examples show that even when a file is removed in the snapped filesystem, the file can still be accessed in the snapshot:

```
# rm /mnt/hello
# cat /snap/hello
hello
# ls -l /snap
total 128098
-rw-r--r-  1 root     other      65536000 Mar  9 11:28 64m
-rw-r--r-  1 root     other             6 Mar  9 11:28 hello
drwx-----  2 root     root           8192 Mar  9 11:27 lost+found
# ls -l /mnt
total 128096
-rw-r--r-  1 root     other      65536000 Mar  9 11:28 64m
drwx-----  2 root     root           8192 Mar  9 11:27 lost+found
```

To fully demonstrate how the feature works, consider again the size of the original filesystems. The UFS filesystem is 100MB in size and contains a 64MB file. The snapshot resides on a 10MB VxFS filesystem. The following shows what happens when the 64MB file is removed from the UFS filesystem:

```
# rm /mnt/64m
# df -k
```

```
Filesystem             kbytes    used    avail capacity  Mounted on
/dev/dsk/c0t0d0s0    15121031 1653877 13315944    12%    /
/proc                       0       0        0     0%    /proc
fd                          0       0        0     0%    /dev/fd
mnttab                      0       0        0     0%    /etc/mnttab
swap                  4705000      16  4704984     1%    /var/run
swap                  4705000      16  4704984     1%    /tmp
/dev/vx/dsk/fs1         95983       9    86376     1%    /mnt
/dev/vx/dsk/snap1       10240    1245     8440    13%    /snap-space
/dev/fssnap/0          95983   64050    22335    75%    /snap
```

Note that the although the 64MB file was removed, there is little increase in the amount of space used by the snapshot. Because the data blocks of the 64m file were freed but not overwritten, there is no need to copy them to the snapshot device at this stage. However, if dd is run to create another file in the UFS filesystem as follows:

```
# dd if=/dev/zero of=/mnt/64m bs=65536 count=1000
1000+0 records in
1000+0 records out
```

a new file is created and, as blocks are allocated to the file and overwritten, the original contents must be copied to the snapshot. Because there is not enough space to copy 64MB of data, the snapshot runs out of space resulting in the following messages on the system console. Note that the VxFS filesystem first reports that it is out of space. Because no more data can be copied to the snapshot, the snapshot is no longer intact and is automatically deleted.

```
Mar  9 11:30:03 gauss vxfs: [ID 332026 kern.notice]
NOTICE: msgcnt 2 vxfs: mesg 001: vx_nospace /dev/vx/dsk/snap1 file system
full (1 block extent)
Mar  9 11:30:03 gauss fssnap: [ID 443356 kern.warning]
WARNING: fssnap_write_taskq: error writing to backing file.  DELETING
SNAPSHOT 0, backing file path /snap-space/snapshot0, offset 13729792
bytes, error 5.
Mar  9 11:30:03 gauss fssnap: [ID 443356 kern.warning]
WARNING: fssnap_write_taskq: error writing to backing file.  DELETING
SNAPSHOT 0, backing file path /snap-space/snapshot0, offset 12648448
bytes, error 5.
Mar  9 11:30:03 gauss fssnap: [ID 894761 kern.warning]
WARNING: Snapshot 0 automatically deleted.
```

To confirm the out-of-space filesystem, df is run one last time:

```
# df -k
Filesystem             kbytes    used    avail capacity  Mounted on
/dev/dsk/c0t0d0s0    15121031 1653878 13315943    12%    /
/proc                       0       0        0     0%    /proc
fd                          0       0        0     0%    /dev/fd
mnttab                      0       0        0     0%    /etc/mnttab
swap                  4704824      16  4704808     1%    /var/run
swap                  4704824      16  4704808     1%    /tmp
```

```
/dev/vx/dsk/fs1        95983    64049    22336    75%    /mnt
/dev/vx/dsk/snap1      10240    10240        0   100%    /snap-space
/dev/fssnap/0          95983    64050    22335    75%    /snap
```

UFS snapshots are a useful way to create a stable image of the filesystem prior to running a backup. Note, however, that the size of the filesystem on which the snapshot resides must be large enough to accommodate enough copied blocks for the duration of the backup.

UFS Logging

Solaris UFS, starting with Solaris 7, provides a journaling capability referred to as *UFS Logging*. Unfortunately, there is little documentation outside of Sun to show how logging works.

To enable logging, the mount command should be invoked with the logging option. The amount of space used for logging is based on the size of the filesystem. 1MB is chosen for each GB of filesystem space up to a maximum of 64MB. As with VxFS, the log is circular. Wrapping or reaching the tail of the log involves flushing transactions that are held in the log.

As with VxFS journaling (described in the section *VxFS Journaling* earlier in this chapter) by using UFS logging the log can be replayed following a system crash to bring it back to a consistent state.

The ext2 and ext3 Filesystems

The first filesystem that was developed as part of Linux was a Minix filesystem clone. At this time, the Minix filesystem stored its block addresses in 16-bit integers that restricted the size of the filesystem to 64MB. Also, directory entries were fixed in size and therefore filenames were limited to 14 characters. Minix filesystem support was replaced in 1992 by the *ext* filesystem, which supported filesystem sizes up to 2GB and filename sizes up to 255 characters. However, ext inodes did not have separate access, modification, and creation time stamps, and linked lists were used to manage free blocks and inodes resulting in fragmentation and less-than-ideal performance.

These inadequacies were addressed by both the *Xia* filesystem and the *ext2* filesystem (which was modelled on the BSD Fast File System), both of which provided a number of enhancements, including a better on-disk layout for managing filesystem resources. The improvements resulting in ext2 far outweighed those of Xia, and in ext2 became the defacto standard on Linux.

The following sections first describe the ext2 filesystem, followed by a description of how the filesystem has evolved over time to produce the ext3 filesystem which supports journaling and therefore fast recovery.

Features of the ext2 Filesystem

Shown below are the main features supported by ext2:

4TB filesystems. This required changes within the VFS layer. Note that the maximum file and filesystem size are properties of the underlying filesystem and the kernel implementation.

255-byte filenames. Directory entries are variable in length with a maximum size of 255 bytes.

Selectable file semantics. With a mount option, the administrator can choose whether to have BSD or SVR4 file semantics. This has an effect on the group ID chosen when a file is created. With BSD semantics, files are created with the same group ID as the parent directory. For System V semantics, if a directory has the set group ID bit set, new files inherit the group ID bit of the parent directory and subdirectories inherit the group ID and set group ID bit; otherwise, files and directories inherit the primary group ID of the calling process.

Multiple filesystem block sizes. Block sizes of 1024, 2048, and 4096 bytes can be specified as an option to mkfs.

Reserved space. Up to 5 percent of the filesystem can be reserved for root-only files, allowing some recovery in the case of a full filesystem.

Per-file attributes. Attributes can be set on a file or directory to affect subsequent file access. This is described in detail in the next section.

BSD-like synchronous updates. A mount option ensures that all meta-data (inodes, bitmaps, indirects and directories) are written to disk synchronously when modified. This increases filesystem integrity although at the expense of performance.

Periodic filesystem checks. To enforce filesystem integrity, ext2 has two ways of ensuring that a full fsck is invoked on the filesystem. A count is kept of how many times the filesystem is mounted read/write. When it reaches a specified count, a full fsck is invoked. Alternatively, a time-based system can be used to ensure that the filesystem is cleaned on a regular basis.

Fast symbolic links. As with VxFS, symbolic links are stored in the inode itself rather than in a separate allocated block.

The following sections describe some of these features in more detail.

Per-File Attributes

In addition to the features listed in the last section, there is a set of per-file attributes which can be set using the chattr command and displayed using the lsattr command. The supported attributes are:

EXT2_SECRM_FL. With this attribute set, whenever a file is truncated the data blocks are first overwritten with random data. This ensures that once a file is deleted, it is not possible for the file data to resurface at a later stage in another file.

EXT2_UNRM_FL. This attribute is used to allow a file to be undeleted.

EXT2_SYNC_FL. With this attribute, file meta-data, including indirect blocks, is always written synchronously to disk following an update. Note, though, that this does not apply to regular file data.

EXT2_COMPR_FL. The file is compressed. All subsequent access must use compression and decompression.

EXT2_APPEND_FL. With this attribute set, a file can only be opened in append mode (O_APPEND) for writing. The file cannot be deleted by anyone.

EXT2_IMMUTABLE_FL. If this attribute is set, the file can only be read and cannot deleted by anyone.

Attributes can be set on both regular files and directories. Attributes that are set on directories are inherited by files created within the directory.

The following example shows how the immutable attribute can be set on a file. The passwd file is first copied into the current directory and is shown to be writable by root. The chattr command is called to set the attribute, which can then displayed by calling lsattr. The two operations following show that it is then no longer possible to remove the file or extend it:

```
# cp /etc/passwd .
# ls -l passwd
-rw-r--r--    1 root       root        960 Jan 28 17:35 passwd
# chattr +i passwd
# lsattr passwd
---i--------passwd
# rm passwd
rm: cannot unlink 'passwd': Operation not permitted
# cat >> passwd
bash: passwd: Permission denied
```

Note that at the time of writing, not all of the file attributes are implemented.

The ext2 Disk Layout

The layout of structures on disk is shown in Figure 9.6. Aside from the boot block, the filesystem is divided into a number of fixed size *block groups*. Each block group manages a fixed set of inodes and data blocks and contains a copy of the superblock that is shown as follows. Note that the first block group starts at an offset of 1024 bytes from the start of the disk slice or volume.

```
struct ext2_super_block {
    unsigned long  s_inodes_count;          /* Inodes count (in use)*/
```

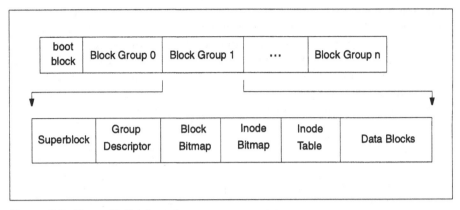

Figure 9.6 The ext2 disk layout.

```
unsigned long  s_blocks_count;        /* Blocks count (in use) */
unsigned long  s_r_blocks_count;      /* Reserved blocks count */
unsigned long  s_free_blocks_count;   /* Free blocks count */
unsigned long  s_free_inodes_count;   /* Free inodes count */
unsigned long  s_first_data_block;    /* First Data Block */
unsigned long  s_log_block_size;      /* Block size */
long           s_log_frag_size;       /* Fragment size */
unsigned long  s_blocks_per_group;    /* # Blocks per group */
unsigned long  s_frags_per_group;     /* # Fragments per group */
unsigned long  s_inodes_per_group;    /* # Inodes per group */
unsigned long  s_mtime;               /* Mount time */
unsigned long  s_wtime;               /* Write time */
unsigned short s_mnt_count;           /* Mount count */
short          s_max_mnt_count;       /* Maximal mount count */
unsigned short s_magic;               /* Magic signature */
unsigned short s_state;               /* File system state */
unsigned short s_errors;              /* Error handling */
unsigned long  s_lastcheck;           /* time of last check */
unsigned long  s_checkinterval;       /* max. time between checks */
};
```

Many of the fields shown here are self explanatory and describe the usage of inodes and data blocks within the block group. The magic number for ext2 is 0xEF58. The fields toward the end of the superblock are used to determine when a full fsck should be invoked (either based on the number of read/write mounts or a specified time).

When writing sequentially to a file, ext2 tries to preallocate space in units of 8 contiguous blocks. Unused preallocation is released when the file is closed, so no space is wasted. This is used to help prevent fragmentation, a situation under which the majority of the blocks in the file are spread throughout the disk because contiguous blocks may be unavailable. Contiguous blocks are also good for performance because when files are accessed sequentially there is minimal disk head movement.

It is said that ext2 does not need defragmentation under normal load as long as there is 5 percent of free space on a disk. However, over time continuous addition and removal of files of various size will undoubtedly result in fragmentation to some degree. There is a defragmentation tool for ext2 called defrag but users are cautioned about its use—if a power outage occurs when running defrag, the file system can be damaged.

The block group is described by the following structure:

```
struct ext2_group_desc {
    unsigned long  bg_block_bitmap;      /* Blocks bitmap block */
    unsigned long  bg_inode_bitmap;      /* Inodes bitmap block */
    unsigned long  bg_inode_table;       /* Inodes table block */
    unsigned short bg_free_blocks_count; /* Free blocks count */
    unsigned short bg_free_inodes_count; /* Free inodes count */
    unsigned short bg_used_dirs_count;   /* Directories count */
};
```

This structure basically points to other components of the block group, with the first three fields referencing specific block numbers on disk. By allocating inodes and disk blocks within the same block group, it is possible to improve performance because disk head movement may be reduced. The bg_used_dirs_count field records the number of inodes in the group that are used for directories. This count is used as part of the scheme to balance directories across the different block groups and to help locate files and their parent directories within the same block group.

To better see how the block group structures are used in practice, the following example, using a small ext2 filesystem, shows how structures are set up when a file is allocated. Firstly, a filesystem is made on a floppy disk as follows:

```
# mkfs /dev/fd0
mke2fs 1.24a (02-Sep-2001)
Filesystem label=
OS type: Linux
Block size=1024 (log=0)
Fragment size=1024 (log=0)
184 inodes, 1440 blocks
72 blocks (5.00%) reserved for the super user
First data block=1
1 block group
8192 blocks per group, 8192 fragments per group
184 inodes per group

Writing inode tables: 0/1done
Writing superblocks and filesystem accounting information: done

This filesystem will be automatically checked every 35 mounts or
180 days, whichever comes first.  Use tune2fs -c or -i to override.
```

Analysis of the on-disk structures can be achieved using the debugfs command. The show_super_stats displays the superblock and the disk group structures. With the -h option, only the superblock is displayed:

```
# debugfs /dev/fd0
debugfs 1.24a (02-Sep-2001)
debugfs: show_super_stats -h
Filesystem volume name:   <none>
Last mounted on:          <not available>
Filesystem UUID:          e4e5f20a-f5f3-4499-8fe0-183d9f87a5ba
Filesystem magic number:  0xEF53
Filesystem revision #:    1 (dynamic)
Filesystem features:      filetype sparse_super
Filesystem state:         clean
Errors behavior:          Continue
Filesystem OS type:       Linux
Inode count:              184
Block count:              1440
Reserved block count:     72
Free blocks:              1399
Free inodes:              173
First block:              1
Block size:               1024
Fragment size:            1024
Blocks per group:         8192
Fragments per group:      8192
Inodes per group:         184
Inode blocks per group:   23
Last mount time:          Wed Dec 31 16:00:00 1969
Last write time:          Fri Feb  8 16:11:59 2002
Mount count:              0
Maximum mount count:      35
Last checked:             Fri Feb  8 16:11:58 2002
Check interval:           15552000 (6 months)
Next check after:         Wed Aug  7 17:11:58 2002
Reserved blocks uid:      0 (user root)
Reserved blocks gid:      0 (group root)
First inode:              11
Inode size:               128


Group  0: block bitmap at 3, inode bitmap at 4, inode table at 5
          1399 free blocks, 173 free inodes, 2 used directories
```

The block group information is shown separate from the superblock. It shows the block numbers where the various structural information is held. For example, the inode bitmap for this block group is stored at block 4—recall from the information displayed when the filesystem was made that the block size is 1024 bytes. This is stored in the s_log_block_size field in the superblock.

Further information about the block group can be displayed with the dumpe2fs command as follows:

```
# dumpe2fs /dev/fd0
dumpe2fs 1.24a (02-Sep-2001)
...
Group 0: (Blocks 1 -1439)
  Primary Superblock at 1,  Group Descriptors at 2-2
  Block bitmap at 3 (+2),  Inode bitmap at 4 (+3)
```

```
Inode table at 5-27 (+4)
1399 free blocks, 173 free inodes, 2 directories
Free blocks: 41-1439
Free inodes: 12-184
```

There are 184 inodes per group in the example here. Inodes start at inode number 11 with the lost+found directory occupying inode 11. Thus, the first inode available for general users is inode 12. The following example shows how all inodes can be used but without all of the space being consumed:

```
# cd /mnt
# i=12
# while [ $i -lt 188 ] ; do ; > $i ; i=`expr $i + 1` ; done
bash: 185: No space left on device
bash: 186: No space left on device
bash: 187: No space left on device
# df -k
Filesystem          1k-blocks      Used Available Use% Mounted on
/dev/hda3            19111092   1844084  17267008  10% /
/dev/hda1               21929      3615     17182  18% /boot
shmfs                  127780         0    127780   0% /dev/shm
/dev/fd0                 1412        15      1325   2% /mnt
```

So, although the filesystem is only 2 percent full, all of the inodes have been allocated. This represents one of the difficulties that filesystems have faced over the years where the number of inodes are statically allocated when the filesystem is made.

The following example shows the statistics of an allocated file:

```
# cp /etc/passwd /mnt ; umount /mnt
# debugfs /dev/fd0
debugfs 1.24a (02-Sep-2001)
debugfs: ls -l /
      2  40755      0      0    1024 13-Feb-2002 20:20 .
      2  40755      0      0    1024 13-Feb-2002 20:20 ..
     11  40755      0      0   12288 13-Feb-2002 20:18 lost+found
     12 100644      0      0    2064 13-Feb-2002 20:20 passwd
debugfs: stat <12>
Inode: 12   Type: regular    Mode:  0644   Flags: 0x0   Generation: 59537
User:    0   Group:     0   Size: 2064
File ACL: 0    Directory ACL: 0
Links: 1   Blockcount: 6
Fragment: Address: 0    Number: 0    Size: 0
ctime: 0x3c6b3af9 -Wed Feb 13 20:20:09 2002
atime: 0x3c6b3af8 -Wed Feb 13 20:20:08 2002
mtime: 0x3c6b3af8 -Wed Feb 13 20:20:08 2002
BLOCKS:
(0-2):41-43
TOTAL: 3
```

In this case, the file is displayed by inode number. The size of the file is 2064 bytes which results in three blocks being allocated: blocks 41 to 43. Recall from displaying the block group information shown previously that the first data block started at block 41.

ext2 On-Disk Inodes

The ext2 on-disk inode structure is defined by the ext2_inode structure as follows:

```
struct ext2_inode {
        __u16        i_mode;              /* File mode */
        __u16        i_uid;               /* Low 16 bits of Owner Uid */
        __u32        i_size;              /* Size in bytes */
        __u32        i_atime;             /* Access time */
        __u32        i_ctime;             /* Creation time */
        __u32        i_mtime;             /* Modification time */
        __u32        i_dtime;             /* Deletion Time */
        __u16        i_gid;               /* Low 16 bits of Group Id */
        __u16        i_links_count;       /* Links count */
        __u32        i_blocks;            /* Blocks count */
        __u32        i_flags;             /* File flags */
        __u32        i_block[EXT2_N_BLOCKS];/* Pointers to blocks */
        __u32        i_generation;        /* File version (for NFS) */
        __u32        i_file_acl;          /* File ACL */
        __u32        i_dir_acl;           /* Directory ACL */
        __u32        i_faddr;             /* Fragment address */
        struct {
                __u8    l_i_frag;         /* Fragment number */
                __u8    l_i_fsize;        /* Fragment size */
        } linux2;
};
```

The first several fields are self explanatory. The i_blocks field records the number of blocks that the file has allocated. This value is in 512-byte chunks. These blocks are stored as either direct data blocks in i_block[] or are referenced through indirect blocks within the same array. For example, consider the passwd file copied to an ext2 filesystem as shown above. Because the file is 2064 bytes in size, three 1024 byte blocks are required. The actual block count shown is 6 (512 byte blocks).

The inode i_block[] array has EXT2_N_BLOCKS (15) pointers to blocks of data. The first EXT2_NDIR_BLOCKS (12) entries in the array are direct pointers to data blocks. The i_block[12] element points to an indirect block of pointers to data blocks. The i_block[13] element points to a double indirect block for which each element points to an indirect block. The i_block[14] element points to a triple indirect block of pointers to double indirects.

Various inode numbers are reserved which explains why the first inode allocated has an inode number of 12 (lost+found is 11). Some reserved inodes are:

EXT2_BAD_INO (1). This file contains a list of bad blocks on the file system.

EXT2_ROOT_INO (2). This is the root directory of the file system.

EXT2_ACL_IDX_INO (3). ACL inode.

EXT2_ACL_DATA_INO (4). ACL inode.

EXT2_BOOT_LOADER_INO (5). The file contains the boot loader.

EXT2_UNDEL_DIR_INO (6). This file is used for file undelete.

EXT2_FIRST_INO (11). This is the first inode that does not have a special meaning and can be used for other purposes.

There are many different inode flags that can be stored in i_flags. These map to the file attributes that can be set with chattr.

The i_faddr field is used in the case where the fragment size and block size are not equal. If the file does not require an exact number of filesystem-sized blocks, the last portion of the file data is stored in a fragment. The location of the fragment is stored in this field.

Repairing Damaged ext2 Filesystems

The e2fsck is used to repair filesystem inconsistencies, that can occur following a system crash. The process followed is divided into five separate passes which are listed below. The information shown here is based on material that appears in the *Linux System Administrators Guide* [WIRZ95]:

Pass 1. This phase takes the longest time to execute, because all of the inodes have to be read into memory and checked.

In this phase, e2fsck checks each inode in the filesystem to ensure the file mode is valid and that all of the blocks in the inode are valid block numbers. During pass 1, bitmaps indicating which blocks and inodes are in use are compiled, to be used later.

If e2fsck notices data blocks that are mapped by more than one inode, it can either clone the duplicated blocks so that each inode has its own copy, or remove the blocks from one or more of the inodes.

To reduce the I/O time necessary in future passes, critical filesystem information is cached in memory, including the location on disk of all of the directory blocks on the filesystem. This removes the need to re-read the directory inodes during pass 2.

Pass 2. In this phase directories are validated. Because directory entries do not span disk blocks, each directory block can be checked individually without reference to other directory blocks. The directory blocks are checked to make sure that the directory entries are valid and contain references to inode numbers that are in use (as determined by pass 1).

For the first directory block in each directory inode, the "." and ".." entries are checked to make sure they exist, and that the inode number for the "." entry matches the current directory.

Pass 2 also caches information concerning the parent directory in which each directory is linked. If a directory is referenced by more than one directory, the second reference of the directory is treated as an illegal hard link and is removed.

Note that at the end of pass 2, nearly all disk I/O that e2fsck needs to perform is complete. Information required by passes 3, 4, and 5 are cached in memory; hence, the remaining passes of e2fsck are largely CPU bound and take less than 5 to 10 percent of the total running time.

Pass 3. In this phase, the directory connectivity is checked by tracing the path of each directory back to the root using information that was cached during pass 2. At this time, the ".." entry for each directory is also checked to make sure it is valid. Any directories that can not be traced back to the root are linked to the lost+found directory.

Pass 4. In this phase, e2fsck checks the reference counts for all inodes by iterating over all the inodes and comparing the link counts (which were cached in pass 1) against internal counters calculated during passes 2 and 3. Any undeleted files with a zero link count are placed in lost+found during this pass.

Pass 5. In this last phase e2fsck checks the validity of the filesystem summary information. It compares the block and inode bitmaps which were constructed during the previous passes against the actual bitmaps on the filesystem and corrects the on-disk copies if necessary.

The e2fsck program is designed to run as quickly as possible. Because filesystem checking programs tend to be disk-bound, this was done by optimizing the algorithms used by e2fsck so that filesystem structures are not repeatedly accessed from the disk. In addition, the order in which inodes and directories are checked are sorted by block number, to reduce the amount of time in disk seeks.

Tuning a ext2 Filesystem

The tune2fs program can be used to change the various tunable parameters of an ext2 filesystem. Some of the different tunables that can be changed are:

- -c max-mount-counts. This option adjusts the count of read/write mounts between two filesystem checks.
- -e error-behavior. When errors are detected, the behavior of the ext2 kernel code can be altered with this option. The value of error-behavior can be continue in that the kernel continues with normal execution, remount-ro, which forces the kernel to remount the filesystem read-only, or panic in which case the kernel will panic.
- -u user. This option sets the user who can benefit from the reserved blocks when the filesystem becomes full. The value of user can be a numerical user ID or a user name.

For further information on tune2fs see the tune2fs(8) manual page.

Resizing ext2 Filesystems

The `resize2fs` command can be used to increase or decrease the size of an ext2 filesystem. Note that the filesystem must be unmounted before the resize can take place. The `resize2fs` program does not manipulate the size of underlying partition. To increase the size of a filesystem, the partition must be increased first using `fdisk`. Similarly, to decrease the size of an ext2 filesystem, the partition must be resized with `fdisk` following the call to `resize2fs`.

If an ext2 filesystem resides on an LVM (Logical Volume Manager) volume, the `e2fsadm` command can be used to resize both the filesystem and the underlying logical volume.

The ext3 Filesystem

The ext3 filesystem was introduced to solve one specific problem, namely the amount of time it takes to perform a filesystem check following a system crash.

As described in the section *VxFS Journaling*, earlier in this chapter, these times can be significant, measured in many hours, if the filesystem is very large in size. Note that large in this case is actually a property of the amount of structural data (inodes) and not specifically the size of the filesystem.

Another goal behind ext3 was to make as few changes to the underlying ext2 code base as possible because ext2 is small in size, easy to maintain, robust, and well understood.

The use of ext3 was positioned in such a way that it is easy to transition between ext2 and ext3 filesystems and vice versa.

The actual journaling layer is separate from ext3. The filesystem understands the concepts of transaction (when one starts, when it finishes) but it is not actually responsible for the journaling.

How to Use an ext3 Filesystem

A new ext3 filesystem can be created by `mkfs` or by converting an existing ext2 filesystem. To create a new ext3 filesystem, `mkfs` is called as follows:

```
# mkfs -j /dev/sda5
```

To convert an existing ext2 filesystem to an ext3 filesystem, the `tune2fs` command can be invoked as follows:

```
# tune2fs -j /dev/sda5
```

Note that the command can be invoked on either a mounted or unmounted filesystem. If invoked on a mounted filesystem, the journal will appear as a visible file (`.journal`). If invoked on an unmounted filesystem or if `mkfs -j` is run when making the filesystem, the journal will not be visible.

To actually mount the filesystem, the `ext3` filesystem type must be specified:

```
# mount -t ext3 /dev/sda5 /mnt1
```

Conversion back to ext2 can be achieved by using the `tune2fs` command as follows:

```
# tune2fs -O ^has_journal /dev/sda5
```

or simply by replaying the log to make the filesystem clean and then simply mounting it as an ext2 filesystem.

Data Integrity Models in ext3

As with VxFS, there is a set of choices about the type and level of journaling to be performed. Users can choose among the following options, which are passed to mount.

`data=writeback`. This option limits data integrity guarantees so that file data itself is not journaled. The filesystem, is however, guaranteed to be structurally sound at all times.

`data=ordered`. This mode, which is the default, ensures that data is consistent at all times. The data is actually written to the file before the transaction is logged. This ensures that there is no stale data in any filesystem block after a crash.

`data=journal`. This option writes all file data through the journal. This means that the data is actually written to disk twice. This option provides the best guarantees in terms of filesystem integrity but because data is written through the journal, performance can be significantly impacted and the time for recovery after a crash can be much greater.

How Does ext3 Work?

The design of ext3 was presented in [TWEE98]. To provide a transaction mechanism, all meta-data-related data blocks must be logged in the journal. There are three distinct types of blocks in question:

Journal blocks. An update to an inode, for example, will write the entire filesystem block to which the inode belongs in to the journal. In [TWEE98], Stephen Tweedie claims that this is a relatively cheap method due to the sequential nature in which data is written to the journal, and that by following this simple approach, there is little complexity in the kernel and therefore less CPU overhead.

Descriptor blocks. These blocks describe other journal blocks and are written to the journal before the journal blocks are written. Because the journal blocks are the actual meta-data blocks that must be written, the descriptor blocks are used to record information about the journal blocks, such as the disk block on which they reside.

Header blocks. The header blocks are written throughout the journal. They record the start and end of the journal together with a sequence number that is used during recovery to locate the order in which the blocks were written.

As with VxFS, transactions are delayed in memory to aid performance. With ext3, a set of transactions is batched into a *compound transaction* and committed to the journal on disk. This process is called *checkpointing*. While checkpointing is in progress, a new compound transaction is started, that will record any further changes to the filesystem while the previous compound transaction is being written to disk.

Crash recovery is performed by walking through the journal and writing any journal blocks to their correct location on disk. Because this is an idempotent operation, a crash in the middle of recovery does not matter because the process can be repeated any number of times with exactly the same effect.

Summary

There are many different UNIX filesystems and to scratch the surface on all of them would easily fill a book of this size. The three filesystems described in the chapter represent a good cross section of filesystems from the UNIX and Linux operating systems and cover the commercial filesystem market (VxFS), the most widely documented and ported filesystem (UFS), and the most popular open source filesystems (ext2 and ext3).

Only a few other filesystems have been documented in any detail. [HANC01] describes the AdvFS filesystem developed by Digital which is the main filesystem of their True64 operating system. [KELL96] describes IBM's JFS filesystem.

To understand filesystem internals it is always best to start with one of the simple filesystems such as the original System V filesystem as documented in [LION96]. If studying Linux, the ext2 filesystem on one of the earlier kernels is a good place to start before looking at the more elaborate, and therefore more complex, filesystems.

CHAPTER

10

Mapping Filesystems to Multiprocessor Systems

Once upon a time, filesystem writers (in fact kernel writers in general) didn't have to worry about multiprocessor issues. Certain structures needed protection by locks for the case where a process went to sleep (for example, for an I/O operation) or if interrupts executed code which could attempt to access structures that were being used by the process currently running on the CPU.

All of this changed with the introduction of *Symmetric Multiprocessor* (SMP)-based systems, where multiple CPUs share the same memory and a single kernel runs across all of the CPUs. In this model, one must assume that *threads* of execution could be running within any part of the kernel and could attempt to modify any kernel structure at the same time as another thread.

This chapter follows the evolution of UNIX through the earlier Uni-Processor (UP) days through to today's highly scalable SMP-based UNIX implementations. Different types of MP locks are described, as well as how the VERITAS filesystem, VxFS, uses these locks to manage its set of in-core inodes.

The Evolution of Multiprocessor UNIX

[WAIT87] documents the early years of *Multi-Processor* (MP) development in UNIX. In the mid 1980s the emergence of Sun Microsystems and Apollo

Computing saw the introduction of cheaper workstations, allowing engineers to have their own workstations for the first time. In addition to the well-established computer companies such as DEC, IBM, and Cray, newcomers including Sequent, Alliant, Convex, and Encore started to introduce multiprocessor-based UNIX operating systems and hardware.

The first MP UNIX, named MUNIX, was developed at the Naval Postgraduate School in Monterey [HAWL75]. An MP-based UNIX kernel developed at Purdue University in the late 1970s ran on a VAX computer in a master/slave model whereby the UNIX kernel ran on one processor while user applications ran on the other processors. Within Bell Labs, the UNIX/370 project was formed to create an MP UNIX kernel to run on an MP version of the IBM 370 mainframe. This kernel used semaphores to lock various kernel structures. Members of the Bell Labs team then went on to create an MP UNIX to run on their own 3B20A resulting in a kernel that could perform 70 percent better than the UP version.

One company that would make enormous enhancements to SMP UNIX and that would eventually find its way into SVR4 ES/MP was Sequent Computers, which emerged in the mid 1980s and made significant improvements to both the underlying hardware and the UNIX kernel.

The large number of UNIX systems companies has diminished somewhat with consolidation around systems from Sun, IBM, and HP, all of which are today producing SMP systems with up to 64 CPUs.

Traditional UNIX Locking Primitives

This section examines the earlier uni-processor (UP) UNIX synchronization primitives starting with 5th Edition UNIX and going up to SVR4.0. Over this twenty-year time period, the implementation stayed remarkably similar. As noted in his book *Lions Commentary on UNIX 6th Edition-with Source Code* [LION96], John Lions notes that the early mechanisms for handling critical sections of code were "totally inappropriate in a multi-processor system."

As mentioned earlier, in UP UNIX implementations, the kernel needed to protect data structures in the case when a process went to sleep or when handling interrupts. The reasons a process might sleep include: waiting for I/O, waiting for a lock owned by another process, or giving up the CPU to another process after using up its timeslice.

If a process needs to access some resource such as a buffer cache buffer that is currently in use, it will issue a sleep() call specifying the address of the resource it requires. A swtch() call is made to relinquish control of the CPU, allowing another process to run. For example, to wait on a busy buffer, the following code sequence is made:

```
if (bp->b_flags & B_BUSY) {
    bp->b_flags |= B_WANTED;
    sleep(bp, PRIBIO);
}
```

The address of the structure on which the process is waiting (called the *wait channel*) is stored in the p_wchan field of the proc structure. The priority argument passed to sleep() will be described in more detail later in the chapter. Note for now though that if the priority is greater than or equal to zero, the process may be awoken from a sleep by a signal. A value of less than zero prevents this from happening.

When a process is about to relinquish control of a specific resource, it looks to see if another process is waiting on the resource and issues a corresponding wakeup() call to signal to the process that the resource is now available. In this case, the following code sequence is invoked:

```
if (bp->b_flags & B_WANTED)
    wakeup(bp);
```

To determine which process is sleeping on the resource, a scan is made through the proc table issuing a wakeup() call for each process whose p_wchan field is set to bp.

Hardware and Software Priority Levels

To prevent data structures from being modified by interrupt handling code, *critical sections* were protected by software priority levels. Because interrupts can occur at any time, there is a potential for an interrupt handler to modify the same data structure as the process currently running, resulting in a corrupted variable or linked list. To prevent this from happening, UNIX allows the running process to temporarily disable interrupts while executing critical sections of code. Disabling all interrupts is typically unnecessary, so a number of priority levels were established allowing the kernel to block one or more interrupts depending on the type of operation being performed.

When porting an operating system, notice must be taken of the hardware-assigned priorities for each device. This is a hardware decision for which the operating system developers may have little or no choice. However, by knowing the hardware vector, it is then possible to disable specific interrupts. Each interrupt is assigned a priority such that if an interrupt were to occur while an interrupt handler is running for the same device, the interrupt can be temporarily masked.

For example, Table 10.1 shows the interrupt vector around the time of 5th Edition UNIX.

When an interrupt occurs, the process priority is changed to reflect the type of interrupt. Although the table shows the process and interrupt priorities to be the same, this does not have to occur in practice. If the RK disk driver interrupts, the processor priority will be switched to level 5. This prevents any interrupts from occurring at processor priority less than or equal to 5. Any interrupts that occur at this time with a lower priority will be held (latched) until the current interrupt handling code is finished.

Table 10.1   Hardware and Software Priority Levels in 5th Edition UNIX

PERIPHERAL DEVICE	INTERRUPT PRIORITY	PROCESS PRIORITY
Teletype input	4	4
Teletype output	4	4
Paper tape input	4	4
Paper tape output	4	4
Line printer	4	4
RK disk driver	5	5
Line clock	6	6
Programmable clock	6	6

Typically, the CPU will be running at processor priority level 0. Consider the case within the buffer cache handling code where a process has located the required buffer, but the buffer is currently in the middle of an I/O operation. Because the buffer is busy, the process needs to set the b_flags field to B_WANTED before calling sleep() as shown earlier. In this case the following fragment of code is executed:

```
spl6();
if (bp->b_flags & B_BUSY) {
    bp->b_flags |= B_WANTED;
    sleep(bp, PRIBIO);
    spl0();
} else {
    spl0();
}
```

In this case, the buffer has been found on one of the hash queues. In order to check the b_flags field, this process must block interrupts from the disk driver, thus the initial call to spl6() (set priority level). If B_BUSY is not set, the buffer is not in use and the call is made to spl0() to set the priority level back to 0. If the buffer is in use, B_WANTED can be set safely and the process issues a call to sleep(). One thought that comes to mind here without knowledge of the implementation of sleep() is that, at a glance, it appears as if the process goes to sleep with interrupts blocked. In essence this is true. However, the next process that wakes up will set the priority level to the level at which it went to sleep. Consider the case where another process is waiting for a separate buffer from the one shown above. After it awakes, it knows that it has control of the buffer it slept on, so it will immediately issue an spl0() call as shown above.

After the process that issues the call to sleep() awakes, the priority passed to sleep() is reinstated before sleep() returns.

UP Locking and Pre-SVR4 Filesystems

Now that the old style primitives have been described, consider how this applies to the old filesystem implementation. Recall that there was no File System Switch or VFS architecture at that time. The main concern for filesystem development was the thought of what happens when a process goes to sleep. If the process is in the middle of performing I/O on file A, it would certainly not be a good idea to let another process come along and truncate the file. The section *Putting it All Together*, in Chapter 6, showed how file I/O took place in the research editions of UNIX. At the higher layers of the kernel, most activity involved manipulating per-process data structures such as the user, proc, and file structures and therefore there was no need to protect the process from interrupts or other processes. Furthermore, on read operations, there was no locking within the filesystem handling code per se. The only locking occurred within the buffer cache following calls to bread(), which in turn would invoke getblk(). The same is also true for overwrites whereby a write to the file would overwrite blocks that were already allocated.

File allocation on the other hand had a number of places where there could be contention. The first lock of interest was at the filesystem level. When a call to alloc() was made to allocate a filesystem block, the s_lock field of the mount structure was held to indicate that allocation was taking place. If the s_lock field was already set, a call to sleep() was made passing the address of s_lock. After a block had been allocated (or freed), a call to wakeup() was issued to allow any other process to then allocate/deallocate. The procedure was also followed when allocating or deallocating an inode, by using the s_ilock field of the mount structure.

There is no locking during handling of the write(S) system call above the block allocation layer. For each 512-byte chunk of the write to perform, a call to bmap() is made to locate the block to write to. If the block is not already present in the file, a call to alloc() is made to allocate a new block. The only reason that this process can sleep is if I/O needs to be performed, and this will occur only after a block has been allocated and assigned to the inode. Therefore, no other process can enter the kernel to access the file until the allocating process relinquishes control of the CPU. The same is also true when a process time slice expires due to the result of a clock interrupt. If the process is running in the kernel, it will continue to run until it is about to return to user space; only then can it sleep.

UP Locking and SVR4-Based Filesystems

The period between the research editions of UNIX described previously and the introduction of SVR4 and the VFS/vnode architecture saw only a few differences in the way that locks were managed in the kernel. The sleep() / wakeup() mechanism used throughout the history of UNIX still remained in place together with the software priority mechanism.

The reader/writer lock, implemented by the vop_rwlock() and vop_rwunlock() vnode operations, was introduced with SVR4 to allow the filesystem to manage locks on the inode internally. When a call was made to VOP_RWLOCK(), the filesystem had no knowledge of whether a read or a write was about to follow. This makes sense to a large degree when performing writes, but the implementation did not allow for multiple readers. This mode of operation was still in place by the time that the first MP versions of UNIX started to appear.

The following example shows a fragment of the implementation of vop_rwlock() in an early version of VxFS:

```
while (ip->i_flag & IRWLOCKED) {
    ip->i_flag |= IWANT;
    sleep(ip, PINOD);
}
ip->i_flag |= IRWLOCKED
```

To release a lock on the inode the following code was executed:

```
ip->i_flag &= ~IRWLOCKED;
if (ip->i_flag & IWANT) {
    ip->i_flag &= ~IWANT;
    wakeprocs(ip, PRMPT);
}
```

Note that the code fragment for sleeping also handles the case where the process may be awoken but another process grabbed the lock first.

No additional locks were taken by the kernel prior to a call to VOP_GETPAGE() or VOP_PUTPAGE(). All other filesystem structures were protected by the same sleep()/wakeup() mechanisms.

Symmetric Multiprocessing UNIX

The introduction of SMP hardware and SMP-based UNIX implementations resulted in a completely new set of locking primitives and removal of the old sleep(), wakeup(), and spl() primitives. With an SMP implementation, multiple threads of control can be executing the same piece of kernel code on different processors at the same time. More importantly, these threads can be accessing the same data structures at the same time.

Early SMP implementations were based around a *global kernel lock*. Each time a process entered the kernel it grabbed the kernel lock and ran in an environment similar to the UP kernels described above. Any other processes entering the kernel were required to sleep until the first processes released the kernel lock. For environments where most work was performed in user space with little I/O, this worked well. However, these environments are not very representative of most real world applications.

Over the years, these *coarse grain locks* were replaced by a much *finer grain* locking model. Imagine any number of threads running in the kernel at the same time. Accessing kernel structures in a read-only manner is fine. However, any time a kernel structure needs to be modified you must bear in mind that while the structure, a linked list for example, is in the process of changing, another thread may be in the process of reading the structure. This is obviously undesirable because the reader might see a corrupt linked list, access NULL pointers, and so on. Therefore, structures must be protected by locks while an update is in progress. There are two basic types of locks, *sleep locks* and *spin locks*. The former are similar to the `sleep()` / `wakeup()` calls described in the previous section. Note, however, that the process will go to sleep, yielding to another process that is ready to run. If the critical section of code involves only a few instructions to manipulate a linked list, it can be much cheaper for the waiting process to *spin* (loop) waiting for access to the resource.

At the filesystem interface level, the `vop_rwlock()` interface was changed as shown below:

```
int
vx_rwlock(vp, off, len, fmode, mode)
```

The mode field was set to either `LOCK_SHARED` or `LOCK_EXCL`, which informed the filesystem whether a read or a write vnode operation was about to occur. At a simple level, this allowed the filesystem to support multiple readers or a single writer at the vnode layer. It also allowed filesystems to implement a range-locking model whereby portions of the file could be locked allowing multiple readers and writers. Note that supporting multiple concurrent writers is not a trivial task to perform. Most filesystems allow multiple readers.

The `sleep()`/`wakeup()` mechanism was retired in SVR4 ES/MP and replaced by a number of locks more suitable to MP architectures, including spin locks and reader/writer locks. The following sections highlight the different types of locks and describe the circumstances under which one lock may be used in place of another. Note that the above change at the vnode layer was the only locking change between the filesystem-independent and filesystem-dependent layers of the kernel. Much of the work in improving filesystem scalability in an SMP environment comes from careful analysis of filesystem-specific data structures to ensure that locking occurs at a fine grain level and coarser locks are minimized as much as possible; with 64-way SMP systems, there can be significant contention on locks that are at too high a level.

SMP Lock Types

Rather than describing the whole set of possible locks that are available on the various SMP UNIX implementations, this section highlights the types of locks that can be used in SMP implementations, together with the conditions under which one would use one lock type over another. Following this section, using

VxFS as an example, the types of locks used to manage in-core inodes is described.

Mutex locks. The mutex (*mutual exclusion*) lock has a single owner. An *adaptive mutex* is a variant of the mutex lock under which a thread trying to acquire the mutex can choose to spin (*spin lock*) or sleep. When spinning, the process loops constantly trying to acquire the lock. If the process chooses to sleep, it relinquishes control of the CPU and sleeps until the holding process releases the mutex.

Reader / writer locks. There are many instances where multiple threads can be accessing certain structures or sections of code simultaneously but where only one thread can modify the same structures. One example, as shown previously, is the VOP_RWLOCK() vnode interface. The filesystem can use a reader/writer lock on an inode to allow multiple threads to read from the file simultaneously but only one thread to actually write to a file at any one time.

Sleep locks. Some implementations do not permit holders of mutexes or reader/writer locks to sleep if the locks are held. Instead, sleep locks must be used if the thread wishes to block.

Turnstiles. Different threads in the kernel may be running at different priorities. If threads of different priorities go to sleep on the same lock and the one with the lowest priority is first to grab the lock, *priority inversion* occurs; that is, the lower priority thread runs in preference to the higher priority thread. Another type of priority inversion occurs when a high priority thread blocks on a lock already held by a lower priority thread. To help alleviate the problem, the priority of the higher thread is *inherited* by the lower priority thread, ensuring that it completes its task at the priority of the waiting thread. Turnstile locks provide a mechanism whereby mutexes and reader/writer locks can be used with a priority inheritance mechanism.

Condition variables. This type of lock, also called a *synchronization variable* on some platforms, is a lock acquired based on some predicate. Threads can block on the lock and be woken when the result of the predicate changes. In SMP environments there is a potential for the wakeup to be lost if the condition changes after a thread has checked the condition but just before it goes to sleep. To alleviate this problem, condition variables are typically used in conjunction with a mutex, which must be acquired before checking and is released when the thread sleeps.

Semaphores. A semaphore is used to access a shared resource either as a binary semaphore (a mutex is basically a binary semaphore) or as a counter whereby the semaphore is initialized with a number defining how many threads can access the resource simultaneously. Each time a thread grabs the semaphore, the count is decremented. When it reaches zero, the calling thread blocks until a thread releases the semaphore.

When to use different types of locks is not always obvious and may change from one platform to the next depending on the types of locks available. One decision is the choice between spin locks and sleep locks. Typically, spin locks should only be used for very short durations. In a 64-way SMP system, it is highly undesirable to have a large number of threads spinning waiting for a resource held by one thread on another CPU. On the other hand, the sleep/wakeup mechanism is expensive because it can result in a number of context switches. When using spin locks it is important to determine the right granularity of the lock in relation to the structures that are being locked. Does a whole linked list need to be locked? Can the list be split into a number of separate lists, each protected by a separate lock? Is there a significant enough performance benefit to warrant the complexity that results from breaking structures up at this level of granularity?

Getting the level of locking correct is also dependent on the type of workload. Getting the balance right and making the correct choices can often be the result of many years of study!

Mapping VxFS to SMP Primitives

The VERITAS filesystem, VxFS, has been ported to numerous different architectures. At the time of writing, VERITAS directly supports Solaris, AIX, HP-UX, and Linux using the same code base. Because much of the VxFS code is common across all platforms, a generic set of locks is used, which maps to the underlying operating system locks. VxFS makes use of the following types of locks:

Spin locks. These locks are typically used to modify certain structure flags. The duration of the operation is very small, which makes it acceptable for other threads to spin waiting for the lock.

Sleep locks. The *putpage* lock is a sleep lock since the vnode putpage paths through the filesystem are likely to result in disk I/O, causing the calling process to sleep.

Reader / writer sleep locks. Data structures that support multiple readers but only a single writer use this type of lock. Examples would be the inode read/write lock and the getpage lock. VxFS also uses recursive reader/writer sleep locks.

Synchronization variables. These lock types, also called condition variables, provide MP sleep/wakeup synchronization. They are used in conjunction with a spin lock, which must be obtained prior to deciding whether to sleep or not.

The I/O paths of various operating systems have been described throughout the previous chapters. At the filesystem/kernel interface the only locking performed is through the VOP_RWLOCK() / VOP_RWUNLOCK() vnode operations. The following locks give some indication as to how locks can be used to increase the concurrency to structures, such as the in-core inode.

The VxFS Inode Reader/Writer Lock

First, as described above, when reading from or writing to a file, the read/write lock must be acquired on the file either at the VOP layer or from within the filesystem. This is a shared / exclusive lock allowing a single writer and multiple, concurrent readers.

The lock is always acquired in shared mode for read operations and may also be acquired in shared mode for some write operations. In the case where writes access holes or in the case of extending writes, the lock must then be acquired in exclusive mode. Generally speaking, the lock is held exclusively either if blocks need to be allocated to the file or if the file size needs changing.

Because I/O will occur when reading and writing, the inode read / write lock must also be a sleep lock.

The VxFS Getpage and Putpage Locks

As with the inode read/write lock, there can be multiple threads entering through the VOP_GETPAGE() interface to satisfy page faults. Therefore, the getpage lock is also a reader/writer lock. Some getpage calls may involve block allocation and the lock must then be taken in exclusive mode. This may occur, for example, on a writable mapping over a hole in the file. Because I/O may occur for getpage calls, the lock must also be a sleep lock.

The putpage lock is also a reader/writer sleep lock. Threads that are in the process of allocating to the file will take the putpage lock in exclusive mode to block threads coming in through the VOP_PUTPAGE() vnode interface.

The VxFS Inode Lock and Inode Spin Lock

The preceding locks are primarily concerned with reading from and writing to files. There are other times that inodes are accessed. The *inode lock* is used to protect inode fields when the inode needs to be written to disk and also to protect the in-core copy of the disk inode when changes are needed. This lock is exclusive only.

The *inode spin lock* is used to protect fields of the inode that reside in memory only, for example, various flags fields, and read ahead and flush behind statistics.

The VxFS Inode List Lock

At a minimum, inodes are linked onto the free list or hash queue when in use. The fields used to link the inode onto these lists are held within the inode structure. Moving the inode from one list to another involves manipulating a small number of fields. A spin lock is used in this case.

Summary

It is now not uncommon to see 32- and 64-node SMP systems with many gigabytes of memory. The fact that one single kernel has the ability to scale to that number of CPUs shows how multiprocessor technology has evolved since the early implementations in the 1980s.

For further information on multiprocessor UNIX systems, Curt Schimmel's book *UNIX Systems for Modern Architectures* [SCHI94] is a must read for anyone interested in UNIX multiprocessing and associated hardware. *Solaris Internals—Core Kernel Architecture* by Jim Mauro and Richard McDougall [MAUR01] contains detailed information about SMP locks, including the implementation of locking primitives on Solaris. Uresh Vahalia's book *UNIX Internals—The New Frontiers* [VAHA96] shows various case studies of different multiprocessor implementations, as well as describing some of the classic multiprocessor issues.

Pseudo Filesystems

When people think of filesystems, they tend to think of a file hierarchy of files and directories that are all stored on disk somewhere. However, there are a number of filesystem types that provide a host of useful information but which have no physical backing store (disk storage). The most well known pseudo filesystem is /proc, which is used by the ps command as well as various debuggers.

This chapter describes some of the more well known pseudo filesystem types and provides a basic implementation of the ps command using the Solaris /proc filesystem.

The /proc Filesystem

The /proc filesystem was first introduced in 8th Edition UNIX and was described in Tom Killian's 1984 Usenix paper "Processes as Files" [KILL84].

The /proc filesystem was to replace the ptrace() system call, with the advantage that the full process address space was visible and could be manipulated with read() and write() system calls. This contrasts with the interfaces offered by ptrace(), the system call traditionally used by debuggers, that only provides a word-at-a-time interface.

Roger Faulkner and Ron Gomes ported the research version of /proc to SVR4 and presented their work in another USENIX paper: "The Process File System and Process Model in UNIX System V" [FAUL91]. At that time, Faulkner was with Sun Microsystems and Gomes with AT&T Bell Laboratories. As described in the paper, future work was intended to restructure /proc from a flat file system into a directory hierarchy describing a process. That work was undertaken at both Sun and USL and will be described later.

In the early /proc implementation, whose name is derived from the directory on which it is mounted, there is an entry in the directory for each process in the system. The name of the file displayed corresponds to the process ID, while the size of the file represents the size of the process address space. The file permissions correspond to the user who owns the process.

Figure 11.1 shows at a high level how the /proc filesystem is implemented. Standard file-related system calls such as open(), read(), and write() are handled at the filesystem-independent layer in the same manner as for other filesystem types. Much of the information about a process is held in the process table (traditionally in the array proc[]). To open a specific process file, the /proc filesystem must scan the process table looking for an entry whose p_pid field matches the pathname component passed.

One of the most widely used commands that access /proc is ps. Its role is to open each file in the /proc directory and then access the process status through an ioctl() system call. This was originally represented by the prstatus structure, which could be obtained by opening the file and issuing the PIOCSTATUS ioctl command. With the SVR4 implementation of /proc, there were over 40 different ioctl commands that could be issued, many of which dealt with debugging.

Note that the /proc filesystem does not have to be mounted on the /proc directory. It can in fact be mounted multiple times, which allows it to be used in chroot() environments.

The Solaris /proc Implementation

With the introduction of user-level threads of execution, the notion of /proc changed substantially from the single threaded process-based model of previous versions of UNIX. Each entry in /proc is a directory under which all of the information about a specific process is collected.

As an example, consider the following process, which is run in the background. Using the process ID that is returned, the contents of the /proc/3707 are displayed:

```
$ sleep 10000&
[1] 3707
$ cd /proc/3707
$ ls -l
total 1618
-rw-------   1 spate    fcf          1630208 May 28 21:24 as
-r--------   1 spate    fcf              152 May 28 21:24 auxv
```

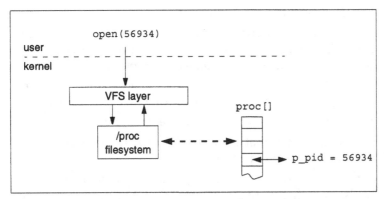

Figure 11.1 Implementation of the /proc filesystem.

```
-r--------   1 spate    fcf            36 May 28 21:24 cred
--w-------   1 spate    fcf             0 May 28 21:24 ctl
lr-x------   1 spate    fcf             0 May 28 21:24 cwd ->
dr-x------   2 spate    fcf          8208 May 28 21:24 fd
-r--r--r--   1 spate    fcf           120 May 28 21:24 lpsinfo
-r--------   1 spate    fcf           912 May 28 21:24 lstatus
-r--r--r--   1 spate    fcf           536 May 28 21:24 lusage
dr-xr-xr-x   3 spate    fcf            48 May 28 21:24 lwp
-r--------   1 spate    fcf          1728 May 28 21:24 map
dr-x------   2 spate    fcf           544 May 28 21:24 object
-r--------   1 spate    fcf          2048 May 28 21:24 pagedata
-r--r--r--   1 spate    fcf           336 May 28 21:24 psinfo
-r--------   1 spate    fcf          1728 May 28 21:24 rmap
lr-x------   1 spate    fcf             0 May 28 21:24 root ->
-r--------   1 spate    fcf          1440 May 28 21:24 sigact
-r--------   1 spate    fcf          1232 May 28 21:24 status
-r--r--r--   1 spate    fcf           256 May 28 21:24 usage
-r--------   1 spate    fcf             0 May 28 21:24 watch
-r--------   1 spate    fcf          2736 May 28 21:24 xmap
```

The contents of some of these files are C structures. For each of the structures that can be accessed, the `procfs.h` header file can be referenced for further information. Where structures are described, the file can be opened and the structure read directly from offset 0 within the file. A primitive ps example, shown in the section *Accessing Files in the Solaris /proc Filesystem*, later in this chapter, demonstrates how this is achieved.

Some of the files make reference to an LWP, a *light weight process*. The LWP model is used to provide support for multiple threads of control within a process. Grouping threads into an LWP alters the scheduling properties of the different threads.

The various files contained within /proc on a per-process basis are:

as. Opening this file gives access to the address space of the process. This allows the caller to find a specific address using `lseek()` and then either read from or write to the address using `read()` and `write()`.

auxv. This file contains dynamic linker information.

cred. The process credentials, defined by the pcred structure, can be found here. This includes information such as the real and effective user IDs, real and effective group IDs, group, and supplementary group information.

ctl. This write-only file is used for process control and accounting. A request may be made to stop or start a process or enable process event tracing.

cwd. This file is a symbolic link to the process' current working directory.

fd. This directory contains files that correspond to the files that the process has open. There is one entry per open file.

lpsinfo, lstatus, lusage. These files give information about each of the process LWPs. Note that there can be multiple LWPs per process; each contains one or more threads.

map. This file contains an array of pmap structures, each of which describes a segment within the virtual address range of the process.

object. Each address space segment maps an underlying file. This directory contains read-only files that are referenced by the map and pagedata files. Opening one of these files gives a file descriptor for the specific mapped file.

pagedata. Opening this file allows the caller to track address space references and modifications on a per-page basis.

psinfo. This file gives general information about the state of the process that is used by the ps command. The psinfo structure, defined in procfs.h, can simply be read from this file.

rmap. Similar to the map file, this file contains an array of prmap structures. These segments are reserved by the operating system for structures such as the stack.

root. This file is a symbolic link to the process' root directory.

sigact. This file contains an array of sigaction structures which define the disposition of signals associated with the traced process.

status. The information stored in this file, underpinned by the pstatus structure, gives a fairly detailed account about the state of the process. This includes a set of flags that indicate whether the process is runnable, stopped, being single-stepped, and so on. Process group and session information, memory size, and tracing data are some of the other types of information that can be found in this file.

usage. This file, underpinned by the prusage structure, gives a wealth of timing-related information about the process.

watch. This file contains an array of pwatch structures, which enable a process to be debugged. The controlling process can set breakpoints in the process by writing a PCWATCH message through the ctl file.

The lwp directory contains further information about each light weight process.

Accessing Files in the Solaris /proc Filesystem

To demonstrate how to access files within /proc, the following simple program gives an idea of how the ps program is implemented. Much of the information that is displayed by ps can be accessed through the psinfo file. Reading from this file returns data underpinned by the psinfo structure. The following program takes a process ID as an argument and reads the corresponding psinfo for that process. It then displays some of the information.

```
#include <fcntl.h>
#include <procfs.h>

main(int argc, char *argv[])
{
        struct psinfo       ps;
        char                fname[256];
        int                 fd;

        sprintf(fname, "/proc/%s/psinfo", argv[1]);
        fd = open(fname, O_RDONLY);
        read(fd, (char *)&ps, sizeof(struct psinfo));
        printf("UID\tPID\tPPID\tCMD\n");
        printf("%d\t%d\t%d\t%s\n",
                ps.pr_uid, ps.pr_pid, ps.pr_ppid, ps.pr_psargs);
}
```

Shown below is a simple run of the program, which displays information about the sleep process shown earlier:

```
$ ./mps 3707
UID     PID  PPID    CMD
824    3707     1    sleep 100000
```

The psinfo file for each /proc entry is readable by anyone. Thus, it is possible for any user to write a more elaborate version of the preceding program that displays entries for all processes.

Tracing and Debugging with /proc

The ctl file allows one process to control another process through a rich set of functions provided by the /proc filesystem. Although all of these functions won't be described here, the aim is to highlight the type of features available and show how a process can be traced or debugged.

Access to the ctl file, which is write only, is achieved by writing an *operational code* to the file together with any additional data required for the operation in question. The controlling process tracks three different types of events, namely:

Signals. A stop based on a signal is handled in all cases where the signal is detected, whether on return from a system call or trap, or during process wakeup.

System calls. The process is stopped either when the kernel is entered to process a system call or is just about to exit from the kernel back to user space after the system call has been processed.

Faults. There are a number of different fault types that can be managed, some of which depend on the type of architecture on which the operating system is running. Fault types include illegal instructions, breakpoints, memory access, and trace traps (used for single stepping).

The `truss` command is a prime example of a utility that controls another process. Its role is to display the system calls made by another process including the system call arguments and return values. The `PCSENTRY` and `PCSEXIT` control functions determine whether a process stops on entry to or exit from a system call. The system calls to be traced are held in the `sysset_t` structure, which is passed along with the `PCSENTRY` and `PCSEXIT` control functions. The `prfillset()` function can be used to build the complete set of system calls, because `truss` will monitor all system calls. For a more controlled trace, the set of system calls monitored can be altered using the `praddset()` and `prdelset()` library functions.

There are a number of different control messages that both stop and start a process. As an example of those functions that are relevant to `truss`, the `PCSTOP` function directs the process to stop on an event of interest and waits for it to stop. An event of interest is defined by invoking `PCSTRACE` (signals to be traced), `PCSFAULT` (faults to be traced), `PCSENTRY` (system call entry), or `PCSEXIT` (system call exit). The `PCRUN` control function makes the process runnable again.

The following pseudo code gives a high-level view of how the `truss` utility can be implemented:

```
prfillset(&syscalls)
PCSENTRY(syscalls)
PCSEXIT(syscalls)
do {
        PCSTOP()
        extract system call arguments
        PCSTART()
        PCSTOP()
        extract system call return value
        display system call type, arguments and return value
        PCSTART()
} while (syscall type != exit);
```

Although this is a simplification, it demonstrates the power of the control functions implemented by the /proc filesystem.

There are a large number of control functions that make a debugger writer's life much easier. If the debugger is interested in fault types, the following are relevant:

`FLTBPT`. A breakpoint trap.

FLTTRACE. A trace trap (used for single stepping).

FLTWATCH. A watchpoint trap (used to trap on memory access).

The PCSFAULT control function can be used to set the faults to be traced. To put a breakpoint on a specific memory access, the PCWATCH function can be used to specify the address to be watched and whether an event should be triggered for read, write, or execute access. This can be used in conjunction with the stop and start control functions.

Anyone wishing to study how a real debugger makes use of /proc should look at the Solaris implementation of gdb, the GNU debugger whose source is freely available.

The Specfs Filesystem

Devices, whether block or character, are represented by special files in the filesystem. As the number of UNIX filesystem types increased, it was found that each filesystem was duplicating effort when managing access to the devices themselves.

Having multiple special files in the namespace caused an additional problem in that there could be multiple buffers in the buffer cache corresponding to the same block on disk. Considering how files are accessed, returning a filesystem vnode for a device file is incorrect. For example, consider the case where the device file resides on a UFS filesystem. Returning a vnode that has the v_op field of the vnode set to the list of UFS vnode operations will lead to problems. First, the *open* vnode operation on UFS or any other filesystem really has no function to perform for regular files. Second, many of the operations that are applicable to regular files are not applicable to device files. To make matters worse, if the vnode goes inactive, the filesystem may attempt to close the device even though it is open through access to another special file that references the same device.

All of these problems can be solved by adding additional logic inside the filesystem. However, consideration must be given on how to handle device access for each vnode operation. Furthermore, reference counting to determine when the last close on a device occurs is left up to the device driver. All in all, this leads to a situation that has a lot of duplication and is prone to errors.

To solve these problems, a new filesystem type, *specfs*, was introduced in SVR4. The specfs filesystem is not visible to users in that it cannot be mounted or seen from within the namespace.

During a VOP_LOOKUP() operation, instead of returning a vnode which corresponds to the special file, the filesystem makes a call to specvp() which returns a new specfs vnode, that the filesystem must return from the lookup operation. This vnode points to a *specfs node* (snode), a private specfs data structure that references the real vnode of the filesystem.

In the case where one device has more than one entry in the namespace, the snode also points to a common specfs vnode. It is through this common vnode that device access actually takes place.

The following example shows the linkage between two device special files and the common specfs vnode that represents both. This is also shown in Figure 11.2. First of all consider the following simple program, which simply opens a file and pauses awaiting a signal:

```
#include <fcntl.h>

main(int argc, char *argv[])
{
        int     fd;

        fd = open(argv[1], O_RDONLY);
        pause();
}
```

As shown below, a new special file is created with the same major and minor number as /dev/null:

```
# ls -l /dev/null
crw-r--r--   1 root     other     13,  2 May 30 09:17 mynull
# mknod mynull c 13 2
# ls -l mynull
crw-r--r--   1 root     other     13,  2 May 30 09:17 mynull
```

and the program is run as follows:

```
# ./dopen /dev/null &
[1]    3715
# ./dopen mynull &
[2]    3719
```

Using crash, it is possible to trace through the list of file related structures starting out at the file descriptor for each process, to see which underlying vnodes they actually reference. First, the process table slots are located where the two processes reside:

```
# crash
dumpfile = /dev/mem, namelist = /dev/ksyms, outfile = stdout
> p ! grep dopen
 336 s  3719  3713  3719  3713    0  46 dopen          load
 363 s  3715  3713  3715  3713    0  46 dopen          load
```

Starting with the process that is accessing the mynull special file, the user area is displayed to locate the open files:

```
> user 336
. . .
OPEN FILES, POFILE FLAGS, AND THREAD REFCNT:
    [0]: F 300106fc690, 0, 0   [1]: F 300106fc690, 0, 0
    [2]: F 300106fc690, 0, 0   [3]: F 300106fca10, 0, 0
. . .
```

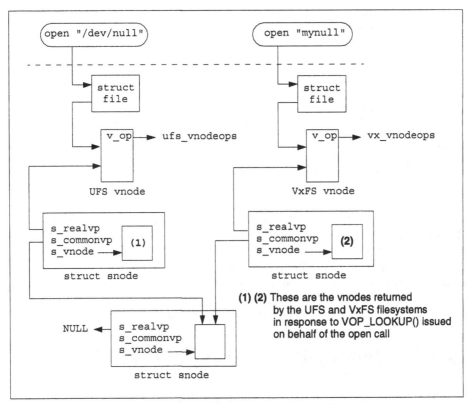

Figure 11.2 Accessing devices from different device special files.

The file structure and its corresponding vnode are then displayed as shown:

```
> file 300106fca10
ADDRESS      RCNT      TYPE/ADDR      OFFSET    FLAGS
300106fca10   1     SPEC/300180a1bd0     0      read
> vnode 300180a1bd0
VCNT VFSMNTED    VFSP      STREAMP VTYPE    RDEV     VDATA    VFILOCKS    VFLAG
  1       0 300222d8578     0       c      13,2  300180a1bc8    0          -

> snode 300180a1bc8
SNODE TABLE SIZE = 256
HASH-SLOT MAJ/MIN    REALVP      COMMONVP    NEXTR  SIZE    COUNT FLAGS
     -         13,2  3001bdcdf50 30001b5d5b0    0     0        0
```

The REALVP field references the vnode for the special file within the filesystem that references mynull.

For the process that opens the /dev/null special file, the same sequence of operations is followed as shown:

```
> user 363
...
OPEN FILES, POFILE FLAGS, AND THREAD REFCNT:
```

```
      [0]: F 300106fc690, 0, 0    [1]: F 300106fc690, 0, 0
      [2]: F 300106fc690, 0, 0    [3]: F 3000502e820, 0, 0
...
> file 3000502e820
ADDRESS    RCNT     TYPE/ADDR        OFFSET    FLAGS
3000502e820   1     SPEC/30001b5d6a0       0    read

> vnode 30001b5d6a0
VCNT VFSMNTED    VFSP     STREAMP VTYPE   RDEV    VDATA    VFILOCKS    VFLAG
  51        0 10458510          0    c   13,2   30001b5d698            0    -
> snode 30001b5d698
SNODE TABLE SIZE = 256
HASH-SLOT MAJ/MIN   REALVP     COMMONVP   NEXTR   SIZE   COUNT FLAGS
     -       13,2   30001638950   30001b5d5b0   0      0        0 up ac
```

Note that for the snode displayed here, the COMMONVP field is identical to the COMMONVP field shown for the process that referenced mynull.

To some readers, much of what has been described may sound like overkill. However, device access has changed substantially since the inception of specfs. By consolidating all device access, only specfs needs to be changed. Filesystems still make the same specvp() call that they were making 15 years ago and therefore have not had to make any changes as device access has evolved.

The BSD Memory-Based Filesystem (MFS)

The BSD team developed an unusual but interesting approach to memory-based filesystems as documented in [MCKU90]. Their goals were to improve upon the various RAM disk-based filesystems that had traditionally been used.

A RAM disk is typically a contiguous section of memory that has been set aside to emulate a disk slice. A RAM disk-based device driver is the interface between this area of memory and the rest of the kernel. Filesystems access the RAM disk just as they would any other physical device. The main difference is that the driver employs memory to memory copies rather than copying between memory and disk.

The paper describes the problems inherent with RAM disk-based filesystems. First of all, they occupy dedicated memory. A large RAM disk therefore locks down memory that could be used for other purposes. If many of the files in the RAM disk are not being used, this is particularly wasteful of memory. One of the other negative properties of RAM disks, which the BSD team did not initially attempt to solve, was the triple copies of data. When a file is read, it is copied from the file's location on the RAM disk into a buffer cache buffer and then out to the user's buffer. Although this is faster than accessing the data on disk, it is incredibly wasteful of memory.

The BSD MFS Architecture

Figure 11.3 shows the overall architecture of the BSD MFS filesystem. To create and mount the filesystem, the following steps are taken:

1. A call to newfs is made indicating that the filesystem will be memory-based.

2. The newfs process allocates an area of memory within its own address space in which to store the filesystem. This area of memory is then initialized with the new filesystem structure.

3. The newfs command call is made into the kernel to mount the filesystem. This is handled by the mfs filesystem type that creates a device vnode to reference the RAM disk together with the process ID of the caller.

4. The UFS mount entry point is called, which performs standard UFS mount time processing. However, instead of calling spec_strategy() to access the device, as it would for a disk-based filesystem, it calls mfs_strategy(), which interfaces with the memory-based RAM disk.

One unusual aspect of the design is that the newfs process does not exit. Instead, it stays in the kernel acting as an intermediary between UFS and the RAM disk.

As requests for read and write operations enter the kernel, UFS is invoked as with any other disk-based UFS filesystem. The difference appears at the filesystem/driver interface. As highlighted above, UFS calls mfs_strategy() in place of the typical spec_strategy(). This involves waking up the newfs process, which performs a copy between the appropriate area of the RAM disk and the I/O buffer in the kernel. After I/O is completed, the newfs process goes back to sleep in the kernel awaiting the next request.

After the filesystem is unmounted the device close routine is invoked. After flushing any pending I/O requests, the mfs_mount() call exits causing the newfs process to exit, resulting in the RAM disk being discarded.

Performance and Observations

Analysis showed MFS to perform at about twice the speed of a filesystem on disk for raw read and write operations and multiple times better for meta-data operations (file creates, etc). The benefit over the traditional RAM disk approach is that because the data within the RAM disk is part of the process address space, it is pageable just like any other process data. This ensures that if data within the RAM disk isn't being used, it can be paged to the swap device.

There is a disadvantage with this approach; a large RAM disk will consume a large amount of swap space and therefore could reduce the overall amount of memory available to other processes. However, swap space can be increased, so MFS still offers advantages over the traditional RAM disk-based approach.

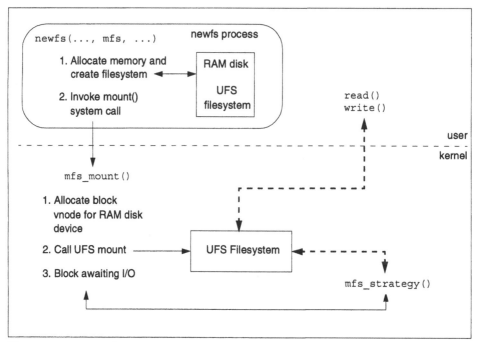

Figure 11.3 The BSD pageable memory-based filesystem.

The Sun tmpfs Filesystem

Sun developed a memory-based filesystem that used the facilities offered by the virtual memory subsystem [SNYD90]. This differs from RAM disk-based filesystems in which the RAM disk simply mirrors a copy of a disk slice. The goal of the design was to increase performance for file reads and writes, allow dynamic resizing of the filesystem, and avoid an adverse effect on performance. To the user, the tmpfs filesystem looks like any other UNIX filesystem in that it provides full UNIX file semantics.

Chapter 7 described the SVR4 filesystem architecture on which tmpfs is based. In particular, the section *An Overview of the SVR4 VM Subsystem* in Chapter 7, described the SVR4/Solaris VM architecture. Familiarity with these sections is essential to understanding how tmpfs is implemented. Because tmpfs is heavily tied to the VM subsystem, it is not portable between different versions of UNIX. However, this does not preclude development of a similar filesystem on the other architectures.

Architecture of the tmpfs Filesystem

In SVR4, files accessed through the read() and write() system calls go through the *seg_map* kernel segment driver, which maintains a cache of recently accessed pages of file data. Memory-mapped files are backed by a *seg_vn* kernel segment that references the underlying vnode for the file. In the case where there is no backing file, the SVR4 kernel provides *anonymous memory* that is backed by swap space. This is described in the section *Anonymous Memory* in Chapter 7.

Tmpfs uses anonymous memory to store file data and therefore competes with memory used by all processes in the system (for example, for stack and data segments). Because anonymous memory can be paged to a swap device, tmpfs data is also susceptible to paging.

Figure 11.4 shows how the tmpfs filesystem is implemented. The vnode representing the open tmpfs file references a tmpfs `tmpnode` structure, which is similar to an inode in other filesystems. Information within this structure indicates whether the file is a regular file, directory, or symbolic link. In the case of a regular file, the `tmpnode` references an anonymous memory header that contains the data backing the file.

File Access through tmpfs

Reads and writes through tmpfs function in a very similar manner to other filesystems. File data is read and written through the seg_map driver. When a write occurs to a tmpfs file that has no data yet allocated, an anon structure is allocated, which references the actual pages of the file. When a file grows the anon structure is extended.

Mapped files are handled in the same way as files in a regular filesystem. Each mapping is underpinned by a segment vnode.

Performance and Other Observations

Testing performance of tmpfs is highly dependent on the type of data being measured. Many file operations that manipulate data may show only a marginal improvement in performance, because meta-data is typically cached in memory. For structural changes to the filesystem, such as file and directory creations, tmpfs shows a great improvement in performance since no disk access is performed.

[SNYD90] also shows a test under which the UNIX kernel was recompiled. The overall time for a UFS filesystem was 32 minutes and for tmpfs, 27 minutes. Filesystems such as VxFS, which provide a *temporary filesystem* mode under which nearly all transactions are delayed in memory, could close this gap significantly.

One aspect that is difficult to measure occurs when tmpfs file data competes for virtual memory with the applications that are running on the system. The amount of memory on the system available for applications is a combination of physical memory and swap space. Because tmpfs file data uses the same memory, the overall memory available for applications can be largely reduced.

Overall, the deployment of tmpfs is highly dependent on the type of workload that is running on a machine together with the amount of memory available.

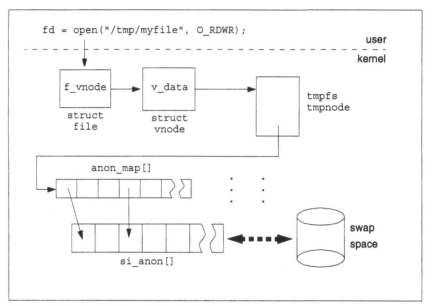

Figure 11.4   Architecture of the tmpfs filesystem.

Other Pseudo Filesystems

There are a large number of different pseudo filesystems available. The following sections highlight some of the filesystems available.

The UnixWare Processor Filesystem

With the advent of multiprocessor-based systems, the UnixWare team introduced a new filesystem type called the *Processor Filesystem* [NADK92]. Typically mounted on the /system/processor directory, the filesystem shows one file per processor in the system. Each file contains information such as whether the processor is online, the type and speed of the processor, its cache size, and a list of device drivers that are bound to the processor (will run on that processor only).

The filesystem provided very basic information but detailed enough to get a quick understanding of the machine configuration and whether all CPUs were running as expected. A write-only control file also allowed the administrator to set CPUs online or offline.

The Translucent Filesystem

The *Translucent Filesystem* (TFS) [HEND90] was developed to meet the needs of software development within Sun Microsystems but was also shipped as part of the base Solaris operating system.

The goal was to facilitate sharing of a set of files without duplication but to allow individuals to modify files where necessary. Thus, the TFS filesystem is mounted on top of another filesystem which has been mounted read only.

It is possible to modify files in the top layer only. To achieve this, a copy on write mechanism is employed such that files from the lower layer are first copied to the user's private region before the modification takes place.

There may be several layers of filesystems for which the view from the top layer is a union of all files underneath.

Named STREAMS

The STREAMS mechanism is a stackable layer of *modules* that are typically used for development of communication stacks. For example, TCP/IP and UDP/IP can be implemented with a single IP STREAMS module on top of which resides a TCP module and a UDP module.

The *namefs* filesystem, first introduced in SVR4, provides a means by which a file can be associated with an open STREAM. This is achieved by calling fattach(), which in turn calls the mount() system call to mount a namefs filesystem over the specified file. An association is then made between the mount point and the STREAM head such that any read() and write() operations will be directed towards the STREAM.

[PATE96] provides an example of how the namefs filesystem is used.

The FIFO Filesystem

In SVR4, named pipes are handled by a loopback STREAMS driver together with the *fifofs* filesystem type. When a call is made into the filesystem to look up a file, if the file is a character or block special file, or if the file is a named pipe, a call is made to specvp() to return a specfs vnode in its place. This was described in the section *The Specfs Filesystem* earlier in this chapter.

In the case of named pipes a call is made from specfs to fifovp() to return a fifofs vnode instead. This initializes the v_op field of the vnode to fifo_vnodeops, which handles all of the file-based operations invoked by the caller of open().

As with specfs consolidating all access to device files, fifofs performs the same function with named pipes.

The File Descriptor Filesystem

The *file descriptor filesystem*, typically mounted on /dev/fd, is a convenient way to access the open files of a process.

Following a call to open(), which returns file descriptor *n*, the following two two system calls are identical:

```
fd = open("/dev/fd/n",mode);
fd = dup(n);
```

Note that it is not possible to access the files of another process through /dev/fd. The file descriptor filesystem is typically used by scripting languages such as the UNIX shells, awk, perl, and others.

Summary

The number of non disk or pseudo-based filesystems has grown substantially since the early 1990s. Although the /proc filesystem is the most widely known, a number of memory-based filesystems are in common use, particularly for use with temporary filesystems and swap management.

It is difficult in a single chapter to do justice to all of these filesystems. For example, the Linux /proc filesystem provides a number of features not described here. The Solaris /proc filesystem has many more features above what has been covered in the chapter. [MAUR01] contains further details of some of the facilities offered by the Solaris /proc filesystem.

Filesystem Backup

Backing up a filesystem to tape or other media is one area that is not typically well documented in the UNIX world. Most UNIX users are familiar with commands such as tar and cpio, which can be used to create a single archive from a hierarchy of files and directories. While this is sufficient for creating a copy of a set of files, such tools operate on a moving target—they copy files while the files themselves may be changing. To solve this problem and allow backup applications to create a consistent image of the filesystem, various snapshotting techniques have been employed.

This chapter describes the basic tools available at the UNIX user level followed by a description of filesystem features that allow creation of snapshots (also called frozen images). The chapter also describes the techniques used by *hierarchical storage managers* to archive file data based on various policies.

Traditional UNIX Tools

There are a number of tools that have been available on UNIX for many years that deal with making copies of files, file hierarchies, and filesystems. The following sections describe tar, cpio, and pax, the best understood utilities for archiving file hierarchies.

This is followed by a description of the dump and restore commands, which can be used for backing up and restoring whole filesystems.

The tar, cpio, and pax Commands

The tar and cpio commands are both used to construct an *archive* of files. The set of files can be a directory hierarchy of files and subdirectories. The tar command originated with BSD while the cpio command came from System V. Because tar is available on just about every platform, including non-UNIX operating systems, cpio will not be mentioned further.

The tar Archive Format

It is assumed that readers are familiar with operation of the tar command. As a quick refresher, consider the following 3 commands:

```
$ tar cvf files.tar /lhome/spate/*
$ tar tvf files.tar
$ tar xvf files.tar
```

The first command (c option) creates a *tar archive* consisting of all files under the directory /lhome/spate. The second command (t option) displays the contents of the archive. The last command (x option) extracts files from the archive.

There are two main tar formats, the original format that originated in BSD UNIX and is shown in Figure 12.1, and the USTAR format as defined by Posix.1. In both cases, the archive consists of a set of *records*. Each record has a fixed size and is 512 bytes. The first entry in the archive is a *header record* that describes the first file in the archive. Next follows zero or more records that hold the file contents. After the first file there is a header record for the second file, records for its contents, and so on.

The header records are stored in a printable ASCII form, which allows tar archives to be easily ported to different operating system types. The end of the archive is indicated by two records filled with zeros. Unused space in the header is left as binary zeros, as will be shown in the next section.

The link field is set to 1 for a linked file, 2 for a symbolic link, and 0 otherwise. A directory is indicated by a trailing slash (/) in its name.

The USTAR tar Archive Format

The USTAR tar format, as defined by POSIX.1, is shown in Figure 12.2. It retains the original tar format at the start of the header record and extends it by adding additional information after the old header information. Presence of the USTAR format can be easily detected by searching for the null-terminated string "ustar" in the *magic* field.

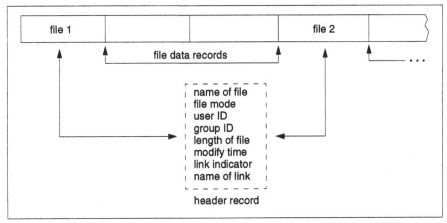

Figure 12.1 The format of the original tar archive.

The information held in the USTAR format matches the information returned by the stat() system call. All fields that are not character strings are ASCII representations of octal numbers.

Shown below are the contents of a tar archive that holds a single file with only a few characters. Some of the fields are highlighted—use the format of the archive shown in Figure 12.2 for reference. The highlighted fields are the file name, the USTAR magic field, the owner, group, and file contents.

```
$ ls -l file
-rw-r--r--   1 spate    fcf           6 Jun  4 21:56 file
$ grep spate /etc/passwd
spate:x:824:119:Steve Pate:/1home/spate:/usr/local/bin/bash
$ grep fcf /etc/group
fcf::119:iwww
$ od -c archive.tar
0000000   f   i   l   e  \0  \0  \0  \0  \0  \0  \0  \0  \0  \0  \0  \0
0000020  \0  \0  \0  \0  \0  \0  \0  \0  \0  \0  \0  \0  \0  \0  \0  \0
*
0000140  \0  \0  \0  \0   0   1   0   0   6   4   4  \0   0   0   0   1
0000160   4   7   0  \0   0   0   0   0   1   6   7  \0   0   0   0   0
0000200   0   0   0   0   0   0   6  \0   0   7   4   7   7   3   1   4
0000220   7   7   3  \0   0   1   0   3   7   4  \0       0  \0  \0  \0
0000240  \0  \0  \0  \0  \0  \0  \0  \0  \0  \0  \0  \0  \0  \0  \0  \0
*
0000400  \0   u   s   t   a   r      \0   s   p   a   t   e  \0  \0
0000420  \0  \0  \0  \0  \0  \0  \0  \0  \0  \0  \0  \0  \0  \0  \0  \0
0000440  \0  \0  \0  \0  \0  \0  \0  \0  \0   f   c   f  \0  \0  \0  \0
0000460  \0  \0  \0  \0  \0  \0  \0  \0  \0  \0  \0  \0  \0  \0  \0  \0
*
0001000   h   e   l   l   o  \n  \0  \0  \0  \0  \0  \0  \0  \0  \0  \0
0001020  \0  \0  \0  \0  \0  \0  \0  \0  \0  \0  \0  \0  \0  \0  \0  \0
*
0024000
```

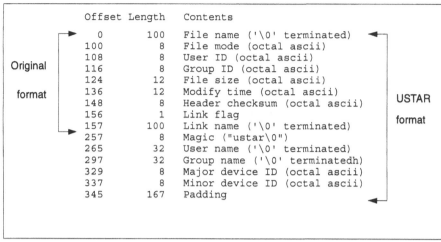

```
              Offset Length    Contents
                   0    100    File name ('\0' terminated)
                 100      8    File mode (octal ascii)
                 108      8    User ID (octal ascii)
  Original      116      8    Group ID (octal ascii)
                 124     12    File size (octal ascii)
  format        136     12    Modify time (octal ascii)
                 148      8    Header checksum (octal ascii)     USTAR
                 156      1    Link flag
                 157    100    Link name ('\0' terminated)       format
                 257      8    Magic ("ustar\0")
                 265     32    User name ('\0' terminated)
                 297     32    Group name ('\0' terminatedh)
                 329      8    Major device ID (octal ascii)
                 337      8    Minor device ID (octal ascii)
                 345    167    Padding
```

Figure 12.2   The USTAR tar format.

Standardization and the pax Command

POSIX.1 defined the pax (*portable archive interchange*) command, which reads and writes archives that conform to the *Archive/Interchange File Format* specified as part of POSIX 1003.1. The pax command can read a number of different, older archive formats including both cpio and tar archives.

For compatibility between different versions of UNIX, the Open Group, which controls the Single UNIX Specification, recommend that users migrate from tar to pax. This is partly due to limitations with the tar format but also to allow operating system vendors to support a single archive format going forward.

Backup Using Dump and Restore

The first *dump* command appeared in 6th Edition UNIX as a means of backing up a complete filesystem. To demonstrate how dump and restore work on a filesystem, this section looks at the VxFS vxdump and vxrestore commands, both of which offer an interface similar to the dump and restore in other filesystems.

The vxdump command can write a filesystem dump either to tape or to a *dumpfile* (a file on the filesystem that holds the image of the dump).

In addition to a number of options that specify tape properties, vxdump operates on dump levels in the range 0 to 9. When a dump level in this range is specified, vxdump backs up all files that changed since the last dump at a lower dump level. For example, if a level 2 dump was taken on Monday and a level 4 dump was taken on Tuesday, a level 3 dump on Wednesday would back up all files that had been modified or added since the level 2 dump on Monday. If a level 0 dump is specified, all files in the filesystem are backed up.

The use of dump levels allows a simple full/incremental approach to backup. As an example, consider the case where a full backup is taken on Sunday, followed by a set of incremental backups on each following day for five days. A dump level of 0 will be specified for the Sunday backup. A level of 1 can be chosen on Monday, 2 on Tuesday, 3 on Wednesday, and so on. This ensures that only files that have been changed since the backup on the previous day will be backed up.

The vxrestore command can be used to restore one or more files from an archive created by vxdump.

In order to provide a simple example of how vxdump and vxrestore work, a simple filesystem with one file is backed up to a dumpfile in /tmp as follows:

```
# ls -l /fs1
total 2
-rw-r--r--   1 root      other          6 Jun  7 15:07 hello
drwxr-xr-x   2 root      root          96 Jun  7 14:41 lost+found
# vxdump -0 -f /tmp/dumpfile /fs1
vxfs vxdump: Date of this level 0 dump: Fri Jun  7 15:08:16 2002
vxfs vxdump: Date of last level 0 dump: the epoch
vxfs vxdump: Dumping /dev/vx/rdsk/fs1 to /tmp/dumpfile
vxfs vxdump: mapping (Pass I) [regular files]
vxfs vxdump: mapping (Pass II) [directories]
vxfs vxdump: estimated 94 blocks (47KB).
vxfs vxdump: dumping (Pass III) [directories]
vxfs vxdump: dumping (Pass IV) [regular files]
vxfs vxdump: vxdump: 41 tape blocks on 1 volumes(s)
vxfs vxdump: Closing /tmp/dumpfile
vxfs vxdump: vxdump is done
```

Using the -t option of vxrestore it is possible to display the contents of the dumpfile prior to issuing any type of restore command:

```
# vxrestore -f /tmp/dumpfile -t
Dump date: Fri Jun  7 15:08:16 2002
Dumped from: the epoch
        2  .
        3  ./lost+found
        4  ./hello
```

This shows the contents of the archive, which is useful in the case where only one or two files need to be restored and confirmation of their existence is required before a restore command is issued. The hello file is restored as follows:

```
# cd /fs1 ; rm hello
# vxrestore -f /tmp/dumpfile -x hello
# ls
hello        lost+found
```

There are a number of other options to vxrestore, including the ability to work interactively. In this mode it is possible to view the contents of the archive using ls and cd commands before deciding which files or directories to extract.

As with other UNIX tools, vxdump works best on a frozen image, the subject of the next few sections.

Frozen-Image Technology

All of the traditional tools described so far can operate on a filesystem that is mounted and in use. Unfortunately, this can lead to backing up some files that are in the process of being written. If files are being changed while the backup runs, an inconsistent image will likely be written to tape or other media.

Ideally, a backup should be run when there is no activity to the filesystem, allowing all files backed up to be in a consistent state. The system administrator does not, however, want to unmount a busy filesystem just to perform a backup. This is where stable snapshot mechanisms come into play.

A *stable snapshot*, or *frozen image*, is a consistent copy of a filesystem that allows a backup application to back up files that are not changing. Even though there still may be activity to the filesystem, the frozen image is guaranteed to be a consistent replica of the filesystem at the time the frozen image was taken.

The following sections describe the two different types of frozen images: snapshots that are not persistent across reboots and snapshots that are persistent across reboots.

Note that there are a number of terms that describe the same concept. *Snapshots*, *frozen-images*, and *point-in-time copies* are used interchangeably in the storage industry to refer to the same thing, a stable image of the filesystem.

Nonpersistent Snapshots

The goal behind any snapshotting technology is to provide a frozen image of the filesystem for the purpose of performing a filesystem backup. Because backups have traditionally been performed within a relatively small window, it was believed that the snapshots only needed to exist for the duration of the backup. If power is lost, or the machine is shutdown, the snapshots are also lost, making them nonpersistent.

The following sections describe how VxFS snapshots are implemented. Sun also provide a snapshot mechanism that is described in the section *UFS Snaphots* in Chapter 9.

VxFS Snapshots

Introduced in the early 1990s, the VxFS snapshot mechanism provided a stable, frozen image of the filesystem for making backups. The *snapshot* is a consistent view of the filesystem (called the *snapped filesystem*) at the time that the snapshot was taken.

VxFS requires a separate device in which to store snapshot data blocks. Using copy-on-write techniques, any blocks that are about to be overwritten in the snapped filesystem are first copied to the snapshot device. By employing a bitmap of all blocks in the snapped filesystem, a read through the snapshot reads the block either from the snapped filesystem or from the snapshot, depending on whether the bitmap indicates that the block has been copied or not.

There can be a number of snapshots of the same filesystem in existence at the same time. Note that each snapshot is a replica of the filesystem at the time the snapshot was taken, and therefore each snapshot is likely to be different. Note also, that there must be a separate device for each snapshot.

The snapshot filesystem is mounted on its own separate directory to the filesystem and looks exactly the same as the snapped filesystem. This allows any UNIX utilities or backup software to work unchanged. Note though, that any backup utilities that use the raw device to make a copy of the filesystem cannot use the raw snapshot device. In place of such utilities, the fscat command can be used to create a raw image of the filesystem. This is described later in the chapter.

A snapshot filesystem is created through a special invocation of the mount command. For example, consider the following 100MB VxFS filesystem. A VxVM volume is created and a filesystem is created on the volume. After mounting, two files are created as follows:

```
# vxassist make fs1 100m
# mkfs -F vxfs /dev/vx/rdsk/fs1 100m
    version 4 layout
    204800 sectors, 102400 blocks of size 1024, log size 1024 blocks
    unlimited inodes, largefiles not supported
    102400 data blocks, 101280 free data blocks
    4 allocation units of 32768 blocks, 32768 data blocks
    last allocation unit has 4096 data blocks
# mount -F vxfs /dev/vx/dsk/fs1 /fs1
# echo hello > /fs1/fileA
# echo goodbye > /fs1/fileB
```

The device on which to create the snapshot is 10MB as shown by a vxassist call to VxVM below. To create the snapshot, mount is called, passing the snapshot device and size with the mount point of the filesystem to be snapped. When df is invoked, the output shows that the two filesystems appear identical, showing that the snapshot presents an exact replica of the snapped filesystem, even though its internal implementation is substantially different.

```
# mkdir /snap
# vxassist make snap 10m
# mount -F vxfs -osnapof=/fs1,snapsize=20480 /dev/vx/dsk/snap /snap
# df -k
...
/dev/vx/dsk/fs1        102400    1135    94943    2%    /fs1
/dev/vx/dsk/snap       102400    1135    94936    2%    /snap
...
```

The size of the snapshot device must be large enough to hold any blocks that change on the snapped filesystem. If the snapshot filesystem runs out of blocks, it is disabled and any subsequent attempts to access it will fail.

It was envisaged that snapshots and a subsequent backup would be taken during periods of low activity, for example, at night or during weekends. During such times, approximately 2 to 6 percent of the filesystem is expected to change. During periods of higher activity, approximately 15 percent of the filesystem may change. Of course, the actual rate of change is highly dependent on the type of workload that is running on the machine at the time. For a snapshot to completely hold the image of a snapped filesystem, a device that is approximately 101 percent of the snapped filesystem should be used.

Accessing VxFS Snapshots

The following example shows how VxFS snapshots work, using the snapshot created in the preceding section. The example shows how the contents of both the snapped filesystem and the snapshot initially look identical. It also shows what happens when a file is removed from the snapped filesystem:

```
# ls -l /fs1
total 4
-rw-r--r--  1 root     other            6 Jun  7 11:17 fileA
-rw-r--r--  1 root     other            8 Jun  7 11:17 fileB
drwxr-xr-x  2 root     root            96 Jun  7 11:15 lost+found
# ls -l /snap
total 4
-rw-r--r--  1 root     other            6 Jun  7 11:17 fileA
-rw-r--r--  1 root     other            8 Jun  7 11:17 fileB
drwxr-xr-x  2 root     root            96 Jun  7 11:15 lost+found
# cat /fs1/fileA
hello
# cat /snap/fileA
hello
# rm /fs1/fileA
# cat /snap/fileA
hello
# df -k
. . .
/dev/vx/dsk/fs1      102400    1134    94944    2%    /fs1
/dev/vx/dsk/snap     102400    1135    94936    2%    /snap
. . .
```

The output from df following the file removal now shows that the two filesystems are different. The snapped filesystem shows more free blocks while the snapshot still retains the exact same properties that it did when the snapshot was created.

Note that while one or more snapshot filesystems are in existence, any changes to the snapped filesystem will result in a block copy to the snapshot if the block has not already been copied. Although reading from the snapped filesystem does not show any performance degradation, there may be a 2 to 3 times increase in the time that it takes to issue a write to a file on the snapped filesystem.

Filesystem Backup   273

Performing a Backup Using VxFS Snapshots

There are a number of ways in which a stable backup may be taken from a snapshot filesystem. First, any of the traditional UNIX tools such as tar and cpio may be used. Because no files are changing within the snapshot, the archive produced with all such tools is an exact representation of the set of files at the time the snapshot was taken. As mentioned previously, if using vxdump it is best to run it on a snapshot filesystem.

The fscat command can be used on a snapshot filesystem in an manner similar to the way in which the dd command can be used on a raw device. Note, however, that running dd on a snapshot device directly will not return a valid image of the filesystem. Instead, it will get the snapshot superblock, bitmap, blockmap, and a series of blocks.

The following example demonstrates how fscat is used. A small 10MB filesystem is created into which two files are created. A snapshot of 5MB is created and fscat is used to copy the image of the filesystem to another device, also 10MB in size.

```
# vxassist make fs1 10m
# vxassist make fs1-copy 10m
# vxassist make snap 5m
# mkfs -F vxfs /dev/vx/rdsk/fs1 10m
    version 4 layout
    20480 sectors, 10240 blocks of size 1024, log size 1024 blocks
    unlimited inodes, largefiles not supported
    10240 data blocks, 9144 free data blocks
    1 allocation units of 32768 blocks, 32768 data blocks
    last allocation unit has 10240 data blocks
# mount -F vxfs /dev/vx/dsk/fs1 /fs1
# echo hello > /fs1/hello
# echo goodbye > /fs1/goodbye
# mount -F vxfs -osnapof=/fs1,snapsize=10240 /dev/vx/dsk/snap /snap
# rm /fs1/hello
# rm /fs1/goodbye
# fscat /dev/vx/dsk/snap > /dev/vx/rdsk/fs1-copy
```

Before issuing the call to fscat the files are removed from the snapped filesystem. Because the filesystem is active at the time that the snapshot is taken, the filesystem superblock flags are marked *dirty* to indicate that it is in use. As a consequence, the filesystem created by fscat will also have its superblock marked dirty, and therefore will need a fsck log replay before it can be mounted. Once mounted, the files originally written to the snapped filesystem are visible as expected.

```
# fsck -F vxfs /dev/vx/rdsk/fs1-copy
log replay in progress
replay complete - marking super-block as CLEAN
# mount -F vxfs /dev/vx/dsk/fs1-copy /fs2
# ls -l /fs2
total 4
```

```
-rw-r--r--   1 root     other        8 Jun  7 11:37 goodbye
-rw-r--r--   1 root     other        6 Jun  7 11:37 hello
drwxr-xr-x   2 root     root        96 Jun  7 11:37 lost+found
# cat /fs2/hello
hello
# cat /fs2/goodbye
goodbye
```

The fscat command is built on top of the VX_SNAPREAD ioctl, which reads a specified block from the filesystem. The bitmap on the snapshot filesystem is consulted to determine whether to return a block from the snapped filesystem or from the snapshot itself. Issuing a truss when running the fscat command shown above will produce the following:

```
13672:  open64("/snap", O_RDONLY)                   = 3
...
13672:  ioctl(3, 0x56584680, 0xFFBEFCF4)            = 5120
13672:  write(1, "\fD5 , nD4F89E 0E6 xDF o".., 5120) = 5120
13672:  ioctl(3, 0x56584680, 0xFFBEFCF4)            = 5120
13672:  write(1, "95DB .9A v04B4938C B  1F".., 5120) = 5120
```

The snapshot filesystem is opened. Following this is a series of VX_SNAPREAD ioctl commands to read blocks from the snapshot followed by a series of writes to standard output.

How VxFS Snapshots Are Implemented

Figure 12.3 shows how VxFS snapshots are laid out on disk. The superblock is a copy, albeit with a small number of modifications, of the superblock from the snapped filesystem at the time the snapshot was made.

The bitmap contains one bit for each block on the snapped filesystem. The bitmap is consulted when accessing the snapshot, to determine whether the block should be read from the snapshot or from the snapped filesystem. The block map also contains an entry for each block on the snapped filesystem. When a block is copied to the snapshot, the bitmap is updated to indicate that a copy has taken place and the block map is updated to point to the copied block on the snapshot device.

To create a snapshot, the filesystem is first *frozen*. This ensures that all data is flushed to disk and any subsequent access is blocked for the duration of the freeze. Once frozen, the superblock of the snapshot is written to disk together with the (empty) bitmap and blockmap. The snapshot is *linked* to the snapped filesystem and the filesystem is then *thawed*, which allows subsequent access.

Persistent Snapshot Filesystems

The snapshot mechanisms discussed so far, such as those provided by VxFS and Solaris UFS, are nonpersistent meaning that they remain for the duration of the mount or while the system is running. Once a reboot occurs, for whatever reason,

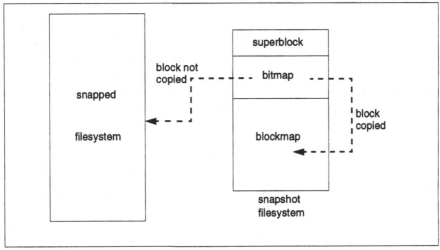

Figure 12.3 Implementation of VxFS snapshots.

the snapshots are no longer valid.

In contrast persistent snapshots remain consistent across a system reboot therefore provide more flexibility, as the following sections will show.

VxFS *storage checkpoints* provide a persistent snapshot mechanism. Unlike VxFS snapshots, they occupy space within the filesystem (disk slice) itself and can be mounted read-only or read/write when required.

Differences between VxFS Storage Checkpoints and Snapshots

Although both storage checkpoints and snapshots provide a stable, point-in-time copy of a filesystem, there are some fundamental differences between the two:

- Snapshots require a separate device in order to hold copy on write blocks. With storage checkpoints, the copy on write blocks are held within the same device in which the snapped/primary filesystem resides.

- Snapshots are read-only while storage checkpoints can be either read-only or read/write.

- Snapshots are nonpersistent in that they are lost following a reboot. Storage checkpoints are persistent and survive a reboot.

- A snapshot filesystem is mounted at the time that it is created and exists for the duration of the mount only. Storage checkpoints remain in existence whether mounted or not. An explicit command must be invoked to remove a storage checkpoint.

- Snapshots track changed blocks in a device-level bitmap. Storage checkpoints track changed blocks on a per-file basis.

How Storage Checkpoints Are Implemented

Most snapshot mechanisms work at the block level. By employing a tracking mechanism such as a bitmap, the filesystem can determine whether copy-on-write blocks have been copied to the snapshot or whether the blocks should be accessed from the filesystem from which the snapshot was taken. Using a simple bitmap technique simplifies operation of the snapshots but limits their flexibility. Typically nonpersistent snapshots are read-only.

VxFS storage checkpoints are heavily tied to the implementation of VxFS. The section *VxFS Disk Layout Version 5*, in Chapter 9, describes the various components of the VxFS disk layout. VxFS mountable entities are called *filesets*. Each fileset has its own inode list including an inode for the root of the fileset, allowing it to be mounted separately from other filesets. By providing linkage between the two filesets, VxFS uses this mechanism to construct a chain of checkpoints, as shown in Figure 12.4.

This linkage is called a *clone chain*. At the head of the clone chain is the *primary fileset*. When a filesystem is created with mkfs, only the primary fileset is created. When a checkpoint is created, the following events occur:

- A new fileset header entry is created and linked into the clone chain. The primary fileset will point downstream to the new checkpoint, and the new checkpoint will point downstream to the next most recent checkpoint. Upstream linkages will be set in the reverse direction. The downstream pointer of the oldest checkpoint will be NULL to indicate that it is the oldest fileset in the clone chain.

- An inode list is created. Each inode in the new checkpoint is an exact copy of the inode in the primary fileset with the exception of the block map. When the checkpoint is created, inodes are said to be *fully overlayed*. In order to read any data from the inode, the filesystem must walk up the clone chain to read the blocks from the inode upstream.

- The in-core fileset structures are modified to take into account the new checkpoint. This is mainly to link the new fileset into the clone chain.

One of the major differences between storage checkpoints and snapshots is that block changes are tracked at the inode level. When a write occurs to a file in the primary fileset, a check must be made to see if the data that exists on disk has already been pushed to the inode in the downstream fileset. If no push has occurred, the block covering the write must be pushed first before the write can proceed. In Figure 12.4, each file shown has four data blocks. Inodes in the primary fileset always access four data blocks. Whether the checkpoint inodes reference the blocks in the primary or not depends on activity on the primary fileset. As blocks are to be written they are pushed to the inode in the downstream checkpoint.

When reading from a checkpoint file, a *bmap* operation is performed at the offset of the read to determine which block to read from disk. If a valid block number is returned, the data can be copied to the user buffer. If an *overlay block* is

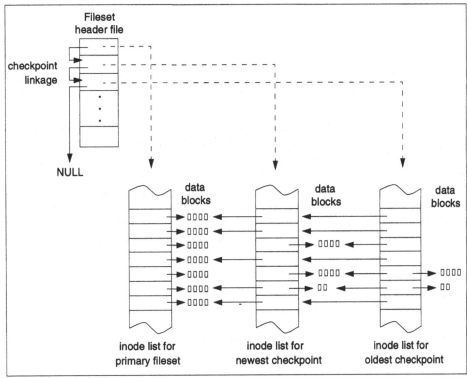

Figure 12.4 The architecture of VxFS storage checkpoints.

returned, the filesystem must walk *upstream* to read from the inode in the next fileset. Over time, blocks will be copied to various files in different filesets in the clone chain. Walking upstream may result in reading blocks from the primary fileset or from one of the filesets within the clone chain.

Using Storage Checkpoints

Checkpoints are created using the fscktpadm command. In order to create a checkpoint, the filesystem from which to create the checkpoint must be mounted. A filesystem is created and two files are added as follows:

```
# mkfs -F vxfs /dev/vx/rdsk/fs1 100m
    version 4 layout
    204800 sectors, 102400 blocks of size 1024, log size 1024 blocks
    unlimited inodes, largefiles not supported
    102400 data blocks, 101280 free data blocks
    4 allocation units of 32768 blocks, 32768 data blocks
    last allocation unit has 4096 data blocks
# mount -F vxfs /dev/vx/dsk/fs1 /fs1
# echo hello > /fs1/hello
# echo goodbye > /fs1/goodbye
# ls -l /fs1
```

```
total 4
-rw-r--r--   1 root     other          8 Jun  9 11:05 goodbye
-rw-r--r--   1 root     other          6 Jun  9 11:05 hello
drwxr-xr-x   2 root     root          96 Jun  9 11:04 lost+found
```

The root directory is displayed in order to view the timestamps, bearing in mind that a storage checkpoint should be an exact replica of the filesystem, including all timestamps.

Two checkpoints are now created. Note that before creation of the second checkpoint, the goodbye file is removed and the hello file is overwritten. One would expect that both files will be visible in the first checkpoint, that the goodbye file will not be present in the second and that the modified contents of the hello file will be visible in the second checkpoint. This will be shown later. Note that changes to the filesystem are being tracked even though the checkpoints are not mounted. Also, as mentioned previously, checkpoints will remain consistent across a umount/mount or a clean or unclean shutdown.

```
# fsckptadm create ckpt1 /fs1
# rm /fs1/goodbye
# echo "hello again" > /fs1/hello
# fsckptadm create ckpt2 /fs1
```

The fsckptadm command can also be used to list all storage checkpoints that belong to a filesystem as follows:

```
# fsckptadm list /fs1
/fs1
ckpt2:
  ctime              = Sun Jun  9 11:06:55 2002
  mtme               = Sun Jun  9 11:06:55 2002
  flags              = none
ckpt1:
  ctime              = Sun Jun  9 11:05:48 2002
  mtime              = Sun Jun  9 11:05:48 2002
  flags              = none
```

Checkpoints can be mounted independently as follows. Note that the device to be specified to mount is a slight variation of the real device. This avoids having multiple mount entries in the mount table that reference the same device.

```
# mkdir /ckpt1
# mkdir /ckpt2
# mount -F vxfs -ockpt=ckpt1 /dev/vx/dsk/fs1:ckpt1 /ckpt1
# mount -F vxfs -ockpt=ckpt2 /dev/vx/dsk/fs1:ckpt2 /ckpt2
```

Finally, the contents of all directories are shown to indicate the specified effects due to adding and removing files:

```
# ls -l /fs1
total 2
```

```
-rw-r--r--   1 root      other         12 Jun  9 11:06 hello
drwxr-xr-x   2 root      root          96 Jun  9 11:04 lost+found
# ls -l /ckpt1
total 4
-rw-r--r--   1 root      other          8 Jun  9 11:05 goodbye
-rw-r--r--   1 root      other          6 Jun  9 11:05 hello
drwxr-xr-x   2 root      root          96 Jun  9 11:04 lost+found
# ls -l /ckpt2
total 0
-rw-r--r--   1 root      other         12 Jun  9 11:06 hello
drwxr-xr-x   2 root      root          96 Jun  9 11:04 lost+found
```

The granularity at which blocks are pushed is generally fixed in size and is a multiple of the system page size. However, there are various optimizations that VxFS can perform. Consider the case where a file in the primary fileset is to be removed and the corresponding checkpoint inode is fully overlayed (no blocks have been pushed). In this case, instead of pushing blocks as the truncation proceeds, it is simpler to swap the block maps. This also has the added advantage that the geometry of the file is preserved.

Fragmentation can occur in the clone inodes as activity in the primary continues—this is largely unavoidable. However, by using the VxFS fsadm command, it is possible to perform extent reorganization on the checkpoint files, which can minimize the fragmentation.

Writable Storage Checkpoints

Frozen images are, just as the name implies, a copy of the filesystem at a specific moment in time. Because the main goal of producing frozen images has been to perform backups, this generally works extremely well. However, there are times at which writing to frozen images would be beneficial. For example, running a database decision support application on a writable checkpoint would be ideal for many environments. Furthermore, this could be performed while the main database is still active.

VxFS storage checkpoints can be mounted for read/write access as well as read-only access.

Block-Level Incremental Backups

When backing up from a frozen image, backup applications need to back up all of the files that have changed since the last backup. In environments where there are large files, this causes an overhead if only a small percentage of blocks within these files has changed. This is particularly true of database environments. By only backing up changed blocks, the *backup window,* the time to take a backup, can be reduced significantly. As the amount of data increases, incremental backups are becoming more critical, particularly in large enterprise environments, because the amount of time to perform a backup increases as the amount of data increases.

An incremental backup does not remove the need for a full backup. It does however avoid the need to produce a full backup on a daily basis. One scenario is to make a full backup once a week followed by an incremental backup on a daily basis. In order to fully restore a filesystem, the full backup needs to be restored, followed by the incremental backups.

VxFS storage checkpoints can be used to enable block level incremental backups. There are two different types of checkpoints that are used to enable this feature, namely:

Datafull checkpoints. The type of checkpoints described in previous sections are all *datafull* checkpoints. When a block is to be changed in a file in the primary fileset, the block is first copied to the file in the downstream checkpoint.

Dataless checkpoints. When a change occurs to a file in the primary fileset with *dataless* checkpoints, the block map of the downstream checkpoint file is modified to indicate the area of change, but no data is pushed.

Figure 12.5 shows the steps involved in creating an incremental backup. The first step is to create a datafull checkpoint from which a full backup is taken. This involves mounting the checkpoint and performing the backup.

Once the full backup is complete, the checkpoint is converted from datafull to dataless. Over the course of a day, changes to files in the primary fileset will be marked in the corresponding files in the checkpoint. When the backup application is run to create the incremental backup it can determine which blocks have changed in each file, so only data that has changed needs to be backed up.

To perform the incremental backup, a new datafull checkpoint is created. For all files that have changed, the backup application can read the modified blocks from the new, datafull checkpoint and write them to tape.

After the incremental backup is complete, the old dataless checkpoint is then removed and the new, datafull checkpoint is converted to a dataless checkpoint. On following days, the same process continues up until a new full backup is taken, at which point the dataless checkpoint is removed and another datafull checkpoint is created.

In large database environments where database files can span hundreds of gigabytes, the saving in time of block-level incremental backups can be significant.

Hierarchical Storage Management

Although not strictly a backup-related feature, *Hierarchical Storage Management* (HSM) provides an archiving facility that can be used in conjunction with backup software to minimize the amount of data that is transferred from the filesystem to tape. This technique is employed by the VERITAS NetBackup (NBU) and Storage Migrator products.

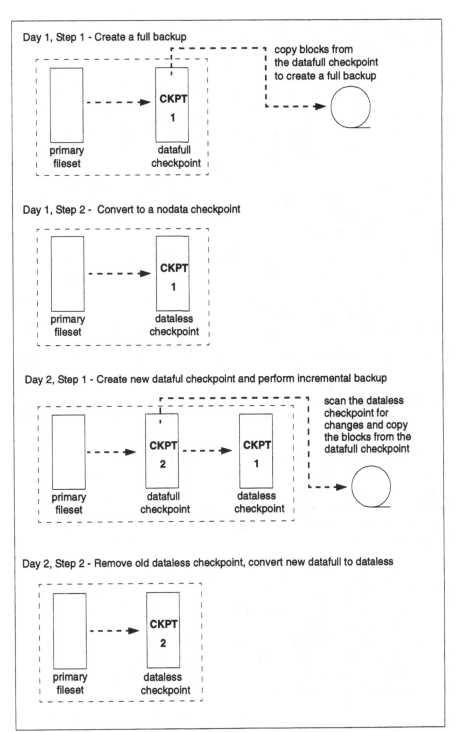

Figure 12.5 Performing an incremental backup using VxFS storage checkpoints.

Introduced many years ago when disk prices were much higher, HSM applications are to physical disks what virtual memory is to physical memory. HSM applications monitor the filesystem and *migrate* files off to tape (or other media) based on a set of policies. For example, an administrator can set a policy that specifies that once the filesystem becomes 80 percent full, files older than 60 days are targets for migration. The HSM application moves the data associated with the file off to tape. The user can still see the files that are migrated and is unaware that the data is no longer on disk. If the user then attempts to access the data, the data is migrated back from tape before the read or write can be processed.

The *Data Management Interfaces Group* (DMIG) [DMIG97] produced a proposal, adopted by X/Open, which provides a set of APIs (DMAPI) that operating system and filesystem developers can implement to ease the job of HSM developers. The main features of the DMAPI are:

- The ability to punch a hole in a file. This operation frees file data blocks but does not change the size of the file.

- Invisible read and write calls. To avoid backup or other applications seeing timestamp changes due to HSM activity, special read and write calls are introduced that avoid updating the timestamps in the inode.

- Support for extended attributes associated with the file. If a file's data blocks have been migrated, there must be some meta-data associated with the file which indicates that a migration has taken place, together with information about where the blocks are held. HSM applications typically tend to keep much of this information in a separate database so only minimal information is usually kept in extended attributes.

- The ability to monitor events on a file. Consider the case where file data has been migrated and a user accesses the file. An event can be posted to the HSM application to signify a read or write. This allows the HSM application to migrate the data back in from tape and perform an invisible write to the file before the user read or write is allowed to succeed.

HSM applications by themselves do not actually back up the filesystem. However, for specific filesystems there may be a substantial amount of data already on tape. When a backup application runs, this may result in duplicate copies of the data being written to tape.

It is possible for both applications to work together such that if file data has already been migrated to tape, backup software can skip those specific data blocks. This feature is implemented by the VERITAS NetBackup and Storage Migrator products, as shown in Figure 12.6.

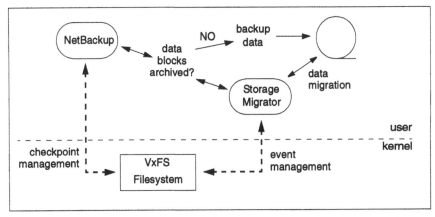

Figure 12.6   Backup and HSM applications working together to minimize data transfers.

Summary

There are numerous different ways in which backups can be taken. For smaller environments, a simple snapshot with standard UNIX utilities may suffice. For larger environments with multiple servers and large disk farms, this simple approach doesn't scale and enterprise backup systems are needed. [BAR02] provides a detailed account of how enterprises perform backups, together with an overall account of how storage area networks are employed.

Features such as VxFS storage checkpoints which are not just persistent, but also writable, allow a host of different types of new applications.

Clustered and Distributed Filesystems

With the advent of computer networks, which appeared in the 1970s and became more widespread in the 1980s, the need to share files between machines became essential. Initially, UNIX tools such as uucp and ftp were used to transfer files from one machine to another. However, disks were still relatively expensive; this resulted in a need to access files across the network without local storage.

The 1980s saw a number of different distributed filesystems make an appearance in the UNIX community, including Sun's *Network Filesystem* (NFS), AT&T's *Remote File Sharing* (RFS), and CMU's *Andrew File System* (AFS) which evolved into the DCE *Distributed File Service* (DFS). Some of the distributed filesystems faded as quickly as they appeared. By far, NFS has been the most successful, being used on tens of thousands of UNIX and non-UNIX operating systems throughout the world.

Distributed filesystems operate around a client/server model, with one of the machines owning an underlying disk-based filesystem and serving files to clients through some well-defined protocol. The protocol and means of transferring files to the user is transparent, with UNIX file semantics being a key goal.

Clustered filesystems by contrast treat a collection of machines and disks as a single entity and provide a fully coherent view of the filesystem from any of the nodes. To the user, clustered filesystems present a single coherent view of the filesystem and may or may not offer full UNIX file semantics. Clustered filesystems as well as local filesystems can be exported for use with NFS.

Distributed Filesystems

Unlike local filesystems where the storage is physically attached and only accessible by processes that reside on the same host machine, distributed filesystems allow access to files on a remote machine through use of a well-defined protocol. Distributed filesystems employ a client/server model where a single filesystem server can serve files to multiple clients.

Regardless of the type of distributed filesystem, one goal that is absolutely essential to all of these filesystems is the need to provide UNIX file semantics when accessing remote files from the client.

There have been numerous distributed filesystems developed for UNIX over the last 20 years. Many of them have come and gone. The most successful distributed filesystem by far is the Sun *Network Filesystem* (NFS) which appeared in the mid 1980s. Although not as feature-rich as filesystems such as the DCE *Distributed File Service* (DFS), the simplicity of the NFS protocol, together with the fact that the NFS protocol is in public domain, resulted in it being ported to many different operating systems, UNIX and non-UNIX alike.

The following sections describe some of the main UNIX distributed filesystems with particular emphasis on NFS.

The Network File System (NFS)

With the advent of networks providing connectivity between computers, it became feasible to provide interfaces through which user programs could access files across a network using the same mechanisms by which they accessed files on a local machine.

Hard disks were still relatively expensive in the late 1970s and early 1980s. By providing a client/server file protocol such as NFS, hardware designers were free to build diskless workstations or least workstations with a minimal amount of local storage.

NFS Background and History

The *Network File System* (NFS) was initially developed by Sun Microsystems in the early to mid 1980s and has been a huge success, with ports to just about every operating system, UNIX and non-UNIX alike. In the paper that described the first two versions of NFS [SAND85], the goals of NFS were to:

Provide machine and OS independence. This goal was to ensure that NFS could work on UNIX and non-UNIX operating systems. The client/server protocols were to be simple enough that they could be implemented on PCs—at the time, a DOS-based environment.

Provide resilience to server crashes. If the server crashes, the clients who are currently accessing the server must be able to recover. Furthermore, the client should be unable to tell the difference between a server that crashed and restarted and one that was just slow in responding.

Provide transparent file access. In order for the filesystem to succeed, it was important that applications could access files through NFS in the same manner in which they could access files on a local disk.

Maintain UNIX semantics on the client. To satisfy the above goal in UNIX environments, it was imperative that NFS provide UNIX file semantics to the applications on the client.

Have acceptable performance. As stated in [SAND85] "People will not want to use NFS if it is no faster than the existing network utilities, such as rcp, even if it is easier to use." The performance targets were set at 80 percent of local disk access.

There were three pieces that comprised NFS, the protocol, the client, and the server. All three will be described throughout the following sections.

The original NFS implementation, as described in [SAND85], encompassed both version 1 and 2 of the protocol when it first became available to the public in SunOS 2.0 in 1985. The first version of the protocol was only used internally within Sun.

At the time of writing, NFS implementations adhering to version 3 of the protocol have been in common use for several years and version 4 implementations are starting to appear. NFS is very well understood by tens of thousands of people throughout the world, which is a great testament of its success and an indicator as to why it will still be one of the most dominant of the distributed filesystems for many years to come.

The Version 1 and 2 NFS Protocols

As described in *The Sun VFS/Vnode Architecture* in Chapter 7, the SunOS filesystem architecture was redesigned and implemented to accommodate multiple filesystem types and provide support for NFS. This was not the only feature of the kernel that NFS depended on—it also relied on use of the Sun *Remote Procedure Call* (RPC) infrastructure, that provided a synchronous, cross network mechanism for one process (or the kernel) to call another process on a different machine. This allowed the NFS protocol to be broken down into a set of procedures specifying their arguments, the results, and the effects.

To communicate across the network, NFS used the *User Datagram Protocol* (UDP) on top of the *Internet Protocol* (IP). Because the protocol was designed to be independent of machine architectures and operating systems, the encoding of the protocol messages and their responses was sensitive to issues such as endianess (the order in which bytes are packed into a machine word). This resulted in the use of the *External Data Representation* (XDR) specification.

The use of RPC and XDR are described in the following section. Before describing how they are used, it first helps to describe the actual procedure calls NFS introduced for communication across the network. The version 2 protocol was documented in [RFC1094], which describes the procedure calls shown in

Table 13.1. Most of the operations are self explanatory. The `null` procedure is used to ping the server and can also be used as a means of measuring the round trip time. The `statfs` procedure returns information that can be displayed when making a call to the `df` command.

The file referenced by these procedures is called a *file handle*. This is an opaque data structure provided by the server in response to a lookup request. The client should never try to interpret the contents of the file handle. File handles are constructed using a combination of operating-specific information and information provided by the filesystem. For the latter, the information must provide a means to locate the file, so the file handle is typically a combination of filesystem specific information together with the inode number of the file and its generation count.

Many of the procedures deal with file attributes. Not surprisingly, the attributes correspond to the various fields of the `stat` structure as described in the section *Basic File Properties* in Chapter 2.

The NFS server is *stateless* in that there is no information kept on the server about past requests. This avoids any complicated crash recovery mechanism. If the client does not receive a response from the server within a specific period of time, the request is retried until it succeeds. This tolerates a server crash and reboot, ensuring that the client cannot detect the difference between a server crash and a server that is simply slow in responding.

The version 2 protocol also requires that any file writes are synchronous. This meets the objective of achieving UNIX file semantics.

Within the file handle, the inode generation count is typically encoded. Consider the case when a file is opened and a file handle is returned. If the file is removed on the server and the inode is reused later for a new file, the file handle is no longer valid because it refers to the old file. To distinguish between the old and new files, UNIX filesystems contain a generation count that is incremented each time the inode is reused. By using the generation count within the file handle, the stale file handle will be detected by the server when the deleted file is referenced.

One of the main goals of NFS was to make it portable across different operating systems. [ROSE86] demonstrated early ports to both an SVR2.2-based version of UNIX and the Sequent Dynix operating system, a System V/BSD hybrid. There were a number of different PC (DOS-based) implementations of NFS. [CALL00] describes the various issues encountered with porting NFS to these platforms.

NFS Client/Server Communications

NFS relies on both the *Remote Procedure Call* (RPC) [RFC1057] and *eXternal Data Representation* (XDR) [RFC1014] specifications as a means of communicating between client and server. XDR allows for the description and encoding of different data types. Its goal is to allow communication between machines with

Table 13.1   The NFS Version 2 Protocol Messages

PROCEDURE	ARGUMENTS	RETURN VALUE
null	null	null
lookup	directory_file_handle, name	file_handle, attributes
create	directory_file_handle, name, attributes	new_file_handle, attributes
remove	directory_file_handle, name	status
getattr	file_handle	attributes
setattr	file_handle, attributes	attributes
read	file_handle, offset, count	attributes, data
write	file_handle, offset, count, data	attributes
rename	directory_file_handle, name, to_file_handle, to_name	status
link	directory_file_handle, name, to_file_handle, to_name	status
symlink	directory_file_handle, name, string	status
readlink	file_handle	string
mkdir	directory_file_handle, name, attributes	file_handle, new_attributes
rmdir	directory_file_handle, name	status
readdir	directory_file_handle, cookie, count	entries
statfs	file_handle	filesystem_stats

different underlying architectures. RPC provides an infrastructure for creating client/server applications whereby an application can call a function provided by the server just as it would call a function within its own address space.

The XDR format assumes that bytes (8-bit) are portable in that the encoding of bytes does not change from one architecture or hardware device to another. Building on top of bytes, the XDR specification requires data types to be constructed from multiples of four bytes of data. If data types require a number of bytes that is not exactly divisible by 4, any unused bytes will be zero-filled. The ordering of the bytes is such that, if read from a byte stream, the high order byte is always read first. This is called *big-endian* (the biggest digit in a number comes first). XDR also uses a standard representation for floating point numbers (following the IEEE standard).

To give a simple example of how XDR is used, consider the encoding of an integer that is defined as a 32-bit data type. This is encoded as follows:

So if this data type were being read from a regular file as a series of bytes, byte 0, the most significant byte, would be read first.

The XDR specification defines a number of primitive data types including signed and unsigned integers, booleans, hyper integers (64 bits), fixed and variable length opaque data types, and strings. It also defines a wide range of structured data types including arrays, unions, linked lists, and structures. In basic terms, any data type that can be defined in the most popular high-level languages can be encoded within XDR.

The RPC mechanism used for NFS was derived from Sun RPC, a simple way to provide a remote procedure call mechanism between two processes on different machines. To the caller of such a procedure, there is no difference between calling an RPC function and calling a local function.

The RPC protocol [RFC1057] can be implemented on top of several different transport protocols. In the case of the early NFS implementations, this was based on UDP/IP. Within the last ten years, a move to using TCP/IP has been made in many environments (typically to avoid packet loss when going through routers). Description of the RPC protocol is beyond the scope of this book. The NFS specification [RFC1094] defines the NFS protocol as an RPC program and [CALL00] provides a more detailed description of the protocol itself.

The overall architecture of NFS in a VFS/vnode architecture is shown in Figure 13.1. This shows the placement of NFS, XDR, and RPC within the kernel. To the rest of the kernel, NFS appears as any other filesystem type.

Exporting, Mounting, and Accessing NFS Filesystems

Table 13.1 shows the different NFS protocol procedures. One thing that is missing from this list of functions is the means by which the very first file handle is obtained, the handle of the root directory from which subsequent lookup operations and other procedures can be performed. This is achieved through a separate *mount protocol* that returns the file handle for the root directory.

There were two reasons for separating the mount protocol from the NFS protocol itself (note that both are described in [RFC1094]). First, the means by which access checking is performed on the server is typically implemented in user space, which can make use of a number of different security mechanisms. Because the NFS protocol is implemented within the kernel for performance reasons, it was felt that it was easiest to allow for this separation. The second reason that the protocols were separated was that the designers thought a single pathname to file handle procedure would tie the implementation of NFS too

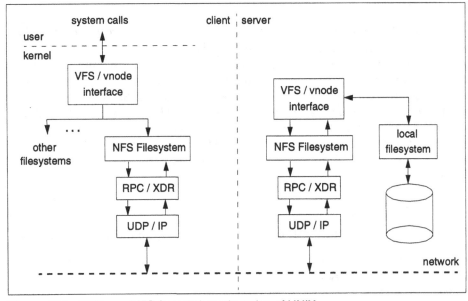

Figure 13.1 NFS on a VFS / vnode based version of UNIX.

closely with UNIX. It was envisaged that the pathname to file handle translation may be implemented by a protocol that differs from the mount protocol.

The initial mount protocol consisted of six different procedures:

MOUNTPROC_NULL. This procedure performs no specific function. It is used to ping the server to measure the round-trip time, which can be used to determine how to time out NFS procedure calls to the server.

MOUNTPROC_MNT. This procedure takes a pathname and returns a file handle that corresponds to the pathname.

MOUNTPROC_DUMP. This function returns a list of clients and the exported filesystems that they have mounted. This is used by the UNIX commands showmount and dfmounts that list the clients that have NFS mounted filesystems together with the filesystems that they have mounted.

MOUNTPROC_UMNT. This procedure is used to inform the server that the NFS filesystem on the client has been unmounted.

MOUNTPROC_UMNTALL. This procedure is sent by a client following a reboot (or after a crash). This prevents the server from maintaining stale mount entries in the event that the client crashed before sending corresponding MOUNTPROC_UMNT messages.

MOUNTPROC_EXPORT. This procedure returns a list of exported filesystems.

The mount protocol remained unchanged for a number of years. Since then, only one additional procedure has been added, MOUNTPROC_PATHCONF, which retrieves additional information from the server allowing NFS filesystems to comply with the POSIX pathconf() system call.

Using NFS

Although the NFS implementations differ from one platform to the next in the way in which filesystems are exported, using NFS is trivial when the appropriate client and server software is running. NFS daemons/threads are typically started when the system bootstraps and enters multiuser mode.

As an example, consider the case in Solaris where a server called srv wishes to export a filesystem mounted on /fs1 to any client. The easiest way to achieve this is to place an entry in /etc/dfs/dfstab that specifies the filesystem to be shared and/or exported. This ensures that the filesystem will be exported for use on each reboot. If no options are needed for this filesystem, the following line is sufficient:

```
share -F nfs /fs1
```

On the client side, a mount call can then be made to mount the filesystem as follows:

```
# mount -F nfs srv:/fs1 /mnt
# mount | grep mnt
/mnt on srv:/fs1 remote/read/write/setuid/dev=2fc004
                                    on Wed Jun 19 07:25:18 2002
```

Once mounted, the filesystem is then usable just as any local filesystem.

The Version 3 NFS Protocol

Despite its huge success, the NFS version 2 protocol was not without problems, leading to the introduction of the NFS version 3 protocol [RFC1813]. The two main problems with the version 2 protocol are highlighted below:

- Only files up to 4GB in size could be accessed. This limitation was exposed early on when running NFS on large machines but was rapidly becoming a problem in most environments.

- Because all writes were required to be written synchronously, write intensive applications suffered a performance bottleneck. There were numerous workarounds for this problem, including some that violated the NFS protocol by performing writes asynchronously.

The goals of those involved in designing NFS version 3 were to solve the two problems described above, tidy up the existing version 2 protocol, and add some minor features, but at the same time limit the scope of the version 3 protocol to avoid it becoming too bloated to be implemented in a timely manner.

[PAWL94] provides an overview of the process the designers of the version 3 protocol went through, the problems inherent in the version 2 protocol, the goals behind the version 3 protocol, the changes introduced with the version 3 protocol, and various implementation and performance-related information. In this paper, they identify twelve main areas in which the protocol was enhanced:

- All arguments within the protocol such as file sizes and file offsets were widened from 32 to 64-bits. This solved the 4GB file restriction.

- The write model was changed to introduce a write/commit phase that allowed for asynchronous writes. (This will be described further).

- A new ACCESS procedure was introduced to solve permission checking problems when mapping the ID of the superuser. This procedure works in the presence of ACLs (Access Control Lists).

- In the original protocol, some of the procedures required a subsequent call in order to retrieve file attributes. In the new protocol, all procedures returned file attributes.

- In the original protocol, writes were limited to 8Kb per procedure call. This restriction was relaxed in the new protocol.

- The READDIRPLUS procedure was introduced that returned both a file handle and attributes. This eliminated some lookup calls when scanning a directory.

- The file handle size in the version 2 protocol was a fixed, 32-byte opaque data type. In version 3, it was changed to be of variable size up to a maximum of 64 bytes.

- The CREATE procedure was modified to allow for exclusive file creates. This solved a workaround in the version 2 protocol whereby a LOOKUP was followed by a CREATE, which left a window in which another client could create the file.

- The version 2 protocol limited the size of filenames and pathnames to 255 and 1024 characters respectively. In version 3, this was replaced by variable length strings which could be agreed on between the client and server.

- The version 3 protocol tightened the errors that could be returned from the server. All error values are iterated, and no errors outside of the list are permitted.

- For the set of file attributes, the `blocksize` field was removed. The `blocks` field was changed to `used` and recorded the total number of bytes used by the file.

- A new error type, `NFS3ERR_JUKEBOX`, was introduced. In a Hierarchical Storage Management (HSM) environment, a request may be made to the server to read a file that has been migrated to tape. The time to read the data back in from tape could be quite large. This error informs the client that the operation is in progress and that the call should be retried. It also allows the client to display a message on the user's console if applicable.

Writes in UNIX are asynchronous by default unless the O_SYNC or O_DSYNC flags are passed to open(). Forcing asynchronous writes to be synchronous inevitably affects performance. With NFS version 3, the client can send a number of asynchronous WRITE requests that it can then commit to disk on the server at a later date by issuing a COMMIT request. Once it receives a COMMIT request, the server cannot return until all data has been flushed to disk. In some regards, the COMMIT request is similar to calling fsync(). The most noticeable difference is that the COMMIT request does not necessarily cover the data for the whole file. It does however allow the client to flush all data when a file is closed or to break up a large synchronous write request into a number of smaller writes, all of which are performed asynchronously but followed by a COMMIT request. This itself is an important enhancement because it allows the filesystem on the server or the disk driver to coalesce a number of writes in a single large write, which is more efficient. The use of asynchronous writes should not affect the crash/recovery properties of NFS because the client is required to keep a copy of all data to be written to the file until a COMMIT is issued.

The READDIRPLUS procedure, while it can be extremely effective, also presents problems. The procedure was introduced to minimize the number of over-the-wire LOOKUP requests once a READDIR procedure had been invoked. This would typically be the case when issuing an ls -F request on a directory.

Because the implementation of READDIRPLUS is significantly more expensive than READDIR, it should be used with caution. Typically, the operation should be performed only when first accessing the directory in order to populate the DNLC (or other name cache, depending on the underlying OS). The operation should then be performed again only in the case where the cache was invalidated for the directory due to a directory modification.

Because many of the goals of NFS version 3 were to improve performance, the proof of its success was therefore dependent on how well it performed. [PAWL94] documented a number of different performance-related tests that showed that the version 3 protocol did in fact meet its objectives.

The NFS Lock Manager Protocol

One decision that the NFS team made when designing the NFS protocol was to omit file locking. One of the main reasons for this was that to support record locking, state would need to be maintained on the server, which would dramatically increase the complexity of NFS implementations.

However, file locking was not something that could be easily overlooked and was therefore implemented in SunOS as the *Network Lock Manager* (NLM). Various iterations of the NLM protocol appeared, with NLM version 3 being the version that was most widely used with NFS version 2. Unfortunately, due to the complexity of implementing support for locking, the NLM protocol was not widely implemented. With the introduction of NFS version 3 [RFC1813], the definition of NLM (version 4) was included with the NFS specification but was still a separate protocol. The NLM protocol also relied on the *Network Status*

Monitor protocol that was required in order to notify clients and servers of a crash such that lock state could be recovered.

Crash/recovery involves coordination between both clients and server as shown here:

Server crash. When locks are handed to clients, the server maintains a list of clients and the locks that they own. If the server crashes, this information is lost. When the server reboots, a *status monitor* runs and sends a message to all known clients. The lock manager on each client is notified and is given an opportunity to reclaim all locks it owns for files on the server. There is a fixed amount of time (or *grace period*) in which the clients can respond. Note however, that this is not an ideal situation as notification of clients may be delayed, because the status monitor typically informs all clients in a serial manner. This window may be reduced by multithreading the status monitor.

Client crash. If the client crashes, any locks that the client holds on the server must be cleaned up. When the client resumes, a message is sent to the server to clean up its locks. Through use of a *client state number*, which is incremented on reboot, the server is able to detect that the client has been rebooted and removes any of the locks that were held by the client before it crashed/rebooted.

Since the NLM was not widely adopted, version 4 of the NFS protocol has been extended to include file locking. This is described in the next section.

The Version 4 NFS Protocol and the Future of NFS

NFS was designed for local area networks and was put in place before the widespread adoption of the World Wide Web. As time goes by there is more of a need to use NFS in wide area networks. This raises questions on security and further highlights the need for NFS to address cross-platform issues. Although one of the goals of the original NFS implementations was to support non-UNIX platforms, the protocol was still heavily geared towards UNIX environments.

The goals of the version 4 protocol are to address the problems highlighted above and to provide additional features that were omitted in the version 3 protocol (version 3 changes were kept to a minimum to ensure that it could be designed and implemented in a timely manner). Although the version 4 protocol involves some substantial changes, the goals are to allow small incremental changes that do not require a complete overhaul of the protocol. The time between the version 2 and 3 protocols was approximately 8 years, which is similar to the time between the version 3 and 4 protocols. A minor revision to the version 4 protocol allows new features to be added to the version 4 protocol in a much more timely manner, say a 1 to 2 year timeframe.

The version 4 protocol is described in [RFC3010]. Following are the main changes that are part of the new protocol. Note that the changes introduced with the version 4 protocol are substantial and only covered briefly here.

Compound procedures. Many file-related operations over NFS require a large number of procedure calls. In a local area network this is not such a great issue. However, when operating in a wide area network the effect on performance is much more noticeable. By combining a number of procedure calls into a single, compound procedure, the amount of over-the-wire communications can be reduced considerably resulting in much better performance.

Internationalization. In previous versions of the protocol, file names were handled as an opaque byte stream. Although they were typically limited to a 7-bit US ASCII representation, they were commonly encoded in 8-bit ISO-Latin-1. Problems occurred because there was no way to specify the type of encoding within XDR. This limited the use of NFS in environments where there may be mixed character sets. To provide better support for internationalization, file and directory names will be encoded with UTF-8.

Volatile file handles. The NFS version 2 and version 3 protocols provided a single file handle type with one set of semantics. This file handle is defined as having a value that is fixed for the lifetime of the filesystem to which it refers. As an example, a file handle on UNIX comprises, amongst other things, the inode number and generation count. Because inodes can be freed and reallocated, the generation count of the inode is increased when reused to ensure that a client file handle that refers to the old file cannot now refer to the new file even though the inode number stays the same. There have also been some implementations that are unable to correctly implement the traditional file handle which inhibits the adoption of NFS on some platforms.

The NFS version 4 protocol divides file handles into both *persistent file handles*, which describe the traditional file handle, and *volatile file handles*. In the case of volatile file handles, the server may not always be able to determine whether the file handle is still valid. If it detects that a file handle is in fact invalid, it returns an NFS4ERR_STALE error message. If however it is unable to determine whether the file handle is valid, it can return an NFS4ERR_FHEXPIRED error message. Clients are able to detect whether a server can handle persistent and volatile file handles and therefore act accordingly.

Attribute classes. The set of attributes that were passed over the wire with earlier versions of the protocol were very UNIX-centric in that the information returned by the server was sufficient to respond to a stat() call on the client. In some environments, these attributes are meaningless, and in some cases, servers are unable to provide valid values.

In NFS version 4, the set of file attributes is divided into three different classes, namely *mandatory, recommended*, and *named* attributes.

The mandatory set of attributes contain information such as the file type and size, information about file handle expiration times, whether hard links and symbolic links are supported, and whether the file has named data streams/attributes.

The set of recommended attributes contain information such as the type of ACLs (Access Control Lists) that the filesystem supports, the ACLs themselves, information about the owner and group, access timestamps, and quota attributes. It also contains information about the filesystem such as free space, total number of files, files available for use, and filesystem limits such as the maximum filename length and maximum number of links.

Named attributes, also called *named data streams*, allow a single file to have multiple streams of opaque bytes unlike the traditional UNIX model of supporting a single stream of bytes per file. To access named data streams over NFS version 4, the OPENATTR procedure can retrieve a *virtual attribute directory* under which READDIR and LOOKUP procedures can be used to view and access the named attributes.

Better namespace handling. Both NFS version 2 and 3 servers export a set of independent pieces of their overall namespace and do not allow NFS clients to cross mountpoints on the server, because NFS expects all lookup operations to stay within a single filesystem. In NFS v4, the server provides a single *root file handle* through which clients can obtain file handles for any of the accessible exports.

NFS v4 servers can be made browsable by bridging exported subtrees of the namespace with a pseudo filesystem and allowing clients to cross server mountpoints. The tree constructed by the server is a logical view of all the different exports.

File locking. As mentioned earlier, locking is not part of the NFS version 2 or version 3 protocols which rely instead on the Network Lock Manager (NLM) protocol, described in the section *The NFS Lock Manager Protocol*, earlier in the chapter. The NLM protocol was not, however, widely adopted.

NFS version 4 provides for both UNIX file-level locking functions and Windows-based share locking functions. NFS version 4 supports both record and byte range locking functions.

Client side caching. Most NFS clients cache both file data and attributes as much as possible. When moving more towards wide area networks, the cost of a cache miss can be significant. The problem with the version 2 and version 3 protocols is that NFS does not provide a means to support cache coherency between multiple clients, which can sometimes lead to invalid file data being read.

NFS version 4 does not provide cache coherency between clients but defines a limited set of caching guarantees to allow locks and share reservations to be used without destructive interference from client-side caching. NFS v4 also provides a *delegation scheme* that allows clients to make decisions that were traditionally made by the server.

The delegation mechanism is an important feature in terms of performance because it limits the number of procedure calls that would typically go between client and server when accessing a file. When another client attempts to access a file for which a delegation has been granted, the server invokes an RPC to the client holding the delegation. The client is then responsible for flushing any file information, including data, that has changed before responding to the recall notice. Only after the first client has responded to the revoke request will the second client be allowed to access the file.

The NFS version 4 specification provides many details for the different types of delegations that can be granted and therefore the type of caching that can be performed on the client.

Built-in security. NFS has relied on the UNIX-centric user ID mechanisms to provide security. This has generally not been a problem because NFS has largely been used within private networks. However, because one of the goals of the version 4 protocol is to widen the use of NFS to wide area networks, this level of security is insufficient. The basic NFS security mechanisms are being extended through use of the RPCSEG_GSS framework. The RPCSEG_GSS mechanisms are implemented at the RPC layer and are capable of providing both private keys schemes, such as Kerboros version 5, and public key schemes.

The NFS version 4 protocol is a significant rework of the version 3 protocol. It provides a wide range of features aimed at continuing its success as it becomes more widely adopted in wide area networks, and it provides better support for building a distributed filesystem for heterogeneous operating systems.

There was a huge amount of investment in NFS prior to version 4. Because NFS version 4 attempts to address many of the prior limitations of the earlier versions, including more attention to non-UNIX operating systems, NFS is likely to grow in popularity.

The NFS Automounter

One feature that is part of some distributed filesystems is the ability to provide a unified namespace across a number of different clients. For example, to see /home/spate on several different clients would require exporting the filesystem from the server on which the filesystem resides and NFS mounting it on all of the required clients. If the mount point is permanent, the appropriate entries must be placed in the vfstab/fstab table. Obviously this model does not scale well when dealing with hundreds of filesystems and a very large number of clients and servers.

This problem was resolved by introduction of the *automounter*. This aids in creation of a unified namespace while keeping the number of mounted filesystems to only those filesystems that are actually in use. The automounter is simple in nature. When a user attempts to access a file that crosses a mount point within the boundaries of the automounter, the NFS filesystem is first mounted prior to allowing the access to proceed. This is shown in Figure 13.2.

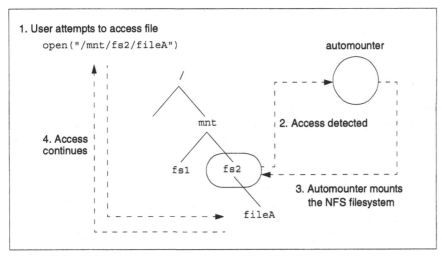

Figure 13.2   Using the automounter to mount an NFS filesystem.

The first automounters were implemented as user space daemons, which typically mount themselves on those directories that require automounter services and masquerade as NFS servers. When an attempt is made to access a file within one of these filesystems, the kernel sends an NFS LOOKUP call to the server, in this case the automounter. The automounter then NFS mounts the real filesystem onto a directory somewhere within its own mount space. The real filesystem is then referenced through symbolic links. For example, in Figure 13.2, the filesystem to be mounted on `fs2` may be mounted on `/auto/f2` and `/mnt/fs1` will be a symbolic link to this directory.

In many environments it is usual to see a combination of standard NFS mounted filesystems and automounted filesystems. The automounter should be used for filesystems that are not accessed frequently, such as manual pages, source code repositories, and so on. User directories and bin directories are examples of directories that are typically mounted through standard NFS means.

Another common use of the automounter is to use it in conjunction with the *Network Information Service* (NIS) in an environment where user home directories are distributed throughout the network. In this way, NIS centrally manages all of the NFS mounts from one of the servers. Although each user's home directory physically resides on only one server, the same server is configured to export the home directory to all hosts on the network. Each host on the network runs the automounter as an NFS client and can therefore mount a user's home directory. This allows the user to log in to any host and have access to his/her home directory. In this environment, file access is enhanced transparently while the use of the automounter avoids the overhead caused by dozens of active but unused NFS mounted filesystems.

Automounter Problems and the Autofs Filesystem

[CALL93] highlighted some of the problems inherent with using the automounter and provided details about autofs, a new automounter that solved the problems described. The type of problems that the original automounter exhibited are as follows:

Symbolic links. The preceding section described how the automounter actually NFS mounts the filesystem on a temporary directory and refers to it through a symbolic link. Because the goal of the automounter is only to mount filesystems when required, it periodically unmounts the filesystem if there is no activity for a predetermined amount of time.

However, if a process issues a getcwd() system call, the real path may be cached which references the temporary directory structure, that is, where the filesystem is actually mounted. If the path is used later, there is no guarantee that the filesystem is still mounted and the automounter is unable to detect that access is being requested. The user process may therefore see the local directory structure and thus unpredictable results.

Adding new mountpoints. The list of filesystems that the automounter manages is consulted only when the automounter first starts. A workaround is to terminate and restart the automounter—obviously not an ideal solution.

Performance. The method of sending NFS requests to the automounter when crossing its mount point, together with the management of symbolic links, is more time consuming than accessing an NFS filesystem directly.

Single threading. Because the automounter is single threaded it can only handle one request at a time. Therefore, when in the process of mounting an NFS filesystem, all subsequent access is blocked.

The autofs filesystem replaced the user-level automounter daemon with an in-kernel filesystem type. The automounter daemon is still retained. However, when it starts, it mounts autofs *in place* for each of the filesystems that is to be managed. In the previous example, the autofs filesystem would be mounted on /mnt. When access is detected to, say /mnt/fs2, autofs invokes an RPC request to communicate with the automounter daemon that NFS mounts the filesystem on /mnt/fs2. Once this is achieved, the autofs filesystem does not intercept any further operations. This eradicates the symbolic link problem and therefore increases the overall performance.

The Remote File Sharing Service (RFS)

At the time Sun was designing NFS, AT&T was working on the development of another distributed filesystem, *Remote File Sharing* (RFS) [RIFK86]. The design goals were quite different for RFS in that they wanted complete UNIX file semantics. This included access to remote devices as well as providing UNIX-level file and record locking. Coverage of different operating systems was not a goal for RFS and thus its implementation was heavily restricted to System V UNIX environments.

The RFS Architecture

In a manner similar to NFS, the RFS client is able to mount a directory that is exported by the server. Exporting of filesystems involved *advertising* a *resource name* with a *name server*. The RFS client could receive details of available resources from the name server and mount a filesystem without prior knowledge of the server which owned the filesystem. RFS required a separate name service protocol in order to manage all resources. Servers would issue an *advertise* procedure to the name server, which then registered the resource in the name server database. When the client requested information about a specific resource, the name server would return the name of the server on which the resource was located. Communication could then take place between client and server to actually mount the filesystem.

RFS also relied on an RPC protocol that provided a procedure on the server for every file-related system call. XDR was used to encode data types but only where the machine architecture of the client and server differed. On the server side, the goal was to *emulate* the environment of the client and provide a context similar to one on the caller to handle the remote procedure calls. This was used to provide management of the process user and group IDs, umask, and so on. This emulation was a little awkward for some operations. For example, when performing a lookup on a pathname, if an RFS mount point was to be crossed, the remainder of the pathname was sent to the server to be resolved. If a series of ".." components took the pathname out of the RFS mounted filesystem, the operation had to be aborted and completed on the client.

To provide for full UNIX semantics including file and record locking, RFS was required to provide a stateful server. This required the server to maintain reference counts for every open call from every client, file and record lock information on the server, and information about the state of named pipes. RFS also maintained a list of all client mounts. If either the server or one of the clients crashed, there was a significant amount of crash/recovery to be performed. If a client crashed, the server was required to remove all traces of the client. Amongst other things, this included decrementing reference counts, releasing any locks that client held, and so on.

Server side failure resulted in the ENOLINK error message being returned when any attempts were made to access files on the server. All inodes/vnodes on the client that accessed RFS files were marked to indicate the failure such that further attempts at access would return ENOLINK without any attempt to communicate with the server.

The overall architecture of RFS is shown in Figure 13.3. Unlike NFS, RFS requires a reliable, virtual circuit transport service. In the figure this is shown as TCP/IP. A virtual circuit is established during the mount and remains in existence for the duration of the mount. For each client/server pair, the virtual circuit is shared if a client mounts more than one RFS filesystem.

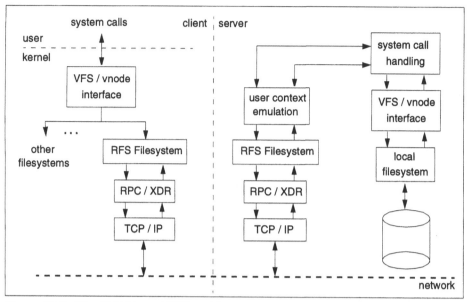

Figure 13.3 The SVR4-based RFS architecture.

Another big difference between RFS and NFS is the support for client-side caching. RFS implements a write-through cache on each server; that is, writes are always sent to the server at the time the write occurs but the data is cached for subsequent access. Obviously this presents a challenge with respect to cache coherency when a write occurs to a file and data is cached on one of more clients. RFS must invalidate cached copies of the data on clients other than the one from which the write is issued. The client-side caching of file data is subsequently disabled either until the process that issued the write closes the file or a predetermined amount of time has passed since the last write to the file.

Differences between RFS and NFS

When RFS was introduced, there were a number of differences between RFS and NFS as defined by the version 2 protocol. Some of these differences were:

- NFS is stateless whereas RFS requires a primary name server that coordinates RFS activity.

- RFS can map user and group IDs from client to server based on presence of a mapping table. NFS by contrast requires that the IDs are the same on both client and server. More specifically, NFS implementations assume the use of NIS to maintain a consistent user database across the network.

- RFS allows access to device files across the network while devices are not accessible across NFS.

- RFS names resources, the directories that are advertised, which are communicated to the primary server. This is not required in NFS.

- RFS requires a connection-mode virtual circuit environment, while NFS runs in a connectionless state.

- RFS provides support for mandatory file and record locking. This is not defined as part of the NFS protocol.

- NFS can run in heterogeneous environments, while RFS is restricted to UNIX environments and in particular System V UNIX.

- RFS guarantees that when files are opened in append mode (O_APPEND) the write is appended to the file. This is not guaranteed in NFS.

- In an NFS environment, the administrator must know the machine name from which the filesystem is being exported. This is alleviated with RFS through use of the primary server.

When reading through this list, it appears that RFS has more features to offer and would therefore be a better offering in the distributed filesystem arena than NFS. However, the goals of both projects differed in that RFS supported full UNIX semantics whereas for NFS, the protocol was *close enough* for most of the environments that it was used in.

The fact that NFS was widely publicized and the specification was publicly open, together with the simplicity of its design and the fact that it was designed to be portable across operating systems, resulted in its success and the rather quick death of RFS, which was replaced by NFS in SVR4.

RFS was never open to the public in the same way that NFS was. Because it was part of the UNIX operating system and required a license from AT&T, it stayed within the SVR3 area and had little widespread usage. It would be a surprise if there were still RFS implementations in use today.

The Andrew File System (AFS)

The *Andrew Filesystem* (AFS) [MORR86] was developed in the early to mid 1980s at Carnegie Mellon University (CMU) as part of *Project Andrew*, a joint project between CMU and IBM to develop an educational-based computing infrastructure. There were a number of goals for the AFS filesystem. First, they required that UNIX binaries could run on clients without modification requiring that the filesystem be implemented in the kernel. They also required a single, unified namespace such that users be able to access their files wherever they resided in the network. To help performance, aggressive client-side caching would be used. AFS also allowed groups of files to be migrated from one server to another without loss of service, to help load balancing.

The AFS Architecture

An AFS network, shown in Figure 13.4, consists of a group of *cells* that all reside under /afs. Issuing a call to ls /afs will display the list of AFS cells. A cell is a collection of servers that are grouped together and administered as a whole. In the

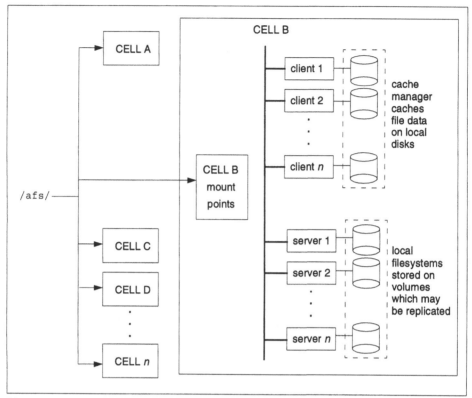

Figure 13.4 The AFS file hierarchy encompassing multiple AFS cells.

academic environment, each university may be a single cell. Even though each cell may be local or remote, all users will see exactly the same file hierarchy regardless of where they are accessing the filesystem.

Within a cell, there are a number of servers and clients. Servers manage a set of *volumes* that are held in the *Volume Location Database* (VLDB). The VLDB is replicated on each of the servers. Volumes can be replicated over a number of different servers. They can also be migrated to enable load balancing or to move a user's files from one location to another based on need. All of this can be done without interrupting access to the volume. The migration of volumes is achieved by *cloning* the volume, which creates a stable snapshot. To migrate the volume, the clone is moved first while access is still allowed to the original volume. After the clone has moved, any writes to the original volume are replayed to the clone volume.

Client-Side Caching of AFS File Data

Clients each require a local disk in order to cache files. The caching is controlled by a local *cache manager*. In earlier AFS implementations, whenever a file was opened, it was first copied in its entirety to the local disk on the client. This quickly became problematic as file sizes increased, so later AFS versions defined the copying to be performed in 64KB chunks of data. Note that, in addition to file data, the cache manager also caches file meta-data, directory information, and symbolic links.

When retrieving data from the server, the client obtains a *callback*. If another client is modifying the data, the server must inform all clients that their cached data may be invalid. If only one client holds a callback, it can operate on the file without supervision of the server until a time comes for the client to notify the server of changes, for example, when the file is closed. The callback is *broken* if another client attempts to modify the file. With this mechanism, there is a potential for callbacks to go astray. To help alleviate this problem, clients with callbacks send *probe* messages to the server on a regular basis. If a callback is missed, the client and server work together to restore cache coherency.

AFS does not provide fully coherent client side caches. A client typically makes changes locally until the file is closed at which point the changes are communicated with the server. Thus, if multiple clients are modifying the same file, the client that closes the file last will write back its changes, which may overwrite another client's changes even with the callback mechanism in place.

Where Is AFS Now?

A number of the original designers of AFS formed their own company Transarc, which went on to produce commercial implementations of AFS for a number of different platforms. The technology developed for AFS also became the basis of DCE DFS, the subject of the next section. Transarc was later acquired by IBM and, at the time of this writing, the history of AFS is looking rather unclear, at least from a commercial perspective.

The DCE Distributed File Service (DFS)

The *Open Software Foundation* started a project in the mid 1980s to define a secure, robust distributed environment for enterprise computing. The overall project was called the *Distributed Computing Environment* (DCE). The goal behind DCE was to draw together the best of breed technologies into one integrated solution, produce the *Application Environment Specification* (AES), and to release source code as an example implementation of the standard. In 1989, OSF put out a *Request For Technology*, an invitation to the computing industry asking them to bid technologies in each of the identified areas. For the distributed filesystem component, Transarc won the bid, having persuaded OSF of the value of their AFS-based technology.

The resulting *Distributed File Service* (DFS) technology bore a close resemblance to the AFS architecture. The RPC mechanisms of AFS were replaced with DCE RPC and the virtual filesystem architecture was replaced with VFS+ that allowed local filesystems to be used within a DFS framework, and Transarc produced the Episode filesystem that provided a wide number of features.

DCE / DFS Architecture

The cell nature of AFS was retained, with a DFS cell comprising a number of servers and clients. DFS servers run services that make data available and monitor and control other services. The DFS server model differed from the original AFS model, with some servers performing one of a number of different functions:

File server. The server that runs the services necessary for storing and exporting data. This server holds the physical filesystems that comprise the DFS namespace.

System control server. This server is responsible for updating other servers with replicas of system configuration files.

Fileset database server. The *Fileset Location Database* (FLDB) master and replicas are stored here. The FLDB is similar to the volume database in AFS. The FLDB holds system and user files.

Backup database server. This holds the master and replicas of the backup database which holds information used to backup and restore system and user files.

Note that a DFS server can perform one or more of these tasks.

The fileset location database stores information about the locations of *filesets*. Each readable/writeable fileset has an entry in the FLDB that includes information about the fileset's replicas and clones (snapshots).

DFS Local Filesystems

A DFS local filesystem manages an *aggregate*, which can hold one or more filesets and is physically equivalent to a filesystem stored within a standard disk partition. The goal behind the fileset concept was to make it smaller than a disk partition and therefore more manageable. As an example, a single filesystem is typically used to store a number of user home directories. With DFS, the aggregate may hold one fileset per user.

Aggregates also supports fileset operations not found on standard UNIX partitions, including the ability to move a fileset from one DFS aggregate to another or from one server to another for load balancing across servers. This is comparable to the migration performed by AFS.

UNIX partitions and filesystems can also be made visible in the DFS namespace if they adhere to the VFS+ specification, a modification to the native VFS/vnode architecture with additional interfaces to support DFS. Note however that these partitions can store only a single fileset (filesystem) regardless of the amount of data actually stored in the fileset.

DFS Cache Management

DFS enhanced the client-side caching of AFS by providing fully coherent client side caches. Whenever a process writes to a file, clients should not see stale data.

To provide this level of cache coherency, DFS introduced a *token manager* that keeps a reference of all clients that are accessing a specific file.

When a client wishes to access a file, it requests a token for the type of operation it is about to perform, for example, a read or write token. In some circumstances, tokens of the same class allow shared access to a file; two clients reading the same file would thus obtain the same class of token. However, some tokens are incompatible with tokens of the same class, a write token being the obvious example. If a client wishes to obtain a write token for a file on which a write token has already been issued, the server is required to revoke the first client's write token allowing the second write to proceed. When a client receives a request to revoke a token, it must first flush all modified data before responding to the server.

The Future of DCE / DFS

The overall DCE framework and particularly the infrastructure required to support DFS was incredibly complex, which made many OS vendors question the benefits of supporting DFS. As such, the number of implementations of DFS were small and adoption of DFS equally limited. The overall DCE program came to a halt in the early 1990s, leaving a small number of operating systems supporting their existing DCE efforts. As NFS evolves and new, distributed filesystem paradigms come into play, the number of DFS installations is likely to decline further.

Clustered Filesystems

With distributed filesystems, there is a single point of failure in that if the server (that owns the underlying storage) crashes, service is interrupted until the server reboots. In the event that the server is unable to reboot immediately, the delay in service can be significant.

With most critical business functions now heavily reliant on computer-based technology, this downtime is unacceptable. In some business disciplines, seconds of downtime can cost a company significant amounts of money.

By making hardware and software more reliable, clusters provide the means by which downtime can be minimized, if not removed altogether. In addition to increasing the reliability of the system, by pooling together a network of interconnected servers, the potential for improvements in both performance and manageability make cluster-based computing an essential part of any large enterprise.

The following sections describe the clustering components, both software and hardware, that are required in order to provide a *clustered filesystem* (CFS). There are typically a large number of components that are needed in addition to filesystem enhancements in order to provide a fully clustered filesystem. After describing the basic components of clustered environments and filesystems, the

VERITAS clustered filesystem technology is used as a concrete example of how a clustered filesystem is constructed.

Later sections describe some of the other clustered filesystems that are available today.

The following sections only scratch the surface of clustered filesystem technology. For a more in depth look at clustered filesystems, you can refer to Dilip Ranade's book *Shared Data Clusters* [RANA02].

What Is a Clustered Filesystem?

In simple terms, a clustered filesystem is simply a collection of servers (also called nodes) that work together to provide a single, unified view of the same filesystem. A process running on any of these nodes sees exactly the same view of the filesystem as a process on any other node. Any changes by any of the nodes are immediately reflected on all of the other nodes.

Clustered filesystem technology is complementary to distributed filesystems. Any of the nodes in the cluster can export the filesystem, which can then be viewed across the network using NFS or another distributed filesystem technology. In fact, each node can export the filesystem, which could be mounted on several clients.

Although not all clustered filesystems provide identical functionality, the goals of clustered filesystems are usually stricter than distributed filesystems in that a single unified view of the filesystem together with full cache coherency and UNIX semantics, should be a property of all nodes within the cluster. In essence, each of the nodes in the cluster should give the appearance of a local filesystem.

There are a number of properties of clusters and clustered filesystems that enhance the capabilities of a traditional computer environment, namely:

Resilience to server failure. Unlike a distributed filesystem environment where a single server crash results loss of access, failure of one of the servers in a clustered filesystem environment does not impact access to the cluster as a whole. One of the other servers in the cluster can take over responsibility for any work that the failed server was doing.

Resilience to hardware failure. A cluster is also resilient to a number of different hardware failures, such as loss to part of the network or disks. Because access to the cluster is typically through one of a number of different routes, requests can be rerouted as and when necessary independently of what has failed. Access to disks is also typically through a shared network.

Application failover. Failure of one of the servers can result in loss of service to one or more applications. However, by having the same application set in a *hot standby* mode on one of the other servers, a detected problem can result in a *failover* to one of the other nodes in the cluster. A failover results in one machine taking the placed of the failed machine. Because a single server failure does not prevent access to the cluster filesystem on another node, the application downtime is kept to a minimum; the only work to perform is to restart the applications. Any form of system restart is largely taken out of the picture.

Increased scalability. Performance can typically be increased by simply adding another node to the cluster. In many clustered environments, this may be achieved without bringing down the cluster.

Better management. Managing a set of distributed filesystems involves managing each of the servers that export filesystems. A cluster and clustered filesystem can typically be managed as a whole, reducing the overall cost of management.

As clusters become more widespread, this increases the choice of underlying hardware. If much of the reliability and enhanced scalability can be derived from software, the hardware base of the cluster can be moved from more traditional, high-end servers to low cost, PC-based solutions.

Clustered Filesystem Components

To achieve the levels of service and manageability described in the previous section, there are several components that must work together to provide a clustered filesystem. The following sections describe the various components that are generic to clusters and cluster filesystems. Later sections put all these components together to show how complete clustering solutions can be constructed.

Hardware Solutions for Clustering

When building clusters, one of the first considerations is the type of hardware that is available. The typical computer environment comprises a set of clients communicating with servers across Ethernet. Servers typically have local storage connected via standards such as SCSI or proprietary based I/O protocols.

While Ethernet and communication protocols such as TCP/IP are unlikely to be replaced as the communication medium between one machine and the next, the host-based storage model has been evolving over the last few years. Although SCSI attached storage will remain a strong player in a number of environments, the choice for storage subsystems has grown rapidly. *Fibre channel*, which allows the underlying storage to be physically separate from the server through use of a fibre channel adaptor in the server and a fibre switch, enables construction of *storage area networks* or SANs.

Figure 13.5 shows the contrast between traditional host-based storage and shared storage through use of a SAN.

Cluster Management

Because all nodes within the cluster are presented as a whole, there must be a means by which the clusters are grouped and managed together. This includes the

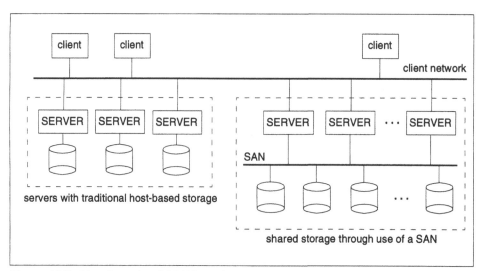

Figure 13.5 Host-based and SAN-based storage.

ability to add and remove nodes to or from the cluster. It is also imperative that any failures within the cluster are communicated as soon as possible, allowing applications and system services to recover.

These types of services are required by all components within the cluster including filesystem, volume management, and lock management.

Failure detection is typically achieved through some type of heartbeat mechanism for which there are a number of methods. For example, a single master node can be responsible for pinging slaves nodes that must respond within a predefined amount of time to indicate that all is well. If a slave does not respond before this time or a specific number of heartbeats have not been acknowledged, the slave may have failed; this then triggers recovery mechanisms.

Employing a heartbeat mechanism is obviously prone to failure if the master itself dies. This can however be solved by having multiple masters along with the ability for a slave node to be promoted to a master node if one of the master nodes fails.

Cluster Volume Management

In larger server environments, disks are typically managed through use of a *Logical Volume Manager*. Rather than exporting physical disk slices on which filesystems can be made, the volume manager exports a set of logical volumes. Volumes look very similar to standard disk slices in that they present a contiguous set of blocks to the user. Underneath the covers, a volume may comprise a number of physically disjointed portions of one or more disks. Mirrored volumes (RAID-1) provide resilience to disk failure by providing one or more identical copies of the logical volume. Each mirrored volume is stored on a different disk.

In addition to these basic volume types, volumes can also be *striped* (RAID 0). For a striped volume the volume must span at least two disks. The volume data is then interleaved across these disks. Data is allocated in fixed-sized units called *stripes*. For example, Figure 13.6 shows a logical volume where the data is striped across three disks with a stripe size of 64KB.

The first 64KB of data is written to disk 1, the second 64KB of data is written to disk 2, the third to disk 3, and so on. Because the data is spread across multiple disks, this increases both read and write performance because data can be read from or written to the disks concurrently.

Volume managers can also implement software RAID-5 whereby data is protected through use of a disk that is used to hold parity information obtained from each of the stripes from all disks in the volume.

In a SAN-based environment where all servers have shared access to the underlying storage devices, management of the storage and allocation of logical volumes must be coordinated between the different servers. This requires a *clustered volume manager*, a set of volume managers, one per server, which communicate to present a single unified view of the storage. This prevents one server from overwriting the configuration of another server.

Creation of a logical volume on one node in the cluster is visible by all other nodes in the cluster. This allows parallel applications to run across the cluster and see the same underlying raw volumes. As an example, Oracle RAC (*Reliable Access Cluster*), formerly *Oracle Parallel Server* (OPS), can run on each node in the cluster and access the database through the clustered volume manager.

Clustered volume managers are resilient to a server crash. If one of the servers crashes, there is no loss of configuration since the configuration information is shared across the cluster. Applications running on other nodes in the cluster see no loss of data access.

Cluster Filesystem Management

The goal of a clustered filesystem is to present an identical view of the same filesystem from multiple nodes within the cluster. As shown in the previous sections on distributed filesystems, providing cache coherency between these different nodes is not an easy task. Another difficult issue concerns lock management between different processes accessing the same file.

Clustered filesystems have additional problems in that they must share the resources of the filesystem across all nodes in the system. Taking a read/write lock in exclusive mode on one node is inadequate if another process on another node can do the same thing at the same time. When a node joins the cluster and when a node fails are also issues that must be taken into consideration. What happens if one of the nodes in the cluster fails? The recovery mechanisms involved are substantially different from those found in the distributed filesystem client/server model.

The local filesystem must be modified substantially to take these considerations into account. Each operation that is provided by the filesystem

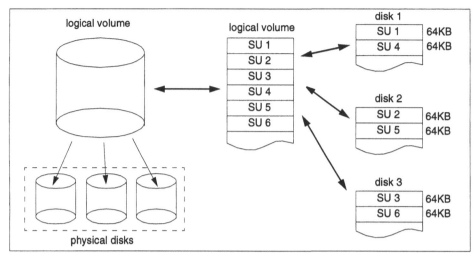

Figure 13.6 A striped logical volume using three disks.

must be modified to become *cluster aware*. For example, take the case of mounting a filesystem. One of the first operations is to read the superblock from disk, mark it *dirty*, and write it back to disk. If the mount command is invoked again for this filesystem, it will quickly complain that the filesystem is dirty and that fsck needs to be run. In a cluster, the mount command must know how to respond to the dirty bit in the superblock.

A transaction-based filesystem is essential for providing a robust, clustered filesystem because if a node in the cluster fails and another node needs to take ownership of the filesystem, recovery needs to be performed quickly to reduce downtime. There are two models in which clustered filesystems can be constructed, namely:

Single transaction server. In this model, only one of the servers in the cluster, the *primary node*, performs transactions. Although any node in the cluster can perform I/O, if any structural changes are needed to the filesystem, a request must be sent from the *secondary node* to the primary node in order to perform the transaction.

Multiple transaction servers. With this model, any node in the cluster can perform transactions.

Both types of clustered filesystems have their advantages and disadvantages. While the single transaction server model is easier to implement, the primary node can quickly become a bottleneck in environments where there is a lot of meta-data activity.

There are also two approaches to implementing clustered filesystems. Firstly, a clustered view of the filesystem can be constructed by layering the cluster components on top of a local filesystem. Although simpler to implement, without knowledge of the underlying filesystem implementation, difficulties can arise in supporting various filesystem features.

The second approach is for the local filesystem to be cluster aware. Any features that are provided by the filesystem must also be made cluster aware. All locks taken within the filesystem must be cluster aware and reconfiguration in the event of a system crash must recover all cluster state.

The section *The VERITAS SANPoint Foundation Suite* describes the various components of a clustered filesystem in more detail.

Cluster Lock Management

Filesystems, volume managers, and other system software require different lock types to coordinate access to their data structures, as described in Chapter 10. This obviously holds true in a cluster environment. Consider the case where two processes are trying to write to the same file. The process which obtains the inode read/write lock in exclusive mode is the process that gets to write to the file first. The other process must wait until the first process relinquishes the lock.

In a clustered environment, these locks, which are still based on primitives provided by the underlying operating system, must be enhanced to provide distributed locks, such that they can be queried and acquired by any node in the cluster. The infrastructure required to perform this service is provided by a *distributed* or *global lock manager* (GLM).

The services provided by a GLM go beyond communication among the nodes in the cluster to query, acquire, and release locks. The GLM must be resilient to node failure. When a node in the cluster fails, the GLM must be able to recover any locks that were granted to the failed node.

The VERITAS SANPoint Foundation Suite

SANPoint Foundation Suite is the name given to the VERITAS Cluster Filesystem and the various software components that are required to support it. *SANPoint Foundation Suite HA* (High Availability) provides the ability to fail over applications from one node in the cluster to another in the event of a node failure.

The following sections build on the cluster components described in the previous sections by describing in more detail the components that are required to build a full clustered filesystem. Each component is described from a clustering perspective only. For example, the sections on the VERITAS volume manager and filesystem only described those components that are used to make them cluster aware.

The dependence that each of the components has on the others is described, together with information about the hardware platform that is required.

CFS Hardware Configuration

A clustered filesystem environment requires nodes in the cluster to communicate with other efficiently and requires each node in the cluster be able to access the underlying storage directly.

For access to storage, CFS is best suited to a *Storage Area Network* (SAN). A SAN is a network of storage devices that are connected via fibre channel hubs and switches to a number of different servers. The main benefit of a SAN is that each of the servers can directly see all of the attached storage, as shown in Figure 13.7. Distributed filesystems such as AFS and DFS require replication to help in the event of a server crash. Within a SAN environment, if one of the servers crashes, any filesystems that the server was managing are accessible from any of the other servers.

For communication between nodes in the cluster and to provide a heartbeat mechanism, CFS requires a private network over which to send messages.

CFS Software Components

In addition to the clustered filesystem itself, there are many software components that are required in order to provide a complete clustered filesystem solution. The components, which are listed here, are described in subsequent sections:

Clustered Filesystem. The clustered filesystem is a collection of cluster-aware local filesystems working together to provide a unified view of the underlying storage. Collectively they manage a single filesystem (from a storage perspective) and allow filesystem access with full UNIX semantics from any node in the cluster.

VCS Agents. There are a number of *agents* within a CFS environment. Each agent manages a specific resource, including starting and stopping the resource and reporting any problems such that recovery actions may be performed.

Cluster Server. The *VERITAS Cluster Server* (VCS) provides all of the features that are required to manage a cluster. This includes communication between nodes in the cluster, configuration, cluster membership, and the framework in which to handle failover.

Clustered Volume Manager. Because storage is shared between the various nodes of the cluster, it is imperative that the view of the storage be identical between one node and the next. The VERITAS *Clustered Volume Manager* (CVM) provides this unified view. When a change is made to the volume configuration, the changes are visible on all nodes in the cluster.

Global Lock Manager (GLM). The GLM provides a cluster-wide lock manager that allows various components of CFS to manage locks across the cluster.

Global Atomic Broadcast (GAB). GAB provides the means to bring up and shutdown the cluster in an orderly fashion. It is used to handle cluster membership, allowing nodes to be dynamically added to and removed from the cluster. It also provides a reliable messaging service ensuring that messages sent from one node to another are received in the order in which they are sent.

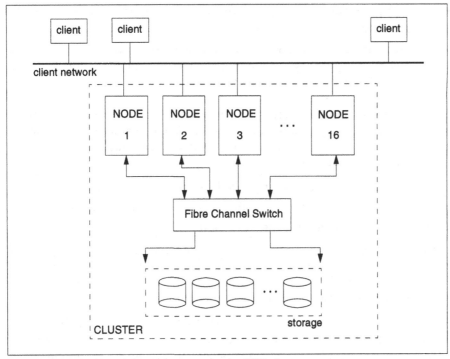

Figure 13.7 The hardware components of a CFS cluster.

Low Latency Transport (LLT). LLT provides a kernel-to-kernel communication layer. The GAB messaging services are built on top of LLT.

Network Time Protocol (NTP). Each node must have the same time

The following sections describe these various components in more detail, starting with the framework required to build the cluster and then moving to more detail on how the clustered filesystem itself is implemented.

VERITAS Cluster Server (VCS) and Agents

The VERITAS Cluster Server provides the mechanisms for managing a cluster of servers. The VCS engine consists of three main components:

Resources. Within a cluster there can be a number of different resources to manage and monitor, whether hardware such as disks and network cards or software such as filesystems, databases, and other applications.

Attributes. Agents manage their resources according to a set of *attributes*. When these attributes are changed, the agents change their behavior when managing the resources.

Service groups. A service group is a collection of resources. When a service group is brought online, all of its resources become available.

In order for the various services of the cluster to function correctly, it is vital that the different CFS components are monitored on a regular basis and that any irregularities that are found are reported as soon as possible in order for corrective action to take place.

To achieve this monitoring, CFS requires a number of different *agents*. Once started, agents obtain configuration information from VCS and then monitor the resources they manage and update VCS with any changes. Each agent has three main entry points that are called by VCS:

Online. This function is invoked to start the resource (bring it online).

Offline. This function is invoked to stop the resource (take it offline).

Monitor. This function returns the status of the resource.

VCS can be used to manage the various components of the clustered filesystem framework in addition to managing the applications that are running on top of CFS. There are a number of agents that are responsible for maintaining the health of a CFS cluster. Following are the agents that control CFS:

CFSMount. Clusters pose a problem in traditional UNIX environments because filesystems are typically mounted before the network is accessible. Thus, it is not possible to add a clustered filesystem to the mount table because the cluster communication services must be running before a cluster mount can take place. The CFSMount agent is responsible for maintaining a cluster-level mount table that allows clustered filesystems to be automatically mounted once networking becomes available.

CFSfsckd. When the primary node in a cluster fails, the failover to another node all happens within the kernel. As part of failover, the new primary node needs to perform a log replay of the filesystem, that requires the user level fsck program to run. On each node in the cluster, a fsck daemon sleeps in the kernel in case the node is chosen as the new primary. In this case, the daemon is awoken so that fsck can perform log replay.

CFSQlogckd. VERITAS Quick Log requires the presence of a QuickLog daemon in order to function correctly. Agents are responsible for ensuring that this daemon is running in environments where QuickLog is running.

In addition to the CFS agents listed, a number of other agents are also required for managing other components of the cluster.

Low Latency Transport (LLT)

Communication between one node in the cluster and the next is achieved through use of the VERITAS *Low Latency Transport Protocol* (LLT), a fast, reliable, peer-to-peer protocol that provides a reliable sequenced message delivery between any two nodes in the cluster. LLT is intended to be used within a single network segment.

Threads register for LLT ports through which they communicate. LLT also monitors connections between nodes by issuing heartbeats at regular intervals.

Group Membership and Atomic Broadcast (GAB)

The GAB service provides cluster group membership and reliable messaging. These are two essential components in a cluster framework. Messaging is built on top of the LLT protocol.

While LLT provides the physical-level connection of nodes within the cluster, GAB provides, through the use of GAB ports, a logical view of the cluster. Cluster membership is defined in terms of GAB ports. All components within the cluster register with a specific port. For example, CFS registers with port F, CVM registers with port V, and so on.

Through use of a global, atomic broadcast, GAB informs all nodes that have registered with a port whenever a node registers or de-registers with that port.

The VERITAS Global Lock Manager (GLM)

The Global Lock Manager (GLM) provides cluster-wide reader/writer locks.

The GLM is built on top of GAB, which in turn uses LLT to communicate between the different nodes in the cluster. Note that CFS also communicates directly with GAB for non-GLM related messages.

The GLM provides shared and exclusive locks with the ability to upgrade and downgrade a lock as appropriate. GLM implements a distributed master/slave locking model. Each lock is defined as having a master node, but there is no single master for all locks. As well as reducing contention when managing locks, this also aids in recovery when one node dies.

GLM also provides the means to *piggy-back* data in response to granting a lock. The idea behind piggy-backed data is to improve performance. Consider the case where a request is made to obtain a lock for a cached buffer and the buffer is valid on another node. A request is made to the GLM to obtain the lock. In addition to granting the lock, the buffer cache data may also be delivered with the lock grant, which avoids the need for the requesting node to perform a disk I/O.

The VERITAS Clustered Volume Manager (CVM)

The VERITAS volume manager manages disks that may be locally attached to a host or may be attached through a SAN fabric. Disks are grouped together into one or more *disk groups*. Within each disk group are one or more logical volumes on which filesystems can be made. For example, the following filesystem:

```
# mkfs -F vxfs /dev/vx/mydg/fsvol 1g
```

is created on the logical volume fsvol that resides in the mydg disk group.

The VERITAS Clustered Volume Manager (CVM), while providing all of the features of the standard volume manager, has a number of goals:

■ Provide uniform naming of all volumes within the cluster. For example, the above volume name should be visible at the same path on all nodes within the cluster.

■ Allow for simultaneous access to each of the shared volumes.

■ Allow administration of the volume manager configuration from each node in the cluster.

■ Ensure that access to each volume is not interrupted in the event that one of the nodes in the cluster crashes.

CVM provides both *private* disk groups and *cluster shareable* disk groups, as shown in Figure 13.8. The private disk groups are accessible only by a single node in the cluster even though they may be physically visible from another node. An example of where such a disk group may be used is for operating system-specific filesystems such as the root filesystem, /var, /usr, and so on. Clustered disk groups are used for building clustered filesystems or for providing shared access to raw volumes within the cluster.

In addition to providing typical volume manager capabilities throughout the cluster, CVM also supports the ability to perform off-host processing. Because volumes can be accessed through any node within the cluster, applications such as backup, decision support, and report generation can be run on separate nodes, thus reducing the load that occurs within a single host/disk configuration.

CVM requires support from the VCS cluster monitoring services to determine which nodes are part of the cluster and for information about nodes that dynamically join or leave the cluster. This is particularly important during volume manager bootstrap, during which device discovery is performed to locate attached storage. The first node to join the cluster gains the role of master and is responsible for setting up any shared disk groups, for creating and reconfiguring volumes and for managing volume snapshots. If the master node fails, the role is assumed by one of the other nodes in the cluster.

The Clustered Filesystem (CFS)

The VERITAS Clustered Filesystem uses a master/slave architecture. When a filesystem is mounted, the node that issues the first mount becomes the *primary* (master) in CFS terms. All other nodes become *secondaries* (slaves).

Although all nodes in the cluster can perform any operation, only the primary node is able to perform transactions—structural changes to the filesystem. If an operation such as creating a file or removing a directory is requested on one of the secondary nodes, the request must be shipped to the primary where it is performed.

The following sections describe some of the main changes that were made to VxFS to make it cluster aware, as well as the types of issues encountered. Figure 13.9 provides a high level view of the various components of CFS.

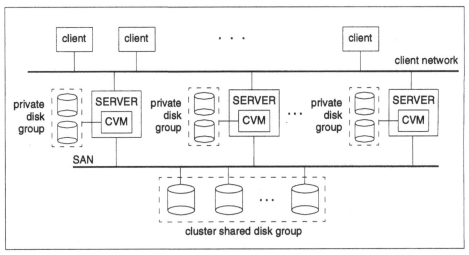

Figure 13.8 CVM shared and private disk groups.

Mounting CFS Filesystems

To mount a VxFS filesystem in a shared cluster, the -o cluster option is specified. Without this option, the mount is assumed to be local only.

The node that issues the mount call first is assigned to be the primary. Every time a node wishes to mount a cluster filesystem, it broadcasts a message to a predefined GAB port. If another node has already mounted the filesystem and assumed primary, it sends configuration data back to the node that is just joining the cluster. This includes information such as the mount options and the other nodes that have mounted the filesystem.

One point worthy of mention is that CFS nodes may mount the filesystem with different mount options. Thus, one node may mount the filesystem read-only while another node may mount the filesystem as read/write.

Handling Vnode Operations in CFS

Because VxFS employs a primary/secondary model, it must identify operations that require a structural change to the filesystem.

For vnode operations that do not change filesystem structure the processing is the same as in a non-CFS filesystem, with the exception that any locks for data structures must be accessed through the GLM. For example, take the case of a call through the VOP_LOOKUP() vnode interface. The goal of this function is to lookup a name within a specified directory vnode and return a vnode for the requested name. The look-up code needs to obtain a global read/write lock on the directory while it searches for the requested name. Because this is a read operation, the lock is requested in shared mode. Accessing fields of the directory may involve reading one or more buffers into the memory. As shown in the next section, these buffers can be obtained from the primary or directly from disk.

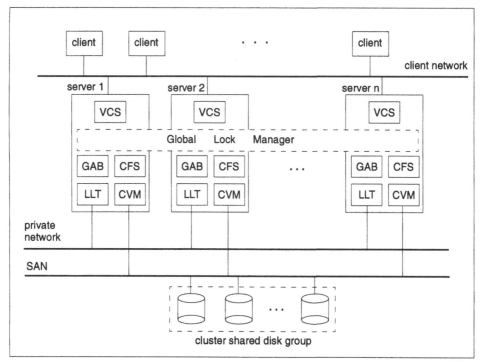

Figure 13.9 Components of a CFS cluster.

For vnode operations that involve any meta-data updates, a transaction will need to be performed, that brings the primary node into play if the request is initiated from a secondary node. In addition to sending the request to the primary, the secondary node must be receptive to the fact that the primary node may fail. It must therefore have mechanisms to recover from primary failure and resend the request to the new primary node. The primary node by contrast must also be able to handle the case where an operation is in progress and the secondary node dies.

The CFS Buffer Cache

VxFS meta-data is read from and written through the VxFS buffer cache, which provides similar interfaces to the traditional UNIX buffer cache implementations. On the primary, the buffer cache is accessed as in the local case, with the exception that global locks are used to control access to buffer cache buffers. On the secondary nodes however, an additional layer is executed to help manage cache consistency by communicating with the primary node when accessing buffers. If a secondary node wishes to access a buffer and it is determined that the primary has not cached the data, the data can be read directly from disk. If the data has previously been accessed on the primary node, a message is sent to the primary to request the data.

The determination of whether the primary holds the buffer is through use of global locks. When the secondary node wishes to access a buffer, it makes a call to obtain a global lock for the buffer. When the lock is granted, the buffer contents will either be passed back as piggy-back data or must be read from disk.

The CFS DNLC and Inode Cache

The VxFS inode cache works in a similar manner to the buffer cache in that access to individual inodes is achieved through the use of global locks.

Unlike the buffer cache, though, when looking up an inode, a secondary node always obtains the inode from the primary. Also recall that the secondary is unable to make any modifications to inodes so requests to make changes, even timestamp updates, must be passed to the primary for processing.

VxFS uses its own DNLC. As with other caches, the DNLC is also clusterized.

CFS Reconfiguration

When a node in the cluster fails, CFS starts the process of *reconfiguration*. There are two types of reconfiguration, based on whether the primary or a secondary dies:

Secondary failure. If a secondary node crashes there is little work to do in CFS other than call the GLM to perform lock recovery.

Primary failure. A primary failure involves a considerable amount of work. The first task is to elect another node in the cluster to become the primary. The new primary must then perform the following tasks:

1. Wake up the `fsck` daemon in order to perform log replay.

2. Call the GLM to perform lock recovery.

3. Remount the filesystem as the primary.

4. Send a broadcast message to the other nodes in the cluster indicating that a new primary has been selected, reconfiguration is complete, and access to the filesystem can now continue.

Of course, this is an oversimplification of the amount of work that must be performed but at least highlights the activities that are performed. Note that each mounted filesystem can have a different node as its primary, so loss of one node will affect only filesystems that had their primary on that node.

CFS Cache Coherency

Processes can access files on any nodes within the cluster, either through `read()` and `write()` system calls or through memory mappings. If multiple processes on multiple nodes are reading the file, they share the file's read/write lock (in this case another global lock). Pages can be cached throughout the cluster.

Cache coherency occurs at the file level only. When a processes requests a read/write lock in exclusive mode in order to write to a file, all cached pages must be destroyed before the lock can be granted. After the lock is relinquished and another process obtains the lock in shared mode, pages may be cached again.

VxFS Command Coordination

Because VxFS commands can be invoked from any node in the cluster, CFS must be careful to avoid accidental corruption. For example, if a filesystem is mounted in the cluster, CFS prevents the user from invoking a mkfs or fsck on the shared volume. Note that non-VxFS commands such as dd are not cluster aware and can cause corruption if run on a disk or volume device.

Application Environments for CFS

Although many applications are tailored for a single host or for a client/server model such as are used in an NFS environment, there are a number of new application environments starting to appear for which clustered filesystems, utilizing shared storage, play an important role. Some of these environments are:

Serial data sharing. There are a number of larger environments, such as video post production, in which data is shared serially between different applications. The first application operates on the data, followed by the second application, and so on. Sharing large amounts of data in such an environment is essential. Having a single mounted filesystem eases administration of the data.

Web farms. In many Web-based environments, data is replicated between different servers, all of which are accessible through some type of load-balancing software. Maintaining these replicas is both cumbersome and error prone. In environments where data is updated relatively frequently, the multiple copies of data are typically out of sync.

By using CFS, the underlying storage can be shared among these multiple servers. Furthermore, the cluster provides better availability in that if one node crashes, the same data is accessible through other nodes.

Off-host backup. Many computing environments are moving towards a 24x7 model, and thus the opportunity to take backups when the system is quiet diminishes. By running the backup on one of the nodes in the cluster or even outside of the cluster, the performance impact on the servers within the cluster can be reduced. In the case where the backup application is used outside of the cluster, mapping services allow an application to map files down to the block level such that the blocks can be read directly from the disk through a frozen image.

Oracle RAC (Real Application Cluster). The Oracle RAC technology, formerly Oracle Parallel Server (OPS), is ideally suited to the VERITAS CFS solution. All of the filesystem features that better enable databases on a single host equally apply to the cluster. This includes providing raw I/O access for multiple readers and writers in addition to features such as filesystem resize that allow the database to be extended.

These are only a few of the application environments that can benefit from clustered filesystems. As clustered filesystems become more prevalent, new applications are starting to appear that can make use of the multiple nodes in the cluster to achieve higher scalability than can be achieved from some SMP-based environments.

Other Clustered Filesystems

A number of different clustered filesystems have made an appearance over the last several years in addition to the VERITAS SanPoint Foundation Suite. The following sections highlight some of these filesystems.

The SGI Clustered Filesystem (CXFS)

Silicon Graphics Incorporated (SGI) provides a clustered filesystem, CXFS, which allows a number of servers to present a clustered filesystem based on shared access to SAN-based storage. CXFS is built on top of the SGI XFS filesystem and the XVM volume manager.

CXFS provides meta-data servers through which all meta-data operations must be processed. For data I/O, clients that have access to the storage can access the data directly. CXFS uses a token-based scheme to control access to various parts of the file. Tokens also allow the client to cache various parts of the file. If a client needs to change any part of the file, the meta-data server must be informed, which then performs the operation.

The Linux/Sistina Global Filesystem

The Global Filesystem (GFS) was a project initiated at the University of Minnesota in 1995. It was initially targeted at postprocessing large scientific data sets over fibre channel attached storage.

Unable to better integrate GFS into the SGI IRIX kernel on which it was originally developed, work began on porting GFS to Linux.

At the heart of GFS is a journaling-based filesystem. GFS is a fully symmetric clustered filesystem—any node in the cluster can perform transactions. Each node in the cluster has its own intent log. If a node crashes, the log is replayed by one of the other nodes in the cluster.

Sun Cluster

Sun offers a clustering solution, including a layered clustered filesystem, which can support up to 8 nodes. Central to Sun Cluster is the *Resource Group Manager* that manages a set of resources (interdependent applications).

The Sun *Global Filesystem* is a layered filesystem that can run over most local filesystems. Two new vnode operations were introduced to aid performance of the global filesystem. The global filesystem provides an NFS-like server that communicates through a secondary server that mirrors the primary. When an update to the primary occurs, the operation is checkpointed on the secondary. If the primary fails, any operations that weren't completed are rolled back.

Unlike some of the other clustered filesystem solutions described here, all I/O goes through a single server.

Compaq/HP True64 Cluster

Digital, now part of Compaq, has been producing clusters for many years. Compaq provides a clustering stack called *TruCluster Server* that supports up to 8 nodes.

Unlike the VERITAS clustered filesystem in which the local and clustering components of the filesystem are within the same code base, the Compaq solution provides a layered clustered filesystem that can sit on top of any underlying local filesystem. Although files can be read from any node in the cluster, files can be written from any node only if the local filesystem is AdvFS (Advanced Filesystem).

Summary

Throughout the history of UNIX, there have been numerous attempts to share files between one computer and the next. Early machines used simple UNIX commands with uucp being commonplace.

As local area networks started to appear and computers became much more widespread, a number of distributed filesystems started to appear. With its goals of simplicity and portability, NFS became the de facto standard for sharing filesystems within a UNIX system.

With the advent of shared data storage between multiple machines, the ability to provide a uniform view of the storage resulted in the need for clustered filesystem and volume management with a number of commercial and open source clustered filesystems appearing over the last several years.

Because both solutions address different problems, there is no great conflict between distributed and clustered filesystem. On the contrary, a clustered filesystem can easily be exported for use by NFS clients.

For further information on NFS, Brent Callaghan's book *NFS Illustrated* [CALL00] provides a detailed account of the various NFS protocols and infrastructure. For further information on the concepts that are applicable to clustered filesystems, Dilip Ranade's book *Shared Data Clusters* [RANA02] should be consulted.

Developing a Filesystem
for the Linux Kernel

Although there have been many programatic examples throughout the book, without seeing how a filesystem works in practice, it is still difficult to appreciate the flow through the kernel in response to the various file- and filesystem-related system calls. It is also difficult to see how the filesystem interfaces with the rest of the kernel and how it manages its own structures internally.

This chapter provides a very simple, but completely functional filesystem for Linux called uxfs. The filesystem is not complete by any means. It provides enough interfaces and features to allow creation of a hierarchical tree structure, creation of regular files, and reading from and writing to regular files. There is a mkfs command and a simple fsdb command. There are several flaws in the filesystem and exercises at the end of the chapter provide the means for readers to experiment, fix the existing flaws, and add new functionality.

The chapter gives the reader all of the tools needed to experiment with a real filesystem. This includes instructions on how to download and compile the Linux kernel source and how to compile and load the filesystem module. There is also detailed information on how to debug and analyze the flow through the kernel and the filesystem through use of printk() statements and the kdb and gdb debuggers. The filesystem layout is also small enough that a new filesystem can be made on a floppy disk to avoid less-experienced Linux users having to partition or repartition disks.

The source code, which is included in full later in the chapter, has been compiled and run on the standard 2.4.18 kernel. Unfortunately, it does not take long before new Linux kernels appear making today's kernels redundant. To avoid this problem, the following Web site:

    www.wiley.com/compbooks/pate

includes uxfs source code for up-to-date Linux kernels. It also contains instructions on how to build the uxfs filesystem for standard Linux distributions. This provides readers who do not wish to download and compile the kernel source the opportunity to easily compile and load the filesystem and experiment. To follow the latter route, the time taken to download the source code, compile, and load the module should not be greater than 5 to 10 minutes.

Designing the New Filesystem

The goal behind designing this filesystem was to achieve simplicity. When looking at some of the smaller Linux filesystems, novices can still spend a considerable amount of time trying to understand how they work. With the uxfs filesystem, small is key. Only the absolutely essential pieces of code are in place. It supports a hierchical namespace and the ability to create, read to, and write from files. Some operations, such as rename and creation of symlinks, have been left out intentionally both to reduce the amount of source code and to give the reader a number of exercises to follow.

Anyone who studies the filesystem in any amount of detail will notice a large number of holes despite the fact that the filesystem is fully functional. The layout of the filesystem is shown in Figure 14.1, and the major design points are detailed as follows:

- The filesystem has only 512-byte blocks. This is defined by the UX_BSIZE constant in the ux_fs.h header file.

- There is a fixed number of blocks in the filesystem. Apart from space for the superblock and inodes, there are 470 data blocks. This is defined by the UX_MAXBLOCKS constant.

- There are only 32 inodes (UX_MAXFILES). Leaving inodes 0 and 1 aside (which are reserved), and using inode 2 for the root directory and inode 3 for the lost+found directory, there are 28 inodes for user files and directories.

- The superblock is stored in block 0. It occupies a single block. Inside the superblock are arrays, one for inodes and one for data blocks that record whether a particular inode or data block is in use. This makes the filesystem source very easy to read because there is no manipulation of bitmaps. The superblock also contain fields that record the number of free inodes and data blocks.

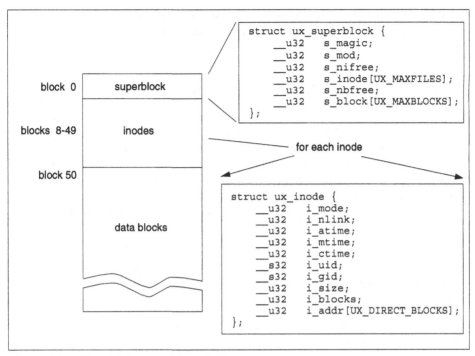

Figure 14.1   The disk layout of the uxfs filesystem.

- There is one inode per data block. The first inode is stored in block 8. Because inodes 0 and 1 are not used, the root directory inode is stored in block 10 and the lost+found directory is stored in block 11. The remaining inodes are stored in blocks 12 through 39.

- The first data block is stored in block 33. When the filesystem is created, block 50 is used to store directory entries for the root directory and block 51 is used to store entries for the lost+found directory.

- Each inode has only 9 direct data blocks, which limits the file size to (9 * 512) = 4608 bytes.

- Directory entries are fixed in size storing an inode number and a 28-byte file name. Each directory entry is 32 bytes in size.

The next step when designing a filesystem is to determine which kernel interfaces to support. In addition to reading and writing regular files and making and removing directories, you need to decide whether to support hard links, symbolic links, rename, and so on. To make this decision, you need to view the different operations that can be exported by the filesystem. There are four vectors that must be exported by the filesystem, namely the super_operations, file_operations, address_space_operations, and inode_operations vectors. In addition to deciding which functions should be supported directly, there are several *generic* functions that can be called in place of providing uxfs specific functions. This eases the job of a creating a filesystem considerably.

Obtaining the Linux Kernel Source

This section shows how to download the Linux kernel source and how to find your way around the kernel source tree to locate files that are of most interest to filesystem development. Later sections show how to configure the kernel to match the hardware on your system, to compile it, and then install the newly built kernel. Both the `LILO` or `GRUB` bootloaders are described.

The Linux kernel source can be retrieved from the following Web site:

```
www.kernel.org
```

The home page of `www.kernel.org` shows the latest versions of the kernel. For example, the following line showed the latest stable version at the time of this writing:

```
The latest stable version of the Linux kernel is: 2.4.18 2002-07-10 00:40
UTC F V VI Changelog
```

The Web site also describes the state of the different kernels including the latest stable version. Click on the kernel version to download the latest kernel. Clicking on `Changelog` will display all of the updates to the latest kernel.

All of the kernels since Linux inception can be found at this site. Follow the links through to the source repositories and locate the kernel of your choice. To use the source in the book as is, you need the 2.4.18 kernel. Alternatively, as described earlier, newer versions of the filesystem can be obtained from the following Web site:

```
www.wiley.com/compbooks/pate
```

Also at the site is information about which Linux kernels and the various Linux distributions that uxfs supports.

To locate the required kernel source, follow the various pointers. As an example, from the home page follow the link to *Linux respository, including kernel source*, then *kernel* and *2.4*. This will take you to the following link:

```
www.kernel.org/pub/linux/kernel/v2.4/
```

The kernel source is a gzipped tar archive. Once the file has been downloaded, it should be unzipped and untarred. The kernel source resides under `/usr/src` although this is not mandatory. One possibility is to untar the archive in `/usr/src` and set a symlink to point to the directory. For example, if the gzipped archive has been placed in `/usr/src`, perform the following steps:

```
# bunzip2 linux-2.4.18.tar.bz2
# mv linux linux.orig
# tar xvf linux-2.4.18.tar
# mv linux linux-2.4.18
# ln -s linux-2.4.18 linux
```

Extracting the files from the tar archive will place them in the directory linux in the current working directory by default. The command to move the old linux directory aside may be replaced with something more suitable to your environment. Alternatively, the soruce can be extracted in a separate directory and then moved into /usr/src/linux-2.4.18. Be careful not to overwrite any existing Linux kernel source trees.

What's in the Kernel Source Tree

There are many files and directories in the Linux kernel source tree. This section provides an overview of how the kernel source tree is laid to allow readers to be able to easily locate the various kernel subsystems or specific files.

arch. This directory contains a directory for each of the different machine architectures that Linux supports including Intel, Sparc, MIPS, and IBM s390.

CREDITS. This file lists all of the major contributors to the kernel together with information about their area of expertise or contribution.

Documentation. There is a whole host of documentation distributed with the kernel source. The filesystems directory contains information about some of the different Linux filesystems in additional to generic filesystem-related information.

drivers. This directory contains all of the Linux device drivers.

fs. This is the directory that will be of most relevance to people interested in filesystems together with the mm directory that contains much of the page cache/data I/O management code. Files in the fs directory implement the dcache, buffer cache, inode cache, and file-related system call handling. Also within the fs directory is a directory for each of the Linux filesystems. Within their respective directories are the filesystem source files themselves.

include. All of the kernel header files can be accessed within this directory. This directory contains architectural-specific header files in addition to header files that are common across all architectures. The common header files can be found in the linux subdirectory. The fs.h header file is of particular importance to filesystem writers. The dcache.h header file defines the structures used by the Linux dcache.

init. This directory contains functions that are executed during kernel bootstrap.

ipc. This directory contains source applicable to System V IPC (Inter Process Communication) including semaphores, shared memory, and message queues.

kdb. If the kdb patch is installed, this directory contains source for the kernel debugger. Note that the kdb patch also changes other files throughout the kernel.

kernel. This directory contains core kernel routines such as process management, system call handling, module management, and so on.

lib. Some of the standard C library functions have counterparts in the kernel. The source can be found in this directory.

MAINTAINERS. This file lists the people who are responsible for various parts of the kernel.

mm. This directory contains all of the memory management code that is not specific to one architecture or another. The Linux page cache managment routines can be found in this directory.

net. All of the networking protocols (TCP, UDP, IP, etc.) are stored in this directory.

There are too many files and directories to decribe here. However, for readers interested in learning about filesystems, the include, fs, and mm directories are where most of the filesystem-related structures and routines can be found. There are also a few interesting files in the drivers/block directory for those wishing to look at the filesystem/driver interfaces in more detail.

Configuring the Kernel

Before building the kernel, it is necessary to determine the kernel configuration. There are many components that are part of the kernel source tree that you will not need as part of your kernel. For example, there are numerous different device drivers for the various SCSI adaptors. If you don't have a need for SCSI access, building support into the kernel is unnecessary. Thus, you need to determine what hardware configuration you have and therefore which kernel components are required.

There are several different methods of defining the configuration. The Linux kernel HOWTO should be consulted in addition to the notes described here. There are multiple copies of the HOWTO available across the World Wide Web. You can find it at the following Web site:

```
www.tldp.org/HOWTO/Kernel-HOWTO.html
```

One of the easiest ways to determine which components of the kernel are needed is to install the kernel source when the Linux operating system is installed. This will result in a configuration file for the installed kernel being available for consultation. It is then possible to copy the configuration file from the installed kernel source tree to the new kernel source tree as follows:

```
# cp /usr/src/linux-2.4.18-3/.config /usr/src/linux-2.4.18/.config
```

Care must be taken here. If the new kernel being installed has a substantially different configuration from the installed kernel, some options may or may not be available. However, this method should suffice in most cases.

One method of defining the configuration is to run the following command for both the installed kernel and the new kernel source. For example, for Red Hat 7.3 run the following:

```
# cd /usr/src/linux-2.4.18-3
# make menuconfig
```

And for the new kernel do the following:

```
# cd /usr/src/linux-2.4.18
# make menuconfig
```

By having both windows side by side it is easy to see which components you need to select for the new kernel by browsing through the configuration of the current kernel. The alternative method is to fully understand what type of hardware you have. When comparing the configurations side by side, it is a safe bet to select everything for the new kernel that is selected in the current kernel.

Items are selected if noted by an asterisk. Loadable kernel modules are denoted by the letter "M." Instructions are available at the top of the screen to indicate how to select. Pressing Enter expands the menu to the next level. Pressing the Escape key takes you back up a level.

Once you have completed changing the configuration, a series of Escape key sequences will prompt you as to whether you wish to save and exit. Note that you do not need to save the configuration for the current kernel. This is particularly important if you have accidently made any changes. After saving the configuration and exiting the program, the following message appears:

```
Saving your kernel configuration...

*** End of Linux kernel configuration.
*** Check the top-level Makefile for additional configuration.
*** Next, you must run 'make dep'
```

Follow the instructions by issuing the following commands:

```
# make dep
# make clean
```

The first step builds all of the necessary kernel dependencies based on the set of options chosen during the kernel configuration process. The next step is to ensure that the build environment is clean such that a subsequent kernel compilation will not pick up any precompiled files that do not match the configuration chosen.

The next step, which is the longest, is to compile the kernel. This can be achieved by typing the following:

```
# make bzImage
...
objcopy -O binary -R .note -R .comment -S compressed/bvmlinux
compressed/bvmlinux.out
tools/build -b bbootsect bsetup compressed/bvmlinux.out CURRENT >
bzImage
Root device is (3, 2)
Boot sector 512 bytes.
Setup is 2536 bytes.
System is 1301 kB
warning: kernel is too big for standalone boot from floppy
make[1]: Leaving directory '/usr/src/linux-2.4.18/arch/i386/boot'
#
```

Once the process is complete, the compressed kernel, which is called bzImage, will be placed in the directory arch/i386/boot. This should be copied to /boot and given a unique name as follows:

```
# cp arch/i386/boot/bzImage /boot/linux.spate
```

Note the name of the file that the kernel was copied to. This should be given an easy to remember name and should not overwrite any existing kernels that are already in /boot. One exception to this rule is when you are building kernels frequently and you know which kernels can be safely overwritten.

Because many of the kernel components were probably selected to be kernel modules, they must be compiled and installed as follows:

```
# make modules
# make modules_install
```

The modules are compiled and installed under the /lib/modules directory. There is one subdirectory for each kernel version. For example, in the case of the kernel being used here, the modules will reside under:

```
/lib/modules/2.4.18
```

It is important to remember to compile and install the modules selected during configuration, a task that is often easy to forget. Without the modules in place, the kernel may not boot.

Installing and Booting the New Kernel

The next step is to configure the boot loader to recognize the new kernel. Most Linux distributions either use LILO or GRUB as the boot loader. This section decribes how to use LILO, the most commonly used boot loader.

Consider the following lines taken from one specific /etc/lilo.conf file that was created as part of Red Hat 7.3 installation:

```
image=/boot/vxlinuz-2.4.18-3
    label=linux
```

```
        initrd=/boot/initrd-2.4.18-3.img
        read-only
        root=/dev/hda2
```

The `image` field specifies the kernel to bootstrap. When `lilo` runs and displays the list of bootable kernels, it displays the names found next to the `label` field, in this case `linux`. The `initrd` field specifies an initial root disk (RAM disk) that will be used prior to checking and mounting the real root filesystem. The `root` field specifies where the root disk can be found.

In order to bootstrap the new kernel, copy these lines to the end of the file and change both the `image` and `label` lines as follows:

```
image=/boot/linux.spate
        label=linux.spate
        initrd=/boot/initrd-2.4.18-3.img
        read-only
        root=/dev/hda2
```

This creates an entry for the new kernel and leaves the existing entry for the default kernel unchanged. Note that it is important not to modify any of the configuration information for the kernel installed as part of the Linux installation. It is imperitive to have a kernel that boots safely because there will be times when building new kernels where device drivers are accidently ommitted. For example, it is not uncommon when building a kernel for the first few times to ommit vital information such as the correct disk drivers, rendering the new kernel unbootable.

The final step is to run `lilo` to install information about the new kernel in the master boot record:

```
# lilo
```

A successful run of `lilo` should not display anything. Once completed, you will see an entry corresponding to your kernel (the `label` field) next time the machine is rebooted.

Using GRUB to Handle Bootstrap

Many Linux distributions are now using the GRUB (*GRand Unified Bootloader*) boot loader. This is extremely rich in features but operates in a different manner to LILO. However, adding a new kernel is not difficult. The `/etc/grub.conf` file is used in a similar manner to `/etc/lilo.conf`. However, adding an entry to this file is sufficient. GRUB does not need to be run to install the information in the master boot record.

For further information on GRUB, see the `grub` manual page.

Booting the New Kernel

The next step is to reboot the machine. Once the machine boots, `lilo` displays the list of kernels that it is able to bootstrap. The newly installed kernel should be visible. This can be selected using the arrow keys and loaded by pressing Enter. If all goes well, the new kernel will boot as expected

To verify that the kernel requested is running, the uname command can be used to display the kernel version as follows:

```
# uname -a
Linux x.y.com 2.4.18 #2 SMP Tue Jul 30 18:55:27 PDT 2002 i686 unknown
```

The kernel version is shown in bold. There will be times when you reboot the machine and lilo automatically boots a kernel by default and you often wonder which kernel is running when you return to the machine. It is typically a good idea to have the default kernel set to the kernel that was installed when the Linux operating system was installed.

Installing Debugging Support

Analyzing the filesystem source code is one way to learn about how filesystems work. However, it is extremely difficult following this method to truly understand the flow through the kernel and filesystem in response to certain operations. There is no better method than installing and using one of the different kernel debuggers allowing you to stop in specific functions, display stack backtraces and function arguments, and print other useful information.

There are three main methods under which a filesystem or indeed any other part of the kernel can be debugged. The first approach involves using the kernel printk() command which is very similar to printf(). The second approach involves using a standalone debugger such as kdb whereby flow can be stopped by placing explicit breakpoints or by entering a special key sequence to enter the debugger. The third approach involves the use of two machines connected through a serial cable and over which gdb can be used for source level debugging.

The following sections describe each of these approaches. The amount of work to perform each task is considerably different with printk() being the simplest approach while the gdb approach involves more time to set up and an additional machine. For readers who wish to experiment and have access to all the available resources it is recommended that you start with printk() first, then move to kdb, and finally to gdb.

The following sections assume some familiarity with debugging concepts.

The printk Approach to Debugging

One of the oldest and easiest styles of debugging is the printf() method. By placing printf() statements throughout the code it is possible to display information about the running program. This is useful for development or simply to follow the flow through the program.

Linux provides the printk() function for kernel/module writers to use.

With the exception of the name change, it can be used in the same manner in which `printf()` can be called. One method employed when writing uxfs was to place a `printk()` at the start of each entry point to the filesystem. When typing various commands at the user prompt, it is then easy to see which functions in the filesystem are called.

Because Linux supports loadable modules, and the time to recompile and reload a module is in the order of seconds, this is the easiest way to watch how the filesystem works in practice and should be the method initially followed by anyone new to kernel development who wants to understand how the kernel works. To get a better idea of how the filesystem-related kernel functions work, `printk()` calls can be placed throughout the kernel, and various structures can be displayed.

Using the SGI kdb Debugger

The `kdb` debugger is a built-in debugger. It must be compiled with the kernel in order for it to be used. It can be used to set breakpoints, display memory, disassemble instructions, and display machine configuration such as the register set. The debugger operates around the kernel symbol table, and therefore functions and structures can be accessed by name.

The source code for `kdb`, which was developed by engineers at SGI (Silicon Graphics Inc), can be downloaded from the SGI Web site. The home page for `kdb` is as follows:

```
http://oss.sgi.com/projects/kdb/
```

Note that when following the link to the download section, the directories displayed are for the versions of `kdb` and not versions of the Linux kernel. For the kernel used to develop uxfs (2.4.18), `kdb` version 2.1 must be used (the latter versions did not support this kernel at the time of writing).

The `README` file in the download directory contains instructions on which files to download. This file should be consulted prior to downloading. Note that there may be several versions for the same kernel. The `README` file specifies how to interpret the version numbers of the patches.

There are two patch files to download. The first is common across all different machine architectures and the second is specific to the machine architecture on which you're running. After downloading the patches, they can be applied as follows:

```
# cd /usr/src/linux-2.4.18
# patch -p1 < ../kdb-v2.1-2.4.18-common-3
patching file kernel/sysctl.c
patching file kernel/ksyms.c
patching file kernel/Makefile
patching file init/main.c
...
patching file Documentation/kdb/kdb_env.man
patching file Documentation/kdb/kdb.mm
```

```
patching file Documentation/kdb/kdb_bp.man
patching file Documentation/kdb/slides
# patch -p2 < ../kdb-v2.1-2.4.18-i386-1
patching file include/asm-i386/hw_irq.h
patching file include/asm-i386/keyboard.h
patching file include/asm-i386/ptrace.h
patching file arch/i386/vmlinux.lds
...
patching file arch/i386/kdb/kdbasupport.c
patching file arch/i386/kdb/ansidecl.h
patching file arch/i386/kdb/bfd.h
patching file arch/i386/kdb/ChangeLog
#
```

Once the patch has been successfully applied, the kernel configuration must be changed to incorporate kdb. Under the section marked *Kernel hacking* , select the option *Built-in Kernel Debugger support* and select the *KDB modules*. The kernel must then be built (make dep ; make bzImage) and reinstalled as described in the section *Configuring the Kernel* earlier in the chapter.

Included with the kdb patch is documentation on how the debugger works, the commands that are available, and so on. The debugger can be entered by pressing the BREAK key. The kdb prompt is then displayed as follows:

```
Entering kdb (current=0xc03b0000,pid 0)on processor 0 due to Keyboard Entry
[0]kdb>
```

The ? command can be used to display the available commands. Shown below is a summary of the more commonly used commands. Examples of how they are used in practice will be shown throughout the chapter.

bp. Set or display a breakpoint.

bph. Set a hardware breakpoint.

bc. Clear a breakpoint.

bl. List the current breakpoints.

bt. Display the stack backtrace for the current process.

go. Exit the debugger and restart kernel execution.

id. Disassemble instructions.

md. Display the contents of the specified address.

mds. Display memory symbolically.

mm. Modify memory.

reboot. Reboot the machine immediately.

rd. Display the register contents.

ss. Single step (instruction at a time).

ssb. Single step the CPU until a branch is reached.

The kdb(8) man page describes the other commands.

Source Level Debugging with gdb

The GNU debugger gdb has been available for many years, typically being used to debug user-level programs. However, by connecting machines together over a serial line in a host/target configuration, gdb can also be used to debug the Linux kernel. This requires a patch to the kernel to include a kgdb driver through which gdb on the host machine can communicate. Although this requires an extra machine and some additional setup work, the ease of use of debugging the kernel at source level is well worth the extra work. It is also easier to see how the kernel works because not only can breakpoints be added to show the flow through the kernel, but function arguments can be displayed along with the source code corresponding to the position at which the breakpoint is hit.

There are multiple patches for kernel-level gdb debugging. The following Web page:

```
http://kgdb.sourceforge.net/
```

is the homepage for kgdb. It references all of the patches and contains detailed instructions on gdb setup. The following sections highlight some of the main points. For complete details, refer to the kgdb homepage.

Connecting the Host and Target Machines

The first step for gdb debugging is to connect the two machines together and verify that data can be passed through the link. The machines must be connected through a standard null modem between the serial ports of the machines as shown in Figure 14.2.

Serial ports support transmission rates from 110 baud up to 115,200 baud. The default baud rate for a serial port is 9,600. This is generally adequate for simple debugging although higher baud rates are preferred if a lot of information will be transmitted over the wire. This will certainly be the case when displaying multiple thread stacks.

Once the link is in place, the speed of the serial port on each machine must be identical. This can be verified on each machine as follows:

```
# stty < /dev/ttyS0
speed 9600 baud; line = 0;
min = 0; time = 10;
-brkint -icrnl -imaxbel
-opost -onlcr
-isig -icanon -iexten -echo -echoe -echok -echoctl -echoke
```

The baud rate is shown here as 9,600. If the baud rate differs between the two machines, the following call to the stty command can set the baud rate:

```
# stty ispeed 9600 ospeed 9600 < /dev/ttyS0
```

Assuming that the baud rate is the same on both machines and the cable is in

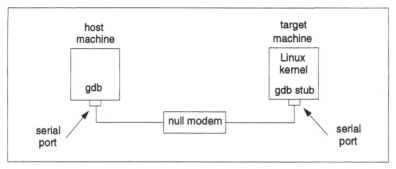

Figure 14.2 Source level kernel debugging with gdb.

place, the link can be tested by simply echoing a string through the cable on one end and reading it on another as follows:

```
Host                                    Target

                                        # cat /dev/ttyS0

# echo hello > /dev/ttyS0

                                        hello
```

If any problems are encountered, review the troubleshooting guide on the kgdb kernel Web site.

Downloading the kgdb Patch

The *download* section of the kgdb kernel Web site contains the kernel patches for specific Linux kernels. Each patch is an ASCII file that contains a set of *diffs*. Once downloaded, the patch to build kgdb into the kernel can be applied to the kernel as follows:

```
# cd /usr/src/linux
# patch -p1 < ../linux-2.4.18-kgdb-1.5.patch
patching file Documentation/Configure.help
patching file Documentation/i386/gdb-serial.txt
patching file Makefile
patching file arch/i386/Makefile
patching file arch/i386/config.in
patching file arch/i386/kernel/Makefile
...
patching file kernel/ksyms.c
patching file kernel/sched.c
```

Once the patch has been applied, the kernel configuration must be updated to include the kgdb options. Under the *Kernel Debugging* section, select the following line:

```
KGDB: Remote (serial) kernel debugging with gdb (NEW)
```

and then select each of the kgdb suboptions. Note that the *Verbose BUG() reporting* option should not be selected.

After saving the kernel configuration, run the following:

```
# make dep
# make clean
# make bzImage
```

to build the new kernel. As described in earlier sections, the kernel will be found under the arch/i386/boot directory.

Installing the kgdb-Modified Kernel

To install the new kernel, the entry in lilo.conf must be changed to instruct the kernel to wait, on bootstrap, for a connection from gdb on the host machine. Shown below is an entry in lilo.conf for the new kernel:

```
image=/boot/linux.gdb
        label=linux.gdb
        initrd=/boot/initrd-2.4.18-3.img
        read-only
        root=/dev/hda2
        append="gdb gdbttyS=0 gdbbaud=9600"
```

This instructs the kgdb stub which serial port to use (/dev/ttyS0) and the baud rate that was established earlier during gdb configuration.

When the new kernel bootstraps, the following message is displayed:

```
Waiting for connection from remote gdb...
```

To connect to the target machine, gdb must be run on the host and the following commands should be entered:

```
# gdb
GNU gdb Red Hat Linux (5.1.90CVS-5)
Copyright 2002 Free Software Foundation, Inc.
GDB is free software, covered by the GNU General Public License, and you
are welcome to change it and/or distribute copies of it under certain
conditions.
Type "show copying" to see the conditions.
There is absolutely no warranty for GDB.  Type "show warranty" for
details.
This GDB was configured as "i386-redhat-linux".
(gdb) target remote /dev/ttyS0
Remote debugging using /dev/ttyS0
0xc011323d in ?? ()
(gdb) c
Continuing.
PCI: PCI BIOS revision 2.10 entry at 0xfbfee, last bus=1
PCI: Using configuration type 1
...
```

The "`target remote`" command specifies the serial port to connect to in order to communicate with the kernel. The c command then continues execution.

To break into the debugger and instruct it where to access the symbolic debugging information, hit Control-C as follows:

```
Program received signal SIGTRAP, Trace/breakpoint trap.
0xc011323d in ?? ()
(gdb) symbol-file /usr/src/linux/vmlinux
Reading symbols from /usr/src/linux/vmlinux...done.
```

The debugger now has enough information to debug the kernel.

gdb and Module Interactions

Because uxfs is a loadable module, gdb knows nothing about the location of the module in memory or where to locate the module's symbolic information.

The `loadmodule` script, also located on the kgdb Web site, must be used to load the module. It is assumed that the module source and binary are located on the host machine and that it is possible to rcp from the host to the target.

Before running `loadmodule`, the GDBSCRIPTS variable, located at the top of the script, must be altered to point to a directory where it can install a script for use with gdb. As an example:

```
GDBSCRIPTS=/home/spate/uxfs/tools/gdbscripts
```

The script can then be run as follows:

```
# loadmodule target-machine ../kern/uxfs
Copying ../kern/uxfs to linux
Loading module ../kern/uxfs
Generating script /home/spate/uxfs/tools/gdbscripts/loadlinuxuxfs
```

Once completed, the module should be loaded on the target machine and the script generated is displayed. This should be run from within gdb. Control-C will get you into gdb from which the script can be executed as follows:

```
Program received signal SIGTRAP, Trace/breakpoint trap.
breakpoint () at gdbstub.c:1177
1177    }
(gdb) so  /home/spate/uxfs/tools/gdbscripts/loadlinuxuxfs
add symbol table from file "/home/spate/uxfs/kern/uxfs" at
        .text_addr = 0xd0854060
        .rodata_addr = 0xd0855c60
        __ksymtab_addr = 0xd085618c
        __archdata_addr = 0xd08562b0
        __kallsyms_addr = 0xd08562b0
        .data_addr = 0xd08568c0
        .bss_addr = 0xd0856a60
```

The setup of gdb is now complete. Control-C can be invoked at any time the debugger needs to be entered to add break points and so on. Use of gdb for kernel-level debugging will be shown throughout the chapter.

Building the uxfs Filesystem

The source code for all of the files that are needed to build the uxfs filesystem for the 2.4.18 kernel is included at the end of the chapter. This includes the source for mkfs and fsdb, the kernel makefile, and the kernel source. The source tree downloaded from www.wiley.com/compbooks/spate is a gzipped tar archive. Download to any directory and issue the following commands:

```
# gunzip uxfs.tar.gz
# tar xvf uxfs.tar
# ls
uxfs.tar  uxfs
# ls uxfs
cmds  kern
```

Commands can be easily built. All that is required is for the uxfs.h header file to be located in the "../kern" directory. To build each of the commands, go to the cmds directory and issue the following:

```
# make fsdb
cc     fsdb.c   -o fsdb
# make fsdb
cc     fsdb.c   -o fsdb
```

The commands can then be used.

The kernel makefile is relatively straightforward as follows:

```
KERNELDIR = /usr/src/linux

include $(KERNELDIR)/.config

FLAGS = -D__KERNEL__  -DMODULE $(VERCFLAGS)
GLOBAL_CFLAGS = -g -I$(KERNELDIR)/include $(FLAGS)

M_OBJS = ux_dir.o ux_alloc.o ux_file.o ux_inode.o

M_TARGET = uxfs

SRCS = $(M_OBJS:.o=.c)

CFLAGS = $(GLOBAL_CFLAGS) $(EXTRA_CFLAGS)

$(M_TARGET) : $(M_OBJS)
    ld -r -o $@ $(M_OBJS)

$(M_OBJS) : %.o : %.c
    $(CC) -c $(CFLAGS) -o $@ $<
```

```
all: uxfs

clean:
    rm -f $(M_OBJS) $(M_TARGET)
```

To build the kernel source, the KERNELDIR variable at the top of the Makefile must be changed to reference the kernel source directory. Figure 14.3 shows how KERNELDIR is set to reference the 2.4.18 source tree.

Once this variable has been set, the kernel can be built as follows:

```
# make uxfs
cc -c -g -I/usr/src/linux/include -D__KERNEL__ -DMODULE -o ux_dir.o ux_dir.c
cc -c -g -I/usr/src/linux/include -D__KERNEL__ -DMODULE -o ux_alloc.o
ux_alloc.c
cc -c -g -I/usr/src/linux/include -D__KERNEL__ -DMODULE -o ux_file.o ux_file.c
cc -c -g -I/usr/src/linux/include -D__KERNEL__ -DMODULE -o ux_inode.o
ux_inode.c
ld -r -o uxfs ux_dir.o ux_alloc.o ux_file.o ux_inode.o
```

This produces the uxfs module that can then be loaded into the kernel. This is shown later in the chapter.

Creating a uxfs Filesystem

The first step when developing a new filesystem is to write a mkfs command to place the intial filesystem layout on disk. This includes the following tasks:

- Create and initialize the filesystem superblock and write it to disk.

- Create a root dirtectory inode and lost+found directory inode. For each of the inodes, ensure that the "." and ".." entries are in place and for the root directory, add an entry for lost+found.

- Account for allocation of the two directories within the inode map.

- Account for allocation of two blocks used for the root and lost+found directories.

The code for mkfs can be found on lines 104 to 262. For uxfs, it is a fairly simple program. As with the kernel, it uses various structure definitions and information from ux_fs.h including superblock structural information, inode formats, directory entries and various filesystem boundaries such as the maximum number of blocks and inodes.

Before the filesystem is implemented, it is important to verify the information that mkfs writes to disk. Thus, the next program to write is fsdb, which can read back and display various superblock and inode information.

The fsdb command (lines 264 to 393) is very simple. It accepts two commands that allow the superblock or a specified inode to be displayed.

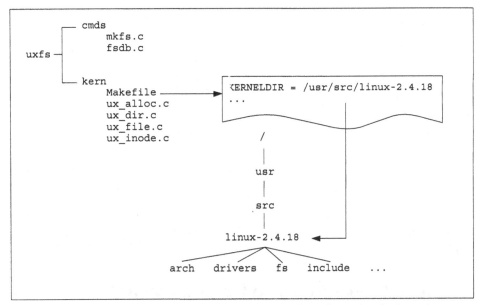

Figure 14.3   The uxfs filesystem source files and makefile referencing the kernel source.

The first task is to read the superblock into memory (lines 365 to 369), validate it, and keep in in memory for the duration of the program. From here, it can access any information it needs to about inodes or data blocks.

The remainder of the main() loop involves reading commands and then calling additional routines. For now, only the superblock or an inode can be displayed. By entering 'q', the program will exit.

The following output from fsdb shows the two commands being run on a newly created filesystem:

```
# ./mkfs /dev/fd0
# ./fsdb /dev/fd0
uxfsdb > s

Superblock contents:
  s_magic   = 0x58494e55
  s_mod     = UX_FSCLEAN
  s_nifree  = 28
  s_nbfree  = 468

uxfsdb > i2

inode number 2
  i_mode    = 41ed
  i_nlink   = 3
  i_atime   = Wed Aug 21 09:55:16 2002
  i_mtime   = Wed Aug 21 09:55:16 2002
  i_ctime   = Wed Aug 21 09:55:16 2002
  i_uid     = 0
```

```
i_gid    = 0
i_size   = 512
i_blocks = 1
i_addr[ 0] = 50  i_addr[ 1] =  0  i_addr[ 2] =  0  i_addr[ 3] =  0
i_addr[ 4] =  0  i_addr[ 5] =  0  i_addr[ 6] =  0  i_addr[ 7] =  0
i_addr[ 8] =  0  i_addr[ 9] =  0  i_addr[10] =  0  i_addr[11] =  0
i_addr[12] =  0  i_addr[13] =  0  i_addr[14] =  0  i_addr[15] =  0

Directory entries:
  inum[ 2],name[.]
  inum[ 2],name[..]
  inum[ 3],name[lost+found]

uxfsdb > q
```

There are many more features that could be added to fsdb. Some of these changes will be imperitive when completing the exercises at the end of the chapter.

Module Initialization and Deinitialization

When writing a loadable kernel module, there are three different things that need to be defined:

- A declaration giving information about the type of module

- A function to be called when the module is loaded. This can perform any initialization functions including registering the filesystem type with the kernel.

- A function to be called when the module is unloaded. This can clean up any remaining filesystem structures and unregister the filesystem.

The various components that are applicable to uxfs are shown in ux_inode.c on lines 1304 to 1317. The module_init() call specifies the function to be run when the module is loaded while the module_exit() function specifies the function to be called when the module is unloaded. Both of these functions perform little work other than registering and unregistering the filesystem driver respectively. The DECLARE_FSTYPE_DEV() macro is shown below:

```
#define DECLARE_FSTYPE(var,type,read,flags) \
struct file_system_type var = { \
        name:       type, \
        read_super: read, \
        fs_flags:   flags, \
        owner:      THIS_MODULE, \
}

#define DECLARE_FSTYPE_DEV(var,type,read) \
        DECLARE_FSTYPE(var,type,read,FS_REQUIRES_DEV)
```

The kernel maintains a list of all such structures, one per filesystem. The entry for uxfs is added when calling `register_filesystem()`. When a mount system call enters the kernel, the filesystem name passed to `mount` is compared with the name field of each `file_system_type` structure. If a match is found, the `read_super` function is called to mount the filesystem.

The `rmmod` command is used to remove a kernel module. If there are still filesystems mounted, the removal will fail; otherwise the kernel calls the module exit function, which in the case of uxfs, is the `exit_uxfs_fs()` function. The only action to perform is to call `unregister_filesystem()`.

Testing the New Filesystem

The following examples show how a uxfs filesystem is created, how the kernel module is loaded, the filesystem is unmounted, and how the module is unloaded. Modules are loaded and unloaded with the `insmod` and `rmmod` commands. Note that by default, the `insmod` command will attempt to look under `/lib/modules/<kernel_version>` to locate the requested module. For example, if the pathname is not specified as shown below, `insmod` will fail even though the requested module is in the current directory. For this reason `"./uxfs"` must be specified.

```
# ./mkfs /dev/fd0
# insmod ./uxfs
# lsmod
Module                  Size  Used by    Not tainted
uxfs                    8608   0   (unused)
ext3                   71968   2   (autoclean)
jbd                    66208   2   (autoclean) [ext3]
# mount -t uxfs /dev/fd0 /mnt
# mount
/dev/hda2 on / type ext3 (rw)
none on /proc type proc (rw)
/dev/hda1 on /boot type ext3 (rw)
none on /dev/pts type devpts (rw,gid=5,mode=620)
/dev/hda5 on /home type ext3 (rw)
none on /dev/shm type tmpfs (rw)
/dev/fd0 on /mnt type uxfs (rw)
# rmmod uxfs
uxfs: Device or resource busy
# umount /mnt
# rmmod uxfs
# lsmod
Module                  Size  Used by    Not tainted
ext3                   71968   2   (autoclean)
jbd                    66208   2   (autoclean) [ext3]
```

The sequence of commands here is merely to illustrate the basics of how to get a uxfs filesystem mounted. The module displayed by `lsmod` is the name of the actual binary and does not bear any resemblance to the source code.

Mounting and Unmounting the Filesystem

The `ux_read_super()` function is called to mount a uxfs filesystem. This function is declared through the `DECLARE_FSTYPE_DEV()` macro and becomes known to the Linux kernel when the filesystem is registered. The code for this function can be found in `ux_inode.c` on lines 1240 to 1302.

The `ux_read_super()` function takes three arguments as shown in `ux_inode.c` on line 1234 and iterated below:

```
ux_read_super(struct super_block *s, void *data, int silent)
```

There is one `super_block` structure per mounted filesystem. One of the tasks to be performed by `ux_read_super()` is to initialize this structure by filling in the following fields:

- `s_magic`. This field holds the magic number of the filesystem, which for uxfs is `0x58494e55`. This field has little practical value.

- `s_blocksize`. This field holds the filesystem block size, which in the case of uxfs is 512 bytes (`UX_BSIZE`).

- `s_op`. This field holds the `super_operations` vector, a set of functions that either deal with the filesystem as a whole or allow inodes to be read, written, and deleted.

- `s_root`. This field is set to reference the `dentry` for the root inode. This is described in more detail later.

The `data` argument is used by the kernel to pass any arguments that were passed to mount. At this stage, uxfs does not accept any command line arguments to mount, so this parameter is ignored. The `silent` argument, if set, allows the filesystem writer to display more detailed information when running. This allows debugging information to be displayed.

The `ux_read_super()` function must also perform the following tasks:

- Call `set_blocksize()` to specify to the underlying driver layer the units of I/O that will be passed through when accessing data through the buffer cache. Note that all subsequent I/O must be in fixed-size chunks.

- Allocate and initialize a root inode for the filesystem. This will be explained in more detail later.

The following example shows how to set a breakpoint in gdb, display a stack backtrace, and show how to display various structures. First of all, after the module is loaded, but before a calling made to mount a filesystem, a breakpoint is set in `ux_read_super()`. Hitting Control-C will enter gdb from which the breakpoint can be set:

```
(gdb) b ux_read_super
Breakpoint 1 at 0xd08557ca: file ux_inode.c, line 237.
```

```
(gdb) c
Continuing.
```

In response to mounting the filesystem, the breakpoint will be hit as follows:

```
# mount -f uxfs /dev/fd0 /mnt

Breakpoint 1, ux_read_super (s=0xcf15a400, data=0x0, silent=0)
    at ux_inode.c:237
237         dev = s->s_dev;
(gdb) list
232         struct ux_fs            *fs;
233         struct buffer_head      *bh;
234         struct inode            *inode;
235         kdev_t                  dev;
236
237         dev = s->s_dev;
238         set_blocksize(dev, UX_BSIZE);
239         s->s_blocksize = UX_BSIZE;
240         s->s_blocksize_bits = UX_BSIZE_BITS;
241
```

The `list` command displays the source code from the point at which the breakpoint has been hit. The `bt` command can be used to display the current stack backtrace as follows:

```
(gdb) bt
#0  ux_read_super (s=0xcf15a400, data=0x0, silent=0) at ux_inode.c:237
#1  0xc0143868 in get_sb_bdev (fs_type=0xd0856a44,
    dev_name=0xccfe8000 "/dev/fd0", flags=0, data=0x0) at super.c:697
#2  0xc0143d2d in do_kern_mount (type=0xccfe9000 "uxfs", flags=0,
    name=0xccfe8000 "/dev/fd0", data=0x0) at super.c:879
#3  0xc0156ff1 in do_add_mount (nd=0xcd011f5c, type=0xccfe9000 "uxfs",
    flags=0, mnt_flags=0, name=0xccfe8000 "/dev/fd0", data=0x0)
    at namespace.c:630
#4  0xc01572b7 in do_mount (dev_name=0xccfe8000 "/dev/fd0",
    dir_name=0xcf80f000 "/mnt", type_page=0xccfe9000 "uxfs",
                flags=3236757504, data_page=0x0) at namespace.c:746
#5  0xc015737f in sys_mount (dev_name=0x805b418 "/dev/fd0",
    dir_name=0x805b428 "/mnt", type=0x805b438 "uxfs", flags=3236757504,
    data=0x0) at namespace.c:779
#6  0xc010730b in system_call ()
```

The arguments to the function at the current position in the stack trace (ux_read_super()) can be displayed with the print (p) command. Note that gdb understands C constructs:

```
(gdb) print *(struct super_block *)0xcf15a400
$1 = {s_list = {next = 0xc0293840, prev = 0xcf6df400}, s_dev = 512,
  s_blocksize = 0, s_blocksize_bits = 0 '\0', s_dirt = 0 '\0',
  s_maxbytes = 2147483647, s_type = 0xd0856a44, s_op = 0x0, dq_op = 0x0,
  s_flags = 0, s_magic = 0, s_root = 0x0, s_umount = {count = -65535,
    wait_lock = {lock = 1}, wait_list = {next = 0xcf15a43c,
```

```
        prev = 0xcf15a43c}}, s_lock = {count = {counter = 0}, sleepers = 0,
        wait = {lock = {lock = 1}, task_list = {next = 0xcf15a450,
        prev = 0xcf15a450}}}, s_count = 1073741824, s_active = {counter = 1},
      s_dirty = 0,
      . . .
```

Later examples show some of the other features of gdb.

Scanning for a Uxfs Filesystem

The first task to perform when mounting the filesystem is to read the superblock from disk. This involves a call to sb_bread() to read block 0 of the device on which the superblock resides. The sb_read() function is merely a wrapper around bread() that extracts the device from the s_dev field of the super_block structure. Thus the following calls are equivalent:

```
bh = sb_bread(sb, block);
bh = bread(sb->s_dev, block, sb->s_blocksize);
```

On return from sb_bread(), a buffer_head structure will reference the data read from the device. Note that each call to sb_read() must be followed at some stage by a call to brelse() to release the buffer. An attempt to reread the same block from disk prior to calling brelse() will cause the filesystem to block. The data read from disk can be referenced by accessing the b_data field. Because the superblock is located at offset 0 within block 0, the ux_superblock structure can be referenced as shown in line 1253:

```
usb = (struct ux_superblock *)bh->b_data;
```

The first check to perform is to validate that this is a uxfs filesystem. Verification is achieved by checking for presence of the uxfs magic number. Assuming that this is detected and the superblock is not marked UX_FSDIRTY, the filesystem can be mounted. Because all of the inode and data block information is stored in the uxfs superblock, it is imperative to keep the superblock in memory at all times. A ux_fs structure is allocated to keep hold of the buffer_head used to read the superblock. This makes it easy to access the ux_superblock structure from either the Linux super_block structure or from a Linux inode. This is shown in Figure 14.4. Note that the buffer is not released until the filesystem is unmounted.

Access to the ux_fs structure can be achieved through either the Linux super_block structure or indirectly from the Linux inode structure as follows:

```
struct super_block      *sb = inode->i_sb;
struct ux_fs            *fs = (struct ux_fs *)sb->s_private;
struct ux_superblock    *usb = fs->u_sb;
```

Because all exported uxfs functions are passed through either the super_block or an inode structure as an argument, it is always possible to get access to the uxfs superblock.

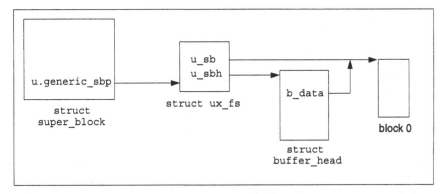

Figure 14.4 Mapping from the Linux super_block structure to the uxfs superblock.

Reading the Root Inode

The final step when mounting the filesystem is to read in the root inode and instantiate it in the dcache. This is achieved through a call to iget() followed by a call to d_alloc_root().

The call to iget() will involve a call back into the filesystem to actually read the inode from disk. Subsequent calls to iget() for the same inode will find the entry in the cache avoiding the need for further filesystem access. For details on how uxfs reads inodes see the section *Reading an Inode from Disk* a little later in the chapter. The Linux kernel calls find_inode() (fs/inode.c) to scan the inode cache for the inode. If not found, a call to get_new_inode() is made.

The call to d_alloc_root() is a wrapper to d_instantiate() that initializes the d_sb field of the dentry structure to reference the new super_block structure. Note that accessing any further inodes will involve access to dentries that already exist and that have been initialized by the kernel.

At this stage, the mount is complete. The super_block structure has been initialized, the root directory is accessible through the Linux inode cache/dcache, and the kernel has access to the the array of functions exported by the root inode through which subsequent operations can be performed.

As another example of how to use gdb, a breakpoint can be set on the ux_read_inode() function as follows:

```
(gdb) b ux_read_inode
Breakpoint 2 at 0xd0855312: file ux_inode.c, line 54.
(gdb) c
Continuing.
```

As with the gdb example earlier, the source code can be displayed at the point where the breakpoint is hit:

```
Breakpoint 2, ux_read_inode (inode=0xcd235460) at ux_inode.c:54
54          unsigned long          ino = inode->i_ino;
(gdb) list
```

```
49    void
50    ux_read_inode(struct inode *inode)
51    {
52        struct buffer_head        *bh;
53        struct ux_inode           *di;
54        unsigned long             ino = inode->i_ino;
55        int                       block;
56
57        if (ino < UX_ROOT_INO || ino > UX_MAXFILES) {
58                printk("uxfs: Bad inode number %lu\n", ino);
```

and the stack backtrace is displayed to locate the flow through the kernel from function to function. In the stack backtrace below, you can see the call from ux_read_super() to iget() to read the root inode. Notice the inode number (2) passed to iget().

```
(gdb) bt
#0  ux_read_inode (inode=0xcd235460) at ux_inode.c:54
#1  0xc015411a in get_new_inode (sb=0xcf15a400, ino=2, head=0xcfda3820,
    find_actor=0, opaque=0x0) at inode.c:871
#2  0xc015439a in iget4 (sb=0xcf15a400, ino=2, find_actor=0, opaque=0x0)
    at inode.c:984
#3  0xd0855bfb in iget (sb=0xcf15a400, ino=2)
    at /usr/src/linux/include/linux/fs.h:1328
#4  0xd08558c3 in ux_read_super (s=0xcf15a400, data=0x0, silent=0)
    at ux_inode.c:272
#5  0xc0143868 in get_sb_bdev (fs_type=0xd0856a44,
    dev_name=0xccf35000 "/dev/fd0", flags=0, data=0x0) at super.c:697
#6  0xc0143d2d in do_kern_mount (type=0xccf36000 "uxfs", flags=0,
...
```

Finally, the inode structure passed to ux_read_inode() can be displayed. Because the inode has not been read from disk, the in-core inode is only partially initialized. The i_ino field is correct, but some of the other fields are invalid at this stage.

```
(gdb) print *(struct inode *)0xcd235460
$2 = {i_hash = {next = 0xce2c7400, prev = 0xcfda3820}, i_list = {
    next = 0xcf7aeba8, prev = 0xc0293d84}, i_dentry = {next = 0xcd235470,
    prev = 0xcd235470}, i_dirty_buffers = {next = 0xcd235478,
    prev = 0xcd235478}, i_dirty_data_buffers = {next = 0xcd235480,
    prev = 0xcd235480}, i_ino = 2, i_count = {counter = 1}, i_dev = 512,
    i_mode = 49663, i_nlink = 1, i_uid = 0, i_gid = 0,
    i_rdev = 512, i_size = 0,
```

Because the address of the inode structure is known, it may be displayed at any time. Simply enter gdb and run the above command once more.

Writing the Superblock to Disk

The uxfs superblock contains information about which inodes and data blocks have been allocated along with a summary of both pieces of information. The superblock resides in a single UX_MAXBSIZE buffer, which is held throughout the duration of the mount. The usual method of ensuring that dirty buffers are flushed to disk is to mark the buffer dirty as follows:

```
mark_buffer_dirty(bh);
```

However, the uxfs superblock is not released until the filesystem is unmounted. Each time the superblock is modified, the s_dirt field of the superblock is set to 1. This informs the kernel that the filesystem should be notified on a periodic basis by the kupdate daemon, which is called on a regular interval to flush dirty buffers to disk. The kupdate() routine can be found in the Linux kernel source in fs/buffer.c. To follow the flow from kupdate() through to the filesystem, the following tasks are performed:

```
# ./mkfs /dev/fd0
# mount -t uxfs /dev/fd0 /mnt
# touch /mnt/file
```

Because a new file is created, a new inode is allocated that requires information in the superblock to be updated. As part of this processing, which will be described in more detail later in the chapter, the s_dirt field of the in-core superblock is set to 1 to indicate that the superblock has been modified.

The ux_write_super() function (lines 1218 to 1229) is called to write the superblock to disk. Setting a breakpoint in ux_write_super() using kdb as follows:

```
Entering  kdb  (current=0xcbe20000,  pid  1320)  on  processor  0  due  to
Keyboard Entry[0]kdb> bp ux_write_super
Instruction(i) BP #1 at 0xd08ab788 ([uxfs]ux_write_super)
    is enabled globally adjust 1
```

and creating the new file as shown will eventually result in the breakpoint being hit, as follows:

```
Entering kdb (current=0xc1464000, pid 7) on processor 0 due to Breakpoint
@ 0xd08ab788
[0]kdb> bt
    EBP          EIP          Function(args)
0xc1465fc4 0xd08ab788 [uxfs]ux_write_super (0xcc53b400, 0xc1464000)
                            uxfs .text 0xd08aa060 0xd08ab788 0xd08ab7c4
          0xc014b242 sync_supers+0x142 (0x0, 0xc1464000)
                            kernel .text 0xc0100000 0xc014b100 0xc014b2c0
0xc1465fd4 0xc0149bd6 sync_old_buffers+0x66 (0xc1464000, 0x10f00,
0xcffe5f9c, 0xc0105000)
                            kernel .text 0xc0100000 0xc0149b70 0xc0149cf0
0xc1465fec 0xc014a223 kupdate+0x273
                            kernel .text 0xc0100000 0xc0149fb0 0xc014a230
          0xc01057c6 kernel_thread+0x26
                            kernel .text
                            0xc0100000 0xc01057a0 0xc01057e0
```

Note the call from kupdate() to sync_old_buffers(). Following through, the kernel code shows an inline function, write_super(), which actually calls into the filesystem as follows:

```
if (sb->s_root && sb->s_dirt)
          if (sb->s_op && sb->s_op->write_super)
               sb->s_op->write_super(sb);
```

Thus, the write_super entry of the superblock_operations vector is called. For uxfs, the buffer holding the superblock is simply marked dirty. Although this doesn't flush the superblock to disk immediately, it will be written as part of kupdate() processing at a later date (which is usually fairly quickly).

The only other task to perform by ux_write_super() is to set the s_dirt field of the in-core superblock back to 0. If left at 1, ux_writer_super() would be called every time kupdate() runs and would, for all intents and purposes, lock up the system.

Unmounting the Filesystem

Dirty buffers and inodes are flushed to disk separately and are not therefore really part of unmounting the filesystem. If the filesystem is busy when an unmount command is issued, the kernel does not communicate with the filesystem before returning EBUSY to the user.

If there are no open files on the system, dirty buffers and inodes are flushed to disk and the kernel makes a call to the put_super function exported through the superblock_operations vector. For uxfs, this function is ux_put_super() (lines 1176 to 1188).

The path when entering ux_put_super() is as follows:

```
Breakpoint 4, ux_put_super (s=0xcede4c00) at ux_inode.c:167
167          struct ux_fs        *fs = (struct ux_fs *)s->s_private;
(gdb) bt
#0   ux_put_super (s=0xcede4c00) at ux_inode.c:167
#1   0xc0143b32 in kill_super (sb=0xcede4c00) at super.c:800
#2   0xc01481db in path_release (nd=0xc9da1f80)
     at /usr/src/linux-2.4.18/include/linux/mount.h:50
#3   0xc0156931 in sys_umount (name=0x8053d28 "/mnt", flags=0)
     at namespace.c:395
#4   0xc015694e in sys_oldumount (name=0x8053d28 "/mnt")
     at namespace.c:406
#5   0xc010730b in system_call ()
```

There are only two tasks to be performed by ux_put_super():

- Mark the buffer holding the superblock dirty and release it.

- Free the structure used to hold the ux_fs structure that was allocated during ux_read_super().

If there are any inodes or buffers used by the filesystem that have not been freed, the kernel will free them and display a message on the console about their existence. There are places within uxfs where this will occur. See the exercises at the end of the chapter for further information.

Directory Lookups and Pathname Resolution

There are three main entry points into the filesystem for dealing with pathname resolution, namely ux_readdir(), ux_lookup(), and ux_read_inode(). One interesting way to see how these three functions work together is to consider the interactions between the kernel and the filesystem in response to the user issuing an ls command on the root directory. When the filesystem is mounted, the kernel already has a handle on the root directory, which exports the following operations:

```
struct inode_operations ux_dir_inops = {
        create:     ux_create,
        lookup:     ux_lookup,
        mkdir:      ux_mkdir,
        rmdir:      ux_rmdir,
        link:       ux_link,
        unlink:     ux_unlink,
};

struct file_operations ux_dir_operations = {
        read:       generic_read_dir,
        readdir:    ux_readdir,
        fsync:      file_fsync,
};
```

The kernel has two calls at a directory level for name resolution. The first is to call ux_readdir() to obtain the names of all the directory entries. After the filesystem is mounted, the only inode in memory is the root inode so this operation can only be invoked on the root inode. Given a filename, the ux_lookup() function can be called to look up a name relative to a directory. This function is expected to return the inode for the name if found.

The following two sections describe each of these operations in more detail.

Reading Directory Entries

When issuing a call to ls, the ls command needs to know about all of the entries in the specified directory or the current working directory if ls is typed without any arguments. This involves calling the getdents() system call. The prototype for getdents() is as follows:

```
int getdents(unsigned int fd, struct dirent *dirp, unsigned int count);
```

The dirp pointer references an area of memory whose size is specified in count. The kernel will try to read as many directory entries as possible. The number of bytes read is returned from getdents(). The dirent structure is shown below:

```
struct dirent
{
    long d_ino;                    /* inode number */
    off_t d_off;                   /* offset to next dirent */
    unsigned short d_reclen;       /* length of this dirent */
    char d_name [NAME_MAX+1];      /* file name (null-terminated) */
}
```

To read all directory entries, ls may need to call getdents() multiple times depending on the size of the buffer passed in relation to the number of entries in the directory.

To fill in the buffer passed to the kernel, multiple calls may be made into the filesystem through the ux_readdir() function. The definition of this function is as follows:

```
int
ux_readdir(struct file *filp, void *dirent, filldir_t filldir)
```

Each time the function is called, the current offset within the directory is increased. The first step taken by ux_readdir() is to map the existing offset into a block number as follows:

```
pos = filp->f_pos;
blk = (pos + 1) / UX+BSIZE;
blk = uip->iaddr[blk];
```

On first entry pos will be 0 and therefore the block to read will be i_addr[0]. The buffer corresponding to this block is read into memory and a search is made to locate the required filename. Each block is comprised of UX_DIRS_PER_BLOCK ux_dirent structures. Assuming that the entry in the block at the appropriate offset is valid (d_ino is not 0), the filldir() routine, a generic kernel function used by all filesystems, is called to copy the entry to the user's address space.

For each directory entry found, or if a null directory entry is encountered, the offset within the directory is incremented as follows:

```
filp->f_pos += sizeof(struct ux_dirent);
```

to record where to start the next read if ux_readdir() is called again.

Filename Lookup

From a filesystem perspective, pathname resolution is a fairly straightforward affair. All that is needed is to provide the lookup() function of the inode_operations vector that is passed a handle for the parent directory and a name to search for. Recall from the ux_read_super() function described in the section *Reading the Root Inode* earlier in the chapter, after the superblock has been read into memory and the Linux super_block structure has been initialized, the root inode must be read into memory and initialized. The uxfs ux_inode_operations vector is assigned to the i_op field of the root inode. From there, filenames may be searched for, and once those directories are brought into memory, a subsequent search may be made.

The ux_lookup() function in ux_dir.c (lines 838 to 860) is called passing the parent directory inode and a partially initialized dentry for the filename to look up. The next section gives examples showing the arguments passed.

There are two cases that must be handled by ux_lookup():

- The name does not exist in the specified directory. In this case an EACCES error is returned in which case the kernel marks the dentry as being *negative*. If another search is requested for the same name, the kernel finds the negative entry in the dcache and will return an error to the user. This method is also used when creating new files and directories and will be shown later in the chapter.

- The name is located in the directory. In this case the filesystem should call iget() to allocate a new Linux inode.

The main task performed by ux_lookup() is to call ux_find_entry() as follows:

```
inum = ux_find_entry(dip, (char *)dentry->d_name.name);
```

Note that the d_name field of the dentry has already been initialized to reference the filename. The ux_find_entry() function in ux_inode.c (lines 1031 to 1054) loops through all of the blocks in the directory (i_addr[]) making a call to sb_bread() to read each appropriate block into memory.

For each block, there can be UX_DIRS_PER_BLOCK ux_dirent structures. If a directory entry is not in use, the d_ino field will be set to 0. Figure 14.5 shows the root directory inode and how entries are laid out within the inode data blocks. For each block read, a check is made to see if the inode number (i_ino) is not zero indicating that the directory entry is valid. If the entry is valid, a string comparison is made between the name requested (stored in the dentry) and the entry in the directory (d_name). If the names match, the inode number is returned.

If there is no match in any of the directory entries, 0 is returned. Note that inode 0 is unused so callers can detect that the entry is not valid.

Once a valid entry is found, ux_lookup() makes a call to iget() to bring the inode into memory, which will call back into the filesystem to actually read the inode.

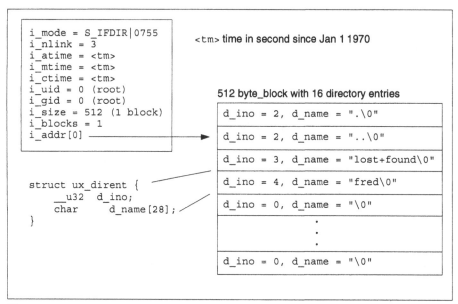

Figure 14.5 uxfs directory entries.

Filesystem/Kernel Interactions for Listing Directories

This section shows the kernel/filesystem interactions when running `ls` on the root directory. The two main entry points into the filesystem for dealing with name resolution, which were described in the last two sections, are `ux_lookup()` and `ux_readdir()`. To obtain further information about a filename, the `ux_read_inode()` must be called to bring the inode into memory. The following example sets a breakpoint on all three functions and then an `ls` is issued on a filesystem that has just been mounted. The filesystem to be mounted has the `lost+found` directory (inode 3) and a copy of the `passwd` file (inode 4). There are no other files.

First, the breakpoints are set in gdb as follows:

```
(gdb) b ux_lookup
Breakpoint 8 at 0xd0854b32: file ux_dir.c, line 367.
(gdb) b ux_readdir
Breakpoint 9 at 0xd0854350
(gdb) b ux_read_inode
Breakpoint 10 at 0xd0855312: file ux_inode.c, line 54.
```

The filesystem is then mounted and the the first breakpoint is hit as follows:

```
# mount -f uxfs /dev/fd0 /mnt

Breakpoint 10, ux_read_inode (inode=0xcd235280) at ux_inode.c:54
54            unsigned long        ino = inode->i_ino;
(gdb) p inode->i_ino
$19 = 2
```

This is a request to read inode number 2 and is called as part of the `ux_read_super()` operation described in the section *Mounting and Unmounting the Filesystem* earlier in the chapter. The `print` (p) command in gdb can be used to display information about any of the parameters passed to the function.

Just to ensure that the kernel is still in the process of mounting the filesystem, a portion of the stack trace is displayed as follows, which shows the call to `ux_read_super()`:

```
(gdb) bt
#0  ux_read_inode (inode=0xcd235280) at ux_inode.c:54
#1  0xc015411a in get_new_inode (sb=0xcf15a400, ino=2, head=0xcfda3820,
    find_actor=0, opaque=0x0) at inode.c:871
#2  0xc015439a in iget4 (sb=0xcf15a400, ino=2, find_actor=0, opaque=0x0)
    at inode.c:984
#3  0xd0855bfb in iget (sb=0xcf15a400, ino=2)
    at /usr/src/linux/include/linux/fs.h:1328
#4  0xd08558c3 in ux_read_super (s=0xcf15a400, data=0x0, silent=0)
    at ux_inode.c:272
...
```

The next step is to run `ls /mnt`, which will result in numerous calls into the filesystem. The first such call is:

```
# ls /mnt

Breakpoint 9, 0xd0854350 in ux_readdir (filp=0xcd39cc60,
dirent=0xccf0dfa0, filldir=0xc014dab0 <filldir64>)
```

This is a request to read directory entries from the root directory. This can be shown by displaying the inode number of the directory on which the operation is taking place. Note how C-like constructs can be used within gdb:

```
(gdb) p ((struct inode *)(filp->f_dentry->d_inode))->i_ino
$20 = 2
```

Here is the stack backtrace:

```
(gdb) bt
#0  0xd0854350 in ux_readdir (filp=0xcd39cc60, dirent=0xccf0dfa0,
    filldir=0xc014dab0 <filldir64>)
#1  0xc014d64e in vfs_readdir (file=0xcd39cc60, filler=0xc014dab0
<filldir64>,
    buf=0xccf0dfa0) at readdir.c:27
#2  0xc014dc2d in sys_getdents64 (fd=3, dirent=0x8058730, count=512)
    at readdir.c:311
#3  0xc010730b in system_call ()
```

Although `ls` may make repeated calls to `getdents()`, the kernel records the last offset within the directory after the previous call to `readdir()`. This can be used by the filesystem to know which directory entry to read next. The `ux_readir()`

routine obtains this offset as follows:

```
pos = filp->f_pos;
```

It can then read the directory at that offset or advance further into the directory if the slot at that offset is unused. Either way, when a valid entry is found, it is copied to the user buffer and the offset is advanced to point to the next entry.

Following this call to ux_readdir(), there are two subsequent calls. Without looking too deeply, one can assume that ls will read all directory entries first.

The next breakpoint hit is a call to ux_lookup() as follows:

```
Breakpoint    8,   ux_lookup   (dip=0xcd235280,   dentry=0xcd1e9ae0)    at
ux_dir.c:367
367            struct ux_inode    *uip = (struct ux_inode *)
```

The dip argument is the root directory and the dentry is a partially initialized entry in the dcache. The name to lookup can be found within the dentry structure as follows:

```
(gdb) p dentry->d_name
$23 = {name = 0xcd1e9b3c "lost+found", len = 10, hash = 4225228667}
```

The section *Filename Lookup* earlier in the chapter showed how the name can be found in the directory and, if found, ux_lookup() will call iget() to read the inode into memory. Thus, the next breakpoint is as follows:

```
Breakpoint 10, ux_read_inode (inode=0xcf7aeba0) at ux_inode.c:54
54          unsigned long         ino = inode->i_ino;
(gdb) p inode->i_ino
$24 = 3
```

The inode number being looked up is inode number 3, which is the inode number for the lost+found directory. The stack backtrace at this point is:

```
(gdb) bt
#0  ux_read_inode (inode=0xcf7aeba0) at ux_inode.c:54
#1  0xc015411a in get_new_inode (sb=0xcf15a400, ino=3, head=0xcfda3828,
    find_actor=0, opaque=0x0) at inode.c:871
#2  0xc015439a in iget4 (sb=0xcf15a400, ino=3, find_actor=0, opaque=0x0)
    at inode.c:984
#3  0xd0854e73 in iget (sb=0xcf15a400, ino=3)
    at /usr/src/linux/include/linux/fs.h:1328
#4  0xd0854b93 in ux_lookup (dip=0xcd235280, dentry=0xcd1e9ae0)
    at ux_dir.c:379
#5  0xc01482c0 in real_lookup (parent=0xcd1e9160,
                              name=0xccf0df5c, flags=0)
    at namei.c:305
#6  0xc0148ba4 in link_path_walk (name=0xcf80f00f "", nd=0xccf0df98)
    at namei.c:590
#7  0xc014943a in __user_walk (name=0x0, flags=8, nd=0xccf0df98)
    at namei.c:841
```

```
#8  0xc0145877 in sys_lstat64 (filename=0xbffff950 "/mnt/lost+found",
    statbuf=0x805597c, flags=1108542220) at stat.c:352
#9  0xc010730b in system_call ()
```

Thus, the ls command has obtained the lost+found directory entry through calling readdir() and is now invoking a stat() system call on the file. To obtain the information to fill in the stat structure, the kernel needs to bring the inode into memory in which to obtain the appropriate information.

There are two more calls to ux_readdir() followed by the next breakpoint:

```
Breakpoint 8, ux_lookup (dip=0xcd235280,dentry=0xcd1e90e0) at ux_dir.c:367
367             struct ux_inode    *uip = (struct ux_inode *)
(gdb) p dentry->d_name
$26 = {name = 0xcd1e913c "passwd", len = 6, hash = 3467704878}
```

This is also invoked in response to the stat() system call. And the final breakpoint hit is:

```
Breakpoint 10, ux_read_inode (inode=0xcd0c4c00) at ux_inode.c:54
54             unsigned long            ino = inode->i_ino;
(gdb) p inode->i_ino
$27 = 4
```

in order to read the inode, to fill in the fields of the stat structure.

Although not shown here, another method to help understand the flow of control when reading directory entries is either to modify the ls source code itself to see the calls it is making or use the ls program (shown in Chapter 2).

Inode Manipulation

Previous sections have already highlighted some of the interactions between the kernel, the inode cache, and the filesystem. When a lookup request is made into the filesystem, uxfs locates the inode number and then calls iget() to read the inode into memory. The following sections describe the inode cache/filesystem interactions in more detail. Figure 14.6 can be consulted for a high-level view of these interactions.

Reading an Inode from Disk

The ux_read_inode() function (lines 1061 to 1109) is called from the kernel iget() function to read an inode into memory. This is typically called as a result of the kernel calling ux_lookup(). A partially initialized inode structure is passed to ux_read_inode() as follows:

```
void
ux_read_inode(struct inode *inode)
```

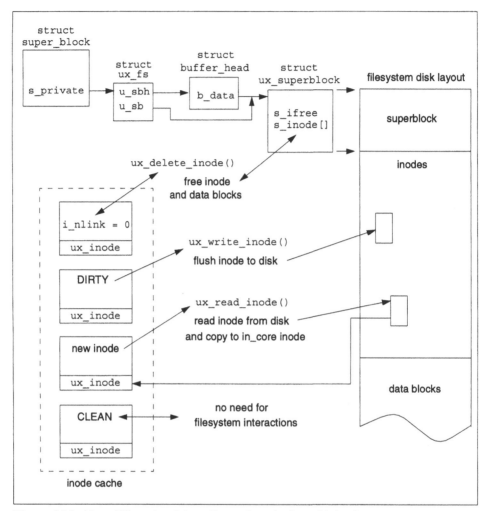

Figure 14.6   Kernel/filesystem interactions when dealing with inodes.

and the inode number of the inode can be found in `inode->i_ino`. The role of `ux_read_inode()` is simply to read the inode into memory and copy relevant fields of the disk portion of the disk-based inode into the `inode` structure passed.

This is a relatively straightforward task in uxfs. The inode number must be converted into a block number within the filesystem and then read through the buffer cache into memory. This is achieved as follows:

```
block = UX_INODE_BLOCK + ino;
bh = sb_bread(inode->i_sb, block)
```

Recall that each uxfs inode is held in its own block on disk and inode 0 starts at the block number defined by `UX_INODE_BLOCK`.

Once read into memory, a copy is made of the inode to the location within the in-core inode defined by the i_private field. This address is at the end of the in-core inode where the union of filesystem dependent information is stored. The i_private field is defined in ux_fs.h as follows:

```
#define i_private u_generic_ip
```

Before freeing the buffer, the in-core inode fields are updated to reflect the on-disk inode. Such information is used by the kernel for operations such as handling the stat() system call.

One additional task to perform in ux_read_inode() is to initialize the i_op, i_fop, and i_mapping fields of the inode structure with the operations applicable to the file type. The set of operations that are applicable to a directory are different to the set of operations that are applicable to regular files. The initialization of both types of inodes can be found on lines 1088 to 1097 and duplicated here:

```
if (di->i_mode & S_IFDIR) {
        inode->i_mode |= S_IFDIR;
        inode->i_op = &ux_dir_inops;
        inode->i_fop = &ux_dir_operations;
} else if (di->i_mode & S_IFREG) {
        inode->i_mode |= S_IFREG;
        inode->i_op = &ux_file_inops;
        inode->i_fop = &ux_file_operations;
        inode->i_mapping->a_ops = &ux_aops;
}
```

Operations such as reading directory entries are obviously not applicable to regular files while various I/O operations are not applicable to directories.

Allocating a New Inode

There is no operation exported to the kernel to allocate a new inode. However, in response to requests to create a directory, regular file, and symbolic link, a new inode needs to be allocated. Because uxfs does not support symbolic links, new inodes are allocated when creating regular files or directories. In both cases, there are several tasks to perform:

- Call new_inode() to allocate a new in-core inode.

- Call ux_ialloc() to allocate a new uxfs disk inode.

- Initialize both the in-core and the disk inode.

- Mark the superblock dirty—the free inode array and summary have been modified.

- Mark the inode dirty so that the new contents will be flushed to disk.

Information about creation of regular files and directories are the subjects of the sections *File Creation and Link Management* and *Creating and Removing Directories* later in the chapter. This section only describes the ux_ialloc() function that can be found in the filesystem source code on lines 413 to 434.

Writing an Inode to Disk

Each time an inode is modified, the inode must be written to disk before the filesystem is unmounted. This includes allocating or removing blocks or changing inode attributes such as timestamps.

Within uxfs itself, there are several places where the inode is modified. The only thing that these functions need to perform is to mark the inode dirty as follows:

```
mark_inode_dirty(inode);
```

The kernel will call the ux_write_inode() function to write the dirty inode to disk. This function, which can be found on lines 1115 to 1141, is exported through the superblock_operations vector.

The following example uses kdb to set a breakpoint on ux_write_inode() in order to see where the function is called from.

```
[0]kdb> bp ux_write_inode
```

The breakpoint can be easily hit by copying files into a uxfs filesystem. The stack backtrace when the breakpoint is encountered is as follows:

```
Instruction(i) BP #0 at 0xd08cd4c8 ([uxfs]ux_write_inode)
    is enabled globally adjust 1
Entering kdb (current=0xc1464000, pid 7) on processor 0 due to Breakpoint
@ 0xd08cd4c8
[0]kdb> bt
    EBP        EIP         Function(args)
0xc1465fc8 0xd08cd4c8 [uxfs]ux_write_inode (0xc77f962c, 0x0, 0xcf9a8868,
                                             0xcf9a8800, 0xc1465fd4)
                            uxfs .text 0xd08cc060 0xd08cd4c8 0xd08cd5c0
          0xc015d738 sync_unlocked_inodes+0x1d8 (0xc1464000)
                            kernel .text 0xc0100000 0xc015d560
0xc015d8e0
0xc1465fd4 0xc0149bc8 sync_old_buffers+0x58 (0xc1464000, 0x10f00,
                                             0xcffe5f9c, 0xc0105000)
                            kernel .text 0xc0100000 0xc0149b70
0xc0149cf0
0xc1465fec 0xc014a223 kupdate+0x273
                            kernel .text 0xc0100000 0xc0149fb0
0xc014a230
          0xc01057c6 kernel_thread+0x26
                                kernel .text 0xc0100000 0xc01057a0
0xc01057e0
```

As with flushing the superblock when dirty, the kupdate daemon locates dirty inodes and invokes ux_write_inode() to write them to disk.

The tasks to be performed by ux_write_inode() are fairly straightfoward:

- Locate the block number where the inode resides. This can be found by adding the inode number to UX_INODE_BLOCK.

- Read the inode block into memory by calling sb_bread().

- Copy fields of interest from the in-core inode to the disk inode, then copy the disk inode to the buffer.

- Mark the buffer dirty and release it.

Because the buffer cache buffer is marked dirty, the periodic run of kupdate will write it to disk.

Deleting Inodes

There are two cases where inodes need to be freed. The first case occurs when a directory needs to be removed; this is described in the section *Creating and Removing Directories* later in the chapter. The second case occurs when the inode link count reaches zero.

Recall that a regular file is created with a link count of 1. The link count is incremented each time a hard link is created. For example:

```
# touch A
# touch B
# ln A C
```

Files A and B are created with a link count of 1. The call to ln creates a directory entry for file C and increments the link count of the inode to which A refers. The following commands:

```
# rm B
# rm A
```

result in calls to the unlink() system call. Because B has a link count of 1, the file will be removed. However, file A has a link count of 2; in this case, the link count is decremented and the directory entry for A is removed, but the file still remains and can be accessed through C.

To show the simple case where a file is created and removed, a breakpoint on ux_write_inode() can be set in kdb as follows:

```
[0]kdb> bp ux_write_inode
Instruction(i) BP #0 at 0xd08cd4c8 ([uxfs]ux_write_inode)
    is enabled globally adjust 1
[0]kdb> go
```

and the following commands are executed:

```
# touch /mnt/file
# rm /mnt/file
```

A regular file (file) is created with a link count of 1. As described in previous chapters of the book, the rm command invokes the unlink() system call. For a file that has a link count of 1, this will result in the file being removed as shown below when the stack backtrace is displayed:

```
Entering kdb (current=0xcaae6000, pid 1398)
                         on processor 0 due to Breakpoint @ 0xd08bc5c0
[0]kdb> bt
EBP        EIP         Function(args)
0xcab81f34 0xd08bc5c0 [uxfs]ux_delete_inode (0xcaad2824, 0xcaad2824,
                                 0xcac4d484, 0xcabc6e0c)
                      uxfs .text 0xd08bb060 0xd08bc5c0 0xd08bc6b4
          0xc015f1f4 iput+0x114 (0xcaad2824, 0xcac4d4e0, 0xcab81f98,
                                 0xcaad2824, 0xcac4d484)
                      kernel .text 0xc0100000 0xc015f0e0 0xc015f3a0
0xcab81f58 0xc015c466 d_delete+0xd6 (0xcac4d484, 0xcac4d56c, 0xcab81f98,
                                 0x0, 0xcabc6e0c)
                      kernel .text 0xc0100000 0xc015c390 0xc015c590
0xcab81f80 0xc01537a8 vfs_unlink+0x1e8 (0xcabc6e0c, 0xcac4d484,
                                 0xcac4d56c, 0xcffefcf8, 0xcea16005)
                      kernel .text 0xc0100000 0xc01535c0 0xc01537e0
0xcab81fbc 0xc0153878 sys_unlink+0x98 (0xbffffc50, 0x2, 0x0,
                                 0xbffffc50, 0x0)
                      kernel .text 0xc0100000 0xc01537e0 0xc01538e0
          0xc01077cb system_call+0x33
                      kernel .text 0xc0100000 0xc0107798 0xc01077d0
```

The call to d_delete() is called to update the dcache first. If possible, the kernel will attempt to make a negative dentry, which will simplify a lookup operation in future if the same name is requested. Inside iput(); if the link count of the inode reaches zero, the kernel knows that there are no further references to the file so the filesystem is called to remove the file.

The ux_delete_inode() function (lines 1148 to 1168) needs to perform the following tasks:

- Free any data blocks that the file references. This involves updating the s_nbfree field and s_block[] fields of the superblock.

- Free the inode by updating the s_nbfree field and s_block[] fields of the superblock.

- Mark the superblock dirty so it will be flushed to disk to reflect the changes.

- Call clear_inode() to free the in-core inode.

As with many functions that deal with inodes and data blocks in uxfs, the tasks performed by ux_delete_inode() and others are greatly simplified because all of the information is held in the superblock.

File Creation and Link Management

Before creating a file, many UNIX utilities will invoke the stat() system call to see is the file exists. This will involve the kernel calling the ux_lookup() function. If the file name does not exist, the kernel will store a negative dentry in the dcache. Thus, if there are additional calls to stat() for the same file, the kernel can see that the file doesn't exist without an additional call to the filesystem.

Shown below is the output from the strace command when using the cp command to copy file to foo:

```
lstat64("foo", 0xbffff8a0) = -1 ENOENT (No such file or directory)
stat64("file", {st_mode=S_IFREG|0644, st_size=0, ...}) = 0
open("file", O_RDONLY|O_LARGEFILE) = 3
open("foo", O_WRONLY|O_CREAT|O_LARGEFILE, 0100644) = 4
```

The cp command invokes the stat() system call on both files before calling open() to create the new file.

The following example shows the call to ux_lookup() in response to the cp command calling the stat() system call:

```
Breakpoint 5, ux_lookup (dip=0xcd73cba0, dentry=0xcb5ed3a0)
                           at ux_dir.c:367
367            struct ux_inode    *uip = (struct ux_inode *)
(gdb) bt
#0  ux_lookup (dip=0xcd73cba0, dentry=0xcb5ed3a0) at ux_dir.c:367
#1  0xc01482c0 in real_lookup (parent=0xcb5ed320, name=0xc97ebf5c,
                               flags=0)
    at namei.c:305
#2  0xc0148ba4 in link_path_walk (name=0xcb0f700b "", nd=0xc97ebf98)
    at namei.c:590
#3  0xc014943a in __user_walk (
                   name=0xd0856920 "\220D\205-,K\205-ÃK\205-<L\205-",
                               flags=9, nd=0xc97ebf98)
    at namei.c:841
#4  0xc0145807 in sys_stat64 (filename=0x8054788 "file",
                             statbuf=0xbffff720, flags=1108542220)
    at stat.c:337
#5  0xc010730b in system_call ()
```

The kernel allocates the dentry before calling ux_lookup(). Notice the address of the dentry which is highlighted above.

Because the file does not exist, the cp command will then call open() to create the file. This results in the kernel invoking the ux_create() function to create the file as follows:

```
Breakpoint 6, 0xd0854494 in ux_create
                        (dip=0xcd73cba0, dentry=0xcb5ed3a0, mode=33188)
(gdb) bt
#0  0xd0854494 in ux_create (dip=0xcd73cba0, dentry=0xcb5ed3a0,
                            mode=33188)
#1  0xc014958f in vfs_create (dir=0xcd73cba0, dentry=0xcb5ed3a0,
                            mode=33188)
    at namei.c:958
#2  0xc014973c in open_namei (pathname=0xcb0f7000 "foo",
                            flag=32834,
    mode=33188, nd=0xc97ebf74) at namei.c:1034
#3  0xc013cd67 in filp_open (filename=0xcb0f7000 "foo",
                            flags=32833,
    mode=33188) at open.c:644
#4  0xc013d0d0 in sys_open (filename=0x8054788 "foo",
                            flags=32833, mode=33188)
    at open.c:788
#5  0xc010730b in system_call ()
```

Note the address of the dentry passed to ux_create(). This is the same as the address of the dentry passed to ux_lookup(). If the file is created successfully, the dentry will be updated to reference the newly created inode.

The ux_create() function (lines 629 to 691) has several tasks to perform:

- Call ux_find_entry() to check whether the file exists. If it does exist, an error is returned.

- Call the kernel new_inode() routine to allocate a new in-core inode.

- Call ux_ialloc() to allocate a new uxfs inode. This will be described in more detail later.

- Call ux_diradd() to add the new filename to the parent directory. This is passed to ux_create() as the first argument (dip).

- Initialize the new inode and call mark_dirty_inode() for both the new inode and the parent inode to ensure that they will be written to disk.

The ux_ialloc() function (lines 413 to 434) is very straightforward working on fields of the uxfs superblock. After checking to make sure there are still inodes available (s_nifree > 0), it walks through the s_inode[] array until it finds a free entry. This is marked UX_INODE_INUSE, the s_ifree field is decremented, and the inode number is returned.

The ux_diradd() (lines 485 to 539) function is called to add the new filename to the parent directory. There are two cases that ux_diradd() must deal with:

- There is space in one of the existing directory blocks. In this case, the name of the new file and its inode number can be written in place. The buffer read into memory, which will hold the new entry, must be marked dirty and released.

- There is no more space in any of the existing directory blocks. In this case, a new block must be allocated to the new directory in which to store the name and inode number. This is achieved by calling the ux_block_alloc() function (lines 441 to 469).

When reading through the existing set of directory entries to locate an empty slot, each directory block must be read into memory. This involves cycling through the data blocks in i_addr[] from 0 to i_blocks.

Creating a hard link involves adding a new filename to the filesystem and incrementing the link count of the inode to which it refers. In some respects, the paths followed are very similar to ux_create() but without the creation of a new uxfs inode.

The ln command will invoke the stat() system call to check whether both filenames already exist. Because the name of the link does not exist, a negative dentry will be created. The ln command then invokes the link() system call, which will enter the filesystem through ux_link(). The prototype for ux_link() is as follows and the source can be found on lines 866 to 887:

```
int
ux_link(struct dentry *old, struct inode *dip, struct dentry *new);
```

Thus when executing the following command:

```
$ ln filea fileb
```

the old dentry refers to filea while new is a negative dentry for fileb, which will have been established on a prior call to ux_lookup().

These arguments can be analyzed by setting a breakpoint on ux_link() and running the above ln command.

```
Breakpoint 11, ux_link (old=0xcf2fe740, dip=0xcf23a240, new=0xcf2fe7c0)
    at ux_dir.c:395
395                 }
(gdb) bt
#0  ux_link (old=0xcf2fe740, dip=0xcf23a240, new=0xcf2fe7c0)
    at ux_dir.c:395
#1  0xc014adc4 in vfs_link (old_dentry=0xcf2fe740, dir=0xcf23a240,
    new_dentry=0xcf2fe7c0) at namei.c:1613
#2  0xc014aef0 in sys_link (oldname=0xbffffc20 "filea",
    newname=0xbffffc26 "fileb") at namei.c:1662
#3  0xc010730b in system_call ()
```

The gdb command can be used to display the arguments passed to ux_link() as follows:

```
(gdb) p new
$9 = (struct dentry *) 0xcf2fe7c0
(gdb) p *old
$10 = {d_count = {counter = 1}, d_flags = 0, d_inode = 0xcd138260,
  d_parent = 0xcb5ed920, d_hash = {next = 0xc2701750, prev = 0xcfde6168},
  d_lru = {next = 0xcf2fe758, prev = 0xcf2fe758}, d_child = {
    next = 0xcb5ed948, prev = 0xcf2fe7e0}, d_subdirs = {next =
0xcf2fe768,
    prev = 0xcf2fe768}, d_alias = {next = 0xcd138270, prev = 0xcd138270},
  d_mounted = 0, d_name = {name = 0xcf2fe79c "filea", len = 5,
    hash = 291007618}, d_time = 0, d_op = 0x0, d_sb = 0xcede4c00,
  d_vfs_flags = 8, d_fsdata = 0x0, d_iname = "filea\0g\0\0\0\0\0\0\0\0"}
(gdb) p old->d_name.name
$11 = (unsigned char *) 0xcf2fe79c "filea"
(gdb) p new->d_name.name
$12 = (unsigned char *) 0xcf2fe81c "fileb"
```

Thus the dentry for old is complely instantiated and references the inode for
filea. The name field of the dentry for new has been set but the dentry has
not been initialized further.

There is not a great deal of work for ux_link() to perform. In addition to
calling ux_diradd() to add the new name to the parent directory, it increments
the link count of the inode, calls d_instantiate() to map the negative
dentry to the inode, and marks it dirty.

The unlink() system call is managed by the ux_unlink() function (lines
893 to 902). All that this function needs to do is decrement the inode link count
and mark the inode dirty. If the link count reaches zero, the kernel will invoke
ux_delete_inode() to actually remove the inode from the filesystem.

Creating and Removing Directories

At this point, readers should be familiar with the mechanics of how the kernel
looks up a filename and creates a negative dentry before creating a file.
Directory creation is a little different in that the kernel performs the lookup rather
than the application calling stat() first. This is shown as follows:

```
Breakpoint 5, ux_lookup (dip=0xcd73cba0, dentry=0xcb5ed420)
                                         at ux_dir.c:367
367         struct ux_inode     *uip = (struct ux_inode *)
(gdb) bt
#0  ux_lookup (dip=0xcd73cba0, dentry=0xcb5ed420) at ux_dir.c:367
#1  0xc01492f2 in lookup_hash (name=0xc97ebf98, base=0xcb5ed320)
    at namei.c:781
#2  0xc0149cd1 in lookup_create (nd=0xc97ebf90, is_dir=1)
    at namei.c:1206
#3  0xc014a251 in sys_mkdir (pathname=0xbffffc1c "/mnt/dir", mode=511)
    at namei.c:1332
#4  0xc010730b in system_call ()
```

Because the filename won't be found (assuming it doesn't already exist), a negative dentry is created is then passed into ux_mkdir() (lines 698 to 780) as follows:

```
Breakpoint 7, 0xd08546d0 in ux_mkdir (dip=0xcd73cba0, dentry=0xcb5ed420,
                                      mode=493)
(gdb) bt
#0  0xd08546d0 in ux_mkdir (dip=0xcd73cba0, dentry=0xcb5ed420, mode=493)
#1  0xc014a197 in vfs_mkdir (dir=0xcd73cba0, dentry=0xcb5ed420,
                            mode=493)
    at namei.c:1307
#2  0xc014a282 in sys_mkdir (pathname=0xbffffc1c "/mnt/dir", mode=511)
    at namei.c:1336
#3  0xc010730b in system_call ()
```

Note that dentry address is the same for both functions.

The initial steps performed by ux_mkdir() are very similar to the steps taken by ux_create(), which was described earlier in the chapter, namely:

- Call new_inode() to allocate a new in-core inode.

- Call ux_ialloc() to allocate a new uxfs inode and call ux_diradd() to add the new directory name to the parent directory.

- Initialize the in-core inode and the uxfs disk inode.

One additional step that must be performed is to allocate a block to the new directory in which to store the entries for "." and "..". The ux_block_alloc() function is called, which returns the block number allocated. This must be stored in i_addr[0], i_blocks must be set to 1, and the size of the inode (i_size) is set to 512, which is the size of the data block.

To remove a directory entry, the ux_rmdir() function (lines 786 to 831) is called. The first step performed by ux_rmdir() is to check the link count of the directory inode. If it is greater than 2, the directory is not empty and an error is returned. Recall that a newly created directory has a link count of 2 when created (for both "." and "..").

The stack backtrace when entering ux_rmdir() is shown below:

```
Breakpoint 8, 0xd0854a0c in ux_rmdir (dip=0xcd73cba0, dentry=0xcb5ed420)
(gdb) bt
#0  0xd0854a0c in ux_rmdir (dip=0xcd73cba0, dentry=0xcb5ed420)
#1  0xc014a551 in vfs_rmdir (dir=0xcd73cba0, dentry=0xcb5ed420)
    at namei.c:1397
#2  0xc014a696 in sys_rmdir (pathname=0xbffffc1c "/mnt/dir")
    at namei.c:1443
#3  0xc010730b in system_call ()
```

The dip argument is for the parent directory and the dentry argument is for the directory to be removed.

The tasks to be performed by ux_rmdir() are as follows:

- Call ux_dirdel() to remove the directory name from the parent directory. This is described in more detail later.

- Free all of the directory blocks.

- Free the inode by incrementing the s_nifree field of the superblock and marking the slot in s_nifree[] to indicate that the inode is free.

The dirdel() function (lines 545 to 576) walks through each of the directory blocks comparing the d_ino field of each ux_dirent structure found with the name passed. If a match is found, the d_ino field is set to 0 to indicate that the slot is free. This is not an ideal solution because if many files are created and removed in the same directory, there will be a fair amount of unused space. However, for the purpose of demonstrating a simple filesystem, it is the easiest solution to implement.

File I/O in uxfs

File I/O is typically one of the most difficult areas of a filesystem to implement. To increase filesystem performance, this is one area where a considerable amount of time is spent. In Linux, it is very easy to provide a fully working filesytem while spending a minimal amount of time of the I/O paths. There are many generic functions in Linux that the filesystem can call to handle all the interactions with the page cache and buffer cache.

The section *File I/O in the 2.4 Linux Kernel* in Chapter 8 describes some of the interactions with the page cache. Because this chapter presents a simplified view of filesystem activity, the page cache internals won't be described. Instead, the following sections show how the kernel interacts with the ux_get_block() function exported by uxfs. This function can be used to read data from a file or allocate new data blocks and write data.

First of all, consider the main entry points into the filesystem for file I/O. These are exported through the file_operations structure as follows:

```
struct file_operations ux_file_operations = {
        llseek:     generic_file_llseek,
        read:       generic_file_read,
        write:      generic_file_write,
        mmap:       generic_file_mmap,
};
```

So for all of the main file I/O related operations, the filesystem defers to the Linux generic file I/O routines. The same is true for operations on any of the mapped file interactions, whether for user-level mappings or for handling operation within the page cache. The address space related operations are:

```
struct address_space_operations ux_aops = {
        readpage:           ux_readpage,
```

```
            writepage:          ux_writepage,
            sync_page:          block_sync_page,
            prepare_write:      ux_prepare_write,
            commit_write:       generic_commit_write,
            bmap:               ux_bmap,
    };
```

For all of the functions defined in this vector, uxfs also makes calls to generic kernel routines. For example, consider the ux_readpage() function (lines 976 to 980), which is also shown here:

```
int
ux_readpage(struct file *file, struct page *page)
{
        return block_read_full_page(page, ux_get_block);
}
```

For each of the uxfs routines exported, uxfs makes a call to a generic kernel function and passes the ux_get_block() routine. Before showing the flow into the filesystem for file I/O, the subject of the next three sections, it is first helpful to show how ux_get_block() (lines 929 to 968) works:

```
int
ux_get_block(struct inode *inode, long block,
            struct buffer_head *bh_result, int create)
```

The ux_getblock() function is called whenever the kernel needs to access part of a file that is not already cached. The block argument is the logical block within the file such that block 0 maps to file offset 0, block 1 maps to file offset 512 and so on. The create argument indicates whether the kernel wants to read from or write to the file. If create is 0, the kernel is reading from the file. If create is 1, the filesystem will need to allocate storage at the offset referenced by block.

Taking the case where block is 0, the filesystem must fill in the appropriate fields of the buffer_head as follows:

```
bh_result->b_dev = inode->i_dev;
bh_result->b_blocknr = uip->i_addr[block];
```

The kernel will then perform the actual read of the data. In the case where create is 1, the filesystem must allocate a new data block by calling ux_block_alloc() and set the appropriate i_addr[] slot to reference the new block. Once allocated, the buffer_head structure must be initialized prior to the kernel performing the I/O operation.

Reading from a Regular File

The filesystem does not do anything specific for reading from regular files. In place of the read operation (file_operations vector), the filesystem specifies the generic_file_read() function.

To show how the filesystem is entered, a breakpoint is set on `ux_get_block()` and the `passwd` file is read from a uxfs filesystem by running the `cat` program. Looking at the size of `passwd`:

```
# ls -l /mnt/passwd
-rw-r--r--    1 root        root          1203 Jul 24 07:51 /etc/passwd
```

there will be three data blocks to access. When the first breakpoint is hit:

```
Breakpoint 1, ux_get_block (inode=0xcf23a420,
                          block=0, bh_result=0xc94f4740, create=0)
    at ux_file.c:21
21          struct super_block *sb = inode->i_sb;
(gdb) bt
#0  ux_get_block (inode=0xcf23a420, block=0, bh_result=0xc94f4740,
                  create=0)
    at ux_file.c:21
#1  0xc0140b1f in block_read_full_page (page=0xc1250fc0,
    get_block=0xd0855094 <ux_get_block>) at buffer.c:1781
#2  0xd08551ba in ux_readpage (file=0xcd1c9360, page=0xc1250fc0)
    at ux_file.c:67
#3  0xc012e773 in do_generic_file_read (filp=0xcd1c9360,
ppos=0xcd1c9380,
    desc=0xc96d1f5c, actor=0xc012eaf0 <file_read_actor>)
    at filemap.c:1401
#4  0xc012ec72 in generic_file_read (filp=0xcd1c9360, buf=0x804eb28 "",
    count=4096, ppos=0xcd1c9380) at filemap.c:1594
#5  0xc013d7c8 in sys_read (fd=3, buf=0x804eb28 "", count=4096)
    at read_write.c:162
#6  0xc010730b in system_call ()
```

there are two uxfs entry points shown. The first is a call to `ux_readpage()`. This is invoked to read a full page of data into the page cache. The routines for manipulating the page cache can be found in mm/`filemap.c`. The second, is the call the `ux_get_block()`. Because file I/O is in multiples of the system page size, the `block_read_full_page()` function is called to fill a page. In the case of the file being read, there are only three blocks of 512 bytes, thus not enough to fill a whole page (4KB). The kernel must therefore read in as much data as possible, and then zero-fill the rest of the page.

The `block` argument passed to `ux_get_block()` is 0 so the filesystem will initialize the `buffer_head` so that the first 512 bytes are read from the file.

The next time that the breakpoint is hit:

```
Breakpoint 1, ux_get_block (inode=0xcf23a420,
                          block=1, bh_result=0xc94f46e0, create=0)
    at ux_file.c:21
21          struct super_block *sb = inode->i_sb;
(gdb) bt
#0  ux_get_block (inode=0xcf23a420, block=1,
                  bh_result=0xc94f46e0, create=0)
    at ux_file.c:21
```

```
#1   0xc0140b1f in block_read_full_page (page=0xc1250fc0,
...
```

the kernel passes `block` 1 so the next 512 bytes will be read from the file. The final call to `ux_get_block()` is shown below:

```
(gdb) bt
#0   ux_get_block (inode=0xcf23a420, block=2,
                   bh_result=0xc94f4680, create=0)
     at ux_file.c:21
#1   0xc0140b1f in block_read_full_page (page=0xc1250fc0,
     get_block=0xd0855094 <ux_get_block>) at buffer.c:1781
#2   0xd08551ba in ux_readpage (file=0xcd1c9360, page=0xc1250fc0)
     at ux_file.c:67
```

The kernel passes `block` 2 so the final 512 bytes will be read from the file.

For uxfs, reading from files is extremely simple. Once the `get_block()` function has been written, there is very little other work for the filesystem to do.

Writing to a Regular File

The mechanisms for writing to files are very similar to those used when reading regular files. Consider the following commands, this time to copy the `passwd` file to a uxfs filesystem:

```
# ls -l /etc/passwd
-rw-r--r--   1 root     root             1336 Jul 24 14:28 /etc/passwd
# cp /etc/passwd /mnt
```

Setting a breakpoint on `ux_get_block()` once more and running the above `cp` command, the first breakpoint is hit as follows:

```
Breakpoint 1, ux_get_block (inode=0xcd710440,
                            block=0, bh_result=0xc96b72a0, create=1)
     at ux_file.c:21
21          struct super_block *sb = inode->i_sb;
(gdb) bt
#0   ux_get_block (inode=0xcd710440, block=0,
                   bh_result=0xc96b72a0, create=1)
     at ux_file.c:21
#1   0xc014074b in __block_prepare_write (inode=0xcd710440,
                          page=0xc125e640, from=0, to=1024,
                          get_block=0xd0855094 <ux_get_block>)
     at buffer.c:1641
#2   0xc0141071 in block_prepare_write (page=0xc125e640, from=0, to=1024,
     get_block=0xd0855094 <ux_get_block>) at buffer.c:1960
#3   0xd08551dd in ux_prepare_write (file=0xcd1c9160, page=0xc125e640,
                          from=0, to=1024)
     at ux_file.c:74
#4   0xc013085f in generic_file_write (file=0xcd1c9160,
```

```
                                        buf=0xbffff160
"root:x:0:0:root:/root:/bin/bash\nbin:x:1:1:bin:/bin:/sbin/nologin\ndaem
on:x:2:2:daemon:/sbin:/sbin/nologin\nadm:x:3:4:adm:/var/adm:/sbin/nologi
n\nlp:x:4:7:lp:/var/spool/lpd:/sbin/nologin\nsync:x:5:0:sync:/"...,
     count=1024, ppos=0xcd1c9180) at filemap.c:3001
#5   0xc013d8e8 in sys_write (fd=4,
     buf=0xbffff160
"root:x:0:0:root:/root:/bin/bash\nbin:x:1:1:bin:/bin:/sbin/nologin\ndaem
on:x:2:2:daemon:/sbin:/sbin/nologin\nadm:x:3:4:adm:/var/adm:/sbin/nologi
n\nlp:x:4:7:lp:/var/spool/lpd:/sbin/nologin\nsync:x:5:0:sync:/"...,
     count=1024) at read_write.c:188
#6   0xc010730b in system_call ()
```

This time the create flag is set to 1, indicating that a block must be allocated to the file. Once the block has been allocated, the buffer_head can be initialized and the first 512 bytes of passwd can be copied to the buffer. If the buffer and inode are marked dirty, both will be flushed to disk.

The next breakpoint is hit, and this time the block argument is set to 1, which will result in another block being allocated to cover the file range 512 to 1023.

```
Breakpoint 1, ux_get_block (inode=0xcd710440,
                              block=1, bh_result=0xc96b7240, create=1)
     at ux_file.c:21
21         struct super_block *sb = inode->i_sb;
(gdb) bt
#0   ux_get_block (inode=0xcd710440, block=1,
                   bh_result=0xc96b7240, create=1)
     at ux_file.c:21
```

The final breakpoint is hit as follows:

```
Breakpoint 1, ux_get_block (inode=0xcd710440, block=2,
                              bh_result=0xc9665900, create=1)
     at ux_file.c:21
21         struct super_block *sb = inode->i_sb;
(gdb) bt
#0   ux_get_block (inode=0xcd710440, block=2,
                   bh_result=0xc9665900, create=1)
     at ux_file.c:21
```

and this time the block argument is set to 2 indicating that the final block which is needed should be allocated. As with reading from regular files, writing to regular files is also an easy function for the filesystem to implement.

Memory-Mapped Files

Although this section won't describe the mechanics of how memory-mapped files work in the Linux kernel, it is easy to show how the filesystem can support mapped files through the same mechanisms used for reading from and writing to regular files.

In place of the mmap function, exported through the file_operations vector, uxfs requests that the generic_file_mmap() will be called. All that the filesystem needs to provide is the get_block() interface.

To demonstrate how the filesystem is involved, a breakpoint is set in ux_get_block() and a file is mapped for read-only access. The first address of the mapping is then touched, which will create a page fault. The stack trace when ux_get_block() is entered is as follows:

```
Breakpoint 1, ux_get_block (inode=0xcf23a420,
                           block=0, bh_result=0xc94bbba0, create=0)
    at ux_file.c:21
21          struct super_block *sb = inode->i_sb;
(gdb) bt
#0  ux_get_block (inode=0xcf23a420, block=0,
                  bh_result=0xc94bbba0, create=0)
    at ux_file.c:21
#1  0xc0140b1f in block_read_full_page (page=0xc1238340,
                               get_block=0xd0855094 <ux_get_block>)
    at buffer.c:1781
#2  0xd08551ba in ux_readpage (file=0xcd1c97e0, page=0xc1238340)
    at ux_file.c:67
#3  0xc012dd92 in page_cache_read (file=0xcd1c97e0, offset=3441203168)
    at filemap.c:714
#4  0xc012ddef in read_cluster_nonblocking (file=0xcd1c97e0,
                               offset=3475219664, filesize=1)
    at filemap.c:739
#5  0xc012f389 in filemap_nopage (area=0xc972a300, address=1073823744,
                               unused=0)
    at filemap.c:1911
#6  0xc012b512 in do_no_page (mm=0xcf996d00, vma=0xc972a300,
              address=1073823744, write_access=0, page_table=0xc91e60a0)
    at memory.c:1249
#7  0xc012b76c in handle_mm_fault (mm=0xcf996d00, vma=0xc972a300,
                               address=1073823744, write_access=0)
    at memory.c:1339
#8  0xc011754a in do_page_fault (regs=0xc952dfc4, error_code=4)
    at fault.c:263
#9  0xc01073fc in error_code ()
```

The kernel is entered, not through a system call, but in response to a fault. Because there are no pages backing the mapped file in the user address space, when the process attempts to access the file, a page fault occurs. The kernel establishes where the page of memory is mapped to and must then fill in the page from the appropriate file.

The ux_readpage() function is entered, which calls back into the memory manager. To fill in the page of data, the kernel will make repeated calls into ux_get_block() until either a page of data has been read or the end of the file has been reached. If the latter occurs, the kernel must zero-fill the page so that, if the process accesses within the same page but beyond the end of the file, it will read zeroes.

The Filesystem Stat Interface

The df command displays information about the filesystem usage such as the number of free and used blocks. Through the super_block operations vector, uxfs exports the ux_statfs() function, which is called in response to df invoking the stafs system call (once for each filesystem). The ux_statfs() function can be found on lines 1194 to 1210. The function prototype is shown below:

```
int
ux_statfs(struct super_block *sb, struct statfs *buf);
```

The df command will make a call to the statfs() system call for each mounted filesystem. Here is the prototype for statfs().

```
int statfs(const char *path, struct statfs *buf);
```

Note that it also uses the statfs structure which is defined below:

```
struct statfs {
        long    f_type;     /* type of filesystem (see below) */
        long    f_bsize;    /* optimal transfer block size */
        long    f_blocks;   /* total data blocks in file system */
        long    f_bfree;    /* free blocks in fs */
        long    f_bavail;   /* free blocks avail to non-superuser */
        long    f_files;    /* total file nodes in file system */
        long    f_ffree;    /* free file nodes in fs */
        fsid_t  f_fsid;     /* file system id */
        long    f_namelen;  /* maximum length of filenames */
};
```

As mentioned earlier in the book, understanding the requirements of user level programs is essential to understanding some of the features that must be provided by filesystems. The information passed through the statfs structure corresponds to filesystem limits, such as the total number of files and blocks in the filesystem, and existing free resources, such as the number of available files and data blocks.

The following example shows a breakpoint being set within kdb to stop when the kernel enters ux_statfs(). The debugger is entered by hitting the Break key as indicated by kdb when it is entered:

```
Entering kdb (current=0xc03b0000, pid 0) on processor 0 due to Keyboard Entry
[0]kdb> bp ux_statfs
Instruction(i) BP #0 at 0xd08bb400 ([uxfs]ux_statfs)
    is enabled globally adjust 1
[0]kdb> bl
Instruction(i) BP #0 at 0xd08bb400 ([uxfs]ux_statfs)
    is enabled globally adjust 1
[0]kdb> go
```

The b1 command displays the existing breakpoints. This is breakpoint number 0 as indicated by "BP #0 ". Thus, to clear the breakpoint, the bc command can be invoked passing 0 as an argument.

```
# df -k /mnt
Filesystem               1k-blocks       Used Available Use% Mounted on
Instruction(i) breakpoint #0 at 0xd08bb400 (adjusted)
0xd08bb400 ux_statfs

Entering kdb (current=0xcd31c000, pid 1509) on processor 0 due to
Breakpoint @ 0xd08bb400
[0]kdb> bt
EBP        EIP        Function(args)
0xcd31df38 0xd08bb400 [uxfs]ux_statfs (0xcc2be400, 0xcd31df50,0xfffffffda,
               uxfs .text 0xd08bb060 0xd08bb400 0xd08bb460
           0xc0141ea2 vfs_statfs+0xa2 (0xcc2be400, 0xcd31df50, 0x43, ...
               kernel .text 0xc0100000 0xc0141e00 0xc0141f20
0xcd31dfbc 0xc0141f58 sys_statfs+0x38 (0x8052bb8, 0xbffff760, ...
               kernel .text 0xc0100000 0xc0141f20 0xc0141fb0
           0xc01077cb system_call+0x33
               kernel .text 0xc0100000 0xc0107798 0xc01077d0
[0]kdb> go
```

When the df command is run and ux_statfs() is reached, the breakpoint is hit and the kernel enters kdb. The bt command can then display the stack backtrace showing that the kernel was entered by a system call that then called through sys_statfs() and vfs_statfs() before entering ux_statfs().

The fields of the statfs structure can be obtained from either predefined defaults in ux_fs.h or from summary information stored in the superblock. Shown below is the result of a call to df following creation of a single directory:

```
# ./mkfs /dev/fd0
# insmod ./uxfs
# mount -t uxfs /dev/fd0 /mnt
# df -k
Filesystem          1k-blocks       Used Available Use% Mounted on
/dev/hda2           15120648    2524836   11827716  18% /
/dev/hda1             102454      11147      86017  12% /boot
/dev/hda5             497829       8240     463887   2% /home
none                 127076          0     127076   0% /dev/shm
/dev/fd0               1000          1        999   1% /mnt
```

In the example that follows, a directory is created. A uxfs directory involves allocating an inode and one data block to hold the "." and ".." entries plus any subsequent entries added to the directory. Note that the single block allocated for the directory is reflected in the information displayed.

```
# mkdir /mnt/dir
# df -k
Filesystem          1k-blocks       Used Available Use% Mounted on
/dev/hda2           15120648    2524836   11827716  18% /
```

```
/dev/hda1            102454      11147      86017   12%  /boot
/dev/hda5            497829       8240     463887    2%  /home
none                127076          0     127076    0%  /dev/shm
/dev/fd0               1000          2        998    1%  /mnt
```

Similarly, df can also display inode allocation information based on the f_files and f_ffree fields of the statfs structure as displayed below:

```
# df -i /mnt
Filesystem            Inodes   IUsed   IFree IUse% Mounted on
/dev/fd0                  32       4      28   13% /mnt
# mkdir /mnt/mydir
# df -i /mnt
Filesystem            Inodes   IUsed   IFree IUse% Mounted on
/dev/fd0                  32       5      27   16% /mnt
```

When first run on an empty filesystem, there are 4 inodes used out of the 32 available (UX_MAXFILES) inodes. By creating a directory an additional inode is used that is returned in the f_ffree field of the statfs structure and displayed by df above.

The Filesystem Source Code

This section displays all of the uxfs source code. All files are included together to make it easier to reference from the different sections of the chapter.

The order in which the files are listed is:

ux_fs.h (lines 1 to 103). This file contains definitions of the structures used by the filesystem. This includes the superblock, inodes, directory entries, and parameters that are global to the filesystem such as the maximum number of files, data blocks, and the location of various structures on disk.

mkfs.c (lines 104 to 263). This file contains the source code to the uxfs mkfs command.

fsdb.c (lines 264 to 394). This file contains the source code to the uxfs fsdb command.

ux_alloc.c (lines 395 to 470). This file contains routines to allocate inodes and data blocks.

ux_dir.c (lines 471 to 912). This file contains the uxfs functions that are exported through the inode_operations vector, including file and directory creation, name resolution, and creation of hard links.

ux_file.c (lines 913 to 1008). This file contains the routines needed for reading from and writing to files. Primarily this includes an allocating bmap interface for retrieving file data blocks and allocating blocks as necessary.

ux_inode.c (lines 1009 to 1317). This file contains routines that work on the filesystem as a whole, including module initialization and deinitialization.

Note that the source code can be accessed through the following Web site:

```
www.wiley.com/compbooks/pate
```

together with modifications and instructions on how to run the filesystem on different versions of Linux.

```
 1 /*----------------------------------------------------------------*/
 2 /*------------------------- ux_fs.h -----------------------*/
 3 /*----------------------------------------------------------------*/
 4
 5 extern struct address_space_operations ux_aops;
 6 extern struct inode_operations ux_file_inops;
 7 extern struct inode_operations ux_dir_inops;
 8 extern struct file_operations ux_dir_operations;
 9 extern struct file_operations ux_file_operations;
10
11
12 #define UX_NAMELEN              28
13 #define UX_DIRS_PER_BLOCK       16
14 #define UX_DIRECT_BLOCKS        16
15 #define UX_MAXFILES             32
16 #define UX_MAXBLOCKS            470
17 #define UX_FIRST_DATA_BLOCK     50
18 #define UX_BSIZE                512
19 #define UX_BSIZE_BITS           9
20 #define UX_MAGIC                0x58494e55
21 #define UX_INODE_BLOCK          8
22 #define UX_ROOT_INO             2
23
24 #define s_private       u.generic_sbp
25 #define i_private       u.generic_ip
26
27 /*
28  * The on-disk superblock. The number of inodes and
29  * data blocks is fixed.
30  */
31
32 struct ux_superblock {
33         __u32       s_magic;
34         __u32       s_mod;
35         __u32       s_nifree;
36         __u32       s_inode[UX_MAXFILES];
37         __u32       s_nbfree;
38         __u32       s_block[UX_MAXBLOCKS];
39 };
40
41 /*
42  * The on-disk inode.
43  */
44
45 struct ux_inode {
46         __u32           i_mode;
47         __u32           i_nlink;
```

```
48          __u32          i_atime;
49          __u32          i_mtime;
50          __u32          i_ctime;
51          __s32          i_uid;
52          __s32          i_gid;
53          __u32          i_size;
54          __u32          i_blocks;
55          __u32          i_addr[UX_DIRECT_BLOCKS];
56 };
57
58 /*
59  * Allocation flags
60  */
61
62 #define UX_INODE_FREE    0
63 #define UX_INODE_INUSE   1
64 #define UX_BLOCK_FREE    0
65 #define UX_BLOCK_INUSE   1
66
67 /*
68  * Filesystem flags
69  */
70
71 #define UX_FSCLEAN       0
72 #define UX_FSDIRTY       1
73
74 /*
75  * FIxed size directory entry.
76  */
77
78 struct ux_dirent {
79          __u32     d_ino;
80          char      d_name[UX_NAMELEN];
81 };
82
83 /*
84  * Used to hold filesystem information in-core permanently.
85  */
86
87 struct ux_fs {
88          struct ux_superblock      *u_sb;
89          struct buffer_head        *u_sbh;
90 };
91
92 #ifdef __KERNEL__
93
94 extern ino_t ux_ialloc(struct super_block *);
95 extern int ux_find_entry(struct inode *, char *);
96 __u32 ux_block_alloc(struct super_block *);
97 extern __u32 ux_block_alloc(struct super_block *);
98 extern int ux_unlink(struct inode *, struct dentry *);
99 extern int ux_link(struct dentry *, struct inode *,
100                    struct dentry *);
101
102 #endif
```

```
103
104 /*------------------------------------------------------------------*/
105 /*------------------------- mkfs.c -------------------------*/
106 /*------------------------------------------------------------------*/
107
108 #include <sys/types.h>
109 #include <unistd.h>
110 #include <stdio.h>
111 #include <fcntl.h>
112 #include <time.h>
113 #include <linux/fs.h>
114 #include <sys/stat.h>
115 #include "../kern/ux_fs.h"
116
117 main(int argc, char **argv)
118 {
119         struct ux_dirent        dir;
120         struct ux_superblock    sb;
121         struct ux_inode         inode;
122         time_t                  tm;
123         off_t                   nsectors = UX_MAXBLOCKS;
124         int                     devfd, error, i;
125         int                     map_blks;
126         char                    block[UX_BSIZE];
127
128         if (argc != 2) {
129                 fprintf(stderr, "uxmkfs: Need to specify device\n");
130                 exit(1);
131         }
132         devfd = open(argv[1], O_WRONLY);
133         if (devfd < 0) {
134                 fprintf(stderr, "uxmkfs: Failed to open device\n");
135                 exit(1);
136         }
137         error = lseek(devfd, (off_t)(nsectors * 512), SEEK_SET);
138         if (error == -1) {
139                 fprintf(stderr, "uxmkfs: Cannot create filesystem"
140                         " of specified size\n");
141                 exit(1);
142         }
143         lseek(devfd, 0, SEEK_SET);
144
145         /*
146          * Fill in the fields of the superblock and write
147          * it out to the first block of the device.
148          */
149
150         sb.s_magic = UX_MAGIC;
151         sb.s_mod = UX_FSCLEAN;
152         sb.s_nifree = UX_MAXFILES - 4;
153         sb.s_nbfree = UX_MAXBLOCKS - 2;
154
155         /*
156          * First 4 inodes are in use. Inodes 0 and 1 are not
157          * used by anything, 2 is the root directory and 3 is
```

```
158            * lost+found.
159            */
160
161           sb.s_inode[0]  = UX_INODE_INUSE;
162           sb.s_inode[1]  = UX_INODE_INUSE;
163           sb.s_inode[2]  = UX_INODE_INUSE;
164           sb.s_inode[3]  = UX_INODE_INUSE;
165
166           /*
167            * The rest of the inodes are marked unused
168            */
169
170           for (i = 4 ; i < UX_MAXFILES ; i++) {
171                   sb.s_inode[i] = UX_INODE_FREE;
172           }
173
174           /*
175            * The first two blocks are allocated for the entries
176            * for the root and lost+found directories.
177            */
178
179           sb.s_block[0] = UX_BLOCK_INUSE;
180           sb.s_block[1] = UX_BLOCK_INUSE;
181
182           /*
183            * The rest of the blocks are marked unused
184            */
185
186           for (i = 2 ; i < UX_MAXBLOCKS ; i++) {
187                   sb.s_block[i] = UX_BLOCK_FREE;
188           }
189
190           write(devfd, (char *)&sb, sizeof(struct ux_superblock));
191
192           /*
193            * The root directory and lost+found directory inodes
194            * must be initialized.
195            */
196
197           time(&tm);
198           memset((void *)&inode, 0, sizeof(struct ux_inode));
199           inode.i_mode = S_IFDIR | 0755;
200           inode.i_nlink = 3;          /* ".", ".." and "lost+found" */
201           inode.i_atime = tm;
202           inode.i_mtime = tm;
203           inode.i_ctime = tm;
204           inode.i_uid = 0;
205           inode.i_gid = 0;
206           inode.i_size = UX_BSIZE;
207           inode.i_blocks = 1;
208           inode.i_addr[0] = UX_FIRST_DATA_BLOCK;
209
210           lseek(devfd, UX_INODE_BLOCK * UX_BSIZE + 1024, SEEK_SET);
211           write(devfd, (char *)&inode, sizeof(struct ux_superblock));
212
```

```
213            memset((void *)&inode, 0 , sizeof(struct ux_inode));
214            inode.i_mode = S_IFDIR | 0755;
215            inode.i_nlink = 2;          /* "." and ".." */
216            inode.i_atime = tm;
217            inode.i_mtime = tm;
218            inode.i_ctime = tm;
219            inode.i_uid = 0;
220            inode.i_gid = 0;
221            inode.i_size = UX_BSIZE;
222            inode.i_blocks = 1;
223            inode.i_addr[0] = UX_FIRST_DATA_BLOCK + 1;
224
225            lseek(devfd, UX_INODE_BLOCK * UX_BSIZE + 1536, SEEK_SET);
226            write(devfd, (char *)&inode, sizeof(struct ux_superblock));
227
228            /*
229             * Fill in the directory entries for root
230             */
231
232            lseek(devfd, UX_FIRST_DATA_BLOCK * UX_BSIZE, SEEK_SET);
233            memset((void *)&block, 0, UX_BSIZE);
234            write(devfd, block, UX_BSIZE);
235            lseek(devfd, UX_FIRST_DATA_BLOCK * UX_BSIZE, SEEK_SET);
236            dir.d_ino = 2;
237            strcpy(dir.d_name, ".");
238            write(devfd, (char *)&dir, sizeof(struct ux_dirent));
239            dir.d_ino = 2;
240            strcpy(dir.d_name, "..");
241            write(devfd, (char *)&dir, sizeof(struct ux_dirent));
242            dir.d_ino = 3;
243            strcpy(dir.d_name, "lost+found");
244            write(devfd, (char *)&dir, sizeof(struct ux_dirent));
245
246            /*
247             * Fill in the directory entries for lost+found
248             */
249
250            lseek(devfd, UX_FIRST_DATA_BLOCK * UX_BSIZE + UX_BSIZE,
251                  SEEK_SET);
252            memset((void *)&block, 0, UX_BSIZE);
253            write(devfd, block, UX_BSIZE);
254            lseek(devfd, UX_FIRST_DATA_BLOCK * UX_BSIZE + UX_BSIZE,
255                  SEEK_SET);
256            dir.d_ino = 2;
257            strcpy(dir.d_name, ".");
258            write(devfd, (char *)&dir, sizeof(struct ux_dirent));
259            dir.d_ino = 2;
260            strcpy(dir.d_name, "..");
261            write(devfd, (char *)&dir, sizeof(struct ux_dirent));
262 }
263
264 /*------------------------------------------------------------------*/
265 /*-------------------------- fsdb.c --------------------------------*/
266 /*------------------------------------------------------------------*/
267
```

```
268 #include <sys/types.h>
269 #include <sys/stat.h>
270 #include <unistd.h>
271 #include <stdio.h>
272 #include <fcntl.h>
273 #include <time.h>
274 #include <linux/fs.h>
275 #include "../kern/ux_fs.h"
276
277 struct ux_superblock     sb;
278 int                      devfd;
279
280 void
281 print_inode(int inum, struct ux_inode *uip)
282 {
283         char                    buf[UX_BSIZE];
284         struct ux_dirent        *dirent;
285         int                     i, x;
286
287         printf("\ninode number %d\n", inum);
288         printf("   i_mode     = %x\n", uip->i_mode);
289         printf("   i_nlink    = %d\n", uip->i_nlink);
290         printf("   i_atime    = %s",
291                 ctime((time_t *)&uip->i_atime));
292         printf("   i_mtime    = %s",
293                 ctime((time_t *)&uip->i_mtime));
294         printf("   i_ctime    = %s",
295                 ctime((time_t *)&uip->i_ctime));
296         printf("   i_uid      = %d\n", uip->i_uid);
297         printf("   i_gid      = %d\n", uip->i_gid);
298         printf("   i_size     = %d\n", uip->i_size);
299         printf("   i_blocks   = %d", uip->i_blocks);
300         for (i=0 ; i<UX_DIRECT_BLOCKS; i++) {
301                 if (i % 4 == 0) {
302                         printf("\n");
303                 }
304                 printf("   i_addr[%2d] = %3d ",
305                         i, uip->i_addr[i]);
306         }
307
308         /*
309          * Print out the directory entries
310          */
311
312         if (uip->i_mode & S_IFDIR) {
313                 printf("\n\n   Directory entries:\n");
314                 for (i=0 ; i < uip->i_blocks ; i++) {
315                         lseek(devfd, uip->i_addr[i] * UX_BSIZE,
316                                 SEEK_SET);
317                         read(devfd, buf, UX_BSIZE);
318                         dirent = (struct ux_dirent *)buf;
319                         for (x = 0 ; x < UX_DIRECT_BLOCKS ; x++) {
320                                 if (dirent->d_ino != 0) {
321                                         printf("    inum[%2d],"
322                                                 "name[%s]\n",
```

```
323                                              dirent->d_ino,
324                                              dirent->d_name);
325                                    }
326                                    dirent++;
327                            }
328                    }
329                    printf("\n");
330            } else {
331                    printf("\n\n");
332            }
333 }
334
335 int read_inode(ino_t inum, struct ux_inode *uip)
336 {
337        if (sb.s_inode[inum] == UX_INODE_FREE) {
338                return -1;
339        }
340        lseek(devfd, (UX_INODE_BLOCK * UX_BSIZE) +
341                (inum * UX_BSIZE), SEEK_SET);
342        read(devfd, (char *)uip, sizeof(struct ux_inode));
343        return 0;
344 }
345
346 main(int argc, char **argv)
347 {
348        struct ux_inode          inode;
349        char                     buf[512];
350        char                     command[512];
351        off_t                    nsectors;
352        int                      error, i, blk;
353        ino_t                    inum;
354
355        devfd = open(argv[1], O_RDWR);
356        if (devfd < 0) {
357                fprintf(stderr, "uxmkfs: Failed to open device\n");
358                exit(1);
359        }
360
361        /*
362         * Read in and validate the superblock
363         */
364
365        read(devfd, (char *)&sb, sizeof(struct ux_superblock));
366        if (sb.s_magic != UX_MAGIC) {
367                printf("This is not a uxfs filesystem\n");
368                exit(1);
369        }
370
371        while (1) {
372                printf("uxfsdb > ") ;
373                fflush(stdout);
374                scanf("%s", command);
375                if (command[0] == 'q') {
376                        exit(0);
377                }
```

```
378                     if (command[0] == 'i') {
379                             inum = atoi(&command[1]);
380                             read_inode(inum, &inode);
381                             print_inode(inum, &inode);
382                     }
383                     if (command[0] == 's') {
384                             printf("\nSuperblock contents:\n");
385                             printf("  s_magic   = 0x%x\n", sb.s_magic);
386                             printf("  s_mod     = %s\n",
387                                     (sb.s_mod == UX_FSCLEAN) ?
388                                     "UX_FSCLEAN" : "UX_FSDIRTY");
389                             printf("  s_nifree  = %d\n", sb.s_nifree);
390                             printf("  s_nbfree  = %d\n\n", sb.s_nbfree);
391                     }
392             }
393 }
394
395 /*-----------------------------------------------------------------*/
396 /*------------------------- ux_alloc.c ----------------------*/
397 /*-----------------------------------------------------------------*/
398
399 #include <linux/module.h>
400 #include <linux/mm.h>
401 #include <linux/slab.h>
402 #include <linux/init.h>
403 #include <linux/locks.h>
404 #include <linux/smp_lock.h>
405 #include <asm/uaccess.h>
406 #include "ux_fs.h"
407
408 /*
409  * Allocate a new inode. We update the superblock and return
410  * the inode number.
411  */
412
413 ino_t
414 ux_ialloc(struct super_block *sb)
415 {
416         struct ux_fs        *fs = (struct ux_fs *)sb->s_private;
417         struct ux_superblock *usb = fs->u_sb;
418         int                 i;
419
420         if (usb->s_nifree == 0) {
421                 printk("uxfs: Out of inodes\n");
422                 return 0;
423         }
424         for (i = 3 ; i < UX_MAXFILES ; i++) {
425                 if (usb->s_inode[i] == UX_INODE_FREE) {
426                         usb->s_inode[i] = UX_INODE_INUSE;
427                         usb->s_nifree--;
428                         sb->s_dirt = 1;
429                         return i;
430                 }
431         }
432         printk("uxfs: ux_ialloc - We should never reach here\n");
```

```
433        return 0;
434 }
435
436 /*
437  * Allocate a new data block. We update the superblock and return
438  * the new block  number.
439  */
440
441 __u32
442 ux_block_alloc(struct super_block *sb)
443 {
444        struct ux_fs          *fs = (struct ux_fs *)sb->s_private;
445        struct ux_superblock  *usb = fs->u_sb;
446        int                   i;
447
448        if (usb->s_nbfree == 0) {
449                printk("uxfs: Out of space\n");
450                return 0;
451        }
452
453        /*
454         * Start looking at block 1. Block 0 is
455         * for the root directory.
456         */
457
458        for (i = 1 ; i < UX_MAXBLOCKS ; i++) {
459                if (usb->s_block[i] == UX_BLOCK_FREE) {
460                        usb->s_block[i] = UX_BLOCK_INUSE;
461                        usb->s_nbfree--;
462                        sb->s_dirt = 1;
463                        return UX_FIRST_DATA_BLOCK + i;
464                }
465        }
466        printk("uxfs: ux_block_alloc - "
467               "We should never reach here\n");
468        return 0;
469 }
470
471 /*----------------------------------------------------------------*/
472 /*-------------------------- ux_dir.c ----------------------------*/
473 /*----------------------------------------------------------------*/
474
475 #include <linux/sched.h>
476 #include <linux/string.h>
477 #include <linux/locks.h>
478
479 #include "ux_fs.h"
480
481 /*
482  * Add "name" to the directory "dip"
483  */
484
485 int
486 ux_diradd(struct inode *dip, const char *name, int inum)
487 {
```

```
488            struct ux_inode        *uip = (struct ux_inode *)
489                                         &dip->i_private;
490            struct buffer_head     *bh;
491            struct super_block     *sb = dip->i_sb;
492            struct ux_dirent       *dirent;
493            __u32                  blk = 0;
494            int                    i, pos;
495
496            for (blk=0 ; blk < uip->i_blocks ; blk++) {
497                    bh = sb_bread(sb, uip->i_addr[blk]);
498                    dirent = (struct ux_dirent *)bh->b_data;
499                    for (i=0 ; i < UX_DIRS_PER_BLOCK ; i++) {
500                            if (dirent->d_ino != 0) {
501                                    dirent++;
502                                    continue;
503                            } else {
504                                    dirent->d_ino = inum;
505                                    strcpy(dirent->d_name, name);
506                                    mark_buffer_dirty(bh);
507                                    mark_inode_dirty(dip);
508                                    brelse(bh);
509                                    return 0;
510                            }
511                    }
512                    brelse(bh);
513            }
514
515            /*
516             * We didn't find an empty slot so need to allocate
517             * a new block if there's space in the inode.
518             */
519
520            if (uip->i_blocks < UX_DIRECT_BLOCKS) {
521                    pos = uip->i_blocks;
522                    blk = ux_block_alloc(sb);
523                    uip->i_blocks++;
524                    uip->i_size += UX_BSIZE;
525                    dip->i_size += UX_BSIZE;
526                    dip->i_blocks++;
527                    uip->i_addr[pos] = blk;
528                    bh = sb_bread(sb, blk);
529                    memset(bh->b_data, 0, UX_BSIZE);
530                    mark_inode_dirty(dip);
531                    dirent = (struct ux_dirent *)bh->b_data;
532                    dirent->d_ino = inum;
533                    strcpy(dirent->d_name, name);
534                    mark_buffer_dirty(bh);
535                    brelse(bh);
536            }
537
538            return 0;
539 }
540
541 /*
542  * Remove "name" from the specified directory.
```

```
543    */
544
545    int
546    ux_dirdel(struct inode *dip, char *name)
547    {
548            struct ux_inode         *uip = (struct ux_inode *)
549                                            &dip->i_private;
550            struct buffer_head      *bh;
551            struct super_block      *sb = dip->i_sb;
552            struct ux_dirent        *dirent;
553            __u32                   blk = 0;
554            int                     i;
555
556            while (blk < uip->i_blocks) {
557                    bh = sb_bread(sb, uip->i_addr[blk]);
558                    blk++;
559                    dirent = (struct ux_dirent *)bh->b_data;
560                    for (i=0 ; i < UX_DIRS_PER_BLOCK ; i++) {
561                            if (strcmp(dirent->d_name, name) != 0) {
562                                    dirent++;
563                                    continue;
564                            } else {
565                                    dirent->d_ino = 0;
566                                    dirent->d_name[0] = '\0';
567                                    mark_buffer_dirty(bh);
568                                    dip->i_nlink--;
569                                    mark_inode_dirty(dip);
570                                    break;
571                            }
572                    }
573                    brelse(bh);
574            }
575            return 0;
576    }
577
578    int
579    ux_readdir(struct file *filp, void *dirent, filldir_t filldir)
580    {
581            unsigned long           pos;
582            struct inode            *inode = filp->f_dentry->d_inode;
583            struct ux_inode         *uip = (struct ux_inode *)
584                                            &inode->i_private;
585            struct ux_dirent        *udir;
586            struct buffer_head      *bh;
587            __u32                   blk;
588
589    start_again:
590            pos = filp->f_pos;
591            if (pos >= inode->i_size) {
592                    return 0;
593            }
594            blk = (pos + 1) / UX_BSIZE;
595            blk = uip->i_addr[blk];
596            bh = sb_bread(inode->i_sb, blk);
597            udir = (struct ux_dirent *)(bh->b_data + pos % UX_BSIZE);
```

```
598
599        /*
600         * Skip over 'null' directory entries.
601         */
602
603        if (udir->d_ino == 0) {
604                filp->f_pos += sizeof(struct ux_dirent);
605                brelse(bh);
606                goto start_again;
607        } else {
608                filldir(dirent, udir->d_name,
609                        sizeof(udir->d_name), pos,
610                        udir->d_ino, DT_UNKNOWN);
611        }
612        filp->f_pos += sizeof(struct ux_dirent);
613        brelse(bh);
614        return 0;
615 }
616
617 struct file_operations ux_dir_operations = {
618        read:                   generic_read_dir,
619        readdir:                ux_readdir,
620        fsync:                  file_fsync,
621 };
622
623 /*
624  * When we reach this point, ux_lookup() has already been called
625  * to create a negative entry in the dcache. Thus, we need to
626  * allocate a new inode on disk and associate it with the dentry.
627  */
628
629 int
630 ux_create(struct inode *dip, struct dentry *dentry, int mode)
631 {
632        struct ux_inode         *nip;
633        struct super_block      *sb = dip->i_sb;
634        struct inode            *inode;
635        ino_t                   inum = 0;
636
637        /*
638         * See if the entry exists. If not, create a new
639         * disk inode, and incore inode. Then add the new
640         * entry to the directory.
641         */
642
643        inum = ux_find_entry(dip, (char *)dentry->d_name.name);
644        if (inum) {
645                return -EEXIST;
646        }
647        inode = new_inode(sb);
648        if (!inode) {
649                return -ENOSPC;
650        }
651        inum = ux_ialloc(sb);
652        if (!inum) {
```

```
653                    iput(inode);
654                    return -ENOSPC;
655            }
656            ux_diradd(dip, (char *)dentry->d_name.name, inum);
657
658            /*
659             * Increment the parent link count and intialize the inode.
660             */
661
662            dip->i_nlink++;
663            inode->i_uid = current->fsuid;
664            inode->i_gid = (dip->i_mode & S_ISGID) ?
665                              dip->i_gid : current->fsgid;
666            inode->i_mtime = inode->i_atime =
667                              inode->i_ctime = CURRENT_TIME;
668            inode->i_blocks = inode->i_blksize = 0;
669            inode->i_op = &ux_file_inops;
670            inode->i_fop = &ux_file_operations;
671            inode->i_mapping->a_ops = &ux_aops;
672            inode->i_mode = mode;
673            inode->i_nlink = 1;
674            inode->i_ino = inum;
675            insert_inode_hash(inode);
676
677            nip = (struct ux_inode *)&inode->i_private;
678            nip->i_mode = mode;
679            nip->i_nlink = 1;
680            nip->i_atime = nip->i_ctime = nip->i_mtime = CURRENT_TIME;
681            nip->i_uid = inode->i_gid;
682            nip->i_gid = inode->i_gid;
683            nip->i_size = 0;
684            nip->i_blocks = 0;
685            memset(nip->i_addr, 0, UX_DIRECT_BLOCKS);
686
687            d_instantiate(dentry, inode);
688            mark_inode_dirty(dip);
689            mark_inode_dirty(inode);
690            return 0;
691 }
692
693 /*
694  * Make a new directory. We already have a negative dentry
695  * so must create the directory and instantiate it.
696  */
697
698 int
699 ux_mkdir(struct inode *dip, struct dentry *dentry, int mode)
700 {
701            struct ux_inode          *nip;
702            struct buffer_head       *bh;
703            struct super_block       *sb = dip->i_sb;
704            struct ux_dirent         *dirent;
705            struct inode             *inode;
706            ino_t                    inum = 0;
707            int                      blk;
```

```
708
709        /*
710         * Make sure there isn't already an entry. If not,
711         * allocate one, a new inode and new incore inode.
712         */
713
714        inum = ux_find_entry(dip, (char *)dentry->d_name.name);
715        if (inum) {
716                return -EEXIST;
717        }
718        inode = new_inode(sb);
719        if (!inode) {
720                return -ENOSPC;
721        }
722        inum = ux_ialloc(sb);
723        if (!inum) {
724                iput(inode);
725                return -ENOSPC;
726        }
727        ux_diradd(dip, (char *)dentry->d_name.name, inum);
728
729        inode->i_uid = current->fsuid;
730        inode->i_gid = (dip->i_mode & S_ISGID) ?
731                        dip->i_gid : current->fsgid;
732        inode->i_mtime = inode->i_atime =
733                        inode->i_ctime = CURRENT_TIME;
734        inode->i_blocks = 1;
735        inode->i_blksize = UX_BSIZE;
736        inode->i_op = &ux_dir_inops;
737        inode->i_fop = &ux_dir_operations;
738        inode->i_mapping->a_ops = &ux_aops;
739        inode->i_mode = mode | S_IFDIR;
740        inode->i_ino = inum;
741        inode->i_size = UX_BSIZE;
742        inode->i_nlink = 2;
743
744        nip = (struct ux_inode *)&inode->i_private;
745        nip->i_mode = mode | S_IFDIR;
746        nip->i_nlink = 2;
747        nip->i_atime = nip->i_ctime
748                     = nip->i_mtime = CURRENT_TIME;
749        nip->i_uid = current->fsuid;
750        nip->i_gid = (dip->i_mode & S_ISGID) ?
751                        dip->i_gid : current->fsgid;
752        nip->i_size = 512;
753        nip->i_blocks = 1;
754        memset(nip->i_addr, 0, 16);
755
756        blk = ux_block_alloc(sb);
757        nip->i_addr[0] = blk;
758        bh = sb_bread(sb, blk);
759        memset(bh->b_data, 0, UX_BSIZE);
760        dirent = (struct ux_dirent *)bh->b_data;
761        dirent->d_ino = inum;
762        strcpy(dirent->d_name, ".");
```

```
763            dirent++;
764            dirent->d_ino = inode->i_ino;
765            strcpy(dirent->d_name, "..");
766
767            mark_buffer_dirty(bh);
768            brelse(bh);
769            insert_inode_hash(inode);
770            d_instantiate(dentry, inode);
771            mark_inode_dirty(inode);
772
773            /*
774             * Increment the link count of the parent directory.
775             */
776
777            dip->i_nlink++;
778            mark_inode_dirty(dip);
779            return 0;
780 }
781
782 /*
783  * Remove the specified directory.
784  */
785
786 int
787 ux_rmdir(struct inode *dip, struct dentry *dentry)
788 {
789            struct super_block      *sb = dip->i_sb;
790            struct ux_fs            *fs = (struct ux_fs *)
791                                    sb->s_private;
792            struct ux_superblock    *usb = fs->u_sb;
793            struct inode            *inode = dentry->d_inode;
794            struct ux_inode         *uip = (struct ux_inode *)
795                                    &inode->i_private;
796            int                     inum, i;
797
798            if (inode->i_nlink > 2) {
799                    return -ENOTEMPTY;
800            }
801
802            /*
803             * Remove the entry from the parent directory
804             */
805
806            inum = ux_find_entry(dip, (char *)dentry->d_name.name);
807            if (!inum) {
808                    return -ENOTDIR;
809            }
810            ux_dirdel(dip, (char *)dentry->d_name.name);
811
812            /*
813             * Clean up the inode
814             */
815
816            for (i=0 ; i<UX_DIRECT_BLOCKS ; i++) {
817                    if (uip->i_addr[i] != 0) {
```

```
818                         usb->s_block[uip->i_addr[i]]
819                                     = UX_BLOCK_FREE;
820                         usb->s_nbfree++;
821                 }
822         }
823
824         /*
825          * Update the superblock summaries.
826          */
827
828         usb->s_inode[dip->i_ino] = UX_INODE_FREE;
829         usb->s_nifree++;
830         return 0;
831 }
832
833 /*
834  * Lookup the specified file. A call is made to iget() to
835  * bring the inode into core.
836  */
837
838 struct dentry *
839 ux_lookup(struct inode *dip, struct dentry *dentry)
840 {
841         struct ux_inode     *uip = (struct ux_inode *)
842                                     &dip->i_private;
843         struct ux_dirent    dirent;
844         struct inode        *inode = NULL;
845         int                 inum;
846
847         if (dentry->d_name.len > UX_NAMELEN) {
848                 return ERR_PTR(-ENAMETOOLONG);
849         }
850
851         inum = ux_find_entry(dip, (char *)dentry->d_name.name);
852         if (inum) {
853                 inode = iget(dip->i_sb, inum);
854                 if (!inode) {
855                         return ERR_PTR(-EACCES);
856                 }
857         }
858         d_add(dentry, inode);
859         return NULL;
860 }
861
862 /*
863  * Called in response to an ln command/syscall.
864  */
865
866 int
867 ux_link(struct dentry *old, struct inode *dip, struct dentry *new)
868 {
869         struct inode        *inode = old->d_inode;
870         int                 error;
871
872         /*
```

```
873             * Add the new file (new) to its parent directory (dip)
874             */
875
876             error = ux_diradd(dip, new->d_name.name, inode->i_ino);
877
878             /*
879              * Increment the link count of the target inode
880              */
881
882             inode->i_nlink++;
883             mark_inode_dirty(inode);
884             atomic_inc(&inode->i_count);
885             d_instantiate(new, inode);
886             return 0;
887  }
888
889  /*
890   * Called to remove a file (decrement its link count)
891   */
892
893  int
894  ux_unlink(struct inode *dip, struct dentry *dentry)
895  {
896             struct inode        *inode = dentry->d_inode;
897
898             ux_dirdel(dip, (char *)dentry->d_name.name);
899             inode->i_nlink--;
900             mark_inode_dirty(inode);
901             return 0;
902  }
903
904  struct inode_operations ux_dir_inops = {
905             create:             ux_create,
906             lookup:             ux_lookup,
907             mkdir:              ux_mkdir,
908             rmdir:              ux_rmdir,
909             link:               ux_link,
910             unlink:             ux_unlink,
911  };
912
913  /*------------------------------------------------------------------*/
914  /*------------------------- ux_file.c ------------------------------*/
915  /*------------------------------------------------------------------*/
916
917  #include <linux/fs.h>
918  #include <linux/locks.h>
919  #include <linux/smp_lock.h>
920  #include "ux_fs.h"
921
922  struct file_operations ux_file_operations = {
923             llseek:    generic_file_llseek,
924             read:      generic_file_read,
925             write:     generic_file_write,
926             mmap:      generic_file_mmap,
927  };
```

```
928
929 int
930 ux_get_block(struct inode *inode, long block,
931             struct buffer_head *bh_result, int create)
932 {
933         struct super_block *sb = inode->i_sb;
934         struct ux_fs      *fs = (struct ux_fs *)
935                                 sb->s_private;
936         struct ux_inode   *uip = (struct ux_inode *)
937                                 &inode->i_private;
938         __u32             blk;
939
940         /*
941          * First check to see if the file can be extended.
942          */
943
944         if (block >= UX_DIRECT_BLOCKS) {
945                 return -EFBIG;
946         }
947
948         /*
949          * If we're creating, we must allocate a new block.
950          */
951
952         if (create) {
953                 blk = ux_block_alloc(sb);
954                 if (blk == 0) {
955                         printk("uxfs: ux_get_block - "
956                                "Out of space\n");
957                         return -ENOSPC;
958                 }
959                 uip->i_addr[block] = blk;
960                 uip->i_blocks++;
961                 uip->i_size = inode->i_size;
962                 mark_inode_dirty(inode);
963         }
964         bh_result->b_dev = inode->i_dev;
965         bh_result->b_blocknr = uip->i_addr[block];
966         bh_result->b_state |= (1UL << BH_Mapped);
967         return 0;
968 }
969
970 int
971 ux_writepage(struct page *page)
972 {
973         return block_write_full_page(page, ux_get_block);
974 }
975
976 int
977 ux_readpage(struct file *file, struct page *page)
978 {
979         return block_read_full_page(page, ux_get_block);
980 }
981
982 int
```

```
983 ux_prepare_write(struct file *file, struct page *page,
984                 unsigned from, unsigned to)
985 {
986         return block_prepare_write(page, from, to, ux_get_block);
987 }
988
989 int
990 ux_bmap(struct address_space *mapping, long block)
991 {
992         return generic_block_bmap(mapping, block, ux_get_block);
993 }
994
995 struct address_space_operations ux_aops = {
996         readpage:        ux_readpage,
997         writepage:       ux_writepage,
998         sync_page:       block_sync_page,
999         prepare_write:   ux_prepare_write,
1000        commit_write:    generic_commit_write,
1001        bmap:            ux_bmap,
1002 };
1003
1004 struct inode_operations ux_file_inops = {
1005        link:            ux_link,
1006        unlink:          ux_unlink,
1007 };
1008
1009 /*------------------------------------------------------------*/
1010 /*------------------------- ux_inode.c -----------------------*/
1011 /*------------------------------------------------------------*/
1012
1013 #include <linux/module.h>
1014 #include <linux/mm.h>
1015 #include <linux/slab.h>
1016 #include <linux/init.h>
1017 #include <linux/locks.h>
1018 #include <linux/smp_lock.h>
1019 #include <asm/uaccess.h>
1020 #include "ux_fs.h"
1021
1022 MODULE_AUTHOR("Steve Pate <spate@veritas.com>");
1023 MODULE_DESCRIPTION("A primitive filesystem for Linux");
1024 MODULE_LICENSE("GPL");
1025
1026 /*
1027  * This function looks for "name" in the directory "dip".
1028  * If found the inode number is returned.
1029  */
1030
1031 int
1032 ux_find_entry(struct inode *dip, char *name)
1033 {
1034         struct ux_inode    *uip = (struct ux_inode *)
1035                                     &dip->i_private;
1036         struct super_block *sb = dip->i_sb;
1037         struct buffer_head *bh;
```

```
1038          struct ux_dirent    *dirent;
1039          int                 i, blk = 0;
1040
1041          for (blk=0 ; blk < uip->i_blocks ; blk++) {
1042                  bh = sb_bread(sb, uip->i_addr[blk]);
1043                  dirent = (struct ux_dirent *)bh->b_data;
1044                  for (i=0 ; i < UX_DIRS_PER_BLOCK ; i++) {
1045                          if (strcmp(dirent->d_name, name) == 0) {
1046                                  brelse(bh);
1047                                  return dirent->d_ino;
1048                          }
1049                          dirent++;
1050                  }
1051          }
1052          brelse(bh);
1053          return 0;
1054 }
1055
1056 /*
1057  * This function is called in response to an iget(). For
1058  * example, we call iget() from ux_lookup().
1059  */
1060
1061 void
1062 ux_read_inode(struct inode *inode)
1063 {
1064          struct buffer_head       *bh;
1065          struct ux_inode          *di;
1066          unsigned long            ino = inode->i_ino;
1067          int                      block;
1068
1069          if (ino < UX_ROOT_INO || ino > UX_MAXFILES) {
1070                  printk("uxfs: Bad inode number %lu\n", ino);
1071                  return;
1072          }
1073
1074          /*
1075           * Note that for simplicity, there is only one
1076           * inode per block!
1077           */
1078
1079          block = UX_INODE_BLOCK + ino;
1080          bh = sb_bread(inode->i_sb, block);
1081          if (!bh) {
1082                  printk("Unable to read inode %lu\n", ino);
1083                  return;
1084          }
1085
1086          di = (struct ux_inode *)(bh->b_data);
1087          inode->i_mode = di->i_mode;
1088          if (di->i_mode & S_IFDIR) {
1089                  inode->i_mode |= S_IFDIR;
1090                  inode->i_op = &ux_dir_inops;
1091                  inode->i_fop = &ux_dir_operations;
1092          } else if (di->i_mode & S_IFREG) {
```

```
1093                    inode->i_mode |= S_IFREG;
1094                    inode->i_op = &ux_file_inops;
1095                    inode->i_fop = &ux_file_operations;
1096                    inode->i_mapping->a_ops = &ux_aops;
1097            }
1098            inode->i_uid = di->i_uid;
1099            inode->i_gid = di->i_gid;
1100            inode->i_nlink = di->i_nlink;
1101            inode->i_size = di->i_size;
1102            inode->i_blocks = di->i_blocks;
1103            inode->i_blksize = UX_BSIZE;
1104            inode->i_atime = di->i_atime;
1105            inode->i_mtime = di->i_mtime;
1106            inode->i_ctime = di->i_ctime;
1107            memcpy(&inode->i_private, di, sizeof(struct ux_inode));
1108            brelse(bh);
1109 }
1110
1111 /*
1112  * This function is called to write a dirty inode to disk.
1113  */
1114
1115 void
1116 ux_write_inode(struct inode *inode, int unused)
1117 {
1118            unsigned long       ino = inode->i_ino;
1119            struct ux_inode     *uip = (struct ux_inode *)
1120                                        &inode->i_private;
1121            struct buffer_head  *bh;
1122            __u32               blk;
1123
1124            if (ino < UX_ROOT_INO || ino > UX_MAXFILES) {
1125                    printk("uxfs: Bad inode number %lu\n", ino);
1126                    return;
1127            }
1128            blk = UX_INODE_BLOCK + ino;
1129            bh = sb_bread(inode->i_sb, blk);
1130            uip->i_mode = inode->i_mode;
1131            uip->i_nlink = inode->i_nlink;
1132            uip->i_atime = inode->i_atime;
1133            uip->i_mtime = inode->i_mtime;
1134            uip->i_ctime = inode->i_ctime;
1135            uip->i_uid = inode->i_uid;
1136            uip->i_gid = inode->i_gid;
1137            uip->i_size = inode->i_size;
1138            memcpy(bh->b_data, uip, sizeof(struct ux_inode));
1139            mark_buffer_dirty(bh);
1140            brelse(bh);
1141 }
1142
1143 /*
1144  * This function gets called when the link count goes to zero.
1145  */
1146
1147 void
```

```
1148 ux_delete_inode(struct inode *inode)
1149 {
1150        unsigned long        inum = inode->i_ino;
1151        struct ux_inode      *uip = (struct ux_inode *)
1152                                   &inode->i_private;
1153        struct super_block   *sb = inode->i_sb;
1154        struct ux_fs         *fs = (struct ux_fs *)
1155                                   sb->s_private;
1156        struct ux_superblock *usb = fs->u_sb;
1157        int                  i;
1158
1159        usb->s_nbfree += uip->i_blocks;
1160        for (i=0 ; i < uip->i_blocks ; i++) {
1161                usb->s_block[uip->i_addr[i]] = UX_BLOCK_FREE;
1162                uip->i_addr[i] = UX_BLOCK_FREE;
1163        }
1164        usb->s_inode[inum] = UX_INODE_FREE;
1165        usb->s_nifree++;
1166        sb->s_dirt = 1;
1167        clear_inode(inode);
1168 }
1169
1170 /*
1171  * This function is called when the filesystem is being
1172  * unmounted. We free the ux_fs structure allocated during
1173  * ux_read_super() and free the superblock buffer_head.
1174  */
1175
1176 void
1177 ux_put_super(struct super_block *s)
1178 {
1179        struct ux_fs         *fs = (struct ux_fs *)s->s_private;
1180        struct buffer_head   *bh = fs->u_sbh;
1181
1182        /*
1183         * Free the ux_fs structure allocated by ux_read_super
1184         */
1185
1186        kfree(fs);
1187        brelse(bh);
1188 }
1189
1190 /*
1191  * This function will be called by the df command.
1192  */
1193
1194 int
1195 ux_statfs(struct super_block *sb, struct statfs *buf)
1196 {
1197        struct ux_fs         *fs = (struct ux_fs *)sb->s_private;
1198        struct ux_superblock *usb = fs->u_sb;
1199
1200        buf->f_type = UX_MAGIC;
1201        buf->f_bsize = UX_BSIZE;
1202        buf->f_blocks = UX_MAXBLOCKS;
```

```
1203            buf->f_bfree = usb->s_nbfree;
1204            buf->f_bavail = usb->s_nbfree;
1205            buf->f_files = UX_MAXFILES;
1206            buf->f_ffree = usb->s_nifree;
1207            buf->f_fsid.val[0] = kdev_t_to_nr(sb->s_dev);
1208            buf->f_namelen = UX_NAMELEN;
1209            return 0;
1210 }
1211
1212 /*
1213  * This function is called to write the superblock to disk. We
1214  * simply mark it dirty and then set the s_dirt field of the
1215  * in-core superblock to 0 to prevent further unnecessary calls.
1216  */
1217
1218 void
1219 ux_write_super(struct super_block *sb)
1220 {
1221         struct ux_fs      *fs = (struct ux_fs *)
1222                                     sb->s_private;
1223         struct buffer_head *bh = fs->u_sbh;
1224
1225         if (!(sb->s_flags & MS_RDONLY)) {
1226                 mark_buffer_dirty(bh);
1227         }
1228         sb->s_dirt = 0;
1229 }
1230
1231 struct super_operations uxfs_sops = {
1232         read_inode:        ux_read_inode,
1233         write_inode:       ux_write_inode,
1234         delete_inode:       ux_delete_inode,
1235         put_super:        ux_put_super,
1236         write_super:       ux_write_super,
1237         statfs:            ux_statfs,
1238 };
1239
1240 struct super_block *
1241 ux_read_super(struct super_block *s, void *data, int silent)
1242 {
1243         struct ux_superblock      *usb;
1244         struct ux_fs             *fs;
1245         struct buffer_head       *bh;
1246         struct inode             *inode;
1247         kdev_t                   dev;
1248
1249         dev = s->s_dev;
1250         set_blocksize(dev, UX_BSIZE);
1251         s->s_blocksize = UX_BSIZE;
1252         s->s_blocksize_bits = UX_BSIZE_BITS;
1253
1254         bh = sb_bread(s, 0);
1255         if(!bh) {
1256                 goto out;
1257         }
```

```
1258            usb = (struct ux_superblock *)bh->b_data;
1259            if (usb->s_magic != UX_MAGIC) {
1260                    if (!silent)
1261                            printk("Unable to find uxfs filesystem\n");
1262                    goto out;
1263            }
1264            if (usb->s_mod == UX_FSDIRTY) {
1265                    printk("Filesystem is not clean. Write and "
1266                            "run fsck!\n");
1267                    goto out;
1268            }
1269
1270            /*
1271             *  We should really mark the superblock to
1272             *  be dirty and write it back to disk.
1273             */
1274
1275            fs = (struct ux_fs *)kmalloc(sizeof(struct ux_fs),
1276                                         GFP_KERNEL);
1277            fs->u_sb = usb;
1278            fs->u_sbh = bh;
1279            s->s_private = fs;
1280
1281            s->s_magic = UX_MAGIC;
1282            s->s_op = &uxfs_sops;
1283
1284            inode = iget(s, UX_ROOT_INO);
1285            if (!inode) {
1286                    goto out;
1287            }
1288            s->s_root = d_alloc_root(inode);
1289            if (!s->s_root) {
1290                    iput(inode);
1291                    goto out;
1292            }
1293
1294            if (!(s->s_flags & MS_RDONLY)) {
1295                    mark_buffer_dirty(bh);
1296                    s->s_dirt = 1;
1297            }
1298            return s;
1299
1300 out:
1301            return NULL;
1302 }
1303
1304 static DECLARE_FSTYPE_DEV(uxfs_fs_type, "uxfs", ux_read_super);
1305
1306 static int __init init_uxfs_fs(void)
1307 {
1308            return register_filesystem(&uxfs_fs_type);
1309 }
1310
1311 static void __exit exit_uxfs_fs(void)
1312 {
```

```
1313          unregister_filesystem(&uxfs_fs_type);
1314 }
1315
1316 module_init(init_uxfs_fs)
1317 module_exit(exit_uxfs_fs)
```

Suggested Exercises

Because the filesystem presents only a basic set of operations, there are several things that can be added to increase functionality. There are also several bugs that exist in the filesystem as it stands that could be fixed. This section contains numerous different exercises that readers can follow either to simply experiment with the filesystem as is or to add additional capabilities.

Simply playing with the filesystem, compiling kernels, and using one of the kernel level debuggers is a significant amount of work in itself. Don't underestimate the amount of time that it can take to achieve these tasks. However, the amount of Linux support information on the World Wide Web is extremely good, so it is usually reasonably easy to find answers to most Linux-related questions.

Beginning to Intermediate Exercises

The exercises in this section can be made to the existing filesystem without changing the underlying disk layout. Some of these exercises involve careful anaysis and some level of testing.

1. What is significant about the uxfs magic number?

2. As a simple way of analyzing the filesystem when running, the silent argument to ux_read_super() can be used to enable debugging. Add some calls to printk() to the filesystem, which are only activated when the silent option is specified. The first step is to determine under what conditions the silent flag is set. The ux_read_super() function provides one example of how silent is used.

3. There are several functions that have not been implemented, such as symbolic links. Look at the various operations vectors and determine which file operations will not work. For each of these functions, locate the place in the kernel where the functions would be called from.

4. For the majority of the operations on the filesystem, various timestamps are not updated. By comparing uxfs with one of the other Linux filesystems—for example ext2—identify those areas where the timestamp updates are missing and implement changes to the filesystem to provide these updates.

5. When the filesystem is mounted, the superblock field s_mod should be set to UX_FSDIRTY and the superblock should be written back to disk. There is already code within ux_read_super() to handle and reject a dirty filesystem. Add this additional feature, but be warned that there is a bug in

ux_read_super() that must be fixed for this feature to work correctly. Add an option to fsdb to mark the superblock dirty to help test this example.

6. Locate the Loopback Filesystem HOWTO on the World Wide Web and use this to build a device on which a uxfs filesystem can be made.

7. There are places in the filesystem where inodes and buffers are not released correctly. When performing some operations and then unmounting the filesystem, warnings will be displayed by the kernel.

Advanced Exercises

The following exercises require more modification to the filesystem and require either substantial modification to the command and/or kernel source:

1. If the system crashes the filesystem could be left in an unstable state. Implement a fsck command that can both detect and repair any such inconsistencies. One method of testing a version of fsck is to modify fsdb to actually *break* the filesystem. Study operations such as directory creation to see how many I/O operations constitute creating the directory. By simulating a subset of these I/O, the filesystem can be left in a state which is not structurally intact.

2. Introduce the concept of indirect, double indirect, and triple indirects. Allow 6 direct blocks, 2 indirect blocks, and 1 triple indirect block to be referenced directly from the inode. What size file does this allow?

3. If the module panics, the kernel is typically able to detect that the uxfs module is at fault and allows the kernel to continue running. If a uxfs filesystem is already mounted, the module is unable to unload because the filesystem is busy. Look at ways in which the filesystem could be unmounted allowing the module to be unloaded.

4. The uxfs filesystem would not work at all well in an SMP environment. By analyzing other Linux filesystems, suggest improvements that could be made to allow uxfs to work in an SMP system. Suggest methods by which coarse grain as well as fine grain locks could be employed.

5. Removing a directory entry leaves a gap within the directory structure. Write a user-level program that enters the filesystem and reorganizes the directory so that unused space is removed. What mechanisms can be used to enter the filesystem?

6. Modify the filesystem to use bitmaps for both inodes and data blocks. Ensure that the bitmaps and blockmaps are separate from the actual superblock. This will involve substantial modifications to both the existing disk layout and in-core structures used to manage filesystem resource.

7. Allow the user to specify the filesystem block size and also the size of the filesystem. This will involve changing the on-disk layout.

8. Study the NFS Linux kernel code and other filesystems to see how NFS file handles are constructed. To avoid invalid file handles due to files being removed and the inode number being reused, filesystems typically employ use of a generation count. Implement this feature in uxfs.

Summary

As the example filesystem here shows, even with the most minimal set of features and limited operations, and although the source code base is small, there are still a lot of kernel concepts to grasp in order to understand how the filesystem works. Understanding which operations need to be supported and the order in which they occur is a difficult task. For those wishing to write a new filesystem for Linux, the initial learning curve can be overcome by taking a simple filesystem and instrumenting it with `printk()` calls to see which functions are invoked in response to certain user-level operations and in what order.

The uxfs filesystem, although very limited in its abilities, is a simple filesystem from which to learn. Hopefully, the examples shown here provide enough information on which to experiment.

I would of course welcome feedback so that I can update any of the material on the Web site where the source code is based:

```
www.wiley.com/compbooks/pate
```

so that I can ensure that it is up-to-date with respect to newer Linux kernels and has more detailed instructions or maybe better information than what is presented here to make it easier for people to experiment and learn. Please send feedback to `spate@veritas.com`.

Happy hacking!

Glossary

Because this is not a general book about operating system principles, there are many OS-related terms described throughout the book that do not have full, descriptive definitions. This chapter provides a glossary of these terms and filesystem-related terms.

/proc. The process filesystem, also called the /proc filesystem, is a pseudo filesystem that displays to the user a hierarchical view of the processes running on the machine. There is a directory in the filesystem per user process with a whole host of information about each process. The /proc filesystem also provides the means to both trace running processes and debug another process.

ACL. Access Control Lists, or more commonly known as ACLs, provide an additional level of security on top of the traditional UNIX security model. An ACL is a list of users who are allowed access to a file along with the type of access that they are allowed.

address space. There are two main uses of the term address space. It can be used to refer to the addresses that a user process can access—this is where the user instructions, data, stack, libraries, and mapped files would reside. One user address space is protected from another user through use of hardware mechanisms. The other use for the term is to describe the instructions, data, and stack areas of the kernel. There is typically only one kernel address space that is protected from user processes.

AFS. The Andrew File System (AFS) is a distributed filesystem developed at CMU as part of the Andrew Project. The goal of AFS was to create a uniform, distributed namespace that spans multiple campuses.

aggregate. UNIX filesystems occupy a disk slice, partition, or logical volume. Inside the filesystem is a hierarchical namespace that exports a single root filesystem that is mountable. In the DFS local filesystem component, each disk slice comprises an aggregate of filesets, each with their own hierarchical namespace and each exporting a root directory. Each fileset can be mounted separately, and in DFS, filesets can be migrated from one aggregate to another.

AIX. This is the version of UNIX distributed by IBM.

allocation unit. An allocation unit, to be found in the VxFS filesystem, is a subset of the overall storage within the filesystem. In older VxFS filesystems, the filesystem was divided into a number of fixed-size allocation units, each with its own set of inodes and data blocks.

anonymous memory. Pages of memory are typically backed by an underlying file in the filesystem. For example, pages of memory used for program code are backed by an executable file from which the kernel can satisfy a page fault by reading the page of data from the file. Process data such as the data segment or the stack do not have backing stored within the filesystem. Such data is backed by anonymous memory that in turn is backed by storage on the swap device.

asynchronous I/O. When a user process performs a read() or write() system call, the process blocks until the data is read from disk into the user buffer or written to either disk or the system page or buffer cache. With asynchronous I/O, the request to perform I/O is simply queued and the kernel returns to the user process. The process can make a call to determine the status of the I/O at a later stage or receive an asynchronous notification. For applications that perform a huge amount of I/O, asynchronous I/O can leave the application to perform other tasks rather than waiting for I/O.

automounter. In many environments it is unnecessary to always NFS mount filesystems. The automounter provides a means to automatically mount an NFS filesystem when a request is made to open a file that would reside in the remote filesystem.

bdevsw. This structure has been present in UNIX since day one and is used to access block-based device drivers. The major number of the driver, as displayed by running ls -l, is used to index this array.

bdflush. Many writes to regular files that go through the buffer cache are not written immediately to disk to optimize performance. When the filesystem is finished writing data to the buffer cache buffer, it releases the buffer allowing it to be used by other processes if required. This leaves a large number of *dirty* (modified) buffers in the buffer cache. A kernel daemon or thread called bdflush runs periodically and flushes dirty buffers to disk freeing space in the buffer cache and helping to provide better data integrity by not caching modified data for too long a period.

block device. Devices in UNIX can be either block or character referring to method through which I/O takes place. For block devices, such as a hard disk, data is transferred in fixed-size blocks, which are typically a minimum of 512 bytes.

block group. As with cylinder groups on UFS and allocations units on VxFS, the ext2 filesystem divides the available space into block groups with each block group managing a set of inodes and data blocks.

block map. Each inode in the filesystem has a number of associated blocks of data either pointed to directly from the inode or from a indirect block. The mapping between the inode and the data blocks is called the block map.

bmap. There are many places within the kernel and within filesystems themselves where there is a need to translate a file offset into the corresponding block on disk. The bmap() function is used to achieve this. On some UNIX kernels, the filesystem exports a bmap interface that can be used by the rest of the kernel, while on others, the operation is internal to the filesystem.

BSD. The Berkeley Software Distribution is the name given to the version of UNIX was distributed by the Computer Systems Research Group (CSRG) at the University of Berkeley.

BSDI. Berkeley Software Design Inc. (BSDI) was a company established to develop and distribute a fully supported, commercial version of BSD UNIX.

buffer cache. When the kernel reads data to and from block devices such as a hard disk, it uses the buffer cache through which blocks of data can be cached for subsequent access. Traditionally, regular file data has been cached in the buffer cache. In SVR4-based versions of UNIX and some other kernels, the buffer cache is only used to cache filesystem meta-data such as directory blocks and inodes.

buffered I/O. File I/O typically travels between the user buffer and disk through a set of kernel buffers whether the buffer cache or the page cache. Access to data that has been accessed recently will involve reading the data from the cache without having to go to disk. This type of I/O is buffered as opposed to direct I/O where the I/O transfer goes directly between the user buffer and the blocks on disk.

cache coherency. Caches can be employed at a number of different levels within a computer system. When multiple caches are provided, such as in a distributed filesystem environment, the designers must make a choice as to how to ensure that data is consistent across these different caches. In an environment where a write invalidates data covered by the write in all other caches, this is a form of strong coherency. Through the use of distributed locks, one can ensure that applications never see stale data in any of the caches.

caching advisory. Some applications may wish to have control over how I/O is performed. Some filesystems export this capability to applications which can select the type of I/O being performed, which allows the filesystem to optimize the I/O paths. For example, an application may choose between sequential, direct, or random I/Os.

cdevsw. This structure has been present in UNIX since day one and is used to access character-based device drivers. The major number of the driver, as displayed by running `ls -l`, is used to index this array.

Chorus. The Chorus microkernel, developed by Chorus Systems, was a popular microkernel in the 1980s and 1990s and was used as the base of a number of different ports of UNIX.

clustered filesystem. A clustered filesystem is a collection of filesystems running on different machines, which presents a unified view of a single, underlying filesystem to the user. The machines within the cluster work together to recover from events such as machine failures.

context switch. A term used in multitasking operating systems. The kernel implements a separate context for each process. Because processes are time sliced or may go to sleep waiting for resources, the kernel switches context to another runnable process.

copy on write. Filesystem-related features such as memory-mapped files operate on a single copy of the data wherever possible. If multiple processes are reading from a mapping simultaneously, there is no need to have multiple copies of the same data. However, when files are memory mapped for write access, a copy will be made of the data (typically at the page level) when one of the processes wishes to modify the data. Copy-on-write techniques are used throughout the kernel.

crash. The `crash` program is a tool that can be used to analyze a dump of the kernel following a system crash. It provides a rich set of routines for examining various kernel structures.

CSRG. The *Computer Systems Research Group*, the group within the University of Berkeley that was responsible for producing the BSD versions of UNIX.

current working directory. Each user process has two associated directories, the root directory and the current working directory. Both are used when performing pathname resolution. Pathnames which start with '/' such as `/etc/passwd` are resolved from the root directory while a pathname such as `bin/myls` starts from the current working directory.

cylinder group. The UFS filesystem divides the filesystem into fixed-sized units called cylinder groups. Each cylinder group manages a set of inodes and data blocks. At the time UFS was created cylinder groups actually mapped to physical cylinders on disk.

data synchronous write. A call to the write() system call typically does not write the data to disk before the system call returns to the user. The data is written to either a buffer cache buffer or a page in the page cache. Updates to the inode timestamps are also typically delayed. This behavior differs from one filesystem to the next and is also dependent on the type of write; extending writes or writes over a hole (in a sparse file) may involve writing the inode updates to disk while overwrites (writes to an already allocated block) will typically be delayed. To force the I/O to disk regardless of the type of write being performed, the user can specify the O_SYNC option to the open() system call. There are times however, especially in the case of overwrites, where the caller may not wish to incur the extra inode write just to update the timestamps. In this case, the O_DSYNC option may be passed to open() in which the data will be written synchronously to disk but the inode update may be delayed.

dcache. The Linux directory cache, or dcache for short, is a cache of pathname to inode structures, which can be used to decrease the time that it takes to perform pathname lookups, which can be very expensive. The entry in the dcache is described by the dentry structure. If a dentry exists, there will always be a corresponding, valid inode.

DCE. The Distributed Computing Environment was the name given to the OSF consortium established to create a new distributed computing environment based on contributions from a number of OSF members. Within the DCE framework was the Distributed File Service, which offered a distributed filesystem.

delayed write. When a process writes to a regular file, the actual data may not be written to disk before the write returns. The data may be simply copied to either the buffer cache or page cache. The transfer to disk is delayed until either the buffer cache daemon runs and writes the data to disk, the pageout daemon requires a page of modified data to be written to disk, or the user requests that the data be flushed to disk either directly or through closing the file.

dentry. An entry in the Linux directory name lookup cache structure is called a dentry, the same name as the structure used to define the entry.

DFS. The Distributed File Service (DFS) was part of the OSF DCE program and provided a distributed filesystem based on the Andrew filesystem but adding more features.

direct I/O. Reads and writes typically go through the kernel buffer cache or page cache. This involves two copies. In the case of a read, the data is read from disk into a kernel buffer and then from the kernel buffer into the user buffer. Because the data is cached in the kernel, this can have a dramatic effect on performance for subsequent reads. However, in some circumstances, the application may not wish to access the same data again. In this case, the I/O can take place directly between the user buffer and disk and thus eliminate an unnecessary copy in this case.

discovered direct I/O. The VERITAS filesystem, VxFS, detects I/O patterns that it determines would be best managed by direct I/O rather than buffered I/O. This type of I/O is called discovered direct I/O and it is not directly under the control of the user process.

DMAPI. The Data Management Interfaces Group (DMIG) was established in 1993 to produce a specification that allowed Hierarchical Storage Management applications to run without repeatedly modifying the kernel and/or filesystem. The resulting Data Management API (DMAPI) was the result of that work and has been adopted by the X/Open group.

DNLC. The Directory Name Lookup Cache (DNLC) was first introduced with BSD UNIX to provide a cache of name to inode/vnode pairs that can substantially reduce the amount of time spent in pathname resolution. Without such a cache, resolving each component of a pathname involves calling the filesystem, which may involve more than one I/O operation.

ext2. The ext2 filesystem is the most popular Linux filesystem. It resembles UFS in its disk layout and the methods by which space is managed in the filesystem.

ext3. The ext3 filesystem is an extension of ext2 that supports journaling.

extended attributes. Each file in the filesystem has a number of fixed attributes that are interpreted by the filesystem. This includes, amongst other things, the file permissions, size, and timestamps. Some filesystems support additional, user-accessible file attributes in which application-specific data can be stored. The filesystem may also use extended attributes for its own use. For example, VxFS uses the extended attribute space of a file to store ACLs.

extent. In the traditional UNIX filesystems data blocks are typically allocated to a file is fixed-sized units equal to the filesystem block size. Extent-based filesystems such as VxFS can allocate a variable number of contiguous data blocks to a file in place of the fixed-size data block. This can greatly improve performance by keeping data blocks sequential on disk and also by reducing the number of indirects.

extent map. *See* block map.

FFS. The Fast File System (FFS) was the name originally chosen by the Berkeley team for developing their new filesystem as a replacement to the traditional filesystem that was part of the research editions of UNIX. Most people know this filesystem as UFS.

file descriptor. A file descriptor is an opaque descriptor returned to the user in response to the open() system call. It must be used in subsequent operations when accessing the file. Within the kernel, the file descriptor is nothing more than an index into an array that references an entry in the system file table.

file handle. When opening a file across NFS, the server returns a file handle, an opaque object, for the client to subsequently access the file. The file handle must be capable of being used across a server reboot and therefore must contain information that the filesystem can always use to access a file. The file handle is comprised of filesystem and non filesystem information. For the filesystem specific information, a filesystem ID, inode number, and generation count are typically used.

fileset. Traditional UNIX filesystems provide a single hierarchical namespace with a single root directory. This is the namespace that becomes visible to the user when the filesystem is mounted. Introduced with the Episode filesystem by Transarc as part of DFS and supported by other filesystems since including VxFS, the filesystem is comprised of multiple, disjoint namespaces called filesets. Each fileset can be mounted separately.

file stream. The standard I/O library provides a rich number of file-access related functions that are built around the FILE structure, which holds the file descriptor in additional to a data buffer. The file stream is the name given to the object through which this type of file access occurs.

filesystem block size. Although filesystems and files can vary in size, the amount of space given to a file through a single allocation in traditional UNIX filesystems is in terms of fixed-size data blocks. The size of such a data block is governed by the filesystem block size. For example, if the filesystem block size is 1024 bytes and a process issues a 4KB write, four 1KB separate blocks will be allocated to the file. Note that for many filesystems the block size can be chosen when the filesystem is first created.

file table. Also called the system file table or even the system-wide file table, all file descriptors reference entries in the file table. Each file table entry, typically defined by a file structure, references either an inode or vnode. There may be multiple file descriptors referencing the same file table entry. This can occur through operations such as dup(). The file structure holds the current read/write pointer.

forced unmount. Attempting to unmount a filesystem will result in an EBUSY if there are still open files in the filesystem. In clustering environments where different nodes in the cluster can access shared storage, failure of one or more resources on a node may require a failover to another node in the cluster. One task that is needed is to unmount the filesystem on the failing node and remount it on another node. The failing node needs a method to forcibly unmount the filesystem.

FreeBSD. Stemming from the official BSD releases distributed by the University of Berkeley, the FreeBSD project was established in the early 1990s to provide a version of BSD UNIX that was free of USL source code licenses or any other licensing obligations.

frozen image. A frozen image is a term used to describe filesystem snapshots where a consistent image is taken of the filesystem in order to perform a reliable backup. Frozen images, or snapshots, can be either persistent or non persistent.

fsck. In a non journaling filesystem, some operations such as a file rename involve changing several pieces of filesystem meta-data. If a machine crashes while part way through such an operation, the filesystem is left in an inconsistent state. Before the filesystem can be mounted again, a filesystem-specific program called fsck must be run to repair any inconsistencies found. Running fsck can take a considerable amount of time if there is a large amount of filesystem meta-data. Note that the time to run fsck is typically a measure of the number of files in the filesystem and not typically related to the actual size of the filesystem.

fsdb. Many UNIX filesystems are distributed with a debugger which can be used to both analyze the on-disk structures and repair any inconsistencies found. Note though, that use of such a tool requires intimate knowledge of how the various filesystem structures are laid out on disk and without careful use, the filesystem can be damaged beyond repair if a great deal of care is not taken.

FSS. An acronym for the File System Switch, a framework introduced in SVR3 that allows multiple different filesystems to coexist within the same kernel.

generation count. One of the components that is typically part of an NFS file handle is the inode number of the file. Because inodes are recycled when a file is removed and a new file is allocated, there is a possibility that a file handle obtained from the deleted file may reference the new file. To prevent this from occurring inodes have been modified to include a generation count that is modified each time the inode is recycled.

gigabyte. A gigabyte (GB) is 1024 megabytes (MB).

gnode. In the AIX kernel, the in-core inode includes a gnode structure. This is used to reference a segment control block that is used to manage a 256MB cache backing the file. All data access to the file is through the per-file segment cache.

hard link. A file's link count is the number of references to a file. When the link count reaches zero, the file is removed. A file can be referenced by multiple names in the namespace even though there is a single on-disk inode. Such a link is called a hard link.

hierarchical storage management. Once a filesystem runs out of data blocks an error is returned to the caller the next time an allocation occurs. HSM applications provide the means by which file data blocks can be *migrated* to tape without knowledge of the user. This frees up space in the filesystem while the file that had been data migrated retains the same file size and other attributes. An attempt to access a file that has been migrated results in a call to the HSM application, which can then migrate that data back in from tape allowing the application to access the file.

HP-UX. This is the version of UNIX that is distributed by Hewlett Packard.

HSM. *See* hierarchical storage management.

indirect data block. File data blocks are accessed through the inode either directly (direct data blocks) or by referencing a block that contains pointers to the data blocks. Such blocks are called indirect data blocks. The inode has a limited number of pointers to data blocks. By the use of indirect data blocks, the size of the file can be increased dramatically.

init. The first process that is started by the UNIX kernel. It is the parent of all other processes. The UNIX operating system runs at a specific init state. When moving through the init states during bootstrap, filesystems are mounted.

inittab. The file that controls the different activities at each init state. Different rc scripts are run at the different init levels. On most versions of UNIX, filesystem activity starts at init level 2.

inode. An inode is a data structure that is used to describe a particular file. It includes information such as the file type, owner, timestamps, and block map. An in-core inode is used on many different versions of UNIX to represent the file in the kernel once opened.

intent log. Journaling filesystems employ an intent log through which transactions are written. If the system crashes, the filesystem can perform log replay whereby transactions specifying filesystem changes are replayed to bring the filesystem to a consistent state.

journaling. Because many filesystem operations need to perform more than one I/O to complete a filesystem operation, if the system crashes in the middle of an operation, the filesystem could be left in an inconsistent state. This requires the fsck program to be run to repair any such inconsistencies. By employing journaling techniques, the filesystem writes transactional information to a log on disk such that the operations can be replayed in the event of a system crash.

kernel mode/space. The kernel executes in a privileged hardware mode which allows it access to specific machine instructions that are not accessible by normal user processes. The kernel data structures are protected from user processes which run in their own protected address spaces.

kilobyte. 1024 bytes.

Linux. A UNIX-like operating system developed by a Finnish college research assistant named Linus Torvalds. The source to the Linux kernel is freely available under the auspices of the GNU public license. Linux is mainly used on desktops, workstations, and the lower-end server market.

Mach. The Mach microkernel was developed at Carnegie Mellon University (CMU) and was used as the basis for the Open Software Foundation (OSF). Mach is also being used for the GNU Hurd kernel.

mandatory locking. Mandatory locking can be enabled on a file if the set group ID bit is switched on and the group execute bit is switched off—a combination that together does not otherwise make any sense. Mandatory locking is seldom used.

megabyte. 1024 * 1024 kilobytes.

memory-mapped files. In addition to using the read() and write() system, calls, the mmap() system call allows the process to map the file into its address space. The file data can then be accessed by reading from and writing to the process address space. Mappings can be either private or shared.

microkernel. A microkernel is a set of services provided by a minimal kernel on which additional operating system services can be built. Various versions of UNIX, including SVR3, SVR4, and BSD have been ported to Mach and Chorus, the two most popular microkernels.

Minix. Developed by Andrew Tanenbaum to teach operating system principles, the Minix kernel source was published in his book on operating systems. A version 7 UNIX clone from the system call perspective, the Minix kernel was very different to UNIX. Minix was the inspiration for Linux.

mkfs. The command used to make a UNIX filesystem. In most versions of UNIX, there is a generic mkfs command and filesystem-specific mkfs commands that enable filesystems to export different features that can be implemented, in part, when the filesystem is made.

mount table. The mount table is a file in the UNIX namespace that records all of the filesystems that have been mounted. It is typically located in /etc and records the device on which the filesystem resides, the mountpoint, and any options that were passed to the mount command.

MULTICS. The MULTICS operating system was a joint project between Bell Labs, GE, and MIT. The goal was to develop a multitasking operating system. Before completion, Bell Labs withdrew from the project and went on to develop the UNIX operating system. Many of the ideas from MULTICS found their way into UNIX.

mutex. A mutex is a binary semaphore that can be used to serialize access to data structures. Only one thread can hold the mutex at any one time. Other threads that attempt to hold the mutex will sleep until the owner relinquishes the mutex.

NetBSD. Frustrated with the way that development of 386/BSD was progressing, others started working on a parallel development path, taking a combination of 386BSD and Net/2 and porting it to a large array of other platforms and architectures.

NFS. The Network File System, a distributed filesystem technology originally developed by Sun Microsystems. The specification for NFS was open to the public in the form of an RFC (request for comments) document. NFS has been adopted by many UNIX and non-UNIX vendors.

OpenServer. SCO OpenServer is the name of the SVR3-based version of UNIX distributed by SCO. This was previously known as SCO Open Desktop.

OSF. The Open Software Foundation was formed to bring together a number of technologies offered by academic and commercial interests. The resulting specification, the distributed computing environment (DCE), was backed by the OSF/1 operating system. The kernel for OSF/1 was based on the Mach microkernel and BSD. OSF and X/Open merged to become the Open Group.

page cache. Older UNIX systems employ a buffer cache, a fixed-size cache of data through which user and filesystem data can be read from or written to. In newer versions of UNIX and Linux, the buffer cache is mainly used for filesystem meta-data such as inodes and indirect data blocks. The kernel provides a page-cache where file data is cached on a page-by-page basis. The cache is not fixed size. When pages of data are not immediately needed, they are placed on the free page list but still retain their identity. If the same data is required before the page is reused, the file data can be accessed without going to disk.

page fault. Most modern microprocessors provide support for virtual memory allowing large address spaces despite there being a limited amount of physical memory. For example, on the Intel x86 architecture, each user process can map 4GB of virtual memory. The different user address spaces are set to map virtual addresses to physical memory but are only used when required. For example, when accessing program instructions, each time an instruction on a different page of memory is accessed, a page-fault occurs. The kernel is required to allocate a physical page of memory and map it to the user virtual page. Into the physical page, the data must be read from disk or initialized according to the type of data being stored in memory.

page I/O. Each buffer in the traditional buffer cache in UNIX referenced an area of the kernel address space in which the buffer data could be stored. This area was typically fixed in size. With the move towards page cache systems, this required the I/O subsystem to perform I/O on a page-by-page basis and sometimes the need to perform I/O on multiple pages with a single request. This resulted in a large number of changes to filesystems, the buffer cache, and the I/O subsystem.

pageout daemon. Similar to the buffer cache `bdflush` daemon, the pageout daemon is responsible for keeping a specific number of pages free. As an example, on SVR4-based kernels, there are two variables, `freemem` and `lotsfree` that are measured in terms of free pages. Whenever `freemem` goes below `lotsfree`, the pageout daemon runs and is required to locate and free pages. For pages that have not been modified, it can easily reclaim them. For pages that have been modified, they must be written to disk before being reclaimed. This involves calling the filesystem `putpage()` vnode operation.

pathname resolution. Whenever a process accesses a file or directory by name, the kernel must be able to resolve the pathname requested down to the base filename. For example, a request to access /home/spate/bin/myls will involve parsing the pathname and looking up each component in turn, starting at home, until it gets to myls. Pathname resolution is often performed one component at a time and may involve calling multiple different filesystem types to help.

Posix. The portable operating system standards group (Posix) was formed by a number of different UNIX vendors in order to standardize the programmatic interfaces that each of them were presenting. Over several years, this effort led to multiple different standards. The Posix.1 standard, which defines the base system call and library routines, has been adopted by all UNIX vendors and many non-UNIX vendors.

proc structure. The proc is one of two main data structures that has been traditionally used in UNIX to describe a user process. The proc structure remains in memory at all times. It describes many aspects of the process including user and group IDs, the process address space, and various statistics about the running process.

process. A process is the execution environment of a program. Each time a program is run from the command line or a process issues a fork() system call, a new process is created. As an example, typing ls at the command prompt results in the shell calling fork(). In the new process created, the exec() system call is then invoked to run the ls program.

pseudo filesystem. A pseudo filesystem is one which does not have any physical backing store (on disk). Such filesystems provide useful information to the user or system but do not have any information that is persistent across a system reboot. The /proc filesystem, which presents information about running processes, is an example of a pseudo filesystem.

quick I/O. The quick I/O feature offered by VERITAS allows files in a VxFS filesystem to appear as raw devices to the user. It also relaxes the locking semantics associated with regular files, so there can be multiple readers and multiple writers at the same time. Quick I/O allows databases to run on the filesystem with raw I/O performance but with all the manageability features provided by the filesystem.

quicklog. The VxFS intent log, through which transactions are first written, is created on the same device that the filesystem is created. The quicklog feature allows intent logs from different filesystems to be placed on a separate device. By not having the intent log on the same device as the filesystem, there is a reduction in disk head movement. This can improve the performance of VxFS

quotas. There are two main types of quotas, user and group, although group quotas are not supported by all versions of UNIX. A quota is a limit on the number of files and data blocks that a user or group can allocate. Once the *soft limit* is exceeded, the user or group has a grace period in which to remove files to get back under the quota limit. Once the grace period expires, the user or group can no longer allocate any other files. A *hard limit* cannot be exceeded under any circumstances.

RAM disk. A RAM disk, as the name implies, is an area of main memory that is used to simulate a disk device. On top of a RAM disk, a filesystem can be made and files copied to and from it. RAM disks are used in two main areas. First, they can be used for temporary filesystem space. Because no disk I/Os are performed, the performance of the system can be improved (of course the extra memory used can equally degrade performance). The second main use of RAM disks is for kernel bootstrap. When the kernel loads, it can access a number of critical programs from the RAM disk prior to the root filesystem being mounted. An example of a critical program is fsck, which may be needed to repair the root filesystem.

raw disk device. The raw disk device, also known as a character device, is one view of the disk storage. Unlike the block device, through which fixed-sized blocks of data can be read or written, I/O can be performed to or from the raw device in any size units.

RFS. At the time that Sun was developing NFS, UNIX System Laboratories, who distributed System V UNIX, was developing its own distributed filesystem technology. The Remote File Sharing (RFS) option was a cache-coherent, distributed filesystem that offered full UNIX semantics. Although technically a better filesystem in some areas, RFS lacked the cross-platform capabilities of NFS and was available only to those who purchased a UNIX license, unlike the open NFS specification.

root directory. Each user process has two associated directories, the root directory and the current working directory. Both are used when performing pathname resolution. Pathnames that start with '/' such as /etc/passwd are resolved from the root directory while a pathname such as bin/myls starts from the current working directory.

root filesystem. The root filesystem is mounted first by the kernel during bootstrap. Although it is possible for everything to reside in the root filesystem, there are typically several more filesystems mounted at various points on top of the root filesystem. By separate filesystems, it is easier to increase the size of the filesystem. It is not possible to increase the size of most root filesystems.

San Point Foundation Suite. The name given to the VERITAS clustered filesystem (FS) and all the clustering infrastructure that is needed to support a clustered filesystem. VERITAS CFS is part of the VERITAS filesystem, VxFS.

SCO. The Santa Cruz Operation (SCO) was the dominant supplier of UNIX to Intel-based PCs and servers. Starting with Xenix, SCO moved to SVR3 and then SVR4 following their acquisition of USL. The SCO UNIX technology was purchased by Caldera in 2001 and SCO changed its name to Tarantella to develop application technology.

Single UNIX Specification. Although standards such as Posix and the various X/Open specifications went a long way to improve application compatibility between different versions of UNIX, each UNIX vendor still implemented different commands, libraries, and system calls. In the early 1990s, a group of companies formed to produce a standard that encompassed Posix, X/Open, and the various additional interfaces. There were initially 1,170 APIs in total, and thus the name originally given to the consortium. The completed specification became known as UNIX95 and has been since superseded by UNIX98.

SMP. Symmetric Multi-Processor (SMP) machines are single-node machines with more than one CPU running concurrently and sharing the same memory. There is a single instance of the kernel running across all of the processors. To the user, the machine appears no different from a uniprocessor machine.

snapshot. A snapshot, also called a frozen image, is a replica of a filesystem. The snapshot looks exactly like the filesystem from which the snapshot was taken. Snapshots can be used to create a stable backup of the filesystem rather than trying to back up a filesystem that is constantly changing.

Solaris. This is the version of UNIX that is distributed by Sun Microsystems. It was derived from SVR4 but has undergone substantial modifications throughout the 1990s.

sparse files. A sparse file is a file that may contain one or more holes. Files are typically backed by data blocks covering the entire range of the file. However, a hole is an area of the file for which there are no data blocks. Users reading across a hole will see a series of zeroes. If a process writes to the file over an area covered by a hole, data blocks will be allocated.

Spec 11/70. *See* Single UNIX Specification.

specfs. The specfs filesystem, introduced with SVR4, is a filesystem that presents devices to the user. To prevent all filesystems having to handle I/O to devices, whenever they see a device in the namespace, they call specfs to return a handle to the device. All I/O will then pass through specfs before going to the device. Inode modifications and calls such as `stat()` will still be passed to the filesystem on which the device node resides.

spin lock. When a process holds a resource such as a buffer cache buffer, another process that wants the same buffer will typically sleep. Because the buffer may be in use for I/O, it could be quite some time before the buffer is freed. Some operations that require the use of locks are for only very short durations, for example, adding an entry to a linked list. Because this operation takes only a few instructions, it does not make sense to make another process that wishes to access the list go to sleep. In this case, the list is protected by a spin lock. The waiting process literally spins around a loop waiting until the lock is released.

standard I/O library. The standard I/O library offers a rich set of functions built on top of the basic file-related system calls such as read() and write(). For processes that are accessing small amounts of data at a time and wish to perform a number of string-related functions on the data, the standard I/O library is more likely to be a better fit to the application.

storage checkpoint. The VERITAS filesystem, VxFS, supports both non persistent and persistent snapshots. Storage checkpoints are persistent snapshots. They survive across a system reboot and are always guaranteed to be structurally intact because all operations to checkpoints are tied in with the VxFS journaling mechanisms. There can be multiple checkpoints for each filesystem, and each can be mounted independently. Storage checkpoints reside in the same device as the filesystem.

strategy function. Each device driver exports a number of functions that are used by filesystems and the rest of the kernel. For block devices, the main entry point into the driver is through an exported strategy interface. Requests for I/O are made through the strategy interface, which is an asynchronous interface. If the caller wishes to wait for the data, it must then make an additional call to block until the I/O is complete.

SunOS. The name given to the Sun version of UNIX prior to Solaris. SunOS was based on BSD UNIX and ran on all Sun workstations and servers up to the early 1990s.

superblock. Each filesystem records basic information about the structure of the filesystem in a superblock. The superblock is always stored in a well-known location on disk so that the filesystem is easily able to find it when the filesystem is to be mounted.

SVID. The set of system calls, library functions, and commands supported by System V UNIX, was documented in the System V Interface Definition (SVID). The last SVID produced was for SVR4.

SVRx. The organizations responsible for the commercial side of UNIX at the Bell Telephone company named their versions of UNIX System V. There were four releases of System V UNIX ending in SVR4 in the late 1980s. The SVR4 technology, at the time SVR4.2MP, was purchased by SCO who carried on development until Caldera bought the technology in the late 1990s.

SVVS. System V UNIX was licensed to several different companies. In order for these companies to use the name "System V" in their own product name, they were required to pass the System V Verification Suite (SVVS).

swap space. The amount of physical memory (RAM) is limited in just about all machines. Because this memory is shared between all applications and the UNIX kernel, an area of disk is used as an extension of physical memory. This area is called the swap space, and there may be multiple different swap spaces in the same system. The UNIX kernel employs daemons or kernel threads, which are responsible for ensuring that there is always a set of free pages of memory at any one time. Older pages are selected for paging and are written to the swap device to free up physical memory. Tables must be kept in memory to record the location of such pages on the swap device.

symbolic link. A symbolic link is a file whose contents are simply a string of characters. This string of characters references another filename. Because the file type is recorded as a symbolic link, also called a symlink, the kernel can use the pathname recorded in the symlink to continue pathname resolution. The resulting name returned will be the file to which the symlink points.

synchronous write. A call to the `write()` system call typically does not write the data to disk before the system call returns to the user. The data is written to either a buffer in the buffer cache or a page in the page cache. Updates to the inode timestamps are also typically delayed. This behavior differs from one filesystem to the next and is also dependent on the type of write; extending writes or writes over a hole (in a sparse file) may involve writing the inode updates to disk while overwrites (writes to an already allocated block) will typically be delayed. To force the I/O to disk regardless of the type of write being performed, the user can specify the `O_SYNC` option to the `open()` system call.

system call. A system call is a special library function that transfers control from user space to the kernel in which to perform a specific operation. The user does not need to typically distinguish between a system call and any other library function that UNIX provides unless performance is of importance, in which case a trade-off between performance and operating-supplied functionality may need to be made.

terabyte. A terabyte (TB) is 1024 gigabytes (GB).

thread. Traditional UNIX systems operate around the concept of a process. Although the process is still the running instance of a user program, modern UNIX kernels support the notion of threads. Each user process may have more than one thread of control, each executing within the same address space, able to access the same data and instructions but running on separate stacks. With the introduction of SMP-based architectures it is possible for the threads to be running concurrently and sharing the process resources. This is often a better solution than having the same tasks performed via separate processes. Within the kernel, there are also likely to be multiple threads running concurrently.

tmpfs. The tmpfs filesystem, provided by Sun Microsystems, is a memory-based filesystem that can be used to provide better performance for applications using temporary files.

True64 UNIX. The 64-bit version of UNIX provided by Digital, now HP/Compaq.

UFS. The UFS filesystem, formerly known as the BSD fast filesystem, is the most widely ported of all UNIX filesystems. Developed to replace the old

UNIX filesystem that was part of the UNIX editions, UFS offered considerably greater performance.

Unix International (UI). Centered around System V UNIX, a number of vendors formed UI, largely in competition to OSF. The goal was to standardize around SVR4 and derivatives. The group was disbanded in the early 1990s.

UnixWare. The version of SVR4-based UNIX produced by Novell. *See* USL.

UP. Uni-Processor (UP) machines have a single processor. *Also see* SMP.

user area. In addition to the proc structure, there is a user structure, also called the user area or uarea, for each running process in UNIX. The user area contains file-related information such as the root and current working directories, and the mapping between file descriptors and the file table.

user mode/space. Each user process runs in its own address space protected from other user processes. There are, however, hardware services that are not accessible in user mode and therefore involve a transition to kernel mode to access. An example would be to access special instructions to initiate a hardware operation.

USG. *See* USL.

USL. The group that started the commercial side of UNIX at Bell Labs went through several different names including the UNIX Systems Group (UGS) and UNIX System Laboratories (USL). This group produced the versions of UNIX up to SVR4. After being acquired by Novell, they went on to produce the UnixWare operating system.

vectored reads/writes. Each time a process issues a read() or write() system call, a single I/O can be performed. The readv() and writev() system calls allow multiple I/Os to be performed in a single system call. In addition to cutting down on system call overhead, it may allow for two or more of the I/Os to be coalesced.

VFS. The Virtual File System (VFS) architecture was the name given to the new filesystem architecture introduced by Sun Microsystems for supporting multiple filesystem types including their new networked filesystem (NFS). Linux has since used the term VFS to refer to their filesystem architecture.

vfstab / fstab. These files, whose names differ between the UNIX variants, hold the filesystems that are to be mounted when the system boots.

VFS-ops. The Sun VFS/vnode interface introduced a set of operations that were applicable to filesystems. Each filesystem must export its own VFS operations that are called by the filesystem-independent layer of the kernel.

vnode. Older UNIX systems used an inode as the structure for representing files both on-disk and in memory. The memory-based inode was often referred to as the in-core inode. With the introduction of the Sun VFS architecture, the in-core inode was replaced with a vnode structure. Albeit a small change, this lead to less confusion all-round.

vnode ops. Whenever the kernel performs a lookup operation to retrieve a file in the filesystem, the vnode is instantiated with a vector of operations that is applicable to the file type. These operations, such as read and write, allow the kernel to call into the filesystem.

VTOC. The Volume Table Of Contents (VTOC) is a label written at the start of the disk to describe the different slices on the disk, where they start, and how many sectors they hold.

VxFS. A journaling filesystem from VERITAS, VxFS is the most successful of the commercially available UNIX filesystems.

VxVM. The VERITAS logical volume manager, VxVM, has been ported to almost all versions of UNIX and Windows NT.

XDR. The eXternal Data Representation is a standard that describes how to represent data types and structures in a machine-independent manner. XDR is used when sending NFS requests and responses over the wire from one machine to another.

Xenix. The version of UNIX developed by both Microsoft and the Santa Cruz Operation (SCO). Xenix was used for Intel-based machines.

X/Open. The X/Open company was established in the U.K. to standardize programmatic interfaces across multiple operating systems. The resulting XPG (X/Open Portability Guide) was originally based on Posix.1.

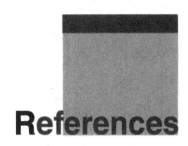

References

[ARMA92]   Armand, F. and Dean, R. (1992). "Data Movement in Kernelized Systems." Proceedings of the Summer 1992 USENIX Conference, pages 238–247.

[BACH86]   Bach, M. (1986). *The Design of the UNIX Operating System.* Englewood Cliffs, NJ: Prentice-Hall.

[BAR01]   Bar, M. (2001). *Linux File Systems.* Berkeley, CA: Osborne/McGraw-Hill.

[BAR02]   Barker, R., and Massiglia, P. (2002). *Storage Area Networking Essentials.* New York: John Wiley & Sons.

[BATL92]   Batlivala, N., Gleeson, B., Hamrick, J., Lurndal, S., Price, D., Soddy, J., and Abrossimov, V. (1992). "Experience with SVR4 over Chorus." Proceedings of the USENIX Workshop on Microkernels & Other Kernel Architectures, April 1992.

[BECK96]   Beck, M., Bohme, H., Dziadzka, M., Kunitz, U., Magnus, R., and Verworner, D. (1996). *Linux Kernel Internals.* Reading, Massachusetts: Addison-Wesley.

[CALL00]   Callaghan, B. (2000). *NFS Illustrated.* Reading, Massachusetts: Addison-Wesley.

[CALL93]   Callaghan, B., and Sing, S. (1993). "The Autofs Automounter." Proceedings of the USENIX Summer 1993 Technical Conference, Cincinnati, Ohio June 21–25, 1993.

[DMIG97]   *CAE Specification Systems Management: Data Storage Management (XDSM) API.* X/Open Document Number: C429 ISBN: 1-85912-190-X

[FAUL91]   Faulkner R., and Gomes R. (1991). "The Process File System and Process Model in UNIX System V." Proceedings of the USENIX Association Winter Conference, Dallas, TX, January 1991.

[GALL95]   Gallmeister, B. (1995). *Posix.4 : Programming for the Real World.* Sebastopol, CA: O'Reilly.

[GING87]   Gingell, R. A., Moran, J. P., and Shannon, W. A. (1987). "Virtual Memory Architecture in SunOS." Proceedings of the USENIX 1987 Summer Conference, pages 81–94.

[GOOD94]   Goodheart, B. and Cox, J. (1994). *The Magic Garden Explained: The Internals of System V Release 4, An Open Systems Design.* Sydney, Australia: Prentice-Hall.

[HANC01]   Hancock, S. (2001). *True64 UNIX Filesystem Administration Handbook.* Woburn, MA: Digital Press.

[HAWL75]   Hawley, J. and Meyer, W. (1975). *MUNIX, a Multiprocessing version of UNIX.* Monterey, California: Naval Postgraduate School.

[HEND90]   Hendricks, D. (1990). "A File System for Software Development." Proceedings of the Summer 1990 USENIX Technical Conference, June 1990, pages 333–340.

[KARE86]   Karels, M. and McKusick, M. (1986). "Toward a Compatible Filesystem Interface." Conference of the European Users' Group, September 1986.

[KELL96]   Kelly, D. (1996). *AIX/6000 Internals and Architecture.* New York, NY: McGraw-Hill.

[KERN78]   Kernighan, B. and Ritchie, D. (1978). *The C Programming Language.* Englewood Cliffs, NJ: Prentice-Hall.

[KILL84]   Killian, T. J. (1988). "Processes as Files." Proc. Summer 1984 USENIX Conference, pages 203–207.

[KLEI86]   Kleiman, S. (1986). "Vnodes: An Architecture for Multiple File System Types in Sun Unix." Proceedings of the Summer 1986 USENIX Conference, pages 238–247.

[LEFF89]   Leffler, S., McKusick, M., Karels, M., and Quarterman, J. (1989). *4.3BSD UNIX Operating System.* Reading, Massachusetts: Addison Wesley.

[LION96]   Lions, J. (1996). *Lions' Commentary on UNIX 6th Edition.* San Jose, CA: Peer-to-Peer Communications.

[MAUR01]   Mauro, J. and McDougall, R. (2001). *Solaris Internals—Core Kernel Architecture.* Palo Alto, CA: Prentice Hall.

[MCKU84]   McKusick, M.K., Joy, W., Leffler, S., and Fabry, R. (1984). "A Fast File System for UNIX." Communications of the ACM, August 1984, pages 181–197.

[MCKU90]   McKusick, M.K., Karels, M.K., and Bostic, K. (1990). "A Pageable Memory Based Filesystem." Proceedings of the Summer 1990 USENIX Technical Conference, June 1990.

[MORR86]   Morris, J.H., Satyanarayanan, M., Conner, M.H., Howard, J.H., Rosenthal, D.S.H., and Smith, F.D. (1986). "Andrew: A Distributed Personal Computing Environment." Communications of the ACM, Volume 29, No. 3, March 1986.

[NADK92]   Nadkarni, A.V. (1992). "The Processor File System in UNIX SVR4.2." Proceedings of the 1992 USENIX Workshop on File Systems, May 1992, pages 131–132.

[PATE96]   Pate, S. D. (1996). *UNIX Internals—A Practical Approach*. Reading, Massachusetts: Addison Wesley.

[PAWL94]   Pawlowski, B., Juszczak, C., Staubach, P., Smith, C., Lebel, D., and Hitz, D. (1994). "NFS Version 3 Design and Implementation." Proceedings of the Summer 1994 Summer USENIX Conference, June 1994, pages 137–151.

[RANA02]   Ranade, D. M. (2002). *Shared Data Clusters*. New York: John Wiley & Sons.

[RFC1014]   Sun Microsystems, Inc., *External Data Representation Specification*. RFC-11014. Menlo Park, CA: DDN Network Information Center, SRI International.

[RFC1057]   Sun Microsystems, Inc. *Remote Procedure Call Specification*. RFC-11057. Menlo Park, CA: DDN Network Information Center, SRI International.

[RFC1094]   Sun Microsystems, Inc. *Network Filesystem Specification*. RFC-11094. Menlo Park, CA: DDN Network Information Center, SRI International.

[RFC1813]   Sun Microsystems, Inc. *NFS Version 3 Protocol Specification*, RFC-1813. Menlo Park, CA: DDN Network Information Center, SRI International.

[RFC2203]   Eisler, M., Chiu, A., and Ling, L. *RPCSEC_GSS Protocol Specification*, RFC-2203, August 1995.

[RFC3010]   IETF Network Working Group. *NFS Version 4 Protocol Specification*. RFC-3010.

[RIFK86]   Rifkin, A.P., Forbes, M.P., Hamilton, R.L., Sabrio, M., Shah, S., and Yueh, K. (1986). "RFS Architectural Overview." Proceedings of the Summer 1986 USENIX Technical Conference, June 1986, pages 248-259.

[RITC74]   Ritchie, D. and Thompson, K. (1974). "The UNIX Timesharing System." Communications of the ACM, July 1974, pages 365-375.

[ROSE86]   Rosen, M. B., Wilde, M. J., and Fraser-Campbell, B. (1986). "NFS Portability." Proceedings of the Summer 1986 USENIX Technical Conference, Atlanta, GA, pages 299–305.

[SALU96]   Salus, P. (1996). *A Quarter Century of UNIX*. Reading, Massachusetts: Addison Wesley.

[SAND85]   Sandberg, R., Goldeberg, D., Kleiman, S., Walsh, D., and Lyon, B. (1985). "Design and Implementation of the Sun Network Filesystem." Proceedings of the Summer 1985 USENIX Conference, Berkeley, CA.

[SCHI93]   Schildt, H. (1993). *The Annotated ANSI C Standard*. Berkeley, CA: Osborne McGraw-Hill.

[SCHI94]   Schimmel, C. (1994). *UNIX Systems for Modern Architectures*, Reading, Massachusetts: Addison-Wesley.

[SNYD90]   Snyder, P. (1990). "tmpfs: A Virtual Memory File System." (1990). Proceedings of the Autumn 1990 European UNIX Users' Group Conference, October 1990, pages 241–248.

[STEV92]   Stevens, R. (1992). *Advanced Programming in the UNIX Environment*. Englewood Cliffs, NJ: Prentice Hall.

[TANE87]   Tanenbaum, A. (1987). *Operating Systems: Design and Implementation*. Englewood Cliffs, NJ: Prentice Hall.

[TWEE98]   Tweedie, S. (1998). "Journaling the Linux ext2fs filesystem." Linux Expo, 1998.

[VAHA96]   Vahalia, U. (1996). *UNIX Internals—The New Frontiers*. Englewood Cliffs, NJ: Prentice Hall.

[WAIT87]   Waite, M. (1987). *UNIX Papers for UNIX Developers and Power Users*. Indianapolis, IN: Howard W. Sams & Company.

[WEBB93]   Webber, N. (1993). "Operating System Support for Portable Filesystem Extensions." USENIX Conference Proceedings, Winter, 1993, pages 219-225.

[WIRZ95]   Wirzenius, L. (1995). *The Linux System Administrators Guide*, version 0.3, August 6th, 1995. Public Domain.

Index